The Developmental Needs Meeting Strategy

An Ego State Therapy for Healing Adults with Childhood Trauma and Attachment Wounds

Shirley Jean Schmidt, MA, LPC

First Edition
Copyright © 2009   All Rights Reserved
Published by DNMS Institute, LLC
6421 Mondean Street San Antonio, Texas, 78240
DNMS@DNMSInstitute.com
www.DNMSInstitute.com
(210) 561-7881

Table of Contents

Acknowledgements

I express my heartfelt thanks for my husband Jurgen, who has supported me without complaint, in every possible way, through the writing of this book. I'm especially grateful for Kevin Quirk, who is (miraculously) both a writing editor and an ego state therapist. He provided essential advice to make the book the best it could be. I'm profoundly thankful for several reviewers who provided critical support and feedback, including Joan Bacon, Cynthia Engel, Donna Stanley, Christine Courtois, Ricky Greenwald, and Carol Forgash. I'm especially thankful for the help I received from Ginger Enrico. Although an experienced DNMS therapist, she was able to critique the book with a beginner's mind – finding and helping me correct passages that might confuse therapists new to the DNMS.

Introduction

When I first began practicing as a psychotherapist I was taught that many of the unwanted behaviors, beliefs, and emotions that clients seek to change, originate with unresolved trauma, often from childhood; and that resolving these traumas would lead to the growth and change clients desire. Consequently I learned to apply the traditional trauma-treatment model – the (roughly) three-stage approach which includes a rapport-building/stabilization stage, a trauma-desensitization stage, and an integration/resolution stage.[1] In the trauma-desensitization stage clients are guided to relive and abreact their traumas with emotionally taxing interventions such as EMDR,[2] flooding,[3] hypnotherapy,[4] and Prolonged Exposure.[5]

After some years practicing therapy with this approach, I observed it was not always helpful. For example, clients who grew up feeling unhappy and insecure did not always have specific childhood "traumas" to desensitize; and some who had actual childhood traumas to target experienced little to no benefit once they were desensitized.

In 2000 I had an interesting conversation with my colleague Merle Yost, a therapist from Oakland. He was working with a very difficult client named Jim – an unemployed diabetic who hoarded. His apartment was filled with junk, which he would not clean or organize. He was not eating properly, which was making him sick, making it hard for him to look for work. Yost told me he had begun experimenting with a needs meeting protocol. He said he invited Jim to think of an internal resource, a nanny, who was able to nurture a young ego state he called Baby Jim; then guided him, starting with infancy, to picture the nanny meeting Baby Jim's needs. They proceeded, developmental stage by stage, meeting needs. By the time they were meeting needs at age three, Jim was cleaning his apartment, working, and eating properly.

His story inspired a significant shift in my view of psychopathology. I suddenly understood how many unwanted behaviors, beliefs, and emotions could originate with unmet developmental needs. I could see that childhood *trauma* was just one of many potential unmet developmental needs – for example, the unmet need for *safety*. So I began experimenting with protocols that might meet clients' unmet childhood needs. I started with the assumption that a good needs meeting protocol would serve to stabilize clients, and prepare them well for the arduous task of trauma desensitization. To my surprise, I eventually observed that meeting developmental needs could gently desensitize traumas – as a side effect of the needs meeting processing. It eliminated the need to guide clients through a separate desensitization process.

A client's own internal Resource ego states are the center of the needs meeting work. The most powerful and effective Resources are those that are anchored in familiar, personal experiences of being effortlessly nurturing and protective; and in significant, personal experiences of a spiritual nature. This part of the model has evolved over the years. In the current protocol design clients establish and connect to a Nurturing Adult Self, a Protective Adult Self, and a Spiritual Core Self. These Resource ego states, not the therapist, meet clients' unmet needs.

Needs meeting processing focuses on *individual wounded ego states* that are stuck in the past – usually in childhood. *The past* is defined as a single or repeated wounding event that involved unmet needs, such as abuse, neglect, rejection, or enmeshment. As the Resources meet needs, the wounded parts of self *fill up on the good things* they did not get in the past (e.g. safety, attunement, connection, validation, love, respect, support, encouragement, etc.). While ego states can become stuck in a traumatic event, the *memory of such an event is not the target* of the needs meeting processing. After getting enough needs met, wounded ego states will become unstuck from the past. As they become unstuck, the associated painful memories will desensitize automatically (as a fortunate side effect).

Many ego state therapies focus a lot of attention on healing wounded parts of self that were the victims of abuse, neglect, rejection, or enmeshment (called reactive parts in the DNMS).[6] This is understandable since clients are often quite vocal about their problematic reactions to stressful events. In the beginning, the DNMS focused on these wounded parts as well, but over time the focus shifted to healing parts of self that *mimic the wounding individuals* who inflicted the abuse, neglect, rejection, or enmeshment (called *maladaptive introjects* in the DNMS). That's because these introjects are the source of many of the problematic reactions clients want to fix. With this shift in processing focus came the welcome discovery that reactive parts will heal automatically as the associated maladaptive introjects heal.

Recent child development research has emphasized the value of a child's secure attachment to loving, attuned caregivers.[7] Because attachment issues are such an important part of child development, in 2006 I developed a DNMS questionnaire, called the *Attachment Needs Ladder*, that would help to systematically direct needs meeting processing to address childhood attachment wounds. The Ladder has four rungs. Each rung is a list of negative beliefs a person might acquire in childhood if attachment needs were not met well. The first rung lists beliefs about existence; the second rung lists beliefs about physical, sexual, and emotional safety; the third rung lists beliefs about sense of self; and the fourth rung lists beliefs about preoccupied and dismissive relationships with others. Clients are asked to rate the believability of each statement in a single rung (starting with Rung1). Those beliefs that feel true to the client (e.g. I don't matter), do so because a maladaptive introject is conveying a wounding message (e.g. You don't matter). These associated introjects are identified and targeted for treatment. A DNMS *Needs Meeting Protocol* is applied to these introjects to get them unstuck from the past. Once complete, clients typically report the negative statements from the targeted rung no longer feel true. This process helps attachment wounds heal.

Clients engaged in any form of psychotherapy, including the DNMS, can experience processing blocks. Maladaptive introjects (parts of self that mimic wounding individuals), are a frequent source of such blocks. In 2005 I developed a brief intervention, called the *Switching the Dominance Protocol*, to help introjects heal. It does not provide complete healing, but can provide enough to stop an introject from conveying someone else's wounding message. Such messages are often at the core of processing blocks. When an interfering, wounding, introject message is silenced, the block will clear. The protocol is simple and elegant, and works without having to challenge the wounding message or associated negative beliefs.

Whether clients seek help for trauma wounds, attachment wounds, or both, the DNMS can help in a remarkably gentle fashion. My colleague Joan Bacon compared it to a popular trauma-focused protocol. She said doing the desensitization protocol is like going to a dentist, while doing the DNMS is like going to a spa.[8] During the DNMS, wounded ego states are only invited forward when one or more Resources are present to provide internal safety and support. Processing only proceeds when permission to do so has been granted from all parts of self.

The successes my DNMS clients have enjoyed over the years have not been merely a function of some unique, personal charisma or talent that I possess. Many therapists have been practicing the DNMS since my first workshop in 2002, and many have shared their success stories on the DNMS professional listserv. A few of their stories are provided below. I offer my heartfelt thanks to those therapists who have submitted client stories to print here. (They are not specifically named here to further ensure client confidentiality.)

- *Bruce, a middle-aged, divorced father, presented for therapy with symptoms of major depression, panic and anxiety, and psychotic thinking; and fear of taking on challenges at work. The symptoms were treated with the DNMS and a host of medications. Bruce grew up experiencing severe physical and emotional abuse and neglect from his father and mother – including some life-threatening traumas. During the DNMS he identified long held beliefs like, "I'm so flawed and needy I shouldn't exist" and "I have to take action on this problem but I can't because I'm flawed and will fail." This helped to uncover introjects delivering wounding parental messages like, "you are inherently flawed and cannot see what is obvious to everyone else, and you put yourself and others at risk every time you attempt something new." Over the course of the DNMS treatment many such introjects were healed with the Needs Meeting Protocol. In his own words: "The DNMS freed me from childish fears and unrealistic expectations that were demands I put on life that would never be met. It taught me to slow my mind's racing thoughts and to use the critical thinking skills I had, but had been buried. It put me in touch with my Resources, who are my Higher Power today. Untangled from past blocks to maturity, my basic thinking patterns have been retrained and while I still have many 'adult' struggles, I maintain a positive outlook toward life and people. My natural patterns of thinking are now optimistic, fearless and calm. Where I used to run from life, I now seek out new challenges. The rewards, as a result, have been incredible. My most profound change has come in my relationship with my father. Unfortunately, he was at the heart of many of my unresolved childhood issues. Today we talk and actually do projects around the house together: a complete miracle. I am no longer alone, as I have fresh new relationships with everyone in my family: mom, brother, and sister as well as my two sons." As a result of the treatment he was also able to take on a significant challenge at work – without anxiety. His success with the project earned him a promotion. He has been symptom-free since terminating therapy, and has titrated off of all medications.*

- *Beth was in her forties when her mother died. The complicated grief that followed brought on an episode of deep depression, cutting, and destructive eating and lifestyle choices. She sought therapy to get her life under control. In childhood she was constantly anxious – at home and school. Beth grew up experiencing neglect and verbal abuse from her father. Her chronic sense of being rejected and abandoned resulted* in an enmeshing and codependent relationship with her mother in childhood, and her husband in adulthood. In the first ten months of treatment her therapist applied a popular trauma desensitization therapy. While it provided some benefit at first, it eventually stopped helping. The therapist switched to the DNMS. Establishing a strong bond to the Resources played a vital role in Beth's ability to move forward again. It allowed her access to painful emotions and memories (including sexual abuse) that she'd felt unprepared to confront before. Using the Attachment Needs Ladder she was able to identify long held beliefs like, "I don't have a right to exist," and "Shame on me for existing." This helped to uncover introjects delivering wounding parental messages like, "You should have been a boy," and "You're not loveable or important." By the time the Needs Meeting Protocol was applied to all the Rung 1 and 2 introjects, she was making significant progress. Her depression had lifted, her cutting behavior had stopped, and her eating and lifestyle choices had significantly improved. For the first time in her life she was able to set and maintain healthy boundaries with intimidating family members. In her own words Beth wrote: "The DNMS process truly has changed my life. Actually changed is not the right word...it is so much more than just changed... maybe reborn, awakened, finally alive...those are more fitting, but yet they too seem not quite 'it'. It was definitely DNMS that allowed me to uncover, process through and un-stick from my past, opening me to both my true heart and self. Now along with the awareness and ever present help of the Resources, I can pretty much handle the day to day events in my life without falling back into old behaviors like raging, self-mutilation and self loathing. I can't put this into some heartfelt and articulate words that conveys the deep gratitude I have for the DNMS process and my DNMS therapist."

- Annabelle, a middle-aged, married, mother, began therapy to deal with a pattern of getting stuck in abusive relationships. She had seen six different counselors (over several years) for cognitive behavioral therapy, and had completed a community domestic violence program. None of these interventions successfully treated the internal conflict and loneliness that fueled her problem. At the time she started the DNMS she had just been badly beaten by her husband of 12 years. She wanted out of this relationship but could not make it happen. She grew up experiencing emotional abuse and neglect from her alcoholic father. Her passive mother did not protect her from his abuse. Using the Attachment Needs Ladder, she was able to identify beliefs like, "Its not safe to exist" and "I must not have needs." Many introjects were found delivering wounding parental messages like, "Shut up and don't talk about it," and "You're not safe unless you appease and please others." After completing all four rungs of the Attachment Needs Ladder, her most painful childhood memories were no longer disturbing to recall. In her own words: "After months of doing the DNMS I learned more about myself and what was driving me to think and feel the way I did. I learned about my child parts who were still looking to get their needs met. I noticed that the periods of chaos were becoming much rarer and that even my family life was improving. I discovered how I thought, and my beliefs about the world, directed my actions - not the other way around. When my mother died, I was able to grieve her loss in a healthy way because of the inner Resources I had developed in therapy. I am very grateful that I had found the inner strengths that were already there to go though that very difficult time. My two daughters began to look up to me as a mother, someone to turn to in times of need, rather than someone they needed to mother. My DNMS therapy has been like a drop of water in a very large pond. The ripples flow outward to quiet all the areas of the pond with peace, joy and inner strength. It has changed my life and the lives of my daughters." As a result of DNMS therapy, she's divorced her abusive husband. She's had no more feelings for him and had no problem staying away.

- Cassandra, a young, single woman, began therapy to deal with the pain of a broken engagement. She had symptoms of major depression with suicidal thoughts. She grew up experiencing harsh criticism and rage reactions from her mother. With the help of the Attachment Needs Ladder she was able to identify beliefs like, "My existence is completely unimportant" and "I must rely on everybody to tell me who I am and constantly reassure me about my appearance, skills, abilities and what I do for them because that makes me of value them." Many introjects were found wounding parental messages like, "If you can't fix the problems of others then you are weak and a failure" and " I am not capable of fixing my own problems because I am incapable so I must fix others." After completing all four rungs of the Attachment Needs Ladder, her most painful childhood memories were no longer disturbing to recall. In her own words: "The process of connecting to my Resources is one I will never forget. I now connect to my Resources regularly. I feel more in control of my self and my life. Having always been insecure, timid, and afraid of conflict, I now have my Resources to draw upon daily to live my life instead of going through the motions. I know that I am my Resources. Knowing they are my purest self has allowed me to take pride in who I am and what I can do in ways I never imagined possible. Just since I've started the DNMS, I've met with rapid success in my professional career and in personal relationships. For the first time in my life I know who I am, what I want, and am convinced that I can make it all happen. The DNMS has given me my life back to live. Instead of being a supporting character in my own story, I now know that I am the lead and the star of the show. This may sound trite, but it is a *way of being that I never thought possible. After years of constant conflict within myself, I am now at peace and fully aware of who I am and the possibilities the journey of my life has to offer."*

- *Julia, a young, single woman, began therapy to deal with major depression and obsessive/compulsive disorder after losing her job and moving back home to live with her parents. She grew up with a verbally abusive mother who could not tolerate even the smallest upsets to her world. She got messages from her parents that they could not love her if she was overweight, late, messy, or in any other way imperfect. She grew up feeling unloved. She started DNMS therapy after doing 3 years of trauma-focused therapy that helped only to a point. The Needs Meeting Protocol was applied to many parental introjects until her most painful childhood memories were no longer disturbing to recall. In her own words: "With each DNMS session, I could tell changes were taking place. At the time, I was actually living with my parents in their home. I was unemployed, and even though I had a master's degree, I was still getting verbal abuse from both parents. The DNMS helped me to change the way I perceived those abusive messages, new and old, from my parents. It gave me the strength to forgive my mother, to be able to talk with her like an adult, and not be scared of her anymore. It almost seemed like magic. For me DNMS was more successful than any thing else I'd tried. It helped me rid my mind of the constant negative messages that were holding me back from going forward in life. I was scared of my parents and now I am not. They don't have power over my thoughts anymore. I can think about a situation and judge it rationally instead of just saying 'well, these people hate me,' or 'I can't do that.' Now I know I can have exactly what I need, which I didn't believe when I went into counseling, and which is the most powerful message I've ever learned." She got another job, moved out of her parents' house, and got married.*

- *Pat, a middle-aged divorced mother, sought therapy to resolve her struggle to establish a romantic relationship. In childhood she was constantly anxious – at home and school. She was afraid to speak out in class and would hide in the bathroom between classes. Her helpless mother believed that, to be secure, women must tolerate men's abuses. She reported that her father was physically and verbally abusive with her, but not with her younger sister. Pat had been married to a physically and verbally abusive man. Although he was wealthy, her lawyers had to pressure him to pay child support. She was constantly fearful of his reactions whenever she had to challenge him. She complained to her mother daily about her plight. She admitted to being a hypochondriac, a condition she'd had since childhood. She believed: "I'm worthless; I'm stupid; there's something terribly wrong with me; I don't deserve to be happy; I'm a loser; and I'll always be alone." At the start of the DNMS, she was blocked from connecting to her Resources. Over a two-month period, many blocking introjects were found. The Switching the Dominance Protocol was applied to each. As the blocks cleared she reported many changes, including: feeling more adult, ceasing the daily calls to her mother, stopping the obsessive thoughts about loneliness and health, an end to feeling intimidated by her ex-husband, setting boundaries with him and her children, stopping smoking, and an overall sense of hope and well being. In addition, she began dating a respectful man and, instead of being focused on pleasing him, she was comfortable being herself and seeing what would develop.*

Here are some comments DNMS clients have made about the benefits of the therapy:

- *"Because of the DNMS I have experienced dramatic changes in affect, both to the stimuli that previously bothered me and to my general level of tension. I have noticed that I no longer go around malls with my hands clenched, my breathing is normal in places when there are a lot of new people, I feel relaxed and also have noticed somatic relief from eczema and irritable bowel syndrome. I have more confidence."*

- *"As a result of working with DNMS, today I live with a stronger sense of reality. I no longer feel like a child trying to figure out the adult world. As a result of this therapy, I am more often in my authentic adult self more of the time."*

- *"My quality of life has improved as a result of DNMS. What held me captive and made me depressed, my low self-esteem and my fear are totally gone. My issues with feeling unworthy to express my feelings are also gone. I feel and know that I am strong, that I am good, that I am worth being taken care of and worth being able to speak up for myself."*

- *"I can see that troubles are temporary now and get through them knowing they will pass. I am not worried about what my coworkers or family members think of me anymore. I do not feel like a failure or a phony. I feel GREAT about myself!"*

- *"Since starting the DNMS, I noticed it's much more peaceful in my head. The part that used to react to any idea with 'you can't make me' or 'you can't stop me,' appears to be gone. What a relief. Once I address an issue, not only does it no longer bother me, but I can't remember what it was. I can remember incidents clearly, but the negative emotional response doesn't exist anymore. This seems to be permanent."*

Contributions to the Development of the Model

Many of my treasured colleagues have contributed to the development of the DNMS – some in direct ways and some in indirect ways. My first thanks go to Sandra Paulsen, who began giving presentations about ego state therapy at EMDR conferences in 1994.[9] These workshops were my first introduction to ego state therapy. I'm appreciative of Francine Shapiro for developing EMDR as a *structured* protocol.[10] I adopted her idea of applying a systematic, step-by-step protocol to accomplish a very specific therapy objective. I'm profoundly grateful to Merle Yost for giving me the foundational premise for the model. He inspired my very first needs meeting protocol, which involved a single, Competent Adult Self meeting the needs of wounded child parts. I was also inspired by Brian Lynn's *Pre-traumatized Self* article in 2000.[11] He proposed clients could connect to a part of self that experienced tranquility in the earliest days in the womb – before the first trauma occurred; and proposed this Pre-Traumatized Self could serve as a resource. After reading about this, I realized I could bring together two internal resources to work as a team – a Competent Adult Self and a Pre-Traumatized Self, which together could form a Resource Sandwich.[12] Child parts would find the center of the sandwich to be a comforting, safe place to get their needs met. (The Pre-Traumatized Self resource has since been replaced by the Spiritual Core Self resource.) In 2002 my colleague Tricia Stevens encouraged me to replace the single Competent Adult Self with two adult Resources, a masculine/protective adult Resource (Protective Adult Self) and a feminine/nurturing adult Resource (Nurturing Adult Self), to mimic a complete family unit.[13] With this change, my colleague Helen Pankowsky wisely suggested replacing the term Resource Sandwich with *Healing Circle*.[14] I'm grateful for Joan Bacon and Richard Holcomb who have, over the years, provided many ideas and suggestions to improve the protocols. I'm also thankful for all the DNMS professional listserv members who have posted questions and problems that have challenged me to keep improving the model.

About this Book

This book provides a wealth of information for any therapist wishing to practice the DNMS. The first chapter opens with a brief overview of the model, followed by important background material. The second chapter provides information about ego state therapy in general, and the DNMS in particular. The third, fourth, fifth and sixth chapters provide detailed descriptions of the Resource Development Protocol, the Switching the Dominance Protocol, the Conference Room Protocol, and the Needs Meeting Protocol respectively. These are the four key protocols that make up the DNMS. The last chapter provides a comprehensive discussion of all the complications and blocks that can arise, in each protocol and procedure. The Appendix offers an abundance of background material, suggestions for working with unstable clients, handouts for clients, and worksheets and forms for therapists. (These handouts, worksheets, and forms are also available to download at www.dnmsinstitute.com/doc/dnmstherapistworksheets.pdf.) The personal pronouns, *he* and *she*, have been alternated throughout the text so that the awkwardness of writing *he/she* could be avoided.

DNMS Research

Two DNMS case-study articles have been published in peer-reviewed journals. (See the abstracts on page 197.) One is a case study about a client of mine with dissociative identity disorder. The other is eight case studies provided by myself and two other therapists. While these published case-studies support my assertion that the DNMS is effective, they do not meet the criteria for *empirical research*. The DNMS has not yet been tested in controlled trials. Until that research has been conducted and published the DNMS cannot be called an *evidence-based therapy*. I look forward to the day when clinical research facilities across the country take the lead in studying the DNMS. Unfortunately it may be difficult to research. For example, it takes much longer to remediate all a client's childhood needs, than to desensitize a single trauma. It may be a challenge to design controlled research protocols that track the treatment benefits and manage the confounding variables, when research subjects receive many months of therapy. I look forward to the day that challenge has been met.

DNMS Support and Training

From 2002 to 2006 I gave many weekend workshops to teach the DNMS to licensed therapists. As the DNMS evolved so did the trainings. By 2006 I realized that the DNMS had become too complicated for most therapists to learn in a weekend workshop, so I began developing a Home Study Course. The Course was completed in 2008, and is now available for any licensed psychotherapist to purchase. The course consists of 16 hours of narrated slide shows – just like one would see at a workshop. The slide shows provide audio tapes of real sessions, so students can learn by hearing how it works. Students can proceed through the slides at their own pace. Study questions are provided with the slides and with the study guide that accompanies the course. Students can get 20 continuing education credits for finishing the course. This type of training provides everything a student needs but facilitated practice. Clinicians who have taken the Home Study Course are eligible to participate in live facilitated practice workshops, to supplement their home study. A full description of the Home Study Course is provided on pages 256-257.

Licensed therapists who purchase this book are eligible for enrollment in the DNMS professional e-mail discussion list. For more information about enrolling in the list, go to www.dnmsinstitute.com/list.html.

References

1. Van der Kolk, B.A., Brown, P., & Van der Hart, O. (1989). Pierre Janet on post-traumatic stress. *Journal of Traumatic Stress, 2*, 365-378.
    Scurfield, R.M. 1985. Post-trauma stress assessment and treatment: Overview and formulations, pp. 219-256. In: C.R. Figley (ed).*Trauma and its wake: The study and treatment of Post-traumatic Stress Disorder*. Brunner/Mazel. New York.
    Putnam, F.W. (1989). *Diagnosis and treatment of multiple personality disorder*. New York: The Guilford Press.
    Phillips, M., & Frederick, C. (1995). *Healing the divided self: Clinical and Ericksonian hypnotherapy for post-traumatic and dissociative conditions*. New York: W.W. Norton & Company.
2. Shapiro, F. (2001). *Eye movement desensitization and reprocessing: Basic principles, protocols, and procedures.* Second edition. New York: Guilford Press.
3. Keane, T.M., Fairbank, J.A., Caddell, J.M., & Zimering, R.T. (1989). Implosive (flooding) therapy reduces symptoms of PTSD in Vietnam combat veterans. *Behavior Therapy, 20,* 245-260.
    4Brown, D. P., & Fromm, E. (1986). *Hypnotherapy and hypnoanalysis*. Hillsdale, NJ: Erlbaum
5. Foa E., Hembree E., and Rothbaum, B. (2007). *Prolonged Exposure Therapy for PTSD: Emotional Processing of Traumatic Experiences Therapist Guide*. Oxford University Press.
6. Assagioli, R. (1975). *Psychosynthesis: A manual of principles and techniques.* London: Turnstone Press.
    Schwartz, R. C. (1995). *Internal family systems therapy*. New York: Guilford Press.
    Stone, H. & Stone, S. (1993). *Embracing our selves: The voice dialogue manual.* Nataraj Publishing.
    Watkins, J. G., & Watkins, H. H. (1997). *Ego states: Theory and therapy.* New York:
7. Cassidy, J. & Shaver, P.R. (2008) Editors, *Handbook of Attachment, Second Edition: Theory, Research, and Clinical Applications*. Guilford Press.
    Cassidy, J. & Shaver, P.R. (1999) Editors, *Handbook of Attachment, First Edition: Theory, Research, and Clinical Applications*. Guilford Press.
8. Personal conversation with Joan Bacon in 2005.
9. Paulsen, S. (1994). *Ego State Disorders: Dissociative but not multiple.* EMDRIA Conference Presentation.
    Paulsen, S. (1996). *Using Internal Dialogue to Achieve Maximum EMDR Results.* EMDRIA Conference Presentation
10. Shapiro, F. (2001). *Eye movement desensitization and reprocessing: Basic principles, protocols, and procedures.* Second edition. New York: Guilford Press.
11. Lynn, B. (2000). Accessing Pre-Traumatic Prenatal Experience Using EMDR: Uncovering a Powerful Resource of Equanimity, Integration, and Self-Esteem in the Pre-Traumatized Self. *EMDRIA Newsletter*, 5:3.
12. Schmidt, S.J. (2001). Meeting needs with a resource sandwich. *EMDRIA Newsletter - Special Edition*, December 2001.
13. Personal conversation with Tricia Stevens in 2002.
14. Personal conversation with Helen Pankowsky in 2002.

Chapter 1
Overview and Background

The DNMS is an ego state therapy – a psychotherapeutic approach for healing wounded adults, based on what is known about how a child's brain develops within a healthy family. It borrows from ego state theory inner-child therapy, self-reparenting therapy, developmental psychology, attachment theory, Eye Movement Desensitization and Reprocessing (EMDR) therapy, and recent developments in neuroscience.

This model is based on the assumption that children have physical, emotional, social, and intellectual needs at each stage of development.[1] When caregivers meet those needs well, children thrive. When caregivers fail to meet needs well enough, they suffer. The degree to which developmental needs were not adequately met is the degree to which a part of self can become stuck in childhood. *Being stuck* means that behaviors, beliefs, or emotions connected to unresolved wounds from the past can get triggered today.[2] For example, you may feel like an adult one minute – then something upsetting happens and suddenly you see the world through the eyes of a sad, angry, or fearful child. The more stuck we are in childhood, the more we have unwanted behaviors, beliefs, and emotions.

The DNMS is designed to treat a wide range of motivated[3] clients, regardless of initial diagnosis or ego strength. This includes clients with complex *trauma wounds* such as those inflicted by verbal, physical, and sexual abuse; and *attachment wounds*, such as those inflicted by parental rejection, neglect, and enmeshment. Clinicians have used the DNMS to treat a wide range of symptoms and issues, including depression, anxiety, panic disorder, social phobia, substance abuse, complex PTSD, relationship trouble, sexual abuse trauma, obsessions/compulsions, eating disorders, dissociative disorders, borderline personality disorder, sexual addiction, self-injurious behaviors, and complicated grief.

Preliminary research supports the efficacy of the DNMS protocols. Two journal articles describe case study data.[4] The first is a single case study report about a client with dissociative identity disorder. The second describes eight case studies from the caseloads of three different DNMS therapists. The two article abstracts are provided in Appendix B, page 197.

Overview of the Key DNMS Protocols & Procedures

This will give you an overview of the model, so as you begin to learn the individual protocols, you'll understand where each fits in the big picture. In the chapters to come, each protocol is explained in detail with many case examples and sample interventions.

© Copyright 2009 by Shirley Jean Schmidt, MA, LPC. All rights reserved. Duplication in any form without permission is prohibited.

Taking a History

Psychotherapy usually begins with getting a history. Before starting the DNMS you'll especially want to find out about a client's most significant relationships – especially those from the developing years. The history-taking should include questions about:
- How family members related to the client (e.g. loving, abusive, neglectful, rejecting, enmeshing).
- How family members related to themselves (e.g. self-critical, self-sabotaging, self-soothing).
- How family members related to each other (e.g. mutually supportive, mutually destructive).
- How family members related to people outside the family (e.g. supportive or destructive).
- How people outside the family related to the client (e.g. supportive or destructive).

Answers to these questions should provide you a pretty good idea of where a client's current strengths and weaknesses have come from. See Appendix D for more information about taking a history and orienting clients for DNMS processing.

The Resource Development Protocol

The DNMS assumes that most adult clients already have within them the skills and abilities to meet a loved one's developmental needs. Such skills might be expressed often or rarely, but if they are present at all clients should be able to access and strengthen them. The Resource Development Protocol is structured to strengthen a client's connection to three Resource parts of self – a Nurturing Adult Self, a Protective Adult Self, and a Spiritual Core Self. When you apply this protocol you'll invite clients to recall real moments of nurturing and protecting a loved one, and peak spiritual experiences – times they experienced the distinct qualities of each Resource. These real experiences anchor three brief, guided meditations that help clients connect to these Resources. For example, during the Nurturing Adult Self meditation a client might recall nurturing her grandson through an illness. During the Protective Adult Self meditation she might recall protecting him by rushing him to the hospital. During the Spiritual Core Self meditation she might recall a peak spiritual experience during a church retreat. By anchoring each meditation with a familiar experience, clients understand their Resources are real parts of self, not just imaginary helpers.

The Healing Circle
Spiritual Core Self

Protective Adult Self   Nurturing Adult Self

Once a client has connected to each Resource, you'll invite her to bring all three to together – to form a *Healing Circle*. In later protocols, these Resources will work together as a team to help wounded parts of self get unstuck from the past.

The Switching the Dominance Protocol

The Switching the Dominance Protocol is a multipurpose intervention – effective at calming and quieting internal conflicts. It can provide immediate relief for certain emotional overreactions and it can help in overcoming processing blocks. It is also an integral part of the DNMS Conference Room Protocol.

The DNMS model posits several types of wounded child parts. The most damaging type, *maladaptive introjects*, mirror the wounding actions and messages of abusers, neglecters, rejecters, or betrayers. Their wounding messages are directed towards other parts of self. This perpetuates the internal conflicts that fuel many unwanted behaviors, beliefs, and emotions.

A maladaptive introject is made up of two components: (1) a mask or costume that mimics a wounding caregiver, and (2) an innocent child self underneath, reluctantly wearing it. When you start this protocol, the introject mask will be dominant. By speaking to the child part under the mask and applying a series of mini-interventions, you will be able to help her understand that the mask is just a recording of the wounding person the mask is mirroring, and not a real threat at all. As the child part begins to understand this, the mask will

© Copyright 2009 by Shirley Jean Schmidt, MA, LPC. All rights reserved. Duplication in any form without permission is prohibited.

appear smaller and less important. Eventually the mask will appear so small and so unimportant that the child part can put the remains of it in her pocket, and feel control over it for the first time. When this occurs the dominance has switched from the mask to the child part that was wearing it.

The Switching the Dominance Protocol often results in an immediate reduction of the associated unwanted targeted behaviors, beliefs, or emotions. Clients typically report less internal conflict. The positive effects may last a long time, a few weeks, or until the next time the client is stressed. While it *helps* introjects to heal, it does not usually complete the process. The Needs Meeting Protocol is usually needed to finish the job.

The Attachment Needs Ladder Questionnaire

In the DNMS model, attachment wounds are considered so important they are systematically identified, addressed, and healed. Attachment wounds are defined as the emotional wounds sustained in childhood with caregivers' day-to-day failures to meet attachment needs by being chronically rejecting, neglectful, enmeshing, invalidating, or unsupportive. They often form in the absence of good things happening, such as a lack of positive attention, loving attunement, or good boundaries. Clients who cannot readily recognize the good things they missed often have difficulty talking about the harm these experiences inflicted.

The DNMS Attachment Needs Ladder questionnaire helps clients articulate the very important negative beliefs associated with attachment wounds. It consists of a list of negative beliefs a client might acquire in childhood if attachment needs were not met well. The beliefs are organized in four categories – listed on the questionnaire in order of importance. The categories include: Rung 1 - Existence, Rung 2 - Basic Safety, Rung 3 - Sense of Self, and Rung 4 - Relationship to Others. You'll ask clients to rate, from 0-10, how true each negative belief on a single Rung feels, at moments they've felt especially vulnerable. Those beliefs that are rated above zero will be addressed by the Conference Room and Needs Meeting Protocols, one Rung at a time.

The Conference Room Protocol

You'll begin the Conference Room Protocol by inviting your client to get a mental picture of the Resources in a conference room, with a conference table and chairs. Next you'll invite into the conference room, to sit on one side of the table, all the parts of self that believe the negative statements that the client rated above zero. These are called *reactive parts*. You'll then ask the most upset reactive part to look across the table to see the maladaptive introject that is mirroring the person at the root of the upset. When an introject appears, you'll switch the dominance. Then you'll ask the next most upset reactive part to look across the table. When the next maladaptive introject appears, you'll switch the dominance. You'll repeat these steps until every reactive part at the table has identified each associated introject, and the dominance of each has been switched. Once this protocol is complete, all parts at the table will feel a sense of relief and the internal disturbance around the targeted issue will be substantially calmed. You'll then invite the client to select one or more introjects and reactive parts from the conference room to begin the Needs Meeting Protocol.

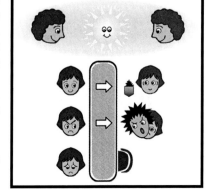

© Copyright 2009 by Shirley Jean Schmidt, MA, LPC. All rights reserved. Duplication in any form without permission is prohibited.

The Needs Meeting Protocol

The Needs Meeting Protocol begins when you invite the introjects and reactive parts, selected from the conference room, into the Healing Circle. Once inside the circle you'll guide the Resources to meet their developmental needs (e.g. safety, love, attunement, nurturing, validation, respect), help them process through painful emotions (e.g. anger and grief), and establish an emotional bond. As the wounded parts make a loving connection to the Resources, they become totally unstuck from the past.

Resources Meet Developmental Needs

Resources Process Painful Emotions

Resources Form an Emotional Bond

Wounded Parts Become Totally Unstuck

Follow-up and Repeat the Process

Once the Needs Meeting Protocol is complete the unwanted behaviors, beliefs, and emotions associated with a targeted issue typically abate. You'll ask the client follow-up questions to verify a healing shift has occurred. For example, you'll ask if the wounding messages that were delivered by the introject masks are still disturbing. The typical answer is "no." You'll ask if the negative belief that felt true in the beginning still feels true. The typical answer is "no." You'll ask if the targeted issue still feels like a problem. The typical answer is "no." When one issue is resolved, you'll invite the client to focus on another. You'll address each problem this way until all therapy goals have been met.

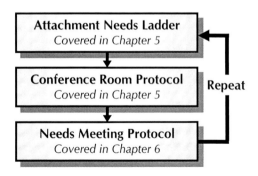

DNMS Limitations

Some presenting problems are related to unmet developmental needs and perpetuated by maladaptive introjects, and some are not. For example, unwanted symptoms can come from organic brain dysfunction (e.g. head

© Copyright 2009 by Shirley Jean Schmidt, MA, LPC. All rights reserved. Duplication in any form without permission is prohibited.

injury), chronic physical stress (e.g. chemotherapy), and inherent temperament (e.g. hypersensitivity). The symptoms associated with such conditions can be exacerbated when wounding messages from a maladaptive introject is compounding a problem. The DNMS can help relieve the portion of unwanted symptoms generated by maladaptive introjects. For example, a person who is inherently hypersensitive may feel driven to anxiety and shame about that by a critical mother introject. If the DNMS heals the mother introject, the anxiety and shame can be eliminated, but the DNMS is not likely to diminish the inherent hypersensitivity.

While many clients are drawn to the DNMS, some are not. Some clients reject the idea of parts of self, some are dead-set on a particular therapy (e.g. EMDR, hypnosis, CBT) and refuse to discuss DNMS, and some need basic help (e.g. personal safety coaching, career counseling) more than DNMS.

Background Material

Developmental Stages

The idea of developmental stages has been around a long time. Sigmund Freud theorized about stages of psychosexual development,[5] Jean Piaget about stages of physical and intellectual development,[6] and John Bowlby about stages of attachment to the caregiver.[7] For the purposes of the DNMS, a developmental stage is defined as a span of time relevant to a baby's, child's, or adolescent's physical, intellectual, social, and emotional maturation.

Erik Erikson theorized that human development unfolds in eight predetermined stages, from infancy to late adulthood, and that each stage involves specific psychosocial developmental tasks.[8] He asserted that progress through each stage was in part determined by the degree of success or failure in all the previous stages. He understood that a person who got their early needs met well, and who successfully mastered developmental tasks, would have certain virtues and psychosocial strengths which would help him lifelong. In contrast, if one's developmental needs were not met well, the person would fail in these tasks and might develop too much of the negative aspect of the task (e.g. too mistrusting), or too much of the positive (e.g. too trusting).

Jean Illsley-Clarke and Connie Dawson[9] wrote *Growing Up Again: Parenting Ourselves, Parenting Our Children* with the dual purpose of teaching parents how to raise their children and of teaching adults how to grow up again. They describe how caregiver behaviors make it more or less possible for children to master the full spectrum of their developmental tasks, needs, and challenges, in order to meet their full potential. They propose nine developmental stages, from pre-birth to old age. The table on the following two pages lists their first seven stages, with corresponding developmental tasks, needs, and clues that needs were not met well. (The table was adapted from Chapter 25 of *Growing up Again*, with permission from the publisher.)

Hierarchy of Needs

Abraham Maslow is best known for his study of human needs. He believed that if a person's developmental needs were not met well enough it could cause one to "fixate" on those unmet needs for the remainder of life. He considered this fixation to be the basis of neurosis. He theorized a hierarchy of basic human needs[10] His hierarchy included:
- Physiological needs – Need for food, water, air, sleep, activity, rest, etc.
- Safety and security needs – Need to be protected from danger.
- Belongingness needs – Need for love, secure attachment, attunement, and connection to others.
- Lower esteem needs – Need to be respected and appreciated by others.
- Higher esteem needs – Need for self-respect, confidence, competence, achievement, and independence.
- Aesthetic needs – Need for symmetry, order, and beauty.

See Appendix B, page 198 for Maslow's Hierarchy of Needs pyramid, and for a table that integrates Maslow's needs with Erikson's stages of development.

© Copyright 2009 by Shirley Jean Schmidt, MA, LPC. All rights reserved. Duplication in any form without permission is prohibited.

Illsley-Clarke and Dawson: Developmental Stages, Tasks, and Needs

	Developmental Tasks	Developmental Needs	Clues Needs Were Not Met Well
Prenatal Stage: Conception to Birth	• To grow • To experience being separate and connected to mom • To accept nourishment, love • To move around • To get familiar with mom • To make decisions about trust • To initiate and complete the birth process	• Mother gets proper nutrition, exercise, rest, medical care • Mother's basic needs are met • Parents resolve their own prenatal traumas or grief from earlier miscarriages • Parents prepare to welcome the child for who she is • Parents lovingly talk, sing to baby • Parents joyful about baby coming • Family prepared to welcome baby • Parents prepare place for baby • Mother arranges for a safe birth • Parents plan good care for baby • Parents plan how to meet their own needs after baby is born	• An unaccounted-for incompleteness of self • Lack of joyfulness not otherwise accounted for • Unable to start things • Addictions or compulsions • Strong desire to be in or avoid water • Struggle to get food or wanting to be served food • Need to sleep all curled up • Reacting against someone wanting to get too close • Excessive independence • Starting things and not finishing • Feeling grandiose or worthless
Stage 1: Birth to 6 Months	• To call for care • To cry or signal to get needs met • To accept touch • To accept nurturance • To bond emotionally • To learn to trust caring adults and self • To decide to live, to be	• Developmental achievements affirmed • Loving, consistent care • Appropriate response to needs • Parents thinking of baby • Holding and looking at baby while feeding • Talking to and echoing baby • Nurturing touch, gaze, talk, song • Parents who seek help as needed • Reliable and trustworthy caregivers • Parents who can meet their own needs	• Not trusting others • Wanting others to anticipate needs • Not aware of needs • Not needing anything • Feeling numb • Others needs are more important • Not wanting to be touched • Compulsive, joyless sexual touching • Unwilling to self-disclose, especially negative information
Stage 2: 6 to 18 Months	• To explore and experience the environment • To develop sensory awareness • To signal needs • To trust others and self • To continue forming secure attachments with parents • To get help when distressed • To learn there are options, not all problems are easily solved • To develop initiative • To continue tasks from Stage 1	• Developmental achievements affirmed • Loving, consistent care • Safe environment • Protection from harm • Food, nurturing, touch • Two yeses for every no • Many sensory experiences • Uninterrupted expression • Validation of experience • Lots of conversation and eye contact • Response to child-initiated play • Parents who can meet their own needs	• Boredom • Reluctance to initiate • Being overactive or too quiet • Perfectionism or avoidance • Compulsively neat • Doubting familiar knowledge • Believing it's okay not to be safe, supported, protected
Stage3: 18 Months to 3 Years	• To establish an ability to think for self • To test reality, to push against boundaries and other people • To learn to solve problems with cause-and-effect logic • To learn words like: stop, go there, come here, stay here • To express emotions like anger • To separate from parents without losing their love • To develop initiative • To begin ending ego-centricity • To continue tasks from earlier stages	• Developmental achievements affirmed • Love, safety, and protection • Help transitioning between activities • Clear, simple instructions • Encouragement and praise • Words like: stop, come, stay, go there • Reasonable limits enforced well • Celebration of ability to think • Time and space to organize thinking • Permission to express positive and negative feelings • Reasons and information • Help naming things • Harmony, not conflict • Even-tempered caregivers • Parents who can meet their own needs	• Inappropriate rebellion • Preference to be right over successful • Fear and sadness covered with anger or bullying • Egocentric • Fear of anger in self or others • Saying no or yes without thinking • Trouble setting boundaries • Letting others dominate • Expression of anger indirectly

© Copyright 2009 by Shirley Jean Schmidt, MA, LPC. All rights reserved. Duplication in any form without permission is prohibited.

Illsley-Clarke and Dawson: Developmental Stages, Tasks, and Needs

	Developmental Tasks	Developmental Needs	Clues Needs Were Not Met Well
Stage 4: 3 Years to 6 Years	• To assert an identity separate from others • To acquire information about world, self, body, and gender • To learn that behaviors have consequences • To discover one's effect on others and one's place in groups • To learn to exert power to affect relationships • To practice socially appropriate behavior • To separate fantasy from reality • To learn extent of personal power • To continue learning earlier developmental tasks	• Developmental achievements affirmed • Love, safety, and protection • Support for exploring the world of things, people, ideas, feelings • Encouragement to express feelings and connect feelings and thinking • Information about the environment • Answers to questions • Appropriate (loving) positive or negative consequences for actions • Age-appropriate responsibility • Encouragement of fantasy and separation of fantasy from reality • Praise for appropriate behavior • Age-appropriate information about world, self, body, and gender	• Having to be in a position of power • Afraid of or reluctant to use power • Unsure of personal adequacy • Identity confusion – needing to define self by a job or relationship • Feeling driven to achieve • Overuse of outlandish dress or behavior • Frequently comparing self to others and needing to come off better • Wanting or expecting magical solutions or effects
Stage 5: 6 Years to 12 Years	• To learn skills, learn from mistakes, and decide to be adequate • To learn to listen, collect information and think • To practice thinking and doing • To reason about wants and needs • To check out family rules and learn about structures outside the family • To learn the relevancy of rules • To learn consequences of breaking rules • To disagree with others and still feel loved • To test ideas and values • To develop internal controls • To learn age-appropriate responsibility • To learn when to flee, when to flow, and when to stand firm • To learn to cooperate • To test abilities against others • To identify with one's own gender • To continue to learn from earlier tasks	• Developmental achievements affirmed • Love, safety, and protection • Affirmation for learning in own style • Love and praise for developing skills • Reliable sources and accurate information about people, world, sex • Challenges to negative behavior/thinking • Encouragement for cause-and-effect thinking • Clearly defined, age-appropriate responsibilities • Affirmations for logical/creative thinking • Problem solving help/tools • Help discerning when to flee, flow, or fight • Appropriate negotiable and non-negotiable rules • Experience of natural consequences • Sense of connection in spite of disagreement • Encouragement of accurate reporting • Encouragement of age-appropriate behaviors • Encouragement and help being responsible for own decisions, thinking, and feelings • Teachers to develop skills of interest	• Having to be part of a gang or only functioning well as a loner • Not understanding the relevance of rules • Not understanding the freedom rules can give • Unwillingness to examine own values or morals. • Needing to be king or queen of the hill • Trusting the thinking of others more than trusting own intuition • Expecting one has to know how to do things without learning how, finding out, or being taught how • Reluctance to learn new things or be productive
Stage 6: 12 to 19 Years	• To take more steps towards independence • To achieve a clearer emotional separation from family • To emerge gradually as a separate, independent person with own identity and values • To be competent and responsible for own needs, feelings, and behaviors • To integrate sexuality into earlier developmental tasks	• Developmental achievements affirmed • Love, safety, and protection • Acceptance of feelings • Discussion about sexuality • Unacceptable behavior confronted • Clear boundaries about drug use and sexual activity • Support for moves towards independence • Help reworking tasks from earlier developmental stages • Encouragement of the development of true-to-self unique identity based on socially acceptable behaviors	• Preoccupation with sex, body, clothes, appearance, friends, or sex role • Unsure of own values; vulnerable to peer pressure • Problems with starting and ending jobs, roles, and relationships • Over-dependence on or alienation from family or others • Irresponsibility • Trouble making /keeping commitments • Looking to others to define self • Confusing sex with nurturing • Unsure of sexual identity • Unsure of lovability

© Copyright 2009 by Shirley Jean Schmidt, MA, LPC. All rights reserved. Duplication in any form without permission is prohibited.

Well-Intentioned Caregivers Can Fail to Meet Needs

Unmet developmental needs are not limited to incidents of outright child abuse and neglect. It is possible for well-intentioned, reasonably educated, highly motivated, loving caregivers to fail to meet all the needs of a child. This can happen when a child's needs are particularly complex or obscure; caregivers are ill-informed about the specific needs of the child at a given developmental stage, and unknowingly make poor choices in feeding, limit setting, discipline, child care, managing sibling rivalries, etc.; caregivers have unresolved emotional issues; caregivers are under extreme stress or suffering hardships, such as financial problems, health problems, natural disasters, or war, which make it impossible for them to meet needs they would otherwise be able to meet.

Ego State Theory

The DNMS is an ego state therapy based on ego state theory. This section provides you an overview of ego state theory. Chapter 2 will discuss the application of ego state therapy. Ego state theory posits that we all have different sub-personalities, parts of self, or ego states. To understand ego states, you must first understand states of mind.

A state of mind consists of behaviors, beliefs, emotions, and body sensations evoked by the environment at a given moment in time.[11] You're always in a state of mind. You're in a state of mind right now. Hopefully it's relaxed, alert, and curious. States of mind are temporary, and constantly changing. For example, you may wake up one morning in a calm and rested state of mind, then shift into a vigilant state of mind when a suicidal client calls in crisis. Later you may shift back into a calm state of mind when your client is admitted to a hospital.

According to Daniel Siegel, a state of mind can become *engrained* when a positive event is experienced repeatedly (e.g. when a parent consistently supports and encourages a child's self-expression); when a negative event is experienced repeatedly (e.g. when a parent consistently punishes a child's self-expression); or when the mind cannot make sense of a traumatic event (e.g. when a child is assaulted by a parent and cannot understand why).[12] An engrained state of mind can become an ego state, or a part of self with a point of view. An ego state is more enduring than a temporary state of mind. When a person is in a particular ego state, all the emotions, beliefs, and/or body sensations that were present when that state of mind became engrained are present again.

Healthy ego states form in response to positive, affirming relationships with role models who are loving and attuned. They live in the present; feel and manage the full range of emotions; hold positive beliefs about self and world; engage in appropriate/desirable behaviors; and have an adaptive point of view.

Wounded ego states form in response to traumas; and to negative, wounding relationships with role models who are abusive, neglectful, rejecting, and enmeshing. They live in the past; are stuck in painful emotions; hold negative, irrational beliefs about self and world; engage in unwanted or inappropriate behaviors; and have a maladaptive point of view.

Ego states can change over time – usually becoming more engrained as new events are interpreted based on past experience and bias. Healthy ego states typically adapt well to new experiences, while wounded ego states do not. In fact, wounded parts of self may feel more powerless as their poor decisions lead to more problems. But wounded ego states can heal and grow if they can get nurturing from adult parts of self, and process through their traumas and losses.

An individual can have many ego states – both healthy and wounded. The term self-system refers to the "family" of ego states within an individual.[13] Ego states, just like family members, may communicate with each other effectively or ineffectively, or interact cooperatively or uncooperatively.[14] The nature of ego state interactions within the self-system is influenced by the nature of *ego state boundaries* – which may be permeable, semi-permeable, or rigid. These boundaries affect the way ego states communicate with each other.[15]

© Copyright 2009 by Shirley Jean Schmidt, MA, LPC. All rights reserved. Duplication in any form without permission is prohibited.

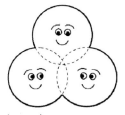

When boundaries are *permeable*, communication between ego states is open, and cooperative.

When boundaries are *semi-permeable* communication between ego states is problematic, and marked by a lack of internal cooperation, and difficulty resolving internal conflicts.

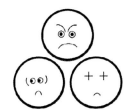

When boundaries are *rigid*, communication between ego states is minimal or non-existent, and marked by un-resolvable internal conflicts.

The degree of ego state permeability is a reflection of ego state integration. Ego states are more or less *integrated* or *dissociated*. This occurs on a continuum – from *adaptive differentiation* to *pathological dissociation*.[16] At the left of the continuum fall the well-adjusted individuals experiencing healthy integration or the *adaptive differentiation* of ego states. For example the drill sergeant who has one state of mind for training soldiers, another state of mind for playing with his infant son, and another state of mind for romancing his wife. These ego state boundaries are permeable. At the center of the continuum fall clients with *defensive* dissociation. They have internal conflicts that are difficult to manage. They present with problems, such as PTSD, eating disorders, panic disorder, depression, obsessive-compulsive disorder, and so forth.[17] These ego state boundaries are semi-permeable. At the right of the continuum fall the clients with pathological dissociation. They have ego states, or alters, that may not know of each other's existence. These clients present with dissociative identity disorder. These ego state boundaries are rigid.

Continuum: Adaptive Differentiation – Pathological Dissociation

Adaptive Differentiation - - - - - - - - - - - - - *Defensive* - - - - - - - - - - - - - *Pathological Dissociation*

Normal Well-Adjusted	Conflicted Ego States	Ego State Disorders	Complex PTSD & DDNOS	Dissociative Identity Disorder

Permeable Boundaries - - - - - - - - *Semi-permeable Boundaries* - - - - - - - - - - - - - *Rigid Boundaries*

An individual's ego state boundary permeability will not necessarily be uniform across the self-system, as this continuum might suggest. An individual may have ego states with permeable boundaries, semi-permeable boundaries, and/or rigid boundaries – all at the same time. An individual may have some ego states that co-exist in harmony, while others exist in hostile conflict.

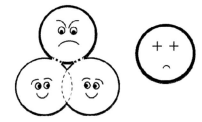

Wounded Ego States Formed by the Firing of Mirror Neurons

The DNMS focuses a lot of attention on healing the most damaging wounded ego states – maladaptive introjects. To really understand the nature of introjects, it helps to understand how they form. New research in the area of *mirror neurons* appears to provide a possible explanation for introjection. Neurophysiologist Vittorio Gallese and colleagues from the University of Parma observed that when one monkey performs a specific action with his hand, specific neurons fire in association with that action. A second monkey, observing that action, will involuntarily fire the same neurons (mirror neurons) that he would need to perform that same task.[18] This discovery, made in the mid 1990s, has spurred a flood of research into the nature and role of a mirror neuron system in humans.

© Copyright 2009 by Shirley Jean Schmidt, MA, LPC. All rights reserved. Duplication in any form without permission is prohibited.

Neuroimaging studies have demonstrated that certain neural circuits get activated in a person who is carrying out an action, expressing an emotion, or experiencing a sensation, and in a person who is observing that person's action, emotion, or sensation.[19]

For example, certain neural circuits are activated in the brain of this happy woman (to right) waving her hat. The same neural circuits become activated in the brain of this child observing the happy woman waving her hat.

Likewise, certain neural circuits are activated in the brain of this unhappy woman pulling her hair (below). The same neural circuits become activated in the brain of this child observing the unhappy woman pulling her hair. This is called *shared activation*.

Mirror neurons appear to get activated when we observe characters in a movie. We feel fear when a character is in danger. We feel sad when a character loses a loved one. We feel aroused when a character is aroused. We feel happy when the boy wins the girl. Of course mirror neurons can get activated in real life dramas as well.

Two Examples of *Shared Activation*

UCLA professor Marco Iacoboni's studies suggest that mirror neurons can send messages to the limbic system making it possible for humans to read each other's feelings.[20] That appears to account for empathy. Studies suggest that the mirror neurons activated while observing others' actions, emotions, or sensations, also respond to their intentions.[21]

Mirror neurons may help us make predictions about others' behavior and emotions. They may help us learn from each other how best to survive. Neuroscientist V.S. Ramachandran suggests that mirror neurons in primitive clans may have enabled innovations such as language and tool use to spread quickly, because they were hardwired to mimic each other.[22]

Gallese believes that the shared activation that arises as mirror neurons fire leads to *embodied simulation*.[23] He writes: "By means of embodied simulation we do not just 'see' an action, an emotion, or a sensation (of another). Side by side with the sensory description of the observed social stimuli, internal representations of the body states associated with these actions, emotions, and sensations are evoked in the observer, 'as if' he or she were doing a similar action or experiencing a similar emotion or sensation."

So this child (to right) is not just observing the happy woman waving a hat, she is also creating an internal representation of being in a happy mood waving a hat. Likewise, the child (below) is not just observing the unhappy woman pulling her hair; she is also creating an internal representation of being in an unhappy mood pulling hair.

As discussed above, we are always in a state of mind. A state of mind can be temporary or engrained. A state of mind can become engrained when a significant event is experienced repeatedly, or when a person cannot make sense of a trauma. The DNMS model presumes that a state of mind associated with the firing of mirror neurons can likewise be temporary or engrained.

A temporary state of mind evoked by the firing of mirror neurons might feel comfortable or uncomfortable. For example, the joy a person feels when a movie has a happy ending will dissipate soon after the movie is over. Likewise, the fear a person feels while watching a scary movie will dissipate after the movie is over.

© Copyright 2009 by Shirley Jean Schmidt, MA, LPC. All rights reserved. Duplication in any form without permission is prohibited.

An engrained state of mind evoked by the firing of mirror neurons in response to repeated interactions with a loving, supportive role model over time will be positive, healthy, and enduring. For example, the security a child feels during years of being cared for by a loving, attuned parent, can last a lifetime. The child's sense of security can become engrained along with an embodied simulation of the loving, attuned parent – an *adaptive introject*.

Likewise, an engrained state of mind evoked by the firing of mirror neurons in response to a single or repeated interactions with an abusive, neglectful, rejecting, or enmeshing role model will be negative, wounded, and enduring. For example, the horror a child feels while being assaulted by a parent can linger for years after the event. The child's fear can become engrained – along with an embodied simulation of the wounding parent – a *maladaptive introject*.

Gallese understands *embodied simulation* to be a basic functional mechanism of the brain, which engages automatically and unconsciously, not the result of a willed or conscious cognitive effort, not aimed at interpreting the intentions of others.[24] This is in contrast to *standard simulation*, which relies on explicitly simulating another's internal state, explicitly taking on another's perspective, and introspection.

In the DNMS model, introjection is presumed to be part of a basic neurological mechanism that operates indiscriminately, without a strategic intention, mirroring healthy and unhealthy role models alike – just because they are there. So whether an introjection is adaptive or maladaptive depends entirely on who has been introjected. When we mirror positive, supportive role models we thrive. When we mirror abusive, neglectful, rejecting, or enmeshing role models we suffer.

The mirror neuron system may help us survive as a species, but under certain conditions, it can hurt us as individuals. This is like our immune system, which is generally good for us, but which can wreak havoc in a single individual with an autoimmune disorder. Clients often feel some shame when they face the reality that they mirror the behaviors of wounding role models. But if introjection is truly just a biological reflex – that happens completely outside of our control – there is no basis for shame. Clients deeply appreciate learning they've been mimicking undesirable people because of biology, not bad intentions.

Healing by Neural Integration

According to neuropsychoanalyst Allan Schore, loving, attuned caregivers stimulate and encourage a child's sense of well being, calm and soothe a child's upset feelings, and provide appropriate safety and protection. A child will form a secure attachment to such caregivers.[25] Securely attached children develop the neural networks[26] and pathways[27] needed for the optimal self-regulation of emotion. These *neural networks* are the internal representations of the loving, attuned caregivers. These *neural pathways* link these internal representations to other neural networks in a way that facilitates self-soothing. These children grow to become well-adjusted adults with the ability to form secure attachments, and regulate their own emotions.

Poorly attuned caregivers have an impaired ability to encourage a child's sense of well being, calm and soothe a child's upset feelings, and provide needed safety and protection. A child will form an anxious or insecure attachment to such caregivers. Anxiously-attached children fail to optimally develop the neural networks and pathways needed for the self-regulation of emotion. Children who are anxiously attached to poorly attuned caregivers may become adults with an impaired ability to self-soothe, an impaired ability to recover from loss or trauma, and an increased risk of psychopathology. (Appendix B, page 199, provides a detailed write up of attachment theory and the neurobiology of attachment.)

© Copyright 2009 by Shirley Jean Schmidt, MA, LPC. All rights reserved. Duplication in any form without permission is prohibited.

Many psychotherapy clients lack the neural architecture needed to regulate emotions well. The DNMS endeavors to raise their emotion-regulation skill to the level it would have been, if they'd been securely attached to loving, attuned caregivers from the beginning. It appears to accomplish this by positively impacting the neural networks and neural pathways needed for the regulation of emotion. This has not yet been proven with brain scan technology. For the moment the ideas proposed here are theoretical.

I believe that the Resource Development Protocol can enhance the neural networks containing skills and resources for regulating emotions, and that the Needs Meeting Protocol strengthens the neural pathways that can connect those skills and resources to the neural networks holding unresolved wounds. DNMS therapists have observed that loving, attuned Resources can stimulate and encourage a wounded child part's sense of well being, calm and soothe a child part's upset feelings, and provide appropriate safety and protection, just like loving, attuned parents would. This appears to provide the emotional repair needed to help child parts heal.

The graphic on the right illustrates progress through the DNMS protocols. Before beginning the DNMS, an isolated child part that is stuck in the past holds an unresolved disturbance. (The halo indicates emotional charge.) The part is disconnected from mature Resource parts of self. During the DNMS, a neural pathway connecting the isolated child parts to the Resources is strengthened. This loving, attuned connection helps to resolve the childhood disturbance. By the end of the DNMS process, a solid connection has been established. The child part that had been stuck in the past is now fully integrated with the Resources and is living in present time. All emotional disturbance related to that child part is resolved.

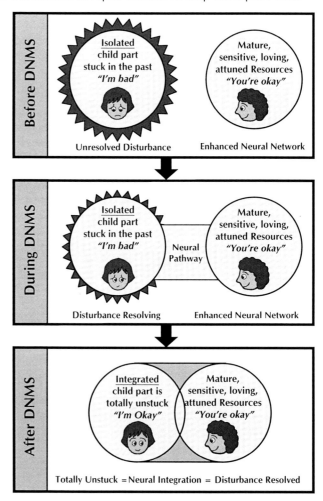

According to Daniel Siegel, self-regulation is accomplished with the process of neural integration, as functional linkages are made between disparate regions of the brain.[28] He suggests that the therapeutic interpersonal experience may actually enable integrative fibers to grow, leading to the attainment of new abilities. Within the DNMS the primary agent for change is the therapeutic intrapersonal relationship between the Resources and wounded child parts.[29] This is akin to what Siegel refers to as *intrapersonal attunement*.[30] This relationship helps child parts of self integrate with adult parts of self, get unstuck from the past, come fully into the present moment, and let go of counterproductive "coping" behaviors, negative beliefs, and painful emotions.

Alternating Bilateral Stimulation (ABS)

Alternating bilateral stimulation (ABS) is used throughout the DNMS to strengthen all positive experiences (e.g. enhancing internal Resources and positive beliefs about self). Francine Shapiro discovered that rapid side-to-side eye movements could be used to facilitate trauma desensitization.[31] Eye movements became a cornerstone of her Eye Movement Desensitization and Reprocessing (EMDR) eight-phase trauma-processing Protocol. Shapiro observed that rapid eye movements could also help strengthen positive beliefs about self.[32] In clinical practice, both alternating bilateral tactile and auditory stimulation were found to be effective alternatives to eye movements. All three modalities are considered forms of ABS.

© Copyright 2009 by Shirley Jean Schmidt, MA, LPC. All rights reserved. Duplication in any form without permission is prohibited.

ABS appears able to strengthen positive traits. Andrew Leeds introduced an EMDR-related protocol, called *Resource Development and Installation* (RDI), which uses ABS to strengthen positive images, memories, and symbols, to prepare clients for EMDR.[33] His RDI protocol was tested in two single-case-design studies with clients with complex PTSD.[34] In the study, ABS was used to enhance a positive felt sense of internal resources and to strengthen the probability clients would use their resources to manage future stressors. Ricky Greenwald proposed using ABS to strengthen a client-generated image representing a psychological resource necessary for successful EMDR processing.[35] In 1999 I developed an ABS protocol for integrating ego state therapy and art therapy.[36] Clients were directed to shift their eyes back and forth between artistic representations of resource ego states and wounded child ego states, to facilitate healing.

Laurel Parnell's book, *Tapping In: A Step-by-Step Guide to Activating Your Healing Resources Through Bilateral Stimulation*, describes a number of ways one can use imagery to *tap into resources*, then strengthen and integrate the resources by *tapping* (applying tactile ABS).[37] She writes about the many ways *resource tapping* can be of benefit, for example by reducing anxiety, coping with trauma and illnesses, improving sleep, and increasing confidence – to name a few.

The Benefits of ABS

Harvard University sleep researcher Robert Stickgold proposed that ABS applied during EMDR therapy may facilitate the memory consolidation that occurs during rapid eye movement (REM) sleep.[38] During REM sleep, associations between neural networks can become activated and strengthened. He postulated that isolated or weakly-associated neural networks can more easily connect to positive adaptive neural networks when ABS is applied. The use of ABS during the DNMS appears to help facilitate communication between wounded ego states and the Resources, and to strengthen positive feelings and beliefs.

ABS Cautions

ABS can suddenly weaken tenuous dissociative barriers, so it should never be used indiscriminately. Sandra Paulsen first wrote about this in 1995 after several EMDR therapists had observed dissociative clients could became overwhelmed during EMDR when ABS was applied.[39] EMDR therapists have observed that: (1) some clients tap into more negative emotions than they can manage, (2) some clients have few internal resources for managing and processing through their negative emotions, and/or (3) ABS does not always process through emotions that get stirred up. To lessen the risk of these things occurring, therapists trained in EMDR now are wisely cautioned to screen for dissociative disorders and to prepare clients well for the intensity of the trauma-processing experience.

ABS is applied during the DNMS almost exclusively to strengthen positives, and to enhance a positive relationship between wounded ego states and the Resources. If a wounded part temporarily loses a supportive connection to the Resources, ABS is stopped until the connection is restored. For this reason, DNMS clients rarely report unfavorable or adverse reactions to ABS. While these above cautions may apply more to EMDR than DNMS, a client's ability to tolerate positive or negative affect should always be considered before applying ABS.

Applying ABS during the DNMS

ABS can be applied as side-to-side eye movements, alternating bilateral auditory stimulation, or alternating bilateral tactile stimulation. The DNMS involves a lot of mental imagery, which most clients prefer to do with eyes closed. Tactile and auditory ABS are popular options. Tactile ABS can be applied manually, by tapping on the client's knees, hands, or feet in an alternating fashion, or with an electronic device called a TheraTapper™. The TheraTapper™ consists of a small control box attached by six-foot wires to two handheld pulsers which vibrate in an alternating fashion. From a six-foot distance, the therapist can change the intensity, length, and speed of the vibrations. (For more information, go to page 255 or www.theratapper.com.) Auditory ABS is best applied with headphones. *Bio*Lateral™ produces a collection of tapes and compact discs with a variety of sounds and music with alternating bilateral tones. (For more information, go to www.biolateral.com.)

ABS Does Not Make the DNMS a Variation of EMDR

The addition of ABS to a therapeutic intervention does not make the intervention an "EMDR therapy." So even though the DNMS uses ABS, it is not EMDR or a variation of EMDR. These approaches are distinctly different.

© Copyright 2009 by Shirley Jean Schmidt, MA, LPC. All rights reserved. Duplication in any form without permission is prohibited.

DNMS protocols are focused primarily on repairing developmental deficits, while EMDR protocols are focused primarily on resolving trauma memories. Other than the use of ABS, the DNMS and EMDR protocol steps share little in common. While clinical observation suggests DNMS clients may process more deeply or quickly when ABS is present, it is not an essential component of the protocols. DNMS sessions without ABS have also been successful. ABS does not appear to be as important to the DNMS protocols as it is to the EMDR and RDI protocols.

How Long Does DNMS Therapy Take?

While the DNMS does appear to resolve symptoms with far greater efficiency than traditional talk therapy, it is not always "brief" therapy. Generally speaking, the more ego strength and fewer unmet developmental needs a client has the more quickly she will progress through the DNMS. Those with a history of chronic *attachment wounds* tend to proceed more slowly than those with *trauma wounds* alone. Clients with attachment wounds *and* trauma wounds usually proceed the most slowly.

Several personal factors can affect the length of the therapy including a client's level of motivation, ability to get and stay focused on DNMS protocols, natural inclination to process quickly versus slowly, eagerness to disclose processing blocks, and ease with resolving processing blocks. Several logistical factors can play a role, such as the frequency of sessions (sessions spaced weeks apart are usually less efficient), and the length of sessions (90-minute sessions are usually more efficient than 50-minute sessions).

Some clients can establish Resources in a single session while others take many months. Those who generally accomplish this quickly and easily had at least one positive childhood role model, and/or have now, or had in the past, a personal experience of being a competent caregiver. Clients with ambivalence about growth and change, no positive childhood role models, and/or no competent caregiver experiences, will take the longest to develop Resources. Some clients need a lot of time to fully access their caregiver skills and/or spiritual core. Some have many basic fears and blocks to change to overcome. But even when it takes a long time to work through processing fears and blocks, the steps to mobilizing Resources can be very ego strengthening, especially for fragile clients. It can be an important part of the overall healing process.

Chapter Summary

This chapter provided an introduction to the DNMS model, including a brief description of each key protocol and procedure. It also provided background information about developmental stages and needs, ego state theory, and mirror neurons. It explained the theoretical foundation and provided a detailed discussion about alternating bilateral stimulation.

Chapter 1 Notes and References

1.   Erikson, E.H. (1950). *Childhood and Society*. New York: Norton.
     Illsley-Clarke, J. & Dawson, C. (1998). *Growing up again: Parenting ourselves, parenting our children*. Hazelden Information Education.
     Maslow, A.H. (1968). *Toward a Psychology of Being*. D. Van Nostrand Company.
2.   Bowlby, J. (1988). *A secure base*. New York: Basic Books.
3.   A motivated client is defined as someone who is prepared to seriously work towards insight and change. A motivated client may have processing blocks and complications arise, but is determined to work through them. An unmotivated client does not intend to seriously work towards change. This includes clients who want the therapist to be "mommy" or simply "take all the pain away." It includes clients who have been unwillingly sent to therapy by a spouse or parole officer, clients who are not ready to open up, and clients who refuse to work through processing blocks. Unmotivated clients do not respond well to any psychodynamic therapy.
4.   Schmidt, S.J. (2004) Developmental Needs Meeting Strategy: A new treatment approach applied to dissociative identity disorder. *Journal of Trauma and Dissociation*, 5(4), 55-78.

© Copyright 2009 by Shirley Jean Schmidt, MA, LPC. All rights reserved. Duplication in any form without permission is prohibited.

Schmidt, S.J., & Hernandez, A. (2007). The Developmental Needs Meeting Strategy: Eight case studies. *Traumatology*. 13:27-48.

5. Freud, S. (1923/1961). The ego and the id. In J Strachey (Ed. and Trans.), *The standard edition of the complete psychological works of Sigmund Freud* (Vol.19). London: Hogarth Press. (Original work published in 1923)

6. Piaget, J. & Inhelder, B (1969). *The Psychology of the Child*, New York: Basic Books.

7. Bowlby, J. (1988). *A secure base.* New York: Basic Books.

8. Erikson, E.H. (1950). *Childhood and Society.* New York: Norton.

9. Illsley-Clarke, J. & Dawson, C. (1998). *Growing up again: Parenting ourselves, parenting our children.* Hazelden Information Education.

10. Maslow, A.H. (1968). *Toward a Psychology of Being.* D. Van Nostrand Company

11. Siegel, D.J. (1999). *The developing mind: Toward a neurobiology of interpersonal experience.* New York: Guilford Press.

12. Siegel, D.J. (1999). *The developing mind: Toward a neurobiology of interpersonal experience.* New York: Guilford Press.

13. Paulsen, S. (2000). *EMDR and the Divided Self: EMDR and ego state therapy for non-dissociative and dissociative clients.* All-day workshop in San Antonio, Texas, April, 2000.

14. Phillips, M., & Frederick, C. (1995). *Healing the divided self: Clinical and Ericksonian hypnotherapy for post-traumatic and dissociative conditions.* New York: W.W. Norton & Company.
    Schwartz, R. C. (1995). *Internal family systems therapy.* New York: Guilford Press.
    Watkins, J.G., & Watkins, H.H. (1997). *Ego states: Theory and therapy.* New York: Norton.

15. Watkins, J.G., & Watkins, H.H. (1997). *Ego states: Theory and therapy.* New York: Norton.

16. Braun, B. (1988). The BASK model of dissociation. *DISSOCIATION, 1,* 4-23
    Watkins, J.G., & Watkins, H.H. (1997). *Ego states: Theory and therapy.* New York: Norton.

17. Phillips, M., & Frederick, C. (1995). *Healing the divided self: Clinical and Ericksonian hypnotherapy for post-traumatic and dissociative conditions.* New York: W.W. Norton & Company.

18. Gallese V., Eagle M.E., and Migone P. (2007). Intentional attunement: Mirror neurons and the neural underpinnings of interpersonal relations. *Journal of the American Psychoanalytic Association, 55:* 131-176

19. Gallese V., Fadiga L., Fogassi L., and Rizzolatti G. (1996). Action recognition in the premotor cortex. *Brain* 119: 593-609.

20. Iacoboni, M., (2005). Understanding others: Imitation, language, empathy. In: *Perspectives on imitation: from cognitive neuroscience to social science,* Hurley, S., and Chater, N. (Eds), Cambridge, MA: MIT Press.

21. Iacoboni, M., Molnar-Szakacs, I., Gallese, V., Buccino, G., Mazziotta, J.C., and, Rizzolatti, G. (2005). Grasping the intentions of others with one's own mirror neuron system. *PLoS Biology* Vol. 3, No. 3.

22. Ramachandran, V.S. (2000) Mirror neurons and imitation learning as the driving force behind "the great leap forward" in human evolution. www.edge.org/documents/archive/edge69.html.

23. Gallese V., Eagle M.E., and Migone P. (2007). Intentional attunement: Mirror neurons and the neural underpinnings of interpersonal relations. *Journal of the American Psychoanalytic Association, 55:* 131-176.

24. Gallese V., Eagle M.E., and Migone P. (2007). Intentional attunement: Mirror neurons and the neural underpinnings of interpersonal relations. *Journal of the American Psychoanalytic Association, 55:* 131-176.

25. Schore, A. (1994). *Affect regulation and the origin of self: The neurobiology of emotional development.* Hillsdale, NJ: Erlbaum.

26. Definition of *neural network* from Wikipedia, January 2009: http://en.wikipedia.org/wiki/Biological_neural_network "In neuroscience, a neural network describes a population of physically interconnected neurons or a group of disparate neurons whose inputs or signaling targets define a recognizable circuit. Communication between neurons often involves an electrochemical process. The interface through which they interact with surrounding neurons usually consists of several dendrites (input connections), which are connected via synapses to other neurons, and one axon (output connection). If the sum of the input signals surpasses a certain threshold, the neuron sends an action potential (AP) at the axon hillock and transmits this electrical signal along the axon."

27. Definition of neural pathway from Wikipedia, January 2009: http://en.wikipedia.org/wiki/Neural_pathway "A neural pathway is a neural tract connecting one part of the nervous system with another, usually consisting of bundles of elongated, myelin-insulated neurons, known collectively as white matter. Neural pathways serve to connect relatively distant areas of the brain or nervous system."

28. Siegel, D.J. (2003). An interpersonal neurobiology of psychotherapy: The developing mind and the resolution of trauma. In M. F. Solomon & D. J. Siegel (Eds.), *Healing trauma: attachment, mind, body and brain* (pp. 1-56). New York: Norton.

29. Because the relationship wounded child parts have with the Resources is the primary agent for change, transference issues tend to be less important in the DNMS. Child parts learn to look to the Resources to meet needs, rather than looking to the therapist.

30. Siegel, D.J. (2007). *The Mindful Brain: Reflection and Attunement in the Cultivation of Well-Being.* New York: Norton.

31. Shapiro, F. (2001). *Eye movement desensitization and reprocessing: Basic principles, protocols, and procedures.* Second edition. New York: Guilford Press.

32. Only the use of eye movements in EMDR has been well researched. Parker and Davidson, the authors of a 2001 meta-analysis, concluded that EMDR-with-eye movements was no different than EMDR-without- eye movements. Davidson, P.R., & Parker, K.C.H. (2001). Eye movement desensitization and reprocessing (EMDR): A meta-analysis. *Journal of Consulting and Clinical Psychology, 69*(2), 305-316.

© Copyright 2009 by Shirley Jean Schmidt, MA, LPC. All rights reserved. Duplication in any form without permission is prohibited.

However, many other studies have come to the opposite conclusion, such as:

Barrowcliff, A.L., Gray, N.S., MacCulloch, S. Freeman, T.C.A., & MacCulloch, M.J. (2003). Horizontal rhythmical eye-movements consistently diminish the arousal provoked by auditory stimuli. British Journal of Clinical Psychology. 42 (3), pp. 289-302.

Christman, S.D., Garvey, K.J., Propper, R.E. & Phaneuf, K.A. (2003). Bilateral eye movements enhance the retrieval of episodic memories. Neuropsychology.17(2):221-9.

While these studies are very relevant to the trauma-focused EMDR protocols, they likely have little bearing on the application of ABS during the DNMS. That is because the DNMS and EMDR protocols are very different. Research to test the effectiveness of ABS during the DNMS has not yet been conducted.

33. Leeds, A. (1998). Lifting the burden of shame: Using EMDR resource installation to resolve a therapeutic impasse. In P. Manfield (Ed.) *Extending EMDR*. New York: Norton.

34. Korn, D.L., & Leeds, A.M. (2002). Preliminary evidence of efficacy for EMDR resource development and installation in the stabilization phase of treatment of complex posttraumatic stress disorder. *Journal of Clinical Psychology, 58,* (12), 1465-1487.

35. Greenwald, R. (1993). Magical installations can help clients to slay their dragons. *EMDR Network Newsletter,* 3(2),16-17.

36. Schmidt, S.J. (1999) Resource-Focused EMDR: Integration of Ego State Therapy, Alternating Bilateral Stimulation, and Art Therapy. *EMDRIA Newsletter,* 4(1), 8-26.

37. Parnell, L. (2008). *Tapping In: A Step-by-Step Guide to Activating Your Healing Resources Through Bilateral Stimulation.* Louisville, Colorado: Sounds True.

38. Stickgold, (2002). EMDR: A putative neurobiological mechanism of action. *Journal of Clinical Psychology, 58,* 61-75.

39. Paulsen, S. (1995). Eye movement desensitization and reprocessing: Its cautious use in the dissociative disorders. *DISSOCIATION, 8*(1), 32-44.

© Copyright 2009 by Shirley Jean Schmidt, MA, LPC. All rights reserved. Duplication in any form without permission is prohibited.

Chapter 2
Ego State Therapy Basics

Ego State Therapy Background

The DNMS is an ego state *therapy* based on ego state *theory*. While Chapter 1 provided an overview of ego state theory, this chapter will focus in detail on ego state therapy. It will lay out some general principles along with specific information you'll need to do the DNMS.

Many therapy approaches have been developed based on ego state theory principles, to treat clients across the dissociative continuum. George Fraser, Richard Kluft, Frank Putnam, and Colin Ross have described hypnosis techniques for treating highly dissociated clients.[1] Approaches such as Psychosynthesis,[2] Gestalt Therapy,[3] Transactional Analysis,[4] Internal Family Systems Therapy,[5] Voice Dialogue,[6] and Inner Child Psychotherapy,[7] have been developed to treat more moderately dissociated clients. The Phillips & Frederick's SARI Model[8] and Watkins & Watkins' Ego State Therapy[9] have both been successful treating both moderately and highly dissociative clients.

These approaches have in common the idea that different personality parts, alters, or ego states can have different views of reality. The aim of each approach is to help individual ego states heal and increase healthy communication and cooperation between ego states. This is the process of ego state *integration*. Watkins & Watkins describe integration as a process of increasing the permeability of ego state boundaries to enhance cooperation so ego states can resolve conflicts.[10] Siegel defines it as the functional clustering of independent self-states into a cohesive whole.[11]

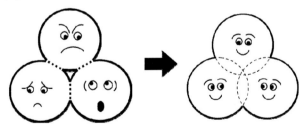

The aim of the DNMS is to identify and heal the wounded ego states most responsible for a client's unwanted behaviors, beliefs, and emotions. The healing occurs as healthy adult Resources connect with wounded child ego states to meet their developmental needs, help them process through painful emotions, and establish emotional bonds. This appears to help ego state boundaries become more permeable.

The integration that occurs during the DNMS as a wounded part of self gets totally unstuck, can be compared to building a road or running a phone line from a city to a remote cabin. Useful, adaptive, healthy information can finally get to the isolated ego states, so they can feel the connection and safety they have longed for. DNMS therapists have observed that once wounded ego states are sufficiently integrated with a client's most adult self, they are no longer a source of unwanted behaviors, beliefs, or emotions.

© Copyright 2009 by Shirley Jean Schmidt, MA, LPC. All rights reserved. Duplication in any form without permission is prohibited.

The DNMS protocols can be effective at treating clients across the dissociative continuum – including those with dissociative identity disorder. (Appendix B provides an abstract from a published DNMS case example of this.)   But this book is oriented to the treatment of clients in the center of the dissociative continuum. Therapists who choose to use DNMS protocols to treat highly dissociative clients should have additional training for addressing their special needs. While that specialty training is outside the scope of this book, Appendix C offers a list of techniques for stabilizing dissociated clients.

Many hypnotherapists advocate working with dissociated ego states while clients are in a hypnotic trance.[12] The DNMS protocols do not include a formal hypnotic induction, because most DNMS clients can easily access their wounded ego states with a little guidance from the therapist. A few clients will naturally go into a deep trance during the DNMS, but most will go into a light trance or no trance at all.

Working with Ego States

Executive Control & Recognizing Ego States in Clients

If you are new to ego state therapy your first challenge may be to simply recognize a client's different ego states. An ego state that is front and center is said to be in executive control.[13] When ego state X is in executive control, we say that the client *is in* X ego state. For example, a client who appears confident, rational, and mature, is probably *in an adult ego state.* She might calmly say, "I understand why you had to reschedule our session. I can work with that." In contrast, a client who appears childlike, irrational, disconnected, or inappropriately afraid is probably *in a child ego state.* She might frown and say in a child-like voice, "I'm very upset you rescheduled my session."

Sometimes two or more ego states will share executive control at the same time. When this happens, usually one is more dominant. For example, an adult self might describe her awareness of an upset child part by calmly stating, "While I understand why you rescheduled our session, a four-year-old part of me is very upset about it." When it is difficult to tell which ego state is making a comment or asking a question, ask something like: "Which part of you is talking now?" or "Is that idea coming from your most adult self?"

You can call out specific ego states. For example, you might ask, "May I speak to the four-year-old that's upset about the appointment change?" When a child part comes forward, the client's posture, body language, and/or voice may change. For example, an ego state stuck at age four may speak in a childlike voice or make childlike gestures. The more dissociated an ego state is, the more likely it will appear and sound different from the client's most adult self. When an adult ego state is also very present, there may be no change in appearance.

A client can usually get a mental picture of an ego state that comes forward. For example, an ego state may appear as self in childhood, as self in adolescence, as self in adulthood, as someone else (e.g. a parent), or as a metaphor (e.g. a monster or witch). An ego state could appear in an angry mood, a sad mood, a fearful mood, assertive mood, trusting mood, mistrusting mood, and so forth. The mental picture of an ego state may evoke a memory and a story of how the part got stuck in the past.

Clients can *voluntarily* and *involuntarily* switch executive control from one ego state to another. A client's ability to switch voluntarily can help you as therapist. For example, you can call forward wounded parts for healing interventions, or call forward a client's Resources to calm upset child parts. However, involuntary switching can cause problems. For example, a war veteran suffering from PTSD may involuntarily switch into a traumatized soldier ego state when he hears a sudden, loud noise in the hall outside the office.

Talking to Individual Parts of Self

Working with ego states involves communicating individually and/or collectively with different parts of self. Since we do not normally communicate this way with others, it could feel odd at first, to you and/or your clients. Once you, and especially your clients, begin to see how effective this is, it will begin to feel more natural.

© Copyright 2009 by Shirley Jean Schmidt, MA, LPC. All rights reserved. Duplication in any form without permission is prohibited.

There are many reasons you might want to call a specific wounded part forward. You might want to get information about an unusual reaction; you might want to provide an upset part with comfort or reassurance; you might need to clear a processing block; or it might be time to start a healing intervention. Sometimes wounded parts come forward, uninvited, when reacting to real or imagined internal or external threats. Either way, when an upset part is front and center, a client might notice unpleasant body sensations, such as a headache, shoulder tension, butterflies in the belly, or difficulty breathing. (See Appendix C for techniques for handling very upset child parts.)

If a part of self comes forward in distress – whether invited or uninvited – welcome and validate it. For example my client Martin said, "I have a teen-aged part that doesn't trust you. He believes you don't really care." After getting permission to speak with the part I said, "Welcome. I'm glad you're here. It sounds like you don't trust me. Considering the many betrayals you experienced growing up, that mistrust makes perfect sense." Then I asked for his age, so I could put the mistrust in historical context. "How old are you?" When he answered "age 14," I understood this was about a particularly bad betrayal by a trusted scout leader. If the source of the mistrust had not been clear, I'd have asked the 14-year-old part to tell me when he first learned to be so mistrusting.

Once a part has fully expressed a concern, provide the needed validation and reassurance. For example, in Martin's case I said, "So 14-year-old, your trusted scout leader, John, repeatedly betrayed you on your campouts together. These experiences have left huge wounds that you've been carrying a long time. It makes sense that you'd expect me to betray you too – and that you would expect that I don't really care. John told you he cared, but in the end he really didn't. Feel free to mistrust me as long as you need to. But if and when you're ready to move forward, I'd like to help you heal those old wounds. Your existence is important. I want you to feel safe here. I want to help you to grow to meet your full potential. When you do, the wounds John inflicted long ago will completely heal, and they won't interrupt your life anymore."

If a client has already established one or more of the DNMS Resources (as discussed in Chapters 1 and 3), you can draw them into a conversation with a wounded part. For example, in Martin's case I also said, "So 14-year-old, ask the Resources if they believe I'm likely to betray you, and tell me what they say." He replied that the Resources believed I wouldn't betray him. Hearing that from the Resources had a calming effect. I encouraged him to seek more reassurance from the Resources, and after some time in dialogue with them, he was much more open to the possibility that I did care and was trustworthy. Eventually he trusted me enough to engage in the work.

If corrective information is not received well, give a child part overt permission to reject it. For example, you might say to a child part: "You should mistrust me as long as you believe that will keep you safe." Then plant a seed for future change. "I hope that one day you will want to let me help you heal."

Always be positive and supportive, even if a part of self is belligerent. Assume anything said to one ego state will be heard by all others. Never argue with a wounded part, no matter how irrational or illogical the point of view, because such opposition will be felt as invalidation – even if your point of view is correct. Only comments that communicate respect and attunement will have a healing effect.

It is often wise to preface a statement or question with the age of the part you're talking to. For example, in the case of Martin, I started my reassurance with: "So *14-year-old*, your trusted scout leader, John, repeatedly betrayed you...." When speaking to young child ego states, use a soft and nurturing voice to help them feel more comfortable. Both of these techniques can help keep the most adult self from answering questions intended for younger parts.

Differing Points of View & Internal Conflicts

The views of a client's most adult state can be very different from the views of a child ego state. For example, if a client expresses an irrational belief, such as "My mother was right - I was born bad," you can ask, "In your most adult state, do you believe you were born bad?" Your client may say, "No, but some other part of me believes it."

Sometimes when you're asking a question of a child ego state, an adult ego state will answer instead. For example, when asked about her alcohol addiction, a client says, "I don't need alcohol - I can do without it."

© Copyright 2009 by Shirley Jean Schmidt, MA, LPC. All rights reserved. Duplication in any form without permission is prohibited.

When you follow-up with, "I know your most adult self believes that, but what does the part of you that drinks heavily every weekend believe?" the client replies, "She needs alcohol to feel confident."

Sometimes you will need to ask a question in a way that will bypass a superficial point of view, to get to a belief deeply held by a wounded child part. Preface a question with, "Close your eyes, and just let your body, not your head, answer the following question..." For example, a question like "Do you believe you deserve to heal?" may evoke a "yes" answer from the head, and a "no" answer from the body. A "no" answer from the body would be connected to a wounded part of self.

Ego states can have *competing agendas* which can lead to internal conflicts . For example, Valerie, an over-weight client, has an adult part of self trying to lose weight while a wounded child part is sabotaging her weight loss efforts. Her wounded child part finds safety in being overweight. This internal conflict creates a *double bind* for Valerie. It forces her to choose between two undesirable options – continue the weight loss program while tolerating the upset child part's irrational fear, or stop the weight loss program to calm the sabotaging child part. Neither option is desirable.

Some clients will tell you about specific parts of self that are generating internal conflicts – for example, the one that drinks too much, the one that's rebellious, or the one that's mean to women. Some clients will tell you their lives would be fine if they could just eliminate the one troublesome part of self. For example, Nellie expressed that all her problems would go away if she could just get rid of her rebellious 18-year-old ego state. I explained that such a plan was not possible, and attempting to do so would certainly lead to more internal conflicts and more problems. I explained that all wounded child parts can heal – even the ones causing very serious problems, like the rebel teen. I asked her if she would let someone amputate her broken leg if she knew it could heal. That helped her understand the 18-year-old part's distress. You'll want to encourage clients to approach disagreeable child parts with compassion instead of hostility. Healing disagreeable child parts will end their disagreeable behaviors, beliefs, and emotions.

Child parts that felt hostility from authority figures in childhood, and feel hostility from authoritarian parts of self now, may also expect hostility to come from the therapist. Consequently those child parts may fear that the therapist will try to annihilate them, or that the therapy interventions will result in their demise. For example, Randy was a client who had a very rough start with the DNMS. With every protocol we tried, a series of unusual complications came up. We eventually tied the complications to a belief held by many child parts that the process of healing would be a process of annihilation. When I finally explained to all the child parts that the healing would not annihilate anyone, but would help each one to grow to meet their full potential, the complications ceased and he was able to smoothly engage with and complete the protocols. (See *System-Wide Announcement* section below.) When you encounter this type of fear, reassure fearful parts that their existence has value, and that the therapy will help them heal so they can grow to meet their full potential. This reassurance can come as a surprise to child parts that are used to being shamed.

Tucking In

Once you've completed a dialogue with a wounded part, it's best to *tuck in* the part.[14] I learned about this from Sandra Paulsen. Tucking in puts the wounded part in a non-active state, so the most adult self can resume executive control. It can be helpful to first ask the part if there's anything she'd like to say or ask before tucking in. Tuck a part in with something like:

> Now find a nice, warm, safe place to tuck in to. Just find a good, safe, place to wait until the next time you're needed.

If a client has already established one or more Resources the child part can be tucked in with the Resources. Tucking in does not necessarily mean putting a part to bed or to sleep. For example, a child part might want to tuck in to a playroom or a playground.

If a wounded child part has trouble imagining a safe place to tuck in, you can help with the construction of one with questions like: "Would the perfect safe place be indoors or outdoors?" "Would the room be large or small?" "Would the room have windows or doors?" "What color would the room be? How would it be furnished?" Once the client has completely described the ideal safe place for the child part to tuck into, invite the part to tuck in to that place.

© Copyright 2009 by Shirley Jean Schmidt, MA, LPC. All rights reserved. Duplication in any form without permission is prohibited.

System-Wide Announcement

A system-wide announcement is a reassuring message conveyed to many wounded parts, at the same time.[15] You can direct it to fearful and mistrusting child parts when you need to build rapport, and calm irrational fears. This is especially helpful when many parts of self harbor fears about being annihilated or invalidated. Tailor your announcement to the problem you need to solve. This example demonstrates how to reassure parts that fear they will be harmed or eliminated. This type of message usually has an instant calming effect.

> I'd like all parts of you to listen now. Each one of you is valuable to me. I don't want to harm any of you, or eliminate any of you. I want to help each of you heal so you can grow to meet your full potential. You get to decide what that is. If you've been stuck in the past, I'd like to help you get unstuck. I'm interested in any concerns or fears you have. We will not do any processing as long as any one of you objects. I'm willing to patiently answer all your questions.

DNMS Ego State Classifications

Different ego state therapy approaches have different ways of conceptualizing the self-system. For example, the Transactional Analysis model conceptualizes *Adult*, *Parent*, and *Child* ego states,[16] the Gestalt model conceptualizes a *top dog* and *underdog*,[17] and the Internal Family Systems model conceptualizes *exile*, *manager*, and *firefighter* ego states.[18] The DNMS conceptualizes two categories of ego states – *reactive parts* and *introjects* – with subsets of ego states in each category. You'll need to be able to recognize each type of ego state, from each category, to effectively navigate the DNMS protocols. Each type is described below.

Reactive Parts

Reactive parts are wounded parts of self that form in reaction to *significant role models*[19] who are abusive, neglectful, rejecting, or enmeshing. They overreact to triggering events in the present. They hold negative beliefs, which are irrational, untrue ideas about self and world. There are several types of reactive parts: powerless reactive parts, controlling reactive parts, and reactive mimics.

Powerless Reactive Parts

Powerless reactive parts hold and cope with painful emotions. They are attached to negative beliefs, such as: "I was born bad," "I am completely vulnerable," "My needs are not important," and "All men are bad." There are several types of powerless reactive parts:

- Some hold raw emotions, like anxiety, terror, anger, sadness, grief, despair, shame, and hopelessness.
- Some hold reactions to specific traumatic experiences.
- Some cope with painful emotions with pain-avoidant behaviors like withdrawing, drinking, or overeating.
- Some cope with painful emotions with self-punishing behaviors like cutting, starving, or isolating.
- Some rebel with risky or self-destructive behaviors like drinking, smoking, or engaging in unprotected sex.
- Some try to manage hurtful people with strategic pleasing behaviors like complying or overachieving.
- Some try to prevent attacks from others by engaging in aggressive behaviors - putting up a façade of strength, intimidation, control, or power.

The maladaptive "coping" behaviors adopted by some reactive parts can fuel external problems, and internal conflicts. However, in spite of this, all reactive parts have good intentions,[20] no matter how counterproductive their behaviors may be.

Most clients can get mental pictures of reactive parts. Reactive parts typically appear looking like the client – usually as the client looked as a child. How old they appear usually reflects the age they were when they were first wounded or most wounded. The mood they're in when they appear provides information about their reaction to the wound.

© Copyright 2009 by Shirley Jean Schmidt, MA, LPC. All rights reserved. Duplication in any form without permission is prohibited.

Sometimes a reactive part appears wearing a mask. Masks can form as part of a coping strategy for dealing with wounding role models. For example, a mask may hide authentic feelings or reactions that are not acceptable to reveal, or may provide a façade of strength to prevent attacks from others. For example, a child who was never permitted by her parents to show anger or sadness may create a phony, happy persona. Or, a child who was often frightened by threatening people may create a protective intimidating mask.

Controlling Reactive Parts

Controlling reactive parts *aim to control the behaviors of other parts of self.* They form for a strategic purpose – to motivate other reactive parts to engage in behaviors that please others, or to stop engaging in behaviors that might upset others. They accomplish this by issuing warnings, threats, commands, or admonitions, such as: "Don't rock the boat," "Keep quiet," "Don't ask for help," and "Put others' needs first." A controlling reactive part will look like the client – usually as the client looked as a child.

Here is an analogy of this concept... Consider the family with a hostile parent who threatens any child who cries, with the wounding message, "Shut up or I'll hit you." When a younger sibling cries, an older sibling, fearing the crying will upset the hostile parent, admonishes her with, "Shhhhh - Be quiet!" The admonition is issued to control the younger sibling's behavior – ultimately to reduce the parental threat. Now consider the client who grew up with a hostile parent threatening her when she cried, with "Shut up or I'll hit you." Because crying was a punishable offense, a *controlling reactive part* formed to admonish other parts of self when they cried. If the controlling reactive part could quiet a part of self that was crying, it might reduce the possibility that the hostile parent would become upset and inflict the dreaded punishment.

| Hostile | Controlling | Powerless |
| Parent | Reactive Part | Reactive Part |

Reactive Mimics

Reactive mimics are a type of reactive part that will strategically mimic a wounding role model for a specific purpose. In childhood a reactive mimic's behavior would be in the service of meeting a caregiver's needs, increasing proximity to a caregiver, and/or minimizing wounding caregiver messages and behaviors. A reactive mimic may look like the client, but more often it will look like the wounding role model. There are many types of reactive mimics. Here are three examples:

- *Hostile reactive mimic:* While growing up, Jason observed that there are two types of people – bullies and victims – and that bullies were safe, and victims were not. In reaction, a hostile reactive mimic formed to act just like the bully he knew best – his dad. This reactive part found safety behind a hostile-dad mask.

- *Pleaser reactive mimic:* While growing up, Rebecca noticed her mother was often in a pleaser mode. Her mother communicated non-verbally that, to earn her love and approval, she must also be a pleaser. In reaction, a pleaser reactive mimic formed to act just like her pleaser mother. This reactive part found safety behind a pleaser-mom mask.

- *Controlling reactive mimic:* This type of reactive part comes up often during DNMS processing. The aim of a controlling reactive mimic is to control other parts of self by mimicking a role model's threatening, rejecting, or devaluing messages, such as: "You'll be punished if you speak," "Don't express emotions if you want to be loved," and "Don't think you're so great."

© Copyright 2009 by Shirley Jean Schmidt, MA, LPC. All rights reserved. Duplication in any form without permission is prohibited.

Using the same analogy as described above... Consider again the family with a hostile parent who threatens any child who cries, with the wounding message, "Shut up or I'll hit you." When a younger sibling cries, an older sibling, fearing the crying will upset the hostile parent, attempts to stop the behavior by mimicking the parent's threat, "Shut up or I'll hit you." The threat is issued to control the younger sibling's behavior – ultimately to reduce the parental threat. Now consider the client who grew up with a hostile parent threatening her when she cried, with "Shut up or I'll hit you." Because crying was a punishable offense a *controlling reactive mimic* formed to threaten other parts of self when they cried. If the controlling reactive mimic could quiet a part of self that was crying, it would reduce the possibility that the hostile parent would become upset and inflict the expected punishment.

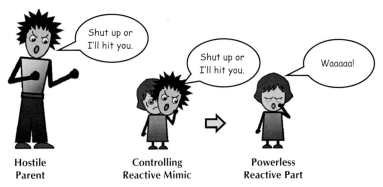

Hostile
Parent

Controlling
Reactive Mimic

Powerless
Reactive Part

Controlling Reactive Parts versus Controlling Reactive Mimics

Controlling reactive parts and controlling reactive mimics both convey harsh messages to other reactive parts with the intent to motivate them to engage in behaviors that might please others, or to stop behaviors that might upset others. Sometimes it is hard to tell them apart.

Controlling reactive parts deliver messages that convey warnings, commands, threats, or admonitions that are clearly in reaction to a wounding role model. They look like the client – usually as the client looked as a child. *Controlling reactive mimics* deliver the same devaluing, upsetting message conveyed by a wounding role model. Clients usually describe them as looking exactly like the role model that is being mimicked.

Controlling Reactive Part

Controlling Reactive Mimic

Introjects

An introject is a part of self that has unconsciously internalized another person's behaviors, ideas, values, or points of view. The DNMS shares this definition with psychotherapy pioneers such as Berne,[21] Freud,[22] Perls,[23] and Watkins & Watkins.[24]

Introjection has often been considered an unconscious process intended to reduce anxiety. Anna Freud considered introjection to be a defense mechanism (along with regression, repression, projection, and sublimation) intended to protect the mind from thoughts, feelings, and conflicts too difficult to cope with consciously.[25] Richard Erskine proposed that the introjection of a parent who is inadequately meeting needs, lessens the external conflict with the parent and provides the illusion of being accepted and loved.[26] Fritz Perls suggested that the "undigested" introjected behaviors and attitudes of others helps a child to adapt to his environment.[27] Laura Perls asserted that conflict with an inadequate caregiver is managed more easily if it is internalized.[28] Watkins & Watkins wrote that a child being abused may introject the perpetrator for the purposes of self-protection.[29] Anna Freud proposed that identification with the aggressor helps one partially conquer fear of abusers by becoming more like them.[30]

© Copyright 2009 by Shirley Jean Schmidt, MA, LPC. All rights reserved. Duplication in any form without permission is prohibited.

This historical understanding of introjection aligns perfectly with the DNMS definition of a reactive mimic. In contrast, the DNMS model presumes introjection to be the result of the involuntary firing of mirror neurons. (Mirror neurons are discussed in detail in Chapter 1, page 9.) It *does not conceptualize* introjection as an intentional helpful adaptation for self protection, reducing anxiety, connecting to others, managing conflicts with others, conquering fears, or anything else for that matter.

Blank Slate

The DNMS conceptualizes the process of introjection as starting with a *blank slate*. A blank slate is a collection of mirror neurons before mirroring begins. It is the brain's potential to mirror someone. The DNMS assumes a blank slate to be a part of self with a point of view. In a developing brain, that point of view embodies a child's good true nature, including: *a natural curiosity, an eagerness to observe and learn from others, and a desire to be in respectful harmony with self and others.*[31]

Adaptive Introjects

When a child spends a lot of time with a role model who is loving, attuned, nurturing, supportive, validating, protective, and able to meet emotional needs, a positive state of mind becomes engrained. This engrained state of mind becomes a helpful internal representation of the positive role model. It becomes an *adaptive introject*. Adaptive introjects will embody a role model's positive behaviors and attitude and will mirror that positive behavior with other people and other parts of self. Because a nurturing role model's point of view is in sync with a person's intrinsic good true nature, a blank slate can easily integrate and mirror these positive behaviors.

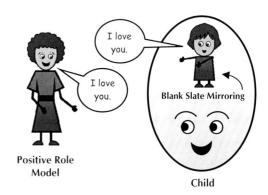

Maladaptive Introjects

Of course role models, such as parents, are not always loving and attuned. Some will deliver very wounding messages. There are three ways wounding messages get conveyed – verbally, non-verbally, or simply inferred by the child. The *verbal messages* are the easiest to understand. For example, a mother says to her child, "I wish you hadn't been born." The *nonverbal messages* involve some interpretation, but can be rather clear. For example a father gives a child a threatening glare, conveying the message "You deserve my wrath." Some *messages are inferred* by a child – that is the child perceives a message that was never actually in the mind of the caregiver. For example, a mother is in a coma for 6 weeks. Because she is not at home, the child assumes she is thinking, "You're not important to me."

When a child spends a lot of time with a wounding role model who is perceived as abusive, neglectful, rejecting, enmeshing, traumatizing, or unable to meet emotional needs, a negative state of mind becomes engrained. Likewise, when a person spends a little time with someone who is very traumatizing (e.g. a kidnapper or rapist), a negative state of mind becomes engrained. Either way, such an engrained state of mind becomes a harmful internal representation of the wounding person. It becomes a *maladaptive introject*. Maladaptive introjects will embody a person's negative behavior and attitude and will mirror that negative behavior.

For many clients wounding introject messages are primarily directed internally – to reactive parts. This leads to unwelcome internal conflict. Because a wounding role model's behavior does not match a child's good true nature, it will integrate superficially. The child part becomes like an actor playing a role that he doesn't like, but cannot stop playing, or wearing a costume or mask that he doesn't like, but cannot take off.

© Copyright 2009 by Shirley Jean Schmidt, MA, LPC. All rights reserved. Duplication in any form without permission is prohibited.

- ### *Simple Maladaptive Introjects*

    Simple introjects mirror caregivers who conveyed wounding messages that contain negative beliefs about self in "I" messages, such as, "I'm powerless" and "I'll never succeed," or faulty notions about the world, such as, "No one is trustworthy" and "Everyone is trustworthy."

    The picture to the right illustrates a wounding role model conveying a wounding "I" message to a child. In the child's brain, mirror neurons take on the wounding caregiver like a mask and reflect back that wounding message. Notice that the blank slate is unwillingly mirroring the role model.

- ### *Oppressive Maladaptive Introjects*

    Oppressive introjects are the easiest to recognize. They mirror caregivers who conveyed wounding threats and "you" messages, such as, "If you make a mistake I'll reject you," "If you seek attention I'll shame you," "You may not say 'no' to others," and "Others are important, you're not."

    The picture to the right illustrates a wounding role model conveying a wounding "you" message to a child. In the child's brain, mirror neurons take on the wounding caregiver like a mask and reflect back that wounding message.

Most of the introjects you will encounter with the DNMS will be oppressive. Some caregivers delivered combination "you" and "I" messages (e.g. "I don't trust men and you shouldn't either," "I must be in control, so you must let me control you," and "I can't meet my own needs, so you must meet them for me."). Introjects that deliver combination messages are classified as oppressive.

Controlling Reactive Mimics versus Maladaptive Introjects

It is easy to confuse maladaptive introjects and reactive mimics, because they both appear wearing a costume that looks like a wounding role model, and they both convey the role model's wounding message. The key difference is found in the point of view of the part of self wearing the mask or costume. To tell them apart, ask the part of self wearing the costume questions like: "Do you like or need this costume?" "Does it serve a useful purpose?" "Would you miss it if it disappeared?" The part of self behind a *reactive mimic mask* will say the mask has a useful purpose. The mask is often perceived as protective or helpful. The part of self behind a *maladaptive introject mask* will say the mask has no purpose, it is not wanted or needed, and it would be wonderful if the mask disappeared.

Controlling Reactive Mimic   **Maladaptive Introject**

The role of mirror neurons in the formation of parts of self, may explain the distinction between reactive mimics and maladaptive introjects. It is the difference between, what Gallese calls *standard simulation* and *embodied simulation.*[32] The DNMS model presumes that reactive mimics form as the result of standard simulation, which involves explicitly simulating a role model's internal state, and explicitly taking on the role

© Copyright 2009 by Shirley Jean Schmidt, MA, LPC. All rights reserved. Duplication in any form without permission is prohibited.

model's perspective, with the help of introspection. Reactive mimics form to solve a problem. The model presumes that introjects form as the result of embodied simulation, which involves the unconscious internalization of a role model, and the result of mirror neurons firing, a process devoid of any strategic intention.

This distinction is important when selecting wounded ego states for processing, because healing introjects helps heal reactive mimics, but healing reactive mimics does not help heal introjects. If a reactive mimic gets unstuck while the associated maladaptive introject is still active the healing effects may not last because the internal threat is still present.

Clues to Classifying Parts of Self

Clues That Differentiate Introjects & Reactive Parts	Powerless Reactive Part	Controlling Reactive Part	Controlling Reactive Mimic	Maladaptive Introject
Part (mask) looks like wounding role model.	No.	No.	Yes.	Yes.
Conveys wounding message (typically a "you" message).	No.	Yes – In reaction to a role model's message.	Yes –Mimicking a role model's message.	Yes –Mimicking a role model's message.
Reacting or mimicking?	Reacting.	Reacting.	Both.	Mimicking.
Mask (or costume) present.	Maybe.	Maybe.	Yes.	Yes.
Issues warnings, threats, commands, or admonitions.	No.	Yes.	Only if the wounding role model issued them.	Only if the wounding role model issued them.
Reveals behaviors, beliefs, or emotions suggestive of being wounded. ("I" statements).	Yes.	No.	No.	Not usually.
Mask is part of a valued coping strategy created by child part wearing it. *	If a mask is present – yes.	If a mask is present – yes.	Yes.*	No.*

*Assessed in Step 2 of the Switching the Dominance Protocol

Reactive Parts and Introjects Interact

Reactive parts form in reaction to external wounding messages, delivered by significant role models – very often parents. These reactive parts can remain stuck, because they continue to react to the internalized wounding messages, delivered now by the maladaptive introjects that mirror the wounding role models.

What Happened in Childhood...

The process begins when a role model, such as a parent, conveys a wounding message. In this example, a parent delivers the wounding message, "Be perfect. I cannot love a bad child." As this message is conveyed, several reactive parts may form. For example, a powerless reactive part, fearful of being imperfect, may form. A controlling reactive part, demanding the powerless reactive part keep quiet, may form. And a reactive mimic, reiterating to the powerless reactive part that she must be perfect to be lovable, may form.

| Parent | Reactive Parts |

© Copyright 2009 by Shirley Jean Schmidt, MA, LPC. All rights reserved. Duplication in any form without permission is prohibited.

But these would not be the only child parts to form when a parent behaves this way. An introject who mirrors the parent's message would also form, and would deliver the parent's message to the same reactive parts that formed in reaction to the parent.

What Happens in Adulthood...

Reactive parts can remain stuck well into adulthood, long after a wounding role model is out of the picture, because the maladaptive introject continues to deliver that role model's wounding message.

The True Source of a Current Problem...

Reactive parts can get triggered when a stressful event occurs. Say, for example, the boss says, "You made a typo. Please correct it." The reactive parts that formed in childhood, in reaction to a wounding parent, might get triggered. A powerless reactive part might be upset because she thinks her boss expects her to be perfect like her mother did. A controlling reactive part might then warn the powerless reactive part to not ask for help, and a reactive mimic might remind the powerless reactive part she that she needs to be perfect to be lovable.

© Copyright 2009 by Shirley Jean Schmidt, MA, LPC. All rights reserved. Duplication in any form without permission is prohibited.

It looks like these three reactive parts got triggered by the boss, and to some degree they did. But something else is also happening. An introject of a wounding parent also got triggered by the boss – a part that is mirroring the parent's wounding message, "Be perfect. I cannot love a bad child." This introject would activate the three reactive parts far more than the boss would.

Boss   Reactive Parts

Healing Wounded Parts of Self

The DNMS is based on the assumption that all present-day issues that originated in unmet needs are perpetuated by maladaptive introjects as they generate internal conflicts with reactive parts. Finding and healing these introjects will help resolve the unwanted behaviors, beliefs, and emotions the internal conflicts evoke. For example, if a client suffers from self loathing because of her mother's rejection, the DNMS can help by healing the introject that mirrors the rejecting mother. If a client bullies others because his father bullied him, the DNMS can help by healing the introject that mirrors the bullying father. If a client is stuck in an unresolved, age-five, parent-inflicted trauma, the DNMS can help heal the trauma by healing the introject that mirrors the traumatizing parents.

Healing Maladaptive Introjects

You'll use two DNMS protocols to help maladaptive introjects heal. You'll apply the Switching the Dominance Protocol first. This helps the wounded parts get partly unstuck from the past. You'll follow this with the Needs Meeting Protocol which will complete the healing by getting parts totally unstuck. (Both protocols, introduced in Chapter 1, will be described in detail in Chapters 4 and 6.)

A maladaptive introject is comprised of two parts: (1) a mask or costume that mirrors a wounding role model, and (2) a silent, emotionless, innocent part of self wearing the mask or costume. Before a healing intervention begins, the mask usually appears in the client's mind as alive, real, and important; while the part wearing it is virtually invisible.

An introject mask is actually just a recording of a wounding role model, and is unable to do any real harm. But because it *feels* real and foreboding to the client, it can elicit painful emotions. This creates the illusion that it is as important and ominous as the person it is mirroring. Because an introject mask is not real, conversations with it are usually counterproductive. In contrast, the quiet part of self wearing it is very real and important, and conversations with this part are very productive. When you apply the DNMS Switching the Dominance Protocol (introduced on page 2) you'll help the part wearing the mask understand that the mask is just a harmless recording. As the part begins to understand this, the mask will get smaller and smaller. When the paradigm shift is complete, and the part fully understands, the mask will become small enough for her to put in a pocket. At this point the dominance will have been switched from the mask to the part that was wearing it.

© Copyright 2009 by Shirley Jean Schmidt, MA, LPC. All rights reserved. Duplication in any form without permission is prohibited.

When you apply the DNMS Needs Meeting Protocol (introduced on page 4) you will guide the client's internal Resources to meet all the wounded part's unmet developmental needs, to help her process through all her unresolved painful emotions, and to form an emotional bond. As this unfolds, the mask will completely disappear and the part will begin to freely express her good true nature (to be in respectful harmony with self and others).

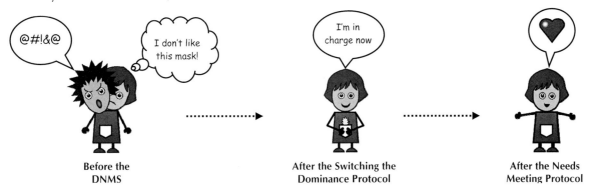

Healing Reactive Parts

As maladaptive introjects heal, the reactive parts that the introject masks had threatened, intimidated, controlled, rejected, or humiliated experience immediate relief. In most cases, they become totally unstuck as soon as the associated introjects become totally unstuck. Since unwanted behaviors, beliefs, and emotions are usually expressed by reactive parts, clients usually report a noticeable improvement in symptoms as each introject is healed.

As an introject becomes unstuck, the associated reactive parts becomes unstuck.

The Benefits of Healing Wounded Parts of Self

As maladaptive introjects heal, your clients will report a greater ability to respond to stressors with adult skills and strengths. So when a stress occurs, like the boss saying, "You made a typo, please correct it," no wounded child parts get triggered. The most adult self simply says, "Sure, I'll have that fixed right away." There is no irrational overreaction.

© Copyright 2009 by Shirley Jean Schmidt, MA, LPC. All rights reserved. Duplication in any form without permission is prohibited.

To be fair, some stressors can be overwhelming, for example, the loss of a child, a life-threatening illness, or a catastrophic flood or fire. Healing maladaptive introjects will not eliminate stress entirely, but it will increase the probability that a client will respond to stressors – whether minor or major – from her most adult self rather than from a wounded child self.

Trauma-Related Introjects

The DNMS protocols can desensitize and heal traumas when there are one or more associated introjects. A *trauma* is defined here as a single, highly disturbing event that produces acute distress, such as a sexual assault, an incident of domestic violence, a car accident, or the loss of a parent. *Trauma wounds* are defined as the unresolved emotional pains associated with a trauma – whether the trauma occurs in childhood or adulthood.

In contrast, *attachment wounds* are defined as the emotional wounds sustained in childhood with caregivers' day-to-day failures to meet attachment needs by being chronically rejecting, neglectful, enmeshing, invalidating, or unsupportive. It is not uncommon for trauma wounds and attachment wounds to intersect.

Childhood traumas always occur in a *context of a relationship* with caregivers, because it is the caregivers' job to foresee dangers to their child, protect their child from foreseen dangers, and soothe their child's painful emotions. The context in which a childhood trauma occurs can substantially influence the intensity of a trauma wound, the child's perception of his own future safety, the child's relationships with his caregivers, and the trauma recovery process. Here is an example that communicates the importance of this context: A four-year-old child is riding in the car with his mother, as she runs errands. When a storm comes up, driving becomes dangerous, and their car gets hit from behind.

- **Scenario #1:** The boy is buckled in his car seat in the back. When it begins to pour, his mother decides to stay off the freeway, and drive home slowly on the streets. They are hit lightly from behind at a stop light. There are no serious injuries, but the boy is traumatized. His mother soothes him and validates his feelings of upset. At home she encourages him to talk about what happened until the painful memory desensitizes naturally.

- **Scenario #2:** The boy is sitting in the front seat, next to his mother – without a seat belt or car seat. When the storm begins she continues to run errands. When he expresses anxiety about the poor visibility, she laughs and tells him there is nothing to fear. They are hit from behind on the freeway. He sustains injuries and is rushed by EMS to the hospital. His mother doesn't sooth him, or validate his feelings of upset. At home, she discourages him from talking about what happened and rewards him for appearing "over it."

In this second scenario, the boy's trauma occurred in the context of his mother's failures to meet needs, including her failure to secure him in a car seat, to take the driving dangers seriously, to validate his fears, to comfort him after he's injured, and to let him talk about the painful experience. Childhood traumas that occur in the context of such caregiver failures are less likely to resolve naturally. This illustrates how trauma-related childhood caregiver failures can occur *before* a trauma has happened, *during* a trauma, and/or *after* a trauma has happened. When caregivers fail to meet trauma-related needs, maladaptive introjects of those caregivers can form.

Unmet Needs before a Trauma Happens

Acts of caregiver neglect can lead to traumas, such as a traumatic injury that occurs because a child was left alone and unsupervised; a catastrophic illness that occurs because a child was not provided timely medical attention; or a sexual assault that occurs because a child was not warned about sexual predators. Such acts of caregiver neglect can form introjects who mirror messages like: "Don't expect me to look after you. You're on your own." "I'm busy, don't bother me. If you feel sick, take an aspirin and go to bed." And "Be a good girl – do whatever adults tell you to do."

© Copyright 2009 by Shirley Jean Schmidt, MA, LPC. All rights reserved. Duplication in any form without permission is prohibited.

Unmet Needs during a Trauma

Acts of caregiver abuse involve failures to meet a child's need for respect and safety, such as a caregiver molesting his child, a caregiver beating his child, or a caregiver locking his child in the basement. Likewise, a caregiver can neglect to intervene to stop a trauma while it is happening. Acts of caregiver abuse can form introjects who mirror messages like, "I can do anything I want to you. You're my property," or "You're a very bad child. You deserve to be locked up." When a caregiver neglects to intervene while a trauma is happening introjects can form who mirror messages like, "I have no power to protect you – you're on your own," and "You're not worth protecting."

Unmet Needs after a Trauma Happens

A child can be further traumatized if a caregiver, who is told of a trauma that has happened, fails to meet the child's post-trauma needs. There are many ways this can occur, for example, when a caregiver fails to provide emotional soothing and reassurance; fails to take action to handle the immediate situation; fails to take action to prevent the trauma from recurring; or fails to take responsibility for any role they might have had in the occurrence of the trauma. A caregiver who is told of a trauma may ignore the incident report, refuse to believe the report, blame the trauma on the child, be overwhelmed by the report, and/or take action which worsens the situation. If a child expects a caregiver to respond inappropriately, she may chose not to talk about a trauma. Poor post-trauma support can be associated with introjects who mirror caregiver messages, such as: "Don't bother me. Your problems are not important." "You're a liar. Stop making up stories." "If you're in trouble it's you're fault – you fix it," "Don't tell me! I can't handle another problem!" and "I will kill anyone who touches you!"

Identifying Trauma-Related Introjects for Processing

Before trauma-processing can begin, all the trauma-related introjects must be identified. This could include introjects of those role models who inflicted the trauma, failed to prevent the trauma, failed to stop a trauma in action, and/or failed to provide needed post-trauma support. While these might not all be caregiver introjects, if the trauma occurred in childhood, the most important introjects will be those that mirror the caregivers who failed to meet trauma-related needs.

- **Example 1:** As a child, Freddy sustained serious injuries when his raging, drunken mother tried to kill them both by running her car off a bridge. She died. He survived. Freddy identified one associated introject, a mother introject conveying the message, "The world is a rotten place. I can't handle it and you can't either. We shouldn't be here."

- **Example 2:** As a child, Sarah was sexually assaulted by her father while her mother was in the next room. She cried out in pain but her mother did not come. Afterwards, when Sarah came out of the room crying, her mother saw blood on her legs and scoffed. She said, "You're a mess, go take a bath." Sarah identified two associated introjects: a father introject conveying the message, "I can do anything I want to you – you're my property," and a mother introject conveying the message, "Men are in charge. We must do what they want because we're their property. There's no use fighting it. So don't expect me to help you."

- **Example 3:** As a child, Nathan was brutally bullied by a classmate at school. When he told his mother about it she showed not interest in listening to him or helping him. He thought about telling his father but decided not to, since his father had a long history of blaming him for things that were not his fault. Nathan identified three associated introjects, a bully introject conveying the message, "I'll hurt you anytime I choose – I have complete power over you," a mother introject conveying the message, "Your problems aren't important – don't tell me about them," and a father introject conveying the message, "If you get into trouble – shame on you. It will always be your fault. You should fix it."

© Copyright 2009 by Shirley Jean Schmidt, MA, LPC. All rights reserved. Duplication in any form without permission is prohibited.

Once all the trauma-related introjects have been identified, you'll apply the DNMS Switching the Dominance and Needs Meeting Protocols. As the introjects are healed, the wounding introject messages will stop playing, and the traumas will fully resolve.

Other Information about Reactive Parts and Introjects

A Part of Self Can Appear as a Metaphor

Not all parts of self appear looking like a person. Sometimes a part of self will appear as a metaphor. For example, a part of self appearing as a rock or an injured animal might represent a powerless reactive part, while a part of self appearing as a monster, witch, darkness, or hostile animal might represent a wounding caregiver. To learn more about a part that appears as a metaphor (e.g. a monster) ask something like:

> Does this (monster) have a message for you?

When the client reveals a message, determine the source by asking:

> Does this message remind you of someone?

If a part of self seems to be mirroring someone ask:

> Is there a little one behind this (monster) costume?

For example, Lucinda reported a part appeared as a fearful shadow holding the belief "I'm not safe." She said it reminded her of hiding from her violent father. This was a powerless reactive part. The next part to appear looked like a crocodile. It was delivering the message "Watch out! I'm coming to get you." It reminded Lucinda of her aggressive, violent father. It was a father introject.

Sometimes an introject that is mirroring a neglectful caregiver will show up as nothingness, blackness, or a void. For example, when Thomas was two years old his handicapped sister was born. His mother was consumed by the needs of her fragile infant and completely ignored him. Thomas felt completely abandoned. When a processing block came up he reported "a darkness" appeared. When I asked who the darkness reminded him of, he cried and said his mother. Her message was "Don't expect me to meet your needs." We found a three-year-old wearing the darkness costume.

Once you have correctly classified a part, it does not matter that it had appeared as a metaphor. Either way, the processing can proceed in the usual way. A reactive part that starts out looking like something other than the client (e.g. rock, animal, shadow) will begin to look more and more like a normal person as the healing process unfolds.

What is a Role Model?

The term role model is used throughout this book to mean any person that a client might introject. A role model is someone who has significantly influenced a client's life – for better or worse. In childhood role models may include parents, grandparents, siblings, neighbors, neighbors, teachers, coaches, scout leaders, and ministers. In adulthood this can include people like spouses, supervisors, and friends. The significant influence may include positive actions, such as loving support, protection, and guidance; or negative actions, such as abuse, neglect, and betrayal. It can also include critical inaction, such as in neglect or abandonment. Brief encounters with strangers can have a significant influence when they are traumatic in nature, such as encounters with bank robbers, muggers, and rapists. While a variety of role models can be influential across the lifespan, childhood caregivers, such as those in a parental role, are considered by far the most important role models because they are 100% responsible for a child's well being. For that reason, this book is focused primarily on the childhood wounds associated with caregiver behaviors.

© Copyright 2009 by Shirley Jean Schmidt, MA, LPC. All rights reserved. Duplication in any form without permission is prohibited.

Introject Mask versus Introject Costume

You will be asking clients to report their mental pictures of introjects as they appear. They may report seeing an introject mask or costume. The term *introject mask* applies when a client reports the introject appears as a part of self wearing a mask with the face of another person. The term *introject costume* applies when an introject appears as a whole person. Throughout this book, these two terms are used interchangeably. Wherever you see the term *mask*, think mask *or* costume.

Child parts wearing introject masks

Child parts wearing introject costumes

Combination Introjects

Most introjects involve a single part of self (usually a child part) wearing a single mask or costume. Occasionally clients encounter a variation of this. For example, a client might report seeing a single ego state that is mirroring more than one person. For example, a single child part might be wearing (a) two masks conveying the messages of two different role models, (b) a composite mask that looks like several role models combined, conveying a combined message, or (c) one mask that looks like one role model that is conveying the message of several role models. Occasionally a client reports two or more child parts wearing a mask or costume. The child parts wearing it might be the same or different ages.

Adulthood Role Models Can Be Introjected

As mentioned above, adults can introject significant role models. Spouses are the most common introjected adulthood role model. Adulthood introjects can be adaptive, as when a spouse is loving and supportive, or maladaptive, as when a spouse is abusive or threatening. Sometimes maladaptive introjects that form in adulthood can generate just as much internal conflict as those formed in childhood. For example, Bobby, a newly divorced 40-year-old man sought therapy to treat irrational fears of overpasses, heights, crowds, and small places. His phobias had developed gradually, over a 12-year period of observing his agoraphobic wife. We found and treated an introject of his anxious wife. Once the introject was totally unstuck, his phobias (which were really just her phobias) vanished.

Sometimes adulthood traumas occur in the context of relationships with individuals in a caregiver role, such as doctors, policemen, lawyers, politicians, etc. Just like parents can fail to meet a child's needs, these adulthood caregivers can fail to meet an adult's needs – resulting in introjected adulthood caregivers. For example, Marcy was in the process of divorcing her threatening, violent husband. The divorce lawyer she had hired failed to protect her from him in many significant ways. The final blow was the day he gave her husband her secret address and phone number. After that day she often observed a menacing man watching her apartment, and got frequent harassing phone calls. Every day she was terrified of being kidnapped or assaulted. In addition to introjecting her abusive husband, she also introjected her lawyer conveying the message, "Your safety is not important. Don't expect me to protect you."

© Copyright 2009 by Shirley Jean Schmidt, MA, LPC. All rights reserved. Duplication in any form without permission is prohibited.

Groups of People Can Be Introjected

Groups of people can be introjected, such as religious groups, racial groups, political groups, corporations, and schoolyard bullies. For example, Phillip, a ex-member of a controlling, cult-like fundamentalist church, introjected his church conveying the message, "You must believe what we believe, or God will punish you in Hell." Edwina, an African-American who grow up in racially segregated Alabama in the early 1960s, introjected the prevailing white community church conveying the message, "You're inferior because you're black." Tess, who had a life-threatening medical illness that required many expensive treatments, introjected her insurance company when they refused to pay their share of her medical bills. Their refusal to pay conveyed the wounding message, "Your health and well-being are not important. We don't care if you die."

Observed Victims Can Be Introjected

DNMS therapist Joan Bacon was the first to observe that we can introject people we have observed being victimized.[33] For example, a child can introject a sibling who is being abused; a soldier can introject someone he killed or someone he saw being killed; a nurse can introject a dying patient or grieving family members. We may be more likely to introject a victim we identify with or feel responsible for. My 50-year-old client, Susan, recalled giving birth to a severely handicapped baby boy at age 25. As she lay in the delivery room watching her motionless newborn across the room, she connected to the many times in childhood that she had been the helpless victim of physical and sexual abuse. We determined that, as she watched the doctors try to resuscitate her son, she had introjected him in his life-threatening state. We identified the 25-year-old part of her that had introjected her helpless newborn, then applied the Switching the Dominance and Needs Meeting Protocols. Once that ego state was totally unstuck, a chronic sense of impending death (that the client had experienced since age 25) was completely gone. She reported immediate and significant improvement in sleep, concentration, anxiety, and depression.

Prenatal Introjection

Although not proven by rigorous scientific means, clinical observation by DNMS therapists suggest that maladaptive introjects may be able to form in the womb. (See Appendix B for a more academic discussion of this.) This appears to happen when a baby's disturbing experience is significant enough to become engrained – whether by abuse, neglect, rejection, or enmeshment. Some clients have reported sensing that they knew before they were born whether or not they were wanted by their mother. If an unborn child can detect rejection, she may also be able to introject her rejecting caregiver. For example, Wilma had done years of cognitive therapy but still felt horrible about herself. She reported that her mother had not wanted a child – especially not a girl. A prenatal-mother introject was found conveying the message, "You shouldn't exist, but if you do, at least be a boy." The child part behind the mom costume was a three-month-old fetus. As the Needs Meeting Protocol unfolded, the client pictured the fetus growing to 6 months, then 9 months, through birth, and then 18 months of age, with different needs getting met at each stage. In the end, the child part appeared as an eight-year-old. Once all the needs were met and she was totally unstuck, the child part reported believing, "I have a right to be here, it's okay to be a girl. I am strong." Following this work, the client reported her sense of being unwanted was gone, and she felt much more in charge of her life.

Morgan, a ministerial school student, reported feeling exhausted and burned out. She had a pattern of anxiously over-preparing for classes and taking on too much work in her church internship placements. She would rarely take rest time for herself. She revealed the belief that "My life script is to save people in pain." Two prenatal mother introjects were found delivering the messages, "I have nothing and you must be my savior," and "Life is so sad, it's your job to make me happy." A womb baby ego state was found behind each mom introject costume. After the Needs Meeting Protocol got both child parts completely unstuck, the client reported feeling separate from others' pain for the first time in her life. She was able to set healthy boundaries in her church work and have realistic expectations surrounding her school performance. She began reconnecting with friends for recreation, scheduled regular massages, and reported feeling unburdened and balanced.

© Copyright 2009 by Shirley Jean Schmidt, MA, LPC. All rights reserved. Duplication in any form without permission is prohibited.

Ego State Therapy Controversy

Some therapists assert that ego state therapy does more harm than good by further fractionating dissociative clients. Others argue that distinguishing some ego states from others, and giving some ego states individual attention, is reifying them, which increases their sense of isolation. Improperly executed ego state work might indeed fractionate a client more, or increase ego state isolation, just as any psychotherapy technique or approach implemented poorly has the potential to fail or do damage. However, properly executed ego state therapy results in much less fractionation and isolation.

The relationships between ego states (or neural networks) can be compared to the relationship between a prosperous city and neighboring towns. Think of a large wealthy city with resources to spare, surrounded by small isolated towns, in economic despair. Each small town will be more or less connected to the city by phone lines, roads, and commerce. The DNMS therapist endeavors to increase communication and cooperation within the self-system. In this analogy that means a benevolent government builds better roads, runs more phone cables, generates more trade, shares resources, and creates good will between the city and towns. It means distributing the city's surplus resources to the towns, so the towns can also prosper. The DNMS focuses on wounded ego state repair, not despair. In this analogy, that means developing the optimal relationship between the city and towns. Focusing treatment on the despair would not likely be as beneficial.

Chapter Summary

This chapter provided basic information about how to work with ego states – from calling ego states forward, to talking to them individually and in groups, to tucking them in. It explained the DNMS ego state classifications of reactive parts and introjects, and the importance of knowing the difference. The difference between maladaptive introjects and reactive parts is like the difference between bullies and the bullied. Maladaptive introjects (bullies) are parts of self that mimic wounding role models. Reactive parts (the bullied) are parts of self that engage in unwanted behaviors, beliefs, and emotions, initially in reaction to the wounding role models, and later in reaction to the maladaptive introjects. This chapter explained just how reactive parts get triggered by maladaptive introjects in adulthood – especially when under stress. It offered a brief overview of how the DNMS helps to heal maladaptive introjects. A description of how the DNMS can desensitize and resolve certain the traumas was also provided.

Chapter 2 Notes and References

1. Fraser, G.A. (1991). The dissociative table technique: A strategy for working with ego states in dissociative disorders and ego-state therapy. *DISSOCIATION, 4,* 205-213.
    Kluft, R.P. (1985). *The childhood antecedents of multiple personality.* Washington, DC: American Psychiatric Press.
    Putnam, F.W. (1989). *Diagnosis and treatment of multiple personality disorder.* New York: The Guilford Press.
    Ross, C.A. (1989). *Multiple Personality Disorder: Diagnosis, Clinical Features, and Treatment.* New York, Toronto: Wiley.
2. Assagioli, R. (1975). *Psychosynthesis: A manual of principles and techniques.* London: Turnstone Press.
3. Perls, F.S., Hefferline, R.F., & Goodman, P. (1951). *Gestalt therapy: Excitement and growth in the human personality.* New York: Dell.
4. Berne, E. (1961). *Transactional analysis in psychotherapy, a systematic individual and social psychiatry.* New York: Grove Press.
5. Schwartz, R. C. (1995). *Internal family systems therapy.* New York: Guilford Press.
6. Stone, H. & Stone, S. (1993). *Embracing our selves: The voice dialogue manual.* Nataraj Publishing.
7. Bradshaw, J. (1990). *Homecoming: Reclaiming and championing you inner child.* Bantam Books.
    Capacchione, L. (1991). *Recovery of Your Inner Child: The Highly Acclaimed Method for Liberating Your Inner Self.* New York: Simon & Schuster/Fireside.
    Napier, N. (1990). *Recreating your self: Building self-esteem through imaging and self-hypnosis.* New York: Norton.
8. Phillips, M., & Frederick, C. (1995). *Healing the divided self: Clinical and Ericksonian hypnotherapy for post-traumatic and dissociative conditions.* New York: W.W. Norton & Company.

© Copyright 2009 by Shirley Jean Schmidt, MA, LPC. All rights reserved. Duplication in any form without permission is prohibited.

9.   Watkins, J. G., & Watkins, H. H. (1997). *Ego states: Theory and therapy*. New York: Norton.

10. Watkins, J. G., & Watkins, H. H. (1997). *Ego states: Theory and therapy*. New York: Norton.

11. Siegel, D.J. (2003). An interpersonal neurobiology of psychotherapy: The developing mind and the resolution of trauma. In M. F. Solomon & D. J. Siegel (Eds.), *Healing trauma: attachment, mind, body and brain* (pp. 1-56). New York: Norton.

12. Fraser, G.A. (1991). The dissociative table technique: A strategy for working with ego states in dissociative disorders and ego-state therapy. *DISSOCIATION, 4,* 205-213.
     Kluft, R.P. (1985). *The childhood antecedents of multiple personality*. Washington, DC: American Psychiatric Press.
     Putnam, F.W. (1989). *Diagnosis and treatment of multiple personality disorder*. New York: The Guilford Press.
     Ross, C.A. (1989). Multiple Personality Disorder: Diagnosis, Clinical Features, and Treatment New York, Toronto: Wiley.

13. Kluft, R.P. (1984). An introduction to multiple personality disorder. *Psychiatric Annals, 14*:19-24.

14. Paulsen, S. (2000). *EMDR and the Divided Self: EMDR and ego state therapy for non-dissociative and dissociative clients*. All-day workshop in San Antonio, Texas, April, 2000.
     Tucking in is similar to Richard Kluft's *therapeutic sleep* – a hypnotic technique that involves putting "overwhelmed alters, or those holding memories or affects intolerable to the alters handling day-to-day functioning, to sleep in between sessions, or even longer." Kluft, R.P. (1993) The initial stages of psychotherapy in the treatment of multiple personality disorder patients. *DISSOCIATION*, 6, p. 158.

15. The DNMS term *system-wide announcement* is akin to what Kluft, Phillips, and Frederick call *talking through* to alters when working with clients with dissociative identity disorder.
     Kluft, R.P. (1982). Varieties of hypnotic interventions in the treatment of multiple personality. *American Journal of Clinical Hypnosis, 24*:230-240.
     Phillips, M., & Frederick, C. (1995). *Healing the divided self: Clinical and Ericksonian hypnotherapy for post-traumatic and dissociative conditions*. New York: W.W. Norton & Company.

16. Berne, E. (1961). *Transactional analysis in psychotherapy, a systematic individual and social psychiatry*. New York: Grove Press.

17. Perls, F.S., Hefferline, R.F., & Goodman, P. (1951). *Gestalt therapy: Excitement and growth in the human personality*. New York: Dell.

18. Schwartz, R. C. (1995). *Internal family systems therapy*. New York: Guilford Press.

19. The term *role model* is defined in this book as any person who has significantly influenced a client's life - for better or worse. In childhood role models may include parents, grandparents, siblings, neighbors, teachers and ministers. In adulthood this can include people like spouses, supervisors and friends. The significant influence may include actions, such as loving support, or inaction, such as an absence of support. A significant influence can also made with brief encounters with strangers, such as bank robbers, muggers, and rapists. While a variety of role models can be influential across the lifespan, childhood caregivers, such as those in a parental role, are considered by far the most important role models because they are 100% responsible for a child's well being. For that reason, this book is focused primarily on childhood wounds associated with caregiver behaviors.

20. Examples of good intentions include: to be authentic; to record and contain traumatic memories; to block pain; to manage internal and external threats; to win approval; to avoid punishment; to express autonomy; and to ensure survival.

21. Berne, E. (1961). *Transactional analysis in psychotherapy, a systematic individual and social psychiatry*. New York: Grove Press.

22. Freud, S. (1923/1961). The ego and the id. In J Strachey (Ed. and Trans.), *The standard edition of the complete psychological works of Sigmund Freud* (Vol.19). London: Hogarth Press. (Original work published in 1923).

23. Perls, F. S. (1973). *The Gestalt approach and eyewitness to therapy*. Science and Behavior Books, Inc.

24. Watkins, J. G., & Watkins, H. H. (1997). *Ego states: Theory and therapy*. New York: Norton.

25. Freud, A. (1966). *The Ego and the Mechanisms of Defense*, vol. 2. Madison, CT: International Universities Press, Inc.

26. Erskine, R.G. (2001). Psychological function, relational needs and transferential resolution: The psychotherapy of an obsession. *Transactional Analysis Journal*, Vol. 31, No. 4, pp. 220-226.

27. Perls, F. S. (1973). *The Gestalt approach and eyewitness to therapy*. Science and Behavior Books, Inc.

28. Perls, L. (1978, Winter). An oral history of Gestalt therapy. Part I: A conversation with Laura Perls, by Edward Rosenfeld. *The Gestalt Journal*, 1, 8-31.

29. Watkins, J. G., & Watkins, H. H. (1997). *Ego states: Theory and therapy*. New York: Norton.

30. Freud, A. (1966). *The Ego and the Mechanisms of Defense*, vol. 2. Madison, CT: International Universities Press, Inc.

31. Montessori, M. (1936). *The Secret of Childhood*. New York: Frederick A. Stokes and Co.

32. Gallese V., Eagle M.E., and Migone P. (2007). Intentional attunement: Mirror neurons and the neural underpinnings of interpersonal relations. *Journal of the American Psychoanalytic Association*, 55: 131-176.

33. Personal communication with Joan Bacon, Psychologist. (2004).

© Copyright 2009 by Shirley Jean Schmidt, MA, LPC. All rights reserved. Duplication in any form without permission is prohibited.

<h1 align="center">Chapter 3</h1>

The Resource Development Protocol

Protocol Overview

The Resource Development Protocol aims to help clients connect to three individual Resource ego states: a Nurturing Adult Self (NAS), a Protective Adult Self (PAS), and a Spiritual Core Self (SCS). When clients connect to these Resources, they are accessing neural networks that hold their best adult caregiver skills – grounded with spirituality. Over the years many ego state therapies and interventions[1] have encouraged adult parts of self to nurture and protect wounded child parts to help them heal. The DNMS goes one step further, providing you a systematic protocol for establishing robust Resource parts of self, so when you call upon them to the help wounded parts heal, they are, without a doubt, fully qualified to competently do the job.

Once each Resource has been mobilized, you'll invite the client to bring all three together to form a team. This team of Resources is called a Healing Circle. These Resources can serve clients in many ways. For example:

- During the DNMS Needs Meeting Protocol wounded parts of self are invited into the Healing Circle where the Resources will meet their needs, process their painful emotions, and form a loving, intimate bond.
- Therapists can refer clients to their compassionate, wise Resources for empathy, reassurance, and advice, at any time, for any topic.
- Clients can invite upset parts of self to wait, in the comfort of the Healing Circle, until a time in the future when their needs can be addressed.
- Clients who feel overwhelmed, both during and between sessions, can go to their Resources for comfort and soothing, which leads to improvements in affect containment and emotion regulation.
- A Healing Circle can serve as a perfect container for holding painful emotions and as a loving Safe Place.
- Clients can establish an ego-strengthening relationship, or intrapersonal attunement, with the Resources.

You'll use alternating bilateral stimulation (ABS) at key moments during this protocol, to enhance ego-strengthening experiences. ABS can be applied to strengthen each individual Resource, and to strengthen the Resource team. The details of ABS application are provided in Chapter 2.

The Healing Circle

Spiritual Core Self

Protective Adult Self   Nurturing Adult Self

You'll start the Resource Development Protocol by describing each Resource to your client. Next you'll encourage him to talk about personal experiences that exemplify the qualities of each Resource, such as being a nurturing and protective grandfather or pet owner. You'll explain how each Resource gets mobilized with a different guided meditation. You'll guide the client in each of the three meditations, and apply ABS to strengthen each Resource connection. Finally, you'll invite all three Resources to join together to form a team – then apply ABS to strengthen the Healing Circle.

A typical client/therapist dialogue is provided at the end of this chapter to illustrate the flow of this protocol. A five-page *Resource Development Protocol Worksheet* is provided in Appendix E. This chapter describes this protocol as it would proceed without complications. Instructions for handling blocks unique to this intervention are covered on pages 166-171 of Chapter 7.

© Copyright 2009 by Shirley Jean Schmidt, MA, LPC. All rights reserved. Duplication in any form without permission is prohibited.

The Nurturing Adult Self and Protective Adult Self

The Nurturing and Protective Adult Selves (NAS & PAS) are considered a person's most mature, caregiver self, expressed in a nurturing role and a protective role. The NAS is a state of mind that can competently nurture a loved one. It predominately embodies qualities like gentleness, compassion, and kindness. The PAS is a state of mind that can competently protect a loved one. It predominately embodies qualities like protection, strength, and courage.

While these two Resources have many skills and abilities, they should not be considered superhuman. Like typical mature adults, they have needs, they are imperfect, they are vulnerable, and they can experience the full range of emotions. But they are very special because they can meet their own needs, manage their vulnerabilities, and regulate their own emotions. They can learn and grow from their mistakes, and continue to mature over time. These skills (and others) make them competent caregivers.

By necessity, the NAS and PAS must be vulnerable and discerning in order to meet physical and emotional needs, solve problems, take action, and be appropriately protective. They are parts of self that are equipped with the skills to handle day-to-day issues of physical survival, such as food, shelter, health, and safety.

Central to the Resource Development Protocol is a list of caregiver skills. This list was constructed over time, from clinical trail and error, and with feedback from clients. While it may or may not be a perfect list, it does appear to cover the most important areas. See the list, complete with definitions, on page 39.

This list of skills and traits becomes the core script for the guided NAS and PAS meditations. The two scripts are the same, except for one key difference. The NAS meditation begins with the word *empathic* and proceeds to the word *protective*, while the PAS meditation begins with the word *protective* and proceeds to the word *empathic*. Both meditations end with the word *grounded*.

Some clients may ask you why the two meditation lists are not completely different. The rationale for using the same list for both Resources is simple: The NAS and PAS will help wounded parts of self heal in much the same way competent parents help children grow and learn. A father typically assumes a protective role, while a mother typically assumes a nurturing role. But a child will benefit the most in their care if both parents have the ability to employ all the skills and traits on the list, even those that are not central to their role. The broader their skill base, the better.

The NAS and PAS are not imaginary, archetypal, or fantasy Resources. They are real parts of self that take up space in the brain in real neural networks. The two meditations serve to heighten clients' awareness of the caregiver skills they already possess. These Resources are no more imaginary than a person's loving concern for a child, grandchild, niece, nephew, or pet is imaginary. Because these two Resources are anchored in a client's real ability to lovingly attune to another person, it means they have the potential to lovingly attune to wounded parts of self.

Discussing Familiar Caregiving Experiences

After describing each Resource, you'll invite your client to discuss personal, successful experiences of being in a nurturing role and a protective role. In particular, you'll want to hear about special moments when *competent caregiver skills were demonstrated naturally, effortlessly, and appropriately, at the same time, while a client was in an adult state of mind.* For example, Lisa recalled patiently playing with her two-year-old niece; Tammie recalled nurturing her treasured terrier; Ginger recalled caring for her cherished granddaughter; Herbert recalled a time at the beach he rescued a stranger from drowning; and Matt recalled a time he pulled a student away from a speeding car. Most clients will be able to recognize their potential to express all the skills and traits needed to be a good-enough nurturer or protector, as they reflect on ordinary, familiar experiences.

© Copyright 2009 by Shirley Jean Schmidt, MA, LPC. All rights reserved. Duplication in any form without permission is prohibited.

The Nurturing Adult Self and Protective Adult Self Skills Defined

Empathic	Able to understand, be aware of, be sensitive to, and vicariously experience the feelings, thoughts, and experiences of others. *
Compassionate	Able to be sympathetically conscious of another's distress, together with a desire to alleviate it. *
Understanding	Able to achieve a grasp of the nature, significance, or explanation of something; able to show a sympathetic or tolerant attitude toward something. *
Accepting	Able to receive willingly, to give admittance or approval to, or to endure without protest or reaction. *
Patient	Able to bear pains or trials calmly or without complaint. Able to manifest forbearance under provocation or strain. Not hasty or impetuous. Steadfast despite opposition, difficulty, or adversity. *
Nurturing	Able to supply nourishment*, both physical and emotional.
Warm	Able to readily show affection, gratitude, cordiality, or sympathy. *
Open	Able to be readily accessible, usually with a generous attitude. Willing to hear and consider. Responsive. Free from reserve or pretense. *
Able To Attune	Able to read nonverbal behavior (body language, tone of voice, and so on) and respond appropriately, with empathy.
Good At Listening	Able to hear something with thoughtful attention and give it consideration. *
Good with Boundaries	Able to set appropriate limits on other's behavior to create safety and comfort for self and others.
Reliable	Able to be relied on, dependable. *
Trustworthy	Able to be trusted. Worthy of confidence, dependable. *
Confident	Self-assured or self-reliant, having confidence in and exercising one's own powers of judgment. *
Respectful	Able to treat someone with respect, giving particular attention or consideration, or showing high regard or esteem. * Able to be courteous.
Appropriately Responsible	Able to answer for one's conduct and obligations. Able to choose between right and wrong.* Not assuming more responsibility than is appropriate.
Problem-Solver	Able to acknowledge a problem and map a plan to get it solved.
Action-Taker	Able to use available resources to take action to solve a problem.
Decision-Maker	Able to select one option, after thoughtful consideration of many.
Logical	Able to reason.* Able to be rational.
Strong	Not easily injured or disturbed, solid; not easily subdued or taken.* Resilient.
Courageous	Able to use mental or moral strength to venture, persevere, and withstand danger, fear, or difficulty. *
Protective	Able to cover or shield from exposure, injury, or destruction. Able to guard. *
Grounded/Centered	Able to be "in the body", in present time, with a sense of peace and stability.

*From Merriam-Webster Online Dictionary, 2002

© Copyright 2009 by Shirley Jean Schmidt, MA, LPC. All rights reserved. Duplication in any form without permission is prohibited.

Clients will typically focus on (a) an ongoing caregiving role with a cherished loved one, such as a child, grandchild, niece, nephew, or pet, or (b) a specific event, such as protecting a loved one, an acquaintance, or a stranger in an emergency situation. Caregiving relationships with other adults (e.g. the friend getting a divorce, the sister with the flu) are usually weak examples. There are exceptions though. My client Abby discovered her adult caregiver skills while looking after a bedridden elderly aunt. As a general rule, it is better for clients to revisit relationships and events that are similar to the type of experiences the Resources will have caring for wounded child ego states.

Most people can easily identify one or more such relationships or events. Even clients who do not often exhibit competent caregiver skills can usually recall one time when they demonstrated all these skills (or maybe two or three times when they collectively demonstrated all the skills). Such real, competent, caregiving experiences can serve as powerful, compelling anchors for mobilizing the NAS and PAS.

Once clients have articulated at least one good example of being a competent nurturer and a competent protector, show them the list of skills defined (from page 39) and ask them to point out any items on the list that are (or were) not present in those special relationships or events. Many clients readily recognize ownership of all 24 items in the context of a special experience.

Clients are often quite surprised to acknowledge how many adult skills and strengths they actually possess. In the course of their daily struggles they are often so over-focused on their unwanted behaviors, beliefs, and emotions they forget how much they can do well. It is not uncommon for a client to say something like, "Wow! I really can do these things. I really can be confident, patient, and reliable. I really am good with my grandkids." Such epiphanies are delightfully ego strengthening.

At a client's request, appropriate substitutions or additions may be made to the list before beginning a meditation. For example a client might prefer the word *rational* over *logical*, or the word *dependable* over *reliable*. When clients have taken a skill to a dysfunctional extreme, the word "appropriately" can be used to qualify it, for example: *appropriately protective*, *appropriately nurturing*, or *appropriately accepting*. A client might choose to add words like *playfulness, sense of humor,* or *intelligence*.

Sometimes a client may wish to drop a trait he thinks he doesn't have. The wounded child parts that the NAS and PAS will be helping to heal need caregivers who have all these traits, so dropping traits from this list is not helpful. Instead, help the client recognize he has already expressed the trait in the past or has the potential to express the trait in the future. If that doesn't work, help him develop the trait. (Read more about that on page 167.)

This discussion of caregiving experiences is very important, because during the guided NAS meditation clients will be invited to reflect on their personal experience of being a skillful nurturer, and during the guided PAS meditation they will be invited to reflect on their personal experience of being a skillful protector. At the conclusion of the meditations, clients' mental pictures of their two adult Resources will be based on these real experiences. This step helps ensure that the NAS and PAS meditations will successfully heighten awareness of competent caregiver skills a client can easily see he already has. In later DNMS processing, if/when processing stalls, reminding clients of these successful experiences can sometimes help clear a block.

Connecting to the Nurturing and Protective Adult Self

You'll mobilize each adult Resource with a two-stage guided meditation. In the first stage you'll invite the client to think about his special experience as a competent caregiver as you name each skill on the list. Just in case an unexpected fear or concern arises in the process, this is done with ABS off. If the client's response to the list is positive, you'll turn ABS on and read the list again – to let the positive experience strengthen all the way. Just before beginning the NAS or PAS meditation, you can explain this to clients with something like this:

> Now we're going to start the (NAS or PAS) meditation. We'll do it in two phases. First I'll guide you through the meditation once, with the TheraTapper off. If your response is positive, I'll guide you through it again, with the TheraTapper on, to let the positive feeling strengthen all the way. When it's time to do the (PAS or NAS) meditation, we'll do it the same way.

© Copyright 2009 by Shirley Jean Schmidt, MA, LPC. All rights reserved. Duplication in any form without permission is prohibited.

The Nurturing Adult Self Meditation

The first part of the NAS meditation goes like this:

> *Think about (that familiar experience of being naturally, effortlessly, and appropriately nurturing) as I name each skill on the list. Nod or say "yes" with each skill you know you possess. Stop me if I name a skill you believe you don't have, or if you feel any discomfort that suggests a block is arising. Close your eyes (if that's comfortable) and take a deep breath. Now get in touch with the following skills and traits, which you already have, including your ability to be empathic... compassionate... understanding... accepting... patient... nurturing... warm... open... able to attune... good at listening... good with boundaries... reliable... trustworthy... confident... respectful... appropriately responsible... problem-solver... action-taker... decision-maker... logical... strong... courageous... protective... and grounded (or centered). Now, bring all these skills together into a single sense of self, your Nurturing Adult Self, and when you're ready, tell me what you notice.*

Clients typically report feeling more confident. Ask how the body feels (if the client does not spontaneously tell you). If the body feels tense or uncomfortable, there is probably a block to identify and clear. If the body feels good, turn on ABS, and read the list again. The second part of the NAS meditation goes like this:

> *Now I'm going to read the list again, with the TheraTapper on. Again I want you to think about (that familiar experience of being naturally, effortlessly, and appropriately nurturing) as I name each skill on the list. You don't have to nod or say "yes" this time, just listen to each item and let each strengthen. Stop me if you feel a discomfort that suggests a block is arising. Now get in touch with the following skills and traits, which you already have, including your ability to be empathic... compassionate... understanding... accepting... patient... nurturing... warm... open... able to attune... good at listening... good with boundaries... reliable... trustworthy... confident... respectful... appropriately responsible... problem-solver... action-taker... decision-maker... logical... strong... courageous... protective... and grounded. Now, bring all these skills together into a single sense of self, your Nurturing Adult Self, and tell me when it's strengthened all the way.*

Once this has strengthened all the way clients typically report an elevated sense of confidence. Ask how the body feels if the client does not spontaneously tell you. If the body feels tense or uncomfortable, there is a problem. Identify and address any associated blocks, then repeat the meditation.

The Protective Adult Self Meditation

Likewise, the first part of the PAS meditation goes like this:

> *Think about (that familiar experience of being naturally, effortlessly, and appropriately protective) as I name each skill on the list. Nod or say "yes" with each skill you know you possess. Stop me if I name a skill you believe you don't have, or if you feel any discomfort that suggests a block is arising. Close your eyes (if that's comfortable) and take a deep breath. Now get in touch with the following skills and traits, which you already have, including your ability to be protective... courageous... strong... logical... decision-maker... action-taker... problem-solver... appropriately responsible... respectful... confident... trustworthy... reliable... good with boundaries... good at listening... able to attune... open... warm... nurturing... patient... accepting... understanding... compassionate... empathic... and grounded (or centered). Now, bring all these skills together into a single sense of self, your Protective Adult Self, and when you're ready, tell me what you notice.*

Again clients typically report feeling more confident. Ask how the body feels (if the client does not spontaneously tell you). If the body feels tense or uncomfortable, there is probably a block to identify and clear. If the body feels good, turn on ABS, and read the list again. The second part of the meditation goes like this:

> *Now I'm going to read the list again, with the TheraTapper on. Again I want you to think about (that familiar experience of being naturally, effortlessly, and appropriately protective) as I name each skill on the list. You don't have to nod or say "yes" this time, just listen to each item and let each strengthen. Stop me if you feel a discomfort that suggests a block is*

© Copyright 2009 by Shirley Jean Schmidt, MA, LPC. All rights reserved. Duplication in any form without permission is prohibited.

arising. Now get in touch with the following skills and traits, which you already have, including your ability to be protective... courageous... strong... logical... decision-maker... action-taker... problem-solver... appropriately responsible... respectful... confident... trustworthy... reliable... good with boundaries... good at listening... able to attune... open... warm... nurturing... patient... accepting... understanding... compassionate... empathic... and grounded (or centered). Now bring all these skills together into a single sense of self, your Protective Adult Self, and let it get as strong as it wants to. Tell me when it's strengthened all the way.

Once this has strengthened all the way clients typically report an elevated sense of confidence. Ask how the body feels if the client does not spontaneously tell you. If the body feels tense or uncomfortable, there is a problem. Identify and address any associated blocks, then repeat the meditation.

Mental Pictures of the Nurturing and Protective Adult Self

At the conclusion of each meditation, ask about the client's mental picture of his Resource (if he does not spontaneously describe it). Ask something like:

Do you get a mental picture of your (NAS or PAS)?

The mental picture of each Resource should correspond directly to the special event or relationship previously discussed. Sometimes a client will report on a mental picture that does not look like self, for example a NAS that looks like an angel, or a PAS that looks like a shaman. In other therapies, or for other therapy purposes, such *Not-Self Resources* can be helpful, meaningful, and valuable. However, in my experience, the wounded child parts that the NAS and PAS will be helping to heal will make notably better progress during the Needs Meeting Protocol if these two Resources look and feel like real parts of self, grounded in familiar experiences. The farther away the NAS and PAS are from ordinary experience, the less robust these healing experiences with the Resources are likely to be.

If a client reports a mental picture of a Not-Self Resource, ask him to picture it side-by-side with a mental image of himself in his special relationship or event, and to report which feels the most comfortable and powerful in the body. Most clients will find the picture of self in the real, familiar experience, to be the more powerful, and will gladly use that picture during DNMS processing. For example, Lacy initially talked about how well she nurtured and protected with her three horses. When we finished the NAS meditation, she reported mentally picturing her PAS as a mother bear protecting her cubs. I asked her to close her eyes and hold her picture of the mother bear protecting her cubs next to a picture of herself protecting her horses. She reported the picture of herself with her horses felt much better and stronger, because it was real. She was glad to use that mental picture for her NAS.

If a client has an aversion to picturing either the NAS or PAS as self, a further investigation will be required to fully understand the nature of the aversion and find a resolution. Fortunately, it is possible to employ a Not-Self Resource as a *Provisional Resource*, which can provide guidance and support while a client is working through processing blocks. Chapter 7 provides details about how to overcome Resource development blocks in general (page 166), and the use of Provisional Resources in particular (page 171).

The Spiritual Core Self

The SCS is a state of mind experienced during meditation, yoga, or prayer; a peak spiritual experience; a transcendent near-death experience; or a moment of clarity while connecting to nature. It is associated with:

- A sense of interconnectedness to all beings
- A sense of completeness and wholeness
- A sense of safety and invulnerability
- No ego, no struggles
- No desires or aversions

- Unconditional, effortless happiness
- Unconditional, effortless acceptance
- Unconditional, effortless loving kindness, compassion
- Timeless, cosmic wisdom and understanding
- Timelessness; present moment is precious and full

© Copyright 2009 by Shirley Jean Schmidt, MA, LPC. All rights reserved. Duplication in any form without permission is prohibited.

The SCS is considered the core of one's being. Some people call it the *soul*. Some believe it is a part of self that may have existed before the body arrived, and may exist after the body dies.

If it is a part of self that will exist after the body dies, then it is an energy flow that will persist no matter what happens to the body. That means it cannot be wounded. As such it would not be concerned about notions of survival in the same way the NAS and PAS are. It can be considered an essential, core part of self that does not change over time – as wise and grounded in adulthood as it was in the womb. A SCS can bring a quality of infinite balance to wounded parts of self which can provide a sense of calm during a storm.

Discussing Spiritual Beliefs & Peak Spiritual Experiences

Invite clients to talk about their spiritual beliefs. Discuss the list of ten qualities associated with this state of mind (listed above). Encourage them to recall moments when they experienced these qualities. By understanding their views on spirituality you can better guide them to disclose their personal, meaningful, peak (spiritual) experiences. Most, but not all clients, will have something to share. For example Gladys, a Catholic who often attends mass, has a deep faith, and prays regularly, was able to describe her experiences of feeling profoundly connected to God when she takes communion. Stephen, a Buddhist, was able to recall an experience of profound calm and connectedness at his first meditation retreat. And Joel, an atheist who loves nature, was able to recall an experience of peace and connectedness on a wilderness campout.

Clients can connect to a SCS whether or not they believe in God, or have a spiritual orientation. Some clients (and some therapists) are indifferent to, or have an aversion to, the subject of spirituality. When a client wants to stay away from this term, you can simply guide him to connect to a *Core Self*. For example, Joel felt more comfortable with the idea of connecting to a Core Self because he was an atheist. Kristin, who believes in God, felt safer connecting to a Core Self because of unresolved priest abuse. My colleague Thomas, a therapist who believes spirituality is just foolishness, guides all his clients to connect to a Core Self.

The DNMS offers clients four alternative SCS meditations. Knowing a client's personal views about spirituality is very important because it can help you select the meditation best suited for each client. For example, three of the four SCS meditations do not contain the word *spiritual*.

Connecting to the Spiritual Core Self

Four alternative meditations are listed below: a Spiritual Core Self Meditation, a Core Self Meditation, a Breath Meditation, and a List Meditation. Only the first of these four uses the word *spiritual*. If one meditation does not appeal to a client, try another. You are welcome to modify these meditations or create your own if any of these miss the mark. Clients who reported having had a peak spiritual or transcendent experience should be invited to think about that special experience during the guided meditation. Whichever meditation you choose to use, read it slowly and tenderly, without ABS.

Regular Spiritual Core Self Meditation

This is the meditation I use most frequently:

> (Think about your special spiritual experience.) *Close your eyes (if that's comfortable) and take a deep breath. Now get in touch with the center of your being... that place within you that is quiet... peaceful... and still. And in this place... it's possible you'll connect to your spiritual core. Your spiritual core has been with you from the beginning... it's the essence of who you are... your core of goodness. Pure... resilient... and whole. And your body knows exactly how to connect you. Notice as you connect to this part of you, and when you're ready, tell me what you notice.*

© Copyright 2009 by Shirley Jean Schmidt, MA, LPC. All rights reserved. Duplication in any form without permission is prohibited.

Core Self Meditation

This is a good choice for those clients who have an aversion to the word *spiritual*:

> (Think about your special transcendent experience.) *Close your eyes (if that's comfortable) and take a deep breath. Now get in touch with the center of your being... that place within you that is quiet... peaceful... and still. And in this place... it's possible you'll connect to your core self. Your core self has been with you from the beginning... it's the essence of who you are... your core of goodness. Pure... resilient... and whole. And your body knows exactly how to connect you. Notice as you connect to this part of you, and when you're ready, tell me what you notice.*

Breath Meditation

My colleague Tom Cloyd[2] has found it is easier for some clients to connect to peace and calmness through the body rather than the mind so he developed the following meditation:

> *There is a place in your mind that is quiet, peaceful, and calm. It's always been there, even though you may never have noticed it. You'll get there by simply watching your breath. First, deliberately inhale, noticing how it takes muscle tension to do this. You have to do a little work to get the air into your lungs. Now release the air, and notice that all you have to do is let go. Just let yourself float down, while the air leaves your body. Notice how good it feels just to let go. Now take another breath, and again notice that muscle tension is needed. Then let go, and just float down. Notice that right at the bottom of your breath, right at the point where you stop exhaling, there is a still moment, a moment where nothing is happening, where all is quiet, calm, peaceful. Okay, now just breathe again, and watch for that point, at the bottom of your breath. Now, breathe again, and this time when you get to the bottom of your breath, just sit there a moment or two, still and quiet, not breathing. Notice what that feels like, what your mind is like: empty, quiet and calm. So, now as you keep breathing, just stay connected to this calm and quiet part of you, now that you've found it... and when you're ready, tell me what you notice.*

List Meditation

This meditation is based on the list of qualities a person typically experiences in their SCS state of mind:

> (Think about your special spiritual experience.) *Close your eyes (if that's comfortable) and take a deep breath. Now get in touch with the center of your being... that place within you that is quiet... peaceful... and still. And in this place... it's possible you'll connect to a sense of interconnectedness to all beings... a sense of completeness and wholeness... of safety and invulnerability. A place where all things and events are equally special... a place of no desires or aversions... no ego or struggles. A place of unconditional effortless happiness, acceptance. A place of loving kindness and compassion. Notice as you connect to this part of you, and when you're ready, tell me what you notice.*

Strengthening the Spiritual Core Self

Notice that the last instruction on each meditation is "tell me what you notice." Clients typically report feeling at peace or calm. Specifically ask how the body feels (if the client does not spontaneously tell you). If the body feels tense or uncomfortable, there is probably a block to identify and clear. If the body feels good, turn on ABS and say:

> *Notice that good feeling. Let it get as strong as it wants to. Tell me when it's strengthened all the way.*

It is not usually necessary to read a meditation again while strengthening with ABS, but it is an option to employ if it helps a client focus. Some clients report connecting to a SCS evokes powerful internal shifts. For example, my client Alexis reported her irrational fears about me abandoning her, or leaving on a trip and never returning, completely disappeared after solidly connecting to her Core Self. Clients appreciate that this

© Copyright 2009 by Shirley Jean Schmidt, MA, LPC. All rights reserved. Duplication in any form without permission is prohibited.

is a state of mind they can bring forward anywhere or anytime they need comfort, support, and reassurance. It is a very ego-strengthening Resource.

Mental Picture of the Spiritual Core Self

At the conclusion of a SCS meditation, ask about the client's mental picture of this Resource (if he does not spontaneously describe it). Ask something like:

> Do you get a mental picture of your Spiritual Core Self?

Clients often say the SCS appears as some sort of light or energy, such as a ball or column of light, a luminous body, a ray of sunlight, or a wave of loving energy. This type of description indicates the client has connected with his spiritual nature. Clients who report a different type of mental picture need to be nudged in the right direction. For example, Beau reported his SCS looked like himself in meditation. I asked him to remove the body from his picture, and to describe what remained. After a few minutes he said a radiant ball of light remained, which looked and felt like his SCS.

Clients with faith in a loving higher power may be inclined to picture their SCS as that higher power. When this happens, help them think of their SCS as a part of self that resonates with love from a higher power. For example, Tony, a church minister, pictured his SCS as Jesus. He didn't understand why it wouldn't strengthen very much. I asked him to put his hand on the part of his body that felt Jesus' love the most. He put his hand on his heart. I then asked him to notice the part of self that was holding that feeling in his heart. He pictured a column of loving white light, receiving Jesus' love. That easily strengthened all the way.

If a client has an aversion to picturing his SCS as some sort of light or energy, a further intervention will be required. Details about how to investigate such mental pictures, and how to handle those connected to processing blocks, are provided in Chapter 7, on page 169.

The Healing Circle of Resources

Once a client has connected to each individual Resource, say something like:

> Picture these three Resources together in a circle, and tell me what you notice. Does it feel like they can work together as a team?

Clients typically report feeling confident and a sense that the Resources can work together as a supportive team. Ask how the body feels (if the client does not spontaneously tell you). If the body feels tense or uncomfortable, there is probably a problem. Identify and address any associated blocks. Once a block has been cleared, invite the client to bring the Resources together again. Once the Healing Circle feels good, say something like:

> Notice you now have a team of Resources to provide comfort, reassurance, and soothing. In the future these Resources will be able to help wounded child parts get all their needs met.

Occasionally a client will report a strong objection to the use of the word "circle," claiming it is suggestive of a satanic or witchcraft ritual. This wording should be adjusted to suit the needs of any client with objections. For example, a term such as *Healing Place* may be a welcome substitute.

Sometimes a client will report the three Resources merging into one Resource. Ordinarily this would not matter, but for the purposes of engaging in healing DNMS interventions with wounded child parts, such a merger is discouraged. Wounded child parts are more likely to feel a greater sense of containment and community when there are three separate Resources. So for the purposes of the DNMS

© Copyright 2009 by Shirley Jean Schmidt, MA, LPC. All rights reserved. Duplication in any form without permission is prohibited.

protocols, encourage clients to picture the Resources as distinct parts of self, with distinct roles – roles which wounded parts of self can recognize benefit from. When a client is experiencing his Resources for any other purpose, inside or outside the session, visualizing the Resource as one merged part of self is not a problem.

Connecting clients to a Healing Circle can have some unexpectedly wonderful results. Some clients report an immediate boost in overall confidence, and a reduction in certain symptoms. For example, Lisa began therapy with me right after as she was released from a psychiatric hospital. She had been admitted after her life fell apart from abusing assorted substances. She was quite depressed and was crying constantly. The only bright spot for her was Libby, her two-year-old niece. She was able to move aside all the wounded parts of self to get in touch with her loving aunt self. Once she has connected to and strengthened each Resource, and established her Healing Circle, her crying jags stopped. She still had a lot of healing to do, but she could see her potential to change and grow, and was able to replace hopelessness with hopefulness.

Complications and Processing Blocks

The Resource Development Protocol does not always unfold smoothly. Complications and blocks can arise at any point in this protocol, for example, while discussing caregiving experiences; discussing the 24 caregiver skills; guiding clients in a Resource meditation; strengthening a Resource after a meditation; asking for a mental picture; and forming a Healing Circle of Resources.

In the DNMS, all processing blocks are GOOD! Clearing blocks does not just make way for DNMS work, it is DNMS work. Blocks can provide valuable information about a client's internal world. They always arise for a reason. The process of clearing blocks helps wounded child parts heal at a moment they feel especially vulnerable. This can be reassuring and ego strengthening. Blocks are not impediments; they are golden opportunities to help clients heal.

Some complications are minor and can be overcome easily by simply educating a client more about the processing, for example, clearing up confusion about what the word *attunement* means. Some are based on *misunderstandings* and faulty assumptions about the outcome of the processing. For example, my client Nancy said, "I'm afraid if I connect to Resources they'll expect me to be perfect like my parents did." Some are due to processing fears rooted in wounding messages and threats received in childhood and conveyed now by *maladaptive introjects*. For example, Phillip said, "I cannot connect to a Nurturing Adult Self because I don't deserve to be nurtured."

Complications generally originate with the client, but they can also originate with the therapist. For example, a client may fail to connect to robust Resources if the therapist is confused about the processing steps or makes a significant technical error.

Some clients have an easy time connecting to Resources. When all goes well it may take as little as 30 minutes. Some clients experience a few processing blocks or confusions that take one or more sessions to clear. Some highly defended clients can experience significant processing blocks that can take a few months to clear. Every intervention that gets a client closer to connecting to Resources has an ego-strengthening benefit – even when the process of working through blocks takes a long time.

Clients are more likely to complete the Resource Development Protocol easily in one to three sessions, with minimal complications, if they (a) had at least one relationship in childhood with a loving, attuned role model or caregiver, and/or (b) have had at least one relationship in adulthood in which they were lovingly, attuned to a cherished loved one (person or animal). Those clients without one or more of these relationships are more likely to encounter processing blocks.

Chapter 7 (pages 166-171) provides a detailed discussion of the types of blocks and complications that can arise during the Resource Development Protocol and interventions for overcoming them.

© Copyright 2009 by Shirley Jean Schmidt, MA, LPC. All rights reserved. Duplication in any form without permission is prohibited.

Preparing Clients to Disclose Processing Blocks

When *unconscious* blocks are present they are often expressed as uncomfortable body sensations. For example, a client might experience the sudden arrival of a headache, stomach ache, butterflies, dissociation, distracting thoughts, numbness, or sleepiness. Because the Resource Development Protocol is usually clients' first experience of the DNMS, it is necessary to prepare them in advance, to disclose blocks that might arise in the process. You might say something like:

> *Sometimes while connecting to Resources, concerns or fears about the processing will arise. Unconscious fears can be expressed by the sudden arrival of a body disturbance such as unpleasant sensations, dissociation, distracting thoughts, numbness, or sleepiness. That may or may not happen to you, but if it does, please tell me about it, even if it doesn't seem important. You're welcome to have concerns or fears – just let me know if they come up. I'll want to address them right away.*

Checking for Blocks before Beginning a Meditation

Just before beginning each meditation you'll check for the presence of a processing block. Ask the client:

> *When you think about beginning the meditation now, to connect you to your (NAS, PAS, or SCS), what do you notice in your body?*

If the client reports the body feels clear (an absence of disturbance), you have a green light to proceed with the protocol. But if an uncomfortable body sensation, numbness, or sleepiness is reported, ask:

> *If this (symptom) could talk, what would it say?*

An answer like: "I'm just excited to see what will come up," suggests the sensation is due to benign nervousness. When this is reported, proceed with the meditation. In contrast, an answer like: "It's not safe for me to feel safe," suggests a processing block is present. Blocks that are revealed in this step must be cleared before beginning a meditation.

Describing Up Front the Switching the Dominance Protocol to Clear Blocks

Tell your clients about reactive parts, introjects, and the Switching the Dominance Protocol, at some point before beginning the first Resource meditation. That way, if you encounter a blocking introject in the middle of a meditation, you can go directly to switching the dominance to clear the block. You won't have to interrupt the processing flow to explain what you're doing. The DNMS Flip Chart offers a convenient way to explain it. (See page 255 for more information about the Flip Chart.) Detailed instructions for applying the Switching the Dominance Protocol are provided in Chapter 4 (page 62). Instructions for applying it to handle a blocking introject are provided in Chapter 7 (page 158).

Cloning the Resources

Sometimes a client needs more than just one of each Resource to solve a particular problem. Fortunately the brain will allow clients to make *clones* of any one Resource or all of them. To clone a Resource, simply invite a client to envision one or more copies of a Resource. Cloning Resources can especially come in handy after handling a processing block. For example, in the middle of the Needs Meeting Protocol, Robert's four-year-old child part interrupted the processing with a question. Once the question was answered, I invited the four-year-old to tuck in.[3] I told the part to envision his very own set of Resources, a set just for him, and to tuck in with them until the next time he was needed. While the four-year-old child part was tucked in with one set of Resources, we resumed the Needs Meeting Protocol with another set.

© Copyright 2009 by Shirley Jean Schmidt, MA, LPC. All rights reserved. Duplication in any form without permission is prohibited.

A Typical Resource Development Protocol Session

The following is a typical client/therapist Resource Development Protocol dialogue that will provide you an example of how to execute and transition between the following steps:

- Discussing caregiving experiences
- Discussing peak spiritual experiences
- Preparing client to disclose processing blocks
- Checking for blocks to prior to starting the first Resource meditation
- Starting the first Resource meditation
- Strengthening the first Resource
- Checking for blocks to prior to starting the second Resource meditation
- Starting the second Resource meditation
- Strengthening the second Resource
- Checking for blocks to prior to starting the third Resource meditation
- Starting the third Resource meditation
- Strengthening the third Resource
- Setting up the Healing Circle
- Strengthening the Healing Circle

Discussing Caregiving Experiences   *ABS Off*

Therapist:	**Tell me about any positive experiences you've had as a parent or caregiver.**
Client:	Okay. Well I had my children when I was very young. I didn't know what I was doing with them. At the time I thought all my mother's ideas about raising kids was right, so I tried to do it her way. It didn't work very well, but it took me years to see it. I loved my children very much and wanted to do the right things, but would say I was not a very good parent.
Therapist:	**Did you say you have a four-year-old granddaughter?**
Client:	Yes. Amy. She's the apple of my eye. She's going to turn five next month.
Therapist:	**Do you ever babysit Amy?**
Client:	Oh sure. My daughter travels a lot for her job. Amy always stays with me whenever her mom's away.
Therapist:	**Would Amy say you're good at taking care of her?**
Client:	Yes... I think so. She adores me – and I adore her. I know a lot more about raising kids now that I can see where I made mistakes with my kids. I'm doing it right with Amy.
Therapist:	**Can you think of a good example of being nurturing or protective of Amy?**
Client:	Yes – bedtime. I've decorated my guest room for her. It's pink – her favorite color. I keep lots of stuffed animals on her bed, and a stack of her books on the dresser. At bedtime we sit on the bed together. I put my arm around her and read her stories. She's starting to read, so sometimes she's reading the book to me. These are wonderful moments. I feel very bonded to her at bedtime.
Therapist:	**That's a great example of being nurturing. Can you think of a good example of being protective of her?**
Client:	Just last Saturday morning we were at the park together. Very few people were there at first. She was playing on the swing. A young boy about 12 showed up with a Pit Bull on a leash. I was a bit alarmed. These dogs have been known to attack children, but I've heard some are very gentle. Pretty soon the boy took the dog off the leash to play Frisbee. I wasn't happy about that. Then some other people showed up with dogs, and suddenly there were lots of dogs just running around the park. I stayed right next to her, in case something happened. Suddenly some of the dogs got in a fight right in front of us – I think the Pit Bull was one of them. Amy started to cry. I picked her up and left the park right away. When we got to the car I asked her why she was crying. She said the dogs scared her. I gave her a big hug and told her they scared me too, which was why we were leaving. I told her it was normal to be scared, but that she would feel better after awhile. She talked about it all the way home. It was most upsetting to her because she loves my dog, Pixie. She'd never seen dogs act like that before.
Therapist:	**That sounds like a good example of being both nurturing and protective.**
Client:	Yeah, I guess it is.

© Copyright 2009 by Shirley Jean Schmidt, MA, LPC. All rights reserved. Duplication in any form without permission is prohibited.

Therapist:	Take a look at this list of caregiver skills. *(She is given the list of NAS & PAS skills.)* **As you read each item, tell me if there is any skill on the list you think <u>you did not</u> have last Saturday when you left the park with Amy.**
Client:	Sometimes I don't feel very confident. When Amy is really upset I try to calm her down. Sometimes if she doesn't stop crying I get anxious and wonder what I'm doing wrong. I feel like I'm failing her.
Therapist:	**When you feel like you're failing her, are you in a child ego state or an adult ego state?**
Client:	Probably a child state.
Therapist:	**It sounds like you were in a pretty adult state in the park with her last Saturday. Were you confident in the park?**
Client:	Yes, yes I was.
Therapist:	**So would you say your most adult self has the ability to be confident with Amy, even when it's difficult to calm her down?**
Client:	Yes... that's true.
Therapist:	**Are there any other skills you think you might not have when you care for Amy?**
Client:	No. When I'm taking care of Amy I have them all.

Discussing Peak Spiritual Experiences   *ABS Off*

Therapist:	**Good. That will come in handy later. Now I want to switch gears and ask you about your spiritual beliefs. Do you have a spiritual practice of some sort?**
Client:	Yes, sort of... off and on. I believe in God, if that's what you mean. As various times in my life I have attended church – especially while I was married. My husband was a church deacon, so we were very active members. After the divorce, he continued to go, but I stopped. I guess I always planned to find a new church, but never did. I'd say I have a pretty strong faith. Spirituality is a lot more important to me than religion.
Therapist:	**A Spiritual Core Self is a state of mind associated with a sense of interconnectedness to all beings; a sense of completeness and wholeness; a sense of safety and invulnerability; no ego, no struggles; no desires or aversions; unconditional, effortless happiness; unconditional, effortless acceptance; unconditional, effortless loving kindness, and compassion; timeless, cosmic wisdom and understanding; and a present moment that is precious and full. Have you ever had an experience when you felt this way?**
Client:	Yes. When I was about 30 our church had a week-long woman's wilderness retreat. One afternoon I took a walk in the woods, alone. I found a spot with a beautiful view, and sat down to pray. As I prayed I felt Jesus right next to me. This was a very difficult time for me. I had two small children and a marriage that was not working. I was regretting every major decision I'd made up to that point. But as I sat in the woods with Jesus sitting next to me, I felt very loved and supported. I felt as though I had a purpose, like there was a bigger plan for me. I experienced a kind of comfort and oneness with Jesus and the world that I cannot describe. I felt a profound peace for days afterwards. Whenever I get very stressed, if I can remember to think about that experience, it calms me down.
Therapist:	**Wow. That sounds like a profoundly important event for you. I'll ask you to refer to it when we get ready to do the Spiritual Core Self meditation. Are you ready to connect to your Resources now?**
Client:	Sure.

Preparing Client to Disclose Processing Blocks   *ABS Off*

Therapist:	**Okay before we get started, I need to explain something. Sometimes while connecting to Resources, concerns or fears about the processing will arise. Unconscious fears can be expressed by the sudden arrival of a body disturbance such as unpleasant sensations, dissociation, distracting thoughts, numbness, or sleepiness. That may or may not happen to you, but if it does, please tell me about it, even if it doesn't seem important. You're welcome to have concerns or fears – just let me know if they come up. I'll want to address them right away. Okay?**
Client:	Okay.
Therapist:	**Which Resource would you like to connect to first?**
Client:	The Nurturing one.

© Copyright 2009 by Shirley Jean Schmidt, MA, LPC. All rights reserved. Duplication in any form without permission is prohibited.

Checking for Blocks to Prior to Starting the Nurturing Adult Self Meditation   *ABS Off*

Therapist: **So when you think about beginning the meditation now, to connect you to your Nurturing Adult Self, what do you notice in your body?**

Client: I feel a little tension in my stomach.

Therapist: **If this sensation could talk what would it say?**

Client: I'm looking forward to doing this.

Starting the Nurturing Adult Self Meditation   *ABS Off*

Therapist: **We're going to do this in two phases. First I'll guide you through the meditation once, with the TheraTapper off. If your response is positive, I'll guide you through it again, with the TheraTapper on, to let the positive feeling strengthen all the way.**

Client: Okay.

Therapist: **Now, I want you to think about your experience of nurturing Amy after she was frightened in the park, as I name each skill on the list. Nod or say 'yes' with each skill you know you possess. Stop me if I name a skill you believe you don't have, or if at any point you experience a disturbance that suggests a block, so we can talk about it. Okay?**

Client: Okay.

Therapist: **Now close your eyes (if that's comfortable) and take a deep breath.** *Pause* **Now get in touch with the following skills and traits, which you already have, starting with your ability to be empathic...**

Client: Yes.

Therapist: **compassionate...**

Client: Yes.

Therapist: **understanding...**

Client: Yes.

Therapist: **accepting...**

Client: Yes.

Therapist: **patient...**

Client: Yes.

Therapist: **nurturing...**

Client: Yes.

Therapist: **warm...**

Client: Yes.

Therapist: **open...**

Client: Yes.

Therapist: **able to attune...**

Client: Now what's that again?

Therapist: **It means you're able to read nonverbal signals, like body language, and respond to them appropriately and empathically.**

Client: Oh yeah. I do that with Amy.

Therapist: **good at listening...**

Client: Okay.

Therapist: **good with boundaries...**

Client: I'm not sure about being good with boundaries.

Therapist: **Were you good at setting boundaries with Amy at the park?**

Client: What do you mean?

Therapist: **Would you have let her walk around the park unsupervised if she had wanted to?**

Client: No.

Therapist: **When you saw the danger would you have let her stay in the park if she had wanted to stay?**

Client: No.

Therapist: **Good. It sounds like you were good with boundaries in the park last week.**

Client: But just about the only time I'm good with boundaries is when I'm looking after Amy.

© Copyright 2009 by Shirley Jean Schmidt, MA, LPC. All rights reserved. Duplication in any form without permission is prohibited.

Therapist:	**That's okay. If you can set good boundaries with Amy you have the potential to express that skill again.**
Client:	Oh. Okay, now I get it.
Therapist:	**Ready to go on?**
Client:	Yeah.
Therapist:	**reliable...**
Client:	Yes.
Therapist:	**trustworthy...**
Client:	Yes.
Therapist:	**confident...**
Client:	Uhmmm...
Therapist:	**In your most adult self...**
Client:	Yes.
Therapist:	**respectful...**
Client:	Yes.
Therapist:	**appropriately responsible...**
Client:	Yes.
Therapist:	**problem solver...**
Client:	Yes.
Therapist:	**action-taker...**
Client:	Yes.
Therapist:	**decision-maker...**
Client:	Yes.
Therapist:	**logical...**
Client:	Yes.
Therapist:	**strong...**
Client:	Yes.
Therapist:	**courageous...**
Client:	Yes.
Therapist:	**protective...**
Client:	Yes.
Therapist:	**and grounded.**
Client:	Yes.
Therapist:	**Now, bring all these skills together into a single sense of self, your Nurturing Adult Self, and when you're ready, tell me what you notice.**
Client:	I see myself smiling in the park with my sweetheart. (*This is her mental picture.*) She's so precious. I know I can take good care of her.
Therapist:	**Good. And what do you notice in your body?**
Client:	My body feels calm and relaxed – confident.
Therapist:	**Good. Now this time we're going to go through the list again with the TheraTapper on. You won't have to nod or say 'yes' this time – just listen and let each word strengthen. Again, think about your experience of nurturing Amy after she was frightened in the park, as I name each skill. Okay?**
Client:	Okay.

Strengthening the Nurturing Adult Self   *ABS On*

Therapist:	**Close your eyes and take a deep breath. Once again get in touch with your ability to be empathic... compassionate... understanding... accepting... patient... nurturing... warm... open... able to attune... good at listening... good with boundaries... reliable... trustworthy... confident... respectful... appropriately responsible... problem-solver... action-taker... decision-maker... logical... strong... courageous... protective... and grounded. Now, bring all these skills together into a single sense of self, your Nurturing Adult Self... let it get as strong as it wants to. Tell me when it's strengthened all the way.**
Client:	Okay.
Therapist:	**What is this like for you?**

© Copyright 2009 by Shirley Jean Schmidt, MA, LPC. All rights reserved. Duplication in any form without permission is prohibited.

Client:	Oh, it feels really nice. I like it. I see myself smiling, confident, happy... able to handle whatever Amy needs.
Therapist:	**Great. Are you ready to connect to the next Resource?**
Client:	Yes.
Therapist:	**Which one would you like to connect to next?**
Client:	The Protective Adult.

Checking for Blocks to Prior to Starting the Protective Adult Self Meditation   *ABS Off*

Therapist:	**Okay. So when you think about beginning the meditation now, to connect you to your Protective Adult Self, what do you notice in your body?**
Client:	I get a little headache.
Therapist:	**Say more about that.**
Client:	You know my father was very protective of us. When we were teenagers he would not let us go to out with friends or date. I was not allowed to drive before I was 18.
Therapist:	**It sounds like you may have "protective" confused with "over-protective." When you think about your experience with Amy at the park, would you say you were appropriately protective with her?**
Client:	Yes, actually I was. I stayed with her the whole time we were there. I let her play on the swings. But we left the moment it was no longer safe.
Therapist:	**Yes! Exactly. How about this... when I list the words, I'll preface "protective" with "appropriately," so you can think about how you were appropriately protective of Amy. How does that sound?**
Client:	Good.
Therapist:	**Good. So, now when you think about beginning the meditation to connect you to your Protective Adult Self, what do you notice in your body?**
Client:	Hey – the headache is gone. I'm relaxed now.

Starting the Protective Adult Self Meditation   *ABS Off*

Therapist:	**Okay. Now, I want you to think about your experience of *protecting* Amy at the park, as I name each skill on the list. Just like before, I want you to nod or say 'yes' with each skill you know you possess. Stop me if I name a skill you believe you don't have, or if at any point you experience a disturbance that suggests a block, so we can talk about it. Now close your eyes (if that's comfortable) and take a deep breath. *Pause* Now get in touch with the following skills and traits, which you already have, starting with your ability to be appropriately protective...**
Client:	Yes.
Therapist:	**courageous...**
Client:	Yes.
Therapist:	**strong...**
Client:	Yes.
Therapist:	**logical...**
Client:	Yes.
Therapist:	**decision-maker...**
Client:	Yes.
Therapist:	**action-taker...**
Client:	Yes.
Therapist:	**problem-solver...**
Client:	Yes.
Therapist:	**appropriately responsible...**
Client:	Yes.
Therapist:	**respectful...**
Client:	Yes.
Therapist:	**confident...**
Client:	Yes.
Therapist:	**trustworthy...**

© Copyright 2009 by Shirley Jean Schmidt, MA, LPC. All rights reserved. Duplication in any form without permission is prohibited.

Client:	Yes.
Therapist:	**reliable...**
Client:	Yes.
Therapist:	**good with boundaries...**
Client:	Yes.
Therapist:	**good at listening...**
Client:	Yes.
Therapist:	**able to attune...**
Client:	Yes.
Therapist:	**open...**
Client:	Yes.
Therapist:	**warm...**
Client:	Yes.
Therapist:	**nurturing...**
Client:	Yes.
Therapist:	**patient...**
Client:	Yes.
Therapist:	**accepting...**
Client:	Yes.
Therapist:	**understanding...**
Client:	Yes.
Therapist:	**compassionate...**
Client:	Yes.
Therapist:	**empathic...**
Client:	Yes.
Therapist:	**and grounded.**
Client:	Yes.
Therapist:	**Now, bring all these skills together into a single sense of self, your Protective Adult Self... and when you're ready, tell me what you notice.**
Client:	Smiling. I like this.
Therapist:	**Good. So what do you notice in your body now?**
Client:	I feel calm and excited at the same time. I like it.

Strengthening the Protective Adult Self   ABS On

Therapist:	**Good. Now we're going to go through the list again with the ABS on. You won't have to nod or say 'yes' this time – just listen and let each word strengthen. Again, think about your experience of *protecting* Amy at the park, as I name each skill. Again, think about being in the park with Amy. Close your eyes and take a deep breath. Once again get in touch with your ability to be appropriately protective... courageous... strong... logical... decision-maker... action-taker... problem-solver... appropriately responsible... respectful... confident... trustworthy... reliable... good with boundaries... good at listening... able to attune... open... warm... nurturing... patient... accepting... understanding... compassionate... empathic... and grounded. Now, bring all these skills together into a single sense of self, your Protective Adult Self... let it get as strong as it wants to. Tell me when it's strengthened all the way.**
Client:	Okay.
Therapist:	**What is this like for you?**
Client:	Oh, my body feels very safe.
Therapist:	**Do you have a mental picture?**
Client:	Yes. I see a mother bear protecting her young. She is gentle with her cubs but she can also be fierce.
Therapist:	**So, just for grins, I want you to hold your image of the mother bear next to an image of you being protective of Amy in the park. Which of these two pictures feels the most powerful or comfortable?**
Client:	Wow. Actually I like the <u>image of me</u> the best. (*This is her mental picture.*)
Therapist:	**Would you have any reservations about using that image of yourself for your Protective Adult Self?**

© Copyright 2009 by Shirley Jean Schmidt, MA, LPC. All rights reserved. Duplication in any form without permission is prohibited.

Client:	No. I really like it.
Therapist:	**Great. So are you ready to connect to your Spiritual Core Self now?**
Client:	Yes.

Checking for Blocks to Prior to Starting the Spiritual Core Self Meditation   *ABS Off*

Therapist:	**Okay. When you think about beginning the meditation now, to connect to your Spiritual Core Self, what do you notice in your body?**
Client:	My body feels good.

Starting the Spiritual Core Self Meditation   *ABS Off*

Therapist:	**Okay. You had mentioned having a peak spiritual experience years ago at a wilderness church retreat. You reported taking a walk in the woods alone to pray. You said that during your prayer you felt an indescribable comfort and oneness with Jesus and the world. Does that sound right?**
Client:	Yes, that's right. It was very powerful. I've felt that love with me ever since.
Therapist:	**I want you to think about that special experience as I read this meditation. Keep in mind that your Spiritual Core Self is not Jesus. It's a part of you that resonates with Jesus' love for you.**
Client:	I understand.
Therapist:	**Okay... Now get in touch with the center of your being... that place within you that is quiet... peaceful... and still. And in this place... it's possible you'll connect to your spiritual core. Your spiritual core has been with you from the beginning... it's the essence of who you are... your core of goodness. Pure... resilient... and whole. And your body knows exactly how to connect you. Notice as you connect to this part of you, and when you're ready, tell me what you notice.**
Client:	Wow. I feel nice and warm inside. I feel that vivid sense of connection to Jesus and the world again.
Therapist:	**Good. Now I'm going to turn the TheraTapper on. Just let it get as strong as it wants to. Tell me when it's strengthened all the way.**

Strengthening the Spiritual Core Self   *ABS On*

Client:	Okay.
Therapist:	**So, do you get a mental picture of this part of you?**
Client:	I see Jesus sitting with me on the mountain.
Therapist:	**Do you feel Jesus' love for you in your body right now?**
Client:	Yes.
Therapist:	**Where do you feel it the most?**
Client:	In my heart.
Therapist:	**So close your eyes and just focus on that sensation. Notice how the energy is moving in your heart as you feel that love. Can you get a picture of that energy?**
Client:	Oh, yes. It's a <u>ball of golden/yellow light</u>. It's beautiful! (*This is her mental picture.*)
Therapist:	**That sounds great. Are you ready to bring all the Resources together now to form a Healing Circle?**
Client:	Yes.

Setting Up the Healing Circle   *ABS Off*

Therapist:	**Now picture these three Resources together in a circle, and tell me what you notice.**
Client:	I feel powerful.
Therapist:	**Does it feel like they can work together as a team?**
Client:	Most definitely!

Strengthening the Healing Circle   *ABS On*

Therapist:	**Good. Notice that. Let it get as strong as it wants to. Tell me when it's strengthened all the way.**
Client:	Wow. That feels great!
Therapist:	**Good. Notice you now have a team of Resources to provide comfort, reassurance, and soothing. In the future these Resources will be able to help wounded child parts get all their needs met.**

© Copyright 2009 by Shirley Jean Schmidt, MA, LPC. All rights reserved. Duplication in any form without permission is prohibited.

Chapter Summary

This chapter described a DNMS protocol for mobilizing three individual Resource ego states – a Nurturing Adult Self (NAS), a Protective Adult Self (PAS), and a Spiritual Core Self (SCS). Clients connect to the NAS and PAS through two meditations which emphasize their most adult skills and strengths, anchored in a real, familiar relationship or event. They connect to a SCS with a meditation that is anchored in a personal peak spiritual experience. Once each individual Resource has been mobilized, they are invited to come together to form a team. This team, a Healing Circle, is the foundation of the other DNMS healing interventions. The *Resource Development Protocol Worksheet*, in Appendix E (page 229), can serve as a helpful guide while you're learning to apply this protocol.

Chapter 3 Notes and References

1. Bradshaw, J. (1990). *Homecoming: Reclaiming and championing you inner child.* Bantam Books.
   Napier, N. (1990). *Recreating your self: Building self-esteem through imaging and self-hypnosis.* New York: Norton.
   Paul, M. (1992). *Inner bonding: Becoming a loving adult to your inner child.* San Francisco: Harper.
   Paulsen, S. (2000). *EMDR and the Divided Self: EMDR and ego state therapy for non-dissociative and dissociative clients.* All-day workshop in San Antonio, Texas, April, 2000.
   Phillips, M., & Frederick, C. (1995). *Healing the divided self: Clinical and Ericksonian hypnotherapy for post-traumatic and dissociative conditions.* New York: W.W. Norton & Company.
   Schwartz, R. C. (1995). *Internal family systems therapy.* New York: Guilford Press.
   Steele, A. (2001). *Introduction to imaginal nurturing with EMDR in the treatment of adult clients with insecure attachment.* Presentation at 2001 EMDRAC Conference in Vancouver, BC.
   Taylor, C.L. (1991). *The inner child workbook: What to do with your past when it just won't go away.* J P Tarcher.
   Watkins, J. G., & Watkins, H. H. (1997). *Ego states: Theory and therapy.* New York: Norton.
   Wildwind, L. (1998). *It's never too late to have a happy childhood.* Presentation at the 1998 EMDRIA Conference in Baltimore, MD.
2. Cloyd, T. (2002). Personal communication.
3. *Tucking in* puts a wounded part in a non-active state so the most adult self can resume executive control. Tuck a part in with something like: "Find a nice, warm, safe place to tuck in to – you can tuck in with the Resources if you like. Just find a good, safe, place to wait until the next time you're needed." Read more about *tucking in* on page 20.

© Copyright 2009 by Shirley Jean Schmidt, MA, LPC. All rights reserved. Duplication in any form without permission is prohibited.

<h1>Chapter 4</h1>

<h1>The Switching the Dominance Protocol</h1>

<h2>Protocol Overview</h2>

The Switching the Dominance Protocol is an ego state intervention helpful for calming internal conflicts, soothing painful emotions, and quieting negative self-talk. In your work with clients, you'll find it can serve a number of purposes. You can use it to provide immediate relief for a simple symptom or problem. It has a role in the DNMS Conference Room Protocol (Chapter 5) which is used for selecting introjects for the Needs Meeting Protocol (Chapter 6). It can also help in overcoming processing blocks (Chapter 7). The set-up for each of these applications is a little different, but otherwise the same protocol steps are used.

The protocol is based on two assumptions: (1) that a reactive part's unwanted behavior, belief, or emotion is fueled by a wounding message conveyed by an introject mask; and (2) that the child part of self wearing the associated introject mask does not like or want the mask.

At the start of the protocol the wounding introject mask is dominant, and the child part wearing it feels subordinate and powerless. The protocol engages in dialogue the part of self wearing a mask, to help her understand that the mask is just a recording of the wounding person it is mirroring, and has no real power to do harm. This is reinforced by loving, supportive Resources, and a realization of being in an adult body now. As that child part begins to understand the truth about the mask, it appears smaller and less important. This helps the part feel stronger and more confident. Eventually the mask will lose all its animation and influence, and the part will be able to put what remains of it in her pocket. When this happens, we say the dominance has been switched from the mask to the part of self that was wearing it.

The Switching the Dominance Protocol often results in an immediate reduction of the targeted reactive parts' unwanted behaviors, beliefs, or emotions. Clients typically report less internal conflict. These positive effects may last a long time, a few weeks, or until the next time the client is stressed. While it helps introjects heal, it does not usually complete the process. The label of *introject* will apply until this part has successfully completed the Needs Meeting Protocol and become totally unstuck from the past.

Two typical client/therapist dialogues are provided at the end of this chapter to illustrate the flow of this protocol. A *Switching the Dominance Protocol Worksheet* is provided in Appendix E. You can use the same worksheet for all three applications of this protocol. This chapter describes this protocol as it would unfold without processing complications or blocks. Instructions for handling complications unique to this protocol are covered on pages 171-178 of Chapter 7.

© Copyright 2009 by Shirley Jean Schmidt, MA, LPC. All rights reserved. Duplication in any form without permission is prohibited.

Switching the Dominance to Treat a Simple Problem

In some cases, the Switching the Dominance Protocol can provide immediate relief for a simple symptom or problem. For example, it may be a helpful intervention when a moderate-to-high functioning client is seeking very brief therapy; when a client who has terminated therapy after resolving core issues, returns to address a simple issue; or when a client's usual progress through a structured DNMS program is interrupted by a very distracting problem.

In this context, this protocol is best used to address *emotional overreactions* to recent triggering events that do not substantially link to complex problems, such as chronic feelings of inadequacy, generally poor ego strength, or dissociative symptoms. While this chapter explains how to switch the dominance of a *single* maladaptive introject causing a *simple* problem, the DNMS Conference Room Protocol (Chapter 5) provides a framework for finding and switching the dominance of *multiple* introjects related to a *complex* problem.

The next five pages provide the instructions you'll need to locate a single introject connected to a specific emotional overreaction, so you can apply the Switching the Dominance Protocol.

Asking About the Client's Experience

Once you have decided to use this protocol to address a current problem, find out more about the client's experience of the problem. For example, you might ask:

> *Does it bring up negative self-talk?*
> *Is it connected to a negative belief about yourself?*
> *What, if any, disturbing body sensations does it evoke?*

Listen for the client's report of an internal voice delivering a wounding message; an irrational, negative belief; or an emotional overreaction. The following describes each of these in detail.

- **An Internal Voice Delivering a Wounding Message**

  A client may report an internal voice conveying a wounding "you" message, such as: "You must never make a mistake," "You may not say 'no' to others," or "Others are important, you're not." A message might contain a threat, such as: "If you make a mistake people will reject you," "You'll be punished if you discuss your feelings," or "Shame on you if you dare to seek attention." Such messages are often preceded by words like; "I hear my father saying...," "I hear my mother yelling..." or "I hear my grandmother whispering...."

- **An Irrational Negative Belief**

  A client may report an irrational negative belief – an untrue, illogical statement about self or world. These are typically "I" statements, such as: "I'm not good enough," "I'm worthless," or "I'm destined to fail." A client may express a negative sentiment such as: "I'm likely to lose my job," "I'm going broke," or "I'm too afraid to date." Such statements are not "negative beliefs," if they are simply true and descriptive. To get to an underlying negative belief, ask something like: "What does it mean about you (*if you lose your job*)." This is intended to elicit any associated negative beliefs, such as: "If I lose my job that will confirm I'm a complete failure."

- **An Emotional Overreaction**

  Clients often report experiencing an emotional overreaction. This is defined as any emotional response considered excessive for the triggering event. For example, a client might report an overly intense reaction to a normally stressful event, such as a paralyzing fear of taking a final exam. Or she might report an overly intense reaction to a normally neutral event, such as a paralyzing fear of folding laundry. Clients do not always recognize when their emotional reactions are abnormally intense.

© Copyright 2009 by Shirley Jean Schmidt, MA, LPC. All rights reserved. Duplication in any form without permission is prohibited.

Connecting to Resources

If your client has successfully completed all or part of the Resource Development Protocol, invite her to connect to her Resources before proceeding. Say something like:

> Connect to your Resources. Tell me when you're connected.

When the client indicates she's connected, apply ABS and say:

> Good. Tell me when that's strengthened all the way.

This brings the Resources front and center so their wisdom and compassion are available to assist when needed. If a client has not yet formally established a NAS, PAS, or SCS, invite her to connect to a Provisional Resource. See page 171 of Chapter 7 for a complete discussion of Provisional Resources.

Inviting Parts of Self Forward

To switch the dominance of an introject you must first contact it. If an introject is *directly* responsible for the problem, it may be easy to access with a simple invitation to come forward. If it is *indirectly* responsible for the problem, you'll need to first invite forward the reactive part the introject is upsetting. The following sample invitations will give you an idea of where to start. Select the invitation that seems the most appropriate considering the aspect of the problem your client is most aware of. If the client has established her Resources, invite the part to *approach the Resources*. If not, just invite the part *forward*.

- ▪ ***Inviting Forward the Part Conveying a Wounding Message***

  If a client is most aware of a voice conveying a wounding message, invite that part of self forward. For example, you might say something like:

  > I'd like to invite, to approach the Resources, the part of self that conveys the message, ('You must be perfect, anything less is failure,'). When you're ready, tell me what you notice. OR

  > I'd like to invite forward the part of self that conveys the message, ('You must be perfect, anything less is failure,'). When you're ready, tell me what you notice.

- ▪ ***Inviting Forward the Part Holding Irrational Negative Belief***

  If a client is most aware of an irrational negative belief, invite forward the part of self holding that belief. For example, you might say something like:

  > I'd like to invite, to approach the Resources, the part of self that believes, ('I'll be a failure if the presentation isn't perfect,'). When you're ready, tell me what you notice. OR

  > I'd like to invite forward the part of self that believes, ('I'll be a failure if the presentation isn't perfect,'). When you're ready, tell me what you notice.

- ▪ ***Inviting Forward the Part Having an Emotional Overreaction***

  If a client is most aware of an emotional overreaction, invite forward the part of self that is highly distressed. For example, you might say something like:

  > I'd like to invite, to approach the Resources, the part of self that (feels overwhelming fear about giving the presentation). When you're ready, tell me what you notice. OR

  > I'd like to invite forward the part of self that (feels overwhelming fear about giving the presentation). When you're ready, tell me what you notice.

© Copyright 2009 by Shirley Jean Schmidt, MA, LPC. All rights reserved. Duplication in any form without permission is prohibited.

Classifying a Part that Comes Forward

You'll want to get a good description of the part that has appeared so you can accurately classify it. It will be a powerless reactive part, a controlling reactive part, or a presumptive introject. When a part is difficult to classify, it may help to ask if the part is reacting to someone or mimicking someone. If the answer is "reacting," it is a reactive part. If the answer is "mimicking," it is a presumptive introject.

- ***Powerless Reactive Part***

  A part of self that looks like the client (usually as the client looked as a child) feeling painful emotions (fear, anger, sadness, hopeless, or pretending to be happy) is a *powerless reactive part*. This part is most likely to come forward when you're inviting a part of self that holds a negative belief or is having an emotional overreaction.

Powerless Reactive Part

- ***Controlling Reactive Part***

  A part of self that looks like the client (usually as the client looked as a child) and is delivering a warning, threat, command, or admonition, is a *controlling reactive part*. This part is most likely to come forward when you're inviting a part that is delivering a wounding message.

Controlling Reactive Part

- ***Presumptive Introject***

  A part of self that looks and acts like the unkind person who conveyed the wounding message (e.g. angry father, rejecting mother) is going to be either a *maladaptive introject* or a *controlling reactive mimic*. These parts are most likely to come forward when you're inviting a part that is delivering a wounding message. Because these both look like introjects, they are called *presumptive introjects*. In Step 2 of the Switching the Dominance Protocol you'll ask the part wearing the mask, "Do you like or need this mask? Does it serve a useful purpose?" If the part does not want the mask, it is the sought-after introject. If the part reveals a need for the mask, you will know it is a reactive mimic.

Controlling Reactive Mimic

Maladaptive Introject

If a presumptive introject comes forward, learn more about it. See the *Collecting Information about a Presumptive Introject* section on page 61.

When a Reactive Part Appears Keep Looking for the Presumptive Introject

If any type of reactive part comes forward, you'll need to keep looking for the introject. Start by asking:

> *May I speak with this little one?*

Then welcome the reactive part with something like:

> *Welcome. I'm glad you're here. How old are you?*

Getting the child part's age is helpful because it provides some context for understanding the material coming up, and it gives you a name to call the child, such as "ten-year-old," or "four-to-six-year-old." When you have the age, say something like:

© Copyright 2009 by Shirley Jean Schmidt, MA, LPC. All rights reserved. Duplication in any form without permission is prohibited.

So (six-year-old), I'm guessing you've been stuck in the past a long time. Is that right? I'd like to help you get unstuck, and you can help. When you're ready, I'd like you to look to the right, where you will see appear the part or parts of self that you're reacting to.[1] When you're ready, tell me what you notice.

Often a part of self that comes forward looks and acts like the person who conveyed the wounding message that led to the problem. This would be a *presumptive introject*. Sometimes the part that appears looks like the client looked as a child delivering the wounding message. This would be a *controlling reactive part.* Occasionally the part of self that appears looks like another child reacting to the message. This would be another *powerless reactive part.*

If a presumptive introject shows up, proceed to the Switching the Dominance Protocol (page 62). If another reactive part shows up, invite the part to look to the right, to see who she is reacting to.

Chain Reaction

It is not unusual to encounter a chain of reactive parts in your search for the introject at the root of a problem. If a reactive part (link 1) looks to the right and sees a maladaptive introject (link 2), the chain is fully mapped.

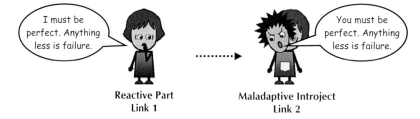

If a reactive part (link 1) looks to the right and sees another reactive part (link 2) that reactive part is welcomed and invited look to the right to see who he/she is reacting to (link 3).

A chain may be short or long. Either way, follow a chain until you find a presumptive introject, then start the Switching the Dominance Protocol.

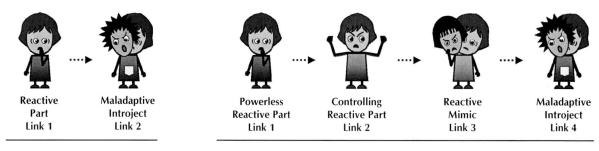

© Copyright 2009 by Shirley Jean Schmidt, MA, LPC. All rights reserved. Duplication in any form without permission is prohibited.

Fortunately, switching the dominance of the introject at the source of a problem will result in a chain reaction of healing, resulting in at least some relief for all the reactive parts.

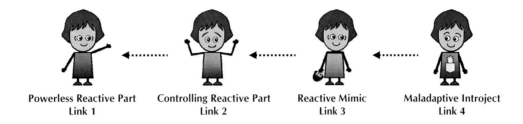

Powerless Reactive Part	Controlling Reactive Part	Reactive Mimic	Maladaptive Introject
Link 1	Link 2	Link 3	Link 4

Collecting Information about a Presumptive Introject

When a presumptive introject appears, your clients may provide varying degrees of information about it. For example, a client or reactive part may provide a lot of information, saying something like: "I see my angry father the way he looked when he'd come home drunk. He's screaming at me to do the dishes. He's calling me a lazy, no-good slut." Or little information may be provided, saying something like: "I see my father."

When little information is provided, probe for details. For example, ask about the wounding message, the mood of the mask, and who the mask looks like. If two masks appear find out if it is one part of self wearing two masks, or two parts of self – each wearing a single mask. If you have no historical context for the particular mask or wounding message disclosed, ask for the back story.

Getting and Rating the Presumptive Introject Message

An introject message should be worded in such a way that it reveals one or more of the following: contempt for the client; a threat to emotional safety (such as threat of rejection, neglect, abandonment, or enmeshment); a threat of physical harm; an inappropriate assignment of responsibility; a person's negative belief about him or herself; and/or a faulty notion about the world.

Introjects can mirror wounding messages that were conveyed both verbally and non-verbally (through facial expressions, body language, broken promises, and failures to meet needs). Likewise, introjects can mirror wounding messages that were inferred from both the actions and inactions of others.

The wounding messages that were conveyed verbally are usually the easiest for the client to report. The non-verbal and inferred messages may need to be coaxed out. Sometimes a client will disclose a message that is worded neutrally or missing specificity. When this happens, encourage further elaboration. For example, Vivian reported seeing her angry mother saying "I'm busy." When asked about an underlying message, she revealed her mother's non-verbal message, "Don't bother me with your problems. Your needs are not important to me." Suggestions for identifying and handling problematic introject messages are provided in Chapter 7, page 171.

A wounding message should evoke a lot of disturbance before the Switching the Dominance Protocol, and little or no disturbance at the end. To measure the change invite the client (or reactive part) to rate, from 0-10, the disturbance evoked by the message before beginning the protocol, and again upon completing the protocol – where 10 is the worst disturbance imaginable and 0 is none at all. For example you might ask something like:

> *When you think about (your father's) message, ('You must be perfect, anything less is failure'), 0-10, how much disturbance comes up now?*

If you forget to get a numerical rating at the start, you can still get one at the end.

© Copyright 2009 by Shirley Jean Schmidt, MA, LPC. All rights reserved. Duplication in any form without permission is prohibited.

Switching the Dominance Protocol

The five pages above provide the instructions you'll need to *locate* a single introject connected to a specific emotional overreaction, so you can apply the Switching the Dominance Protocol, described below. You will also use this protocol in the Conference Room Protocol (see page 94) and to clear processing blocks caused by introjects (see page 158).

To understand the power of this protocol, consider the adage: *The truth will set you free.* As a child part wearing an introject mask comes to understand it is harmless, the mask loses its "power." The size and importance of the mask, at any given moment in the process, is inversely proportional to how completely the child part wearing it understands the truth about it. That means that the more a child part integrates the truth, the less important the mask becomes, until eventually it becomes irrelevant. Keep this in mind as you apply this protocol.

While this section discusses the Switching the Dominance Protocol as it would apply to a wounded child part wearing an introject mask, it can also help when an adult part of self introjects a wounding person (e.g. an abusive spouse or a rapist). The focus here is on child parts, because most DNMS therapy focuses on childhood wounds.

This section discusses the Switching the Dominance Protocol as it would unfold without complications. Instructions for handling protocol complications and blocks are covered in Chapter 7, pages 171-178.

Step 1: Permission to Speak to Child Part Behind the Mask

In Step 1 it may help to set the stage by asking something like:

> *I'm guessing there's a little one behind that mom costume. Is that right?*

Then ask permission to speak to the child part behind the introject mask. It is the simple question:

> *May I speak to the child behind the mask?*

When you get a "yes" answer, go to Step 2.

Step 2: Welcoming the Child Part Behind the Mask

In Step 2 welcome the child part wearing the mask. In a very soft and gentle voice, say:

> *Hey little one, I want you to know I see you, and I know that you're good.[2] And I know the difference between you and this mask. What's it like to hear that?*

Child parts are often surprised and relieved to be seen. Follow up with:

> *Do you like or need this mask? Does it serve a useful purpose?*

If the reply is unclear, ask something like:

> *If the mask were to suddenly disappear would that be a good thing or a bad thing?*

If the child part reports that the mask is wanted or needed, serves a useful purpose, and/or will be missed if gone, then this is a reactive mimic. When this happens, ask the part for her age. (The age can serve as a name.) Then say:

> *So (six-year-old), when you're ready, look to the right, where you'll see appear the part of self that you're reacting to. When you're ready, tell me what you notice.*

Reactive Mimic

© Copyright 2009 by Shirley Jean Schmidt, MA, LPC. All rights reserved. Duplication in any form without permission is prohibited.

When a reactive mimic looks to the right, he or she will often see the introject at the root of the problem. The introject may be mirroring the same person, delivering the same or similar wounding message, or mirroring a completely different person and message. When you find the introject, return to Step 1.

Keep in mind that a child part wearing an introject mask will usually be relatively emotionless in Step 2 of this protocol, except for perhaps a sense of relief at being acknowledged for the first time. In the middle of the protocol, as the dominance begins to switch, the part might begin expressing some painful emotions. In contrast, if in Step 2 a child part wearing a mask feels *overwhelming painful emotions*, it is probably a reactive mimic. Overwhelming emotions (e.g. anger, despair, or fear) are a classic *reaction* to an introject mask.

Step 3: Contrasting the True Nature of the Child with the Dysfunction of the Mask

In Step 3 you'll contrast the true nature of the child part with the dysfunction of the mask. This step starts with the invitation:

Let's talk about the ways that you're different from this mask.

Follow this with about three *tailored questions* which contrast the specific wounding message from the mask with the child's good true nature. For example let's say the mom mask message is: "You'll never be good enough!" The dialogue might go like this:

Therapist:	Do you believe caregivers should always treat children with respect?
Child part:	Yes.
Therapist:	Does the mask agree?
Child part:	No.
Therapist:	Do you believe caregivers should give children positive attention?
Child part:	Yes.
Therapist:	Does the mask agree?
Child part:	No.
Therapist:	Do you believe caregivers should provide loving correction?
Child part:	Yes.
Therapist:	Does the mask agree?
Child part:	No.

After contrasting about three items ask:

Do you see how different you are from the mask? You're nothing like it, are you?

As the child part sees and understands the differences, the mask begins to lose its importance. Here are a few examples of questions tailored for a specific wounding message:

Wounding message:	Questions for child wearing the mask:
I can molest you whenever I want, for as long as I want, and you can't stop me. If you tell I'll kill you.	Do you believe caregivers should always treat children with respect? Do you believe caregivers should cherish and protect children? Do you believe it's appropriate for caregivers to threaten children?
You're not important. Don't bother to ask me for anything, because you won't get it.	Do you believe caregivers should consider children's needs important? Do you believe caregivers should want to meet their children's needs? Do you believe caregivers should be kind, loving, and approachable?
I need you to be here for me. If you don't take care of me I'll fall apart and it will be your fault.	Do you believe children should be responsible for caregiver's emotions? Do you believe children should be expected to meet caregiver's needs? Do you believe adult caregivers should meet their own needs?

Most, but not all, maladaptive introjects mirror wounding *caregivers*. When working with a non-caregiver introject (e.g. sibling, teacher, school yard bully, spouse, etc.) tailor your question accordingly. For example you might need to ask: "Do you believe *siblings* should be supportive of each other?" "Do you believe *teachers* should be protective of their students?" or "Do you believe *classmates* should treat each other with respect?"

© Copyright 2009 by Shirley Jean Schmidt, MA, LPC. All rights reserved. Duplication in any form without permission is prohibited.

Step 4: Getting the Child Part's Age

In Step 4 ask the child part for her age. The age can provide some needed context for Step 5. You might ask:

> So little one, how old are you?

The child part may report a single age, a range of ages, or uncertainty about age. The reported age may have less to do with when the mask was first acquired and more to do with when it was the most influential. For example, Yolanda reported feeling wounded by her mother's non-verbal message "I wish you'd never been born." While her mother conveyed this message from the time she was born, it became especially painful at age four, when she left Yolanda at an orphanage. The child part wearing the mask was age four.

Step 5: Explaining the Illusion of Significance

In Step 5 you'll explain to the child part the truth about the mask's illusion of significance. This starts with a validation of the client's real wounding experiences, then follows with an explanation about the mask being just a recording, an explanation of why the mask evokes an emotional reaction, and a discussion of turning it off. It might sound something like this:

> **Validation:** *When you were age 5, your mother was real, her invalidating, wounding messages were real, and the wounds her messages inflicted were real.*
>
> **Mask as recording:** *While your mother was behaving this way, your brain was making a recording of her; like filming a home movie. That recording became encapsulated in the mask. So the mask looks and sounds like your mother, but it's not your mother. It's just a recording of her behaving this way.*
>
> **Emotional reaction:** *But every time this recording plays, it evokes some very painful emotions. Right? That emotional reaction creates the illusion that the costume is real, important, and wounding, just like your mother was. Now watching a scary movie may make you feel afraid, but that doesn't mean you're really in danger, does it – because a movie is not real life. And this mask isn't real life either.*
>
> **Turning it off:** *If you don't like a movie, you can turn it off. When you understand the truth – that this mask it is no more real than a movie, you can turn it off. How does that sound?*

Child parts are usually intrigued and relieved to hear this.

Step 6: Checking on the Appearance of the Mask

In Step 6 you'll inquire about changes in the appearance of the mask. A client's mental picture of the mask provides crucial information about the process. Ask the child part:

> Does the mask look any different now?

Typically, a mask that looked large and intimidating begins to soften. It often appears smaller, less animated, and/or less important. The first time the mask appears less important say something like:

> See? It already appears less important. That's proof that what I'm saying is true.

If a mask moves away, ask the child part to bring it back in close. If a mask vanishes, ask the child part to hold out her hand and let the remains of the mask appear in the hand. It will usually reappear as a small object. From here on, after each protocol intervention you will return to Step 6 to re-check on the appearance of the mask.

© Copyright 2009 by Shirley Jean Schmidt, MA, LPC. All rights reserved. Duplication in any form without permission is prohibited.

Step 7: Mini-Interventions Help Shift Dominance

In Step 7 you'll apply mini-interventions to help reduce the dominance of the mask. The first two interventions, *Ask the Resources* and *Adult Body*, are the most important. Use one or more of the others if the child part needs more convincing that the mask is harmless. You may improvise your own mini-interventions, if what is offered here is not enough. After each intervention recheck the mask's appearance. When the mask appears to have lost its animation, go to Step 8.

■ ***Ask the Resources***

The *Ask the Resources* intervention gets the child part asking the Resources about the mask. Invite the child part to question the Resources about the nature of the mask. For example, say something like:

> *So little one, ask the Resources if they believe the mask can hurt you now?* OR
>
> *Do the Resources believe the mask is real and important as (<u>wounding role model</u>) was?*

Robust Resources will say the mask is harmless, or that the mask is not real and important. A child part will appreciate hearing this. The Resources can be called upon at any point during this protocol, when the child part needs comforting, reassurance, validation, or information.

■ ***Adult Body Intervention***

The *Adult Body Intervention* informs the child part she is no longer in a child body. Ask the part:

> *Do you know you're in an adult body now?*

Then follow up with:

> *Look at your hands.* (or *Look in this mirror.*) *Is this what you expected to see?*

A child part who reports some surprise in seeing adult hands (or an adult face) is probably pretty stuck in the past. It is very common for parts to be completely unaware, or just partially aware, of being in an adult body. When this happens, explain the downside of being in a child body with something like:

> *As a child your parents were in total control of your life, weren't they? They told you what to eat, when to eat, what to wear, when to sleep. They were in control of who came to the house and who you spent time with. The younger you were, the more control they had. Right?*

Then explain the upside of being in an adult body with something like:

> *But now that you're in an adult body, you make those decisions. You decide what to eat, when to eat it, what to wear, when to sleep. You decide who to spend time with, and who to stay away from. What's it like to think about that?*

A child part will react favorably to this news. Some are quite surprised by this information. A child part who reports expecting to see adult hands (or an adult face) may be fully aware of being in an adult body. Follow up by asking:

> *How is being in an adult body better or different from being in a child body?*

If the part is fully aware of being in an adult body she will be able to easily articulate the difference, which can strengthen her personal power. If the part cannot articulate the difference, she may not be fully aware after all. In such cases, you can explain the downside of being in a child body and the upside of being in an adult body.

Once the child part understands the significance of being in an adult body, recheck the mask's appearance. It will typically appear smaller and less important.

© Copyright 2009 by Shirley Jean Schmidt, MA, LPC. All rights reserved. Duplication in any form without permission is prohibited.

- **Photo Not Dangerous**

The *Photo Not Dangerous* intervention uses a photo metaphor to help the child part better understand that the mask is harmless. In this intervention you will invite the child part to consider the difference between a dangerous creature and a photo of the creature. For example, you might say something like:

> *If I offered to give you to hold a scorpion or a photo of a scorpion, which would you chose?*

A typical child part will understand that a photo is always *harmless*, regardless of the subject. This can help communicate that a mask that imitates a harmful person is harmless – just like a photo of a harmful creature is harmless. You can do this with reference to a rattlesnake, a tarantula, or any other dangerous creature. Once complete, recheck the mask's appearance. It will probably appear smaller and less important.

- **More Metaphors**

Additional metaphors can help convey the message that the mask is just a recording of the wounding caregiver. For example you might explain the mask is like a hologram, a tape recording, or a photograph. Use one of these metaphors or make up your own.

- **Additional Validation**

Some child parts need additional validation that the wounding they experienced in childhood was real and horrible. They need to be reassured that, when you trivialize the importance of the mask, you are not also trivializing their horrible experience. Here is an example of how you can combine an additional validation with another metaphor:

> *When you were little, your mother abused you. That was very real and very horrible for many years. But notice that, unlike your real mother, this costume is no more real than a hologram. And that, unlike your mother, you can pass your hand right through it. See? It has no power at all.*

Once this intervention is complete, recheck the mask's appearance.

- **Playing with the Mask**

Once the mask's animation is all gone, the *Playing with the Mask* intervention can give the child part an opportunity to demonstrate power over the remains of the mask. Invite the child part to play with the mask in a way that helps her discover how truly powerless it is. For example you might say:

> *Throw it to the Resources and play catch. OR   Grab a corner of that fabric and wave it around your head and dance, as the Resources play some peppy music.*

Use this intervention when all the animation is gone but the mask is still too big to fit in the child's pocket. Once complete, recheck the mask's appearance.

- **Drawing on the Power of the Resources**

The *Drawing on the Power of the Resources* intervention is especially helpful when just a little remains of an inanimate mask. It draws on the power of any Resources present, to further process a mask that is not quite ready to pocket. It can be used to reduce a medium-sized mask to pocket-size, or eliminate a caregiver image still visible on a mask.

In this intervention, the involvement of one or more Resources is key. There are many ways to do this. For example, ask the child part to "tape" the remains of the mask to his/her palm and play patty-cake with a Resource; ask the child part to hang on to the remains of the mask while doing the wave with the Resources; or ask the child part to join with a Resource to swing the remains of the mask around.

For example, a threatening father mask has diminished to the size of a notepad. It is inanimate but still holds an image of father's face. Together the child and the NAS swing it around a while. When finished, the mask is the size of a postage stamp, and father's face is gone. Once complete, recheck the mask's appearance.

© Copyright 2009 by Shirley Jean Schmidt, MA, LPC. All rights reserved. Duplication in any form without permission is prohibited.

Step 8: Assessing the Mask's Animation

In Step 8 you'll assess the mask's degree of animation. Each time you recheck the mask's appearance, you'll learn something about the protocol progress. At some point in Step 7 the mask will appear inanimate – often as a lifeless object, such as a sheet of cardboard, a handkerchief, a baseball, a postcard, or a pile of dust. But a mask that appears lifeless may show signs of animation if "provoked." This step provides the provocation needed to check for hidden animation. Ask the child part something like:

> *If I were to poke (shake or wiggle) the mask, what would happen? Would it try to kick me, would it yell at me?*

You could get a wide range of responses. The child part might say the mask vocalizes resistance; reacts with a punch or kick; squeaks or winces; or has no reaction at all. If any animation remains, or if the mask appears larger than a lunchbox, continue with Step 7 interventions. Proceed to Step 9 when the mask appears smaller than a lunchbox, and is inanimate, even when provoked.

Step 9: Highlighting the Child Part's Importance

In Step 9 you'll help the child part fully appreciate her importance and power in contrast to that of the mask. There are at least two ways to implement this.

One way is to invite the child part to:

> *Say to the mask, 'I'm in charge now, you're not.'*
> *Say to the mask, 'I'm alive and real, you're not.'*
> *Say to the mask, 'I'm important, you're not.'*
> *Say to the mask, 'I'm powerful, you're not.'*

Another way is to ask the child part:

> *Who's in charge now, you or what's left of the mask?*
> *Who's alive and real, you or what's left of the mask?*
> *Who's important now, you or what's left of the mask?*
> *Who's powerful now, you or what's left of the mask?*

Child parts typically answer "I am" to each question. Once complete, recheck the mask's appearance. Usually by this time the mask is pocket size. It is helpful to check for any image of the wounding role model present on the mask's remains. For example, the remains of mask might look like a post card with a picture of her critical mother. When this happens, apply the *Drawing on the Power of the Resources* intervention to eliminate the image of mother.

Step 10: Pocketing the Remains

In Step 10 you'll guide the child part to pocket the remains of the mask, in a way that feels empowering. Begin this step once the remains of the mask are *small* enough to fit in a pocket, completely *inanimate*, and devoid of any caregiver images. Start by asking:

> *Would you have any aversion to putting what's left of the mask in your pocket?*

- **No Aversion**

    If the child part has no aversion to putting the mask in a pocket say:

    > *Good. Put it in your pocket. Pat on your pocket and say, 'I'm in charge now.' Does that feel good?*

    If the answer is "yes," strengthen the good feeling with ABS.

© Copyright 2009 by Shirley Jean Schmidt, MA, LPC. All rights reserved. Duplication in any form without permission is prohibited.

■ ***Possible or Definite Aversion***

A child part encouraged or permitted to put an aversive mask in a pocket will ultimately feel invalidated, so be on the lookout for subtle signs of an aversion to pocketing a mask. A child part who says, "I don't want to put it in my pocket," is giving a clear sign. But a response like, "I *could* put it in my pocket," might mean, "I'm happy to put it in my pocket," or it could mean "I could put it in my pocket, but I'd rather not." If a child part says, "I have no aversion," with a hesitation or wince may have an aversion she's trying to keep secret. Such responses must be investigated further. Giving a child part explicit permission to have an aversion may help her feel more comfortable expressing it. If any aversion to pocketing the mask is present, apply one or more additional Step 7 interventions, then come back to Step 10.

When the child part reports no aversion to the mask, you'll tell her to put it in her pocket and say, "I'm in charge now." This means the child is in charge of the mask – the mask is not in charge of her. It does not mean the child part is now in charge of everything. Adult parts of self are still in charge of adult concerns.

A child part that has comfortably pocketed the mask is still somewhat stuck in childhood, and is still considered to be an introject. That label will no longer apply once the child part has successfully completed the Needs Meeting Protocol and become totally unstuck.

Sometimes a child part will want to know why the mask goes in a pocket, not a trash can. An explanation might go something like this:

> *At some point in the future the Resources will help you get completely unstuck from this mask by meeting your developmental needs. If we keep the mask around, you can easily watch it get smaller and smaller until it completely disappears. If you throw it away we might not know what's going on with it.*

Step 11: Orienting the Child Part and Tucking In

In Step 11 you'll orient the introject to future processing with something like:

> *I'd like to help you get totally unstuck from the remains of this mask, at the perfect time. I'm not sure when that will be, hopefully soon.*

If a reactive part had identified the introject, it is appropriate to check in with that reactive part now. For example, you might ask the client something like:

> *How's the* (sad four-year-old), *the one that was reacting to the introject, doing now?*

A reactive part that felt sad, fearful, defensive, or angry before this intervention will typically feel much better. If a reactive part feels better, you might opt to ask the reactive part and the introject something like:

> *Would the two of you like to get together to meet? The Resources can serve you milk and cookies if you like.*

Such a meeting should be an ego-strengthening experience, and can be strengthened with ABS.

A reactive part that continues to feel distressed will likely be reacting to one or more additional introjects. They can be identified by asking the part to look to the right to see who she is reacting to. Reactive parts will feel a great sense of relief once the dominance of each threatening introject is switched.

When it's time to tuck in the parts, say something like:

> *I'd like to help you get totally unstuck at the perfect time. I'm not sure when that will be, hopefully soon. In the meantime I'd like to invite you both to tuck in. Is there anything you'd like to say or ask before you tuck in?*

Then tuck them in with something like:

> *Just find a nice, warm, safe place to tuck in to. You can tuck in with your Resource(s) if you like. Just find a good safe place to wait until the next time you're needed.*

© Copyright 2009 by Shirley Jean Schmidt, MA, LPC. All rights reserved. Duplication in any form without permission is prohibited.

Step 12: Temporary Nature of the Shift

In Step 12 you'll inform the client that switching the dominance is usually a temporary intervention. For example, you might say something like:

> While this intervention has helped this little one get partly unstuck from the mask, we'll have to do the Needs Meeting Protocol later, to help her get totally unstuck. Until then, the mask could reanimate and start delivering the ugly message again. But even if that happens it's STILL harmless, and we can easily switch the dominance back again, in just a few minutes.

It is usually only necessary to tell a client about this once or twice. If at any point an individual child part worries that a mask will reanimate, provide this information on the spot.

Switching the Dominance to Treat a Simple Problem – Follow-up

There are several follow-up questions which can help you assess the success of the Switching the Dominance Protocol to resolve the targeted problem.

- Ask how much disturbance the introject message evokes now with something like:

> Your mom's message was ("You'll never be good enough.") How disturbing is it, to hear that message now?

- Ask for the client's reaction to her current problem with something like:

> When you recall your fears about getting a promotion, is your reaction any different now?

- Ask for the client's reaction to a disturbing past event that is relevant to her problem with something like:

> You cried while telling me you were passed over for that promotion you had worked so hard to get. When you think about failing to get that promotion, is your reaction any different now?

Clients typically report favorable responses to such follow-up questions. If the answers to protocol follow-up questions reveal the problem is only partially resolved, there are two likely reasons. (1) There may be additional introjects related to the problem, and/or (2) the issue might not resolve until after the Needs Meeting Protocol has been applied. The Conference Room Protocol (Chapter 5) can provide a framework for finding and switching the dominance of multiple introjects related to a particular problem. Finding and treating all the associated introjects with the Switching the Dominance Protocol and the Needs Meeting Protocol (Chapter 6) should lead to the desired resolution of the problem.

Other Protocol Issues

Do Not Assault the Mask

During this protocol you have some creative license. But keep in mind that any creative application that does not serve to illuminate the truth about the mask (that it is just a harmless recording), may actually obscure the truth. This includes interventions like yelling at the mask, beating up the mask, or guarding the child part from the mask. Such interventions convey the idea that the mask is ominous, dangerous, or threatening - taking the child part farther away from the truth.

If an angry child part wishes to "assault," "burn," "yell at," "destroy," or "throw away" a mask, encourage her instead to direct anger towards the caregiver the mask is mirroring. Say something like, "Your mother was very critical of you. You were right to grow up angry with her. If I gave you a photo of her right now, would you be angry at the photo or angry at your mom?" The child will probably say "angry at mom." You can follow with: "So does it make more sense to be angry at mom or a mask that looks just like her?" By making this distinction, and directing her anger at the source, the child part is more likely to appreciate how harmless the mask really is.

© Copyright 2009 by Shirley Jean Schmidt, MA, LPC. All rights reserved. Duplication in any form without permission is prohibited.

Working with Two or More Introjects at Once

Sometimes a reactive part looks to the right and sees two or more introjects. For example, a powerless reactive part sees a hostile father introject and an unprotective mother introject. It may be appropriate to switch the dominance of both introjects at the same time. Start by asking to speak to the two child parts behind the two masks. For example, "I want you both to know that I see you and I know that you're good..." From there, each statement or question gets directed to both child parts. Sometimes this works for the whole protocol, sometimes just for part of the protocol. If addressing them together does not work well, change to working with them individually.

More than One Part of Self is Wearing an Introject Mask or Costume

Clients typically report introject costumes being worn by a single part of self – usually a child part. But occasionally, during the Switching the Dominance Protocol, a client will report two or three child parts wearing a single introject mask or costume. The child parts might be the same or different ages. Follow the protocol steps as usual. In Step 10, invite the child parts to split up the remains of the mask or costume – so each can pocket a piece of it.

Step 1 of SDP   **Step 10 of SDP**

The Mask Disappears

Throughout the protocol you'll check on changes in the appearance of the mask. Sometimes a child part will report that a mask has disappeared. When this happens, say:

> Hold out your hand. The remains of the mask will appear in your hand, even if it's just a molecule or two. When you're ready, tell me what you notice.

Usually some small remains appear, but sometimes nothing appears in the hand. It is not uncommon for a mask to disappear around Step 9. This is usually a sign that the processing is going well. Continue with the protocol, but modify Step 9 a bit. Ask the child part questions like:

> Who's in charge now, you or the invisible mask? Who's alive and real, you or the invisible mask? Who's important, you or the invisible mask? Who's powerful, you or the invisible mask?

In Step 10 you'll ask the child part if she has any aversion to putting the *invisible mask* in a pocket. If mask disappears early in the protocol it could indicate a processing block, confusion, or defensiveness. This problem is discussed in Chapter 7, on page 178.

Re-Switching the Dominance

If a client reports that an introject mask or costume has reanimated following a successful switching of the dominance (i.e. in the next session), you should be able to switch it back quite easily. Ask the child part wearing the reanimated mask, something like:

> Do you remember we talked (last week) about the true nature of this mask?

The answer to this allows you to verify that there really is a reanimated mask, and not a new introject that you haven't worked with before. If the child part answers "yes," ask:

> Do you remember what I told you about the mask?

A typical answer would be "yes." If you get a "yes" answer ask:

> What did I tell you about the mask?

© Copyright 2009 by Shirley Jean Schmidt, MA, LPC. All rights reserved. Duplication in any form without permission is prohibited.

A typical answer would be something like "You told me it was just a recording that couldn't do any harm." If you get this type of response, ask:

> And what happens to the mask as you recall that now?

The typical answer would be something like "It's getting small and going back in my pocket." If you don't get these typical replies, you'll need to remind the child part of the mask's illusion of significance. The dominance should re-switch quite readily as you re-inform the child part that the mask is just an illusion and unable to do any real harm.

Incomplete Switch

If a session ends before a child part is comfortable putting the mask in a pocket, the incomplete process must be appropriately closed down so it can be resumed later. Before closing the session, discuss with the child part options for tucking in the mask, in a safe container. A Resource's pocket works well. Then tuck in the child part with the Resource that is holding the mask. If no Resources have been established (not even a Provisional Resource), invite the child part to put the mask in a safe container - such as a safe or a vault. This safe container option is offered because the child part still believes the mask is dangerous, not because it actually is. Then tuck in the child part with the safe container. Later, when you resume the protocol with the child part, the mask will be readily available.

Complications and Processing Blocks

Most clients have an easy time with the Switching the Dominance Protocol, but it does not always unfold smoothly. A client or a child part response that suggests the protocol may be unlikely to end with the mask in the child's pocket, indicates the presence of a *complication or block*. This can happen at any point in this process, for example, while classifying parts of self; while helping the child part see she is different from the mask; while collecting information about changes in the mask's appearance; and when pocketing the mask.

This protocol typically takes as little as 10-20 minutes. Minor processing confusions may take a few extra minutes to clear. Occasionally substantial blocks will arise that take quite a while to work through. If fully developed, robust Resources can be called upon to reassure and encourage child parts that are doubtful a mask is harmless. Even the participation of a single Resource or a Provisional Resource can be beneficial.

Every intervention that resolves a processing block has an ego-strengthening benefit. Detailed instructions for handling all Switching the Dominance Protocol complications and processing blocks – large and small – are provided in Chapter 7, pages 171-178.

Two Switching the Dominance Protocol Sessions

Below you will find two client/therapist Switching the Dominance Protocol dialogues – a simple one and a complex one. Both illustrate treating a simple problem connected to a single introject, and both provide an example of how to execute and transition between the following steps:

- Asking About the Client's Experience
- Connecting to Resources
- Inviting Parts of Self Forward
- Finding the Presumptive Introject
- Getting and Rating the Presumptive Introject Message
- Step 1: Permission to Speak to Child Behind Mask
- Step 2. Welcoming the Child Behind the Mask
- Step 3. Contrasting the True Nature of the Child with the Dysfunction of the Mask
- Step 4. Getting the Child Part's Age

© Copyright 2009 by Shirley Jean Schmidt, MA, LPC. All rights reserved. Duplication in any form without permission is prohibited.

- Step 5. Explaining the Illusion of Significance
- Step 6. Checking on the Appearance of the Mask
- Step 7. Mini-Interventions Help Shift Dominance
- Step 8. Assessing the Mask's Animation
- Step 9. Highlighting the Child Part's Importance
- Step 10. Pocketing the Remains
- Step 11. Orienting the Child and Tucking In
- Step 12. Temporary Nature of the Shift
- Follow-up

Example of a Simple Switching the Dominance Experience

This sample dialogue shows you my most common experience of the Switching the Dominance Protocol. In this example, the maladaptive introject is easy to identify, and the dominance is easily switched. The processing unfolds in an uncomplicated straight line from problem to introject to costume in the pocket.

The Client Discloses a Problem to Address

Client:	I've been offered a promotion at work – a management position. It's a great job for me in every way, except one. I'll have to write reports – weekly, monthly, and yearly reports. I want the job but I don't want to write reports. I get very anxious when I have to write. I'm not very good at it. I so quickly feel defeated. I'm afraid I'm going to have to turn down the offer.

Asking About the Client's Experience

Therapist:	**What kind of thoughts go through your mind when you think about writing reports?**
Client:	I hear my father's voice saying, "You're an idiot." This goes back to grade school and junior high. My father was always checking my homework, especially my writing assignments. I just wasn't very good at school. He tried to help me, but he had no patience. He'd get frustrated and call me an idiot. He was a brilliant college professor and journalist. He loved to read and write. I was just an average student, sometimes below average. I didn't enjoy books the way he did. I loved sports. He couldn't relate to that. It made him angry that I wasn't just like him.
Therapist:	**Would you like to process that today?**
Client:	Absolutely!

Connecting to Resources

Therapist:	**Okay. So start by connecting to your Resources. Tell me when you're connected.**
Client:	Okay.
Therapist:	**Good. Tell me when that's strengthened all the way?** *(Strengthened with ABS.)*
Client:	Okay.

Inviting Parts of Self Forward

Therapist:	**I'd like to invite, to approach the Resources, the part of self that is mimicking your father telling you "You're an idiot." When you're ready, tell me what you notice.**
Client:	I see my angry father telling me, "You're an idiot."

Getting and Rating the Presumptive Introject Message

Therapist:	**How disturbing is his message, 0-10?**
Client:	Ten.

Step 1: Permission to Speak to Child Behind Mask

Therapist:	**I'm guessing there's a little one behind that father costume. Is that right?**
CR part:	Yeah. I think so.
Therapist:	**May I speak to the little one behind the costume?**
CR part:	Yeah.

© Copyright 2009 by Shirley Jean Schmidt, MA, LPC. All rights reserved. Duplication in any form without permission is prohibited.

Step 2. Welcoming the Child Behind the Mask

Therapist:	**Hey little one. Thanks for coming. I want you to know I see you, and I know that you're good. And I know the difference between you and this father costume. What's it like to hear that?**
Child part:	Nice.
Therapist:	**Do you like or need this mask? Does it serve a useful purpose?**
Child part:	None at all.

Step 3. Contrasting the True Nature of the Child with the Dysfunction of the Mask

Therapist:	**Let's talk about the ways you're different from this costume. Do you believe caregivers should always treat children with respect?**
Child part:	Yes.
Therapist:	**Does the costume agree?**
Child part:	No.
Therapist:	**Do you believe caregivers should accept children exactly as they are, regardless of their strengths and weaknesses.**
Child part:	Yes.
Therapist:	**Does the costume agree?**
Child part:	No.
Therapist:	**Do you believe caregivers should encourage children to develop their own unique interests?**
Child part:	Yes.
Therapist:	**Does the costume agree?**
Child part:	No.
Therapist:	**See how different you are from this costume?**
Child part:	Yes.
Therapist:	**You're nothing like it, are you?**
Child part:	No, I'm not.

Step 4. Getting the Child Part's Age

Therapist:	**How old are you little one?**
Child part:	About ten.

Step 5. Explaining the Illusion of Significance

Therapist:	**When you were about ten, your father had a hard time accepting that you were not going to excel at school and writing, like he did. In fact it made him angry. That was very painful and inflicted a deep wound. Now while your father was behaving this way, your brain was making a recording of him - like filming a home movie. That recording of your father behaving this way became encapsulated in this father costume you're wearing. So the costume looks like your father and sounds like your father, but it's not your father. It's just a recording of him behaving this way.**
Child part:	Oh.
Therapist:	**Now every time this recording plays, it evokes some very painful emotions. Right?**
Child part:	Yeah.
Therapist:	**Those painful emotions create the illusion that this costume is real, important, and wounding, just like your father was. But it's not real life. Now if I watch a scary movie I'm going to feel fear, right? But that doesn't mean I'm really in danger, does it? Because a movie is not real life. So just because you're having an emotional reaction, doesn't mean the costume is real. How does that sound?**
Child part:	Good.
Therapist:	**If you don't like a movie, you can turn it off. Right?**
Child part:	Yeah.
Therapist:	**Here's the good news. When you understand the truth about this mask – that it is about as real as a movie, you can turn it off. How does that sound?**
Child part:	Really good.

Step 6. Checking on the Appearance of the Mask

Therapist:	**So with all this new information, does the mask look any different now?**
Child part:	It looks like a life-size cardboard cut out of him.
Therapist:	**Wow. That's quite a change. See? That's proof that what I'm saying is true.**
Child part:	Yeah.

© Copyright 2009 by Shirley Jean Schmidt, MA, LPC. All rights reserved. Duplication in any form without permission is prohibited.

Step 7. Mini-Interventions Help Shift Dominance

Ask the Resources

Therapist:	**So ten-year-old, ask the Resources if they believe the costume can hurt you now like your father hurt you back then.**
Child part:	They say "no," the costume is harmless.
Therapist:	**What's it like to hear that?**
Child part:	I like it.

Adult Body Intervention

Therapist:	**So ten-year-old, do you understand you're in an adult body now?**
Child part:	Ummm. Not sure.
Therapist:	**Take a look in this mirror. Is this what you expected to see?**
Child part:	(Looking in mirror) Ummm. No. Yes, actually no.
Therapist:	**When you were ten, you parents were in total control of your life, weren't they? They told you what to eat, when to eat, what to wear, when to sleep. They were in control of who came to the house and who you spent time with. They made up the rules and they punished you when they thought you broke those rules. Right?**
Child part:	Yeah.
Therapist:	**So now that you're in an adult body you have a lot more power, don't you? You make those decisions. You decide what to eat, when to eat it, what to wear, when to sleep. You decide who to spend time with, and who to stay away from. You make up the rules now, don't you?**
Child part:	Yeah.
Therapist:	**What's it like to think about that?**
Child part:	A relief.

Checking Appearance of the Costume

Therapist:	**So ten-year-old, does the costume look any different now?**
Child part:	It looks like a foot square of cardboard on the floor.

Step 8. Assessing the Mask's Animation

Therapist:	**Very good. So if I were to poke it or shake it, would it have a response? Would it try to kick me, would it yell at me?**
Child part:	No reaction.
Therapist:	**So has it lost all its animation?**
Child part:	Yes.

Step 9. Highlighting the Child Part's Importance

Therapist:	**Very good. So ten-year-old, who's in charge now, you or what's left of the costume?**
Child part:	I am.
Therapist:	**Who's alive and real now, you or what's left of the costume?**
Child part:	I am.
Therapist:	**Who matters now, you or what's left of the costume?**
Child part:	I am.
Therapist:	**Who has power now, you or what's left of the costume?**
Child part:	I do.

Checking Appearance of the Costume

Therapist:	**Is there anything else about the costume's appearance that's changed?**
Child part:	Now it looks like a square of Kleenex™ tissue.
Therapist:	**Does it have an image of your father on it?**
Child part:	No. It's just white.

Step 10. Pocketing the Remains

Therapist:	**Great. Now would you have any aversion to putting what's left of this costume in a pocket?**
Child part:	No.
Therapist:	**So put it in your pocket. Pat on your pocket and say "I'm in charge now."**
Child part:	I'm in charge now.

© Copyright 2009 by Shirley Jean Schmidt, MA, LPC. All rights reserved. Duplication in any form without permission is prohibited.

Therapist:	How does that feel?
Child part:	Wonderful.
Therapist:	**Very good. Notice that good feeling. Take as long as you need to let it strengthen. Tell me when it's strengthened all the way.** *(Strengthened with ABS.)*
Child part:	Okay.

Step 11. Orienting the Child and Tucking In & Step 12. Temporary Nature of the Shift

Therapist:	**So ten-year-old, I'd like to help you get totally unstuck from the remains of this costume, at the perfect time. I'm not sure when that will be, hopefully soon. But for now I'm going to invite you to tuck in. Is there anything you'd like to say or ask before you tuck in?**
Child part:	Will the costume stay in the pocket? How do I know it won't get big again?
Therapist:	**Well it might get big and start calling you an idiot again. But if that happens, keep in mind it's STILL harmless and STILL an illusion. If that does happen, we can easily switch the dominance back again, in just a few minutes. Later, after the Resources have met all your developmental needs, and you've become totally unstuck, it will never return.** *(This is also Step 12.)*
Child part:	Okay.
Therapist:	**Okay. Now find a nice, warm, safe place to tuck in to. You can tuck in with your Resources if you like. Just find a good safe place to wait until the next time you're needed.**
Client:	Okay.

Follow-up

Therapist:	**Now when you think about your father's message, "You're an idiot," how much disturbance does that bring up, 0-10?**
Client:	Well I know I'm not an idiot. There are some things I'm not great at, but that doesn't make me an idiot. It bothers me that he said it – maybe a 1 – but it doesn't feel at all personal now. It's about him, not about me, it's about him.
Therapist:	**So now when you think about taking the promotion and writing weekly, monthly, and yearly reports, is your reaction any different?**
Client:	I don't like to write, and I'm not very good at it, but I can envision myself writing reports now without feeling defeated. Right now I believe I can do it if I have the right kind of help.
Therapist:	**What's it like to think about that?**
Client:	That feels really good!

Example of a Complex Switching the Dominance Experience

This sample dialogue shows you a more complex client experience, illustrating how different reactive parts can come up in your search for the maladaptive introject at the source of a problem. It also shows that, once the introject has been identified, many mini-interventions are sometimes needed to complete the process.

The Client Discloses a Problem to Address

Client:	I'm very distracted today. I got a call from my mother-in-law this morning. She's such a control freak! She's decided to take our kids to Hawaii at Christmas. She's already told them she's taking them and says she's already put airline tickets in the mail. She's just now telling me! She shows me no respect at all. She never asked us if we have plans, she did not ask us for permission. I'm just furious. We've already made plans to visit my family in Kentucky. My parents are putting on a big family reunion. I've already bought the plane tickets and booked the hotel. My kids are not thrilled about going, so this offer to go to Hawaii will sound great to them. They'll hate me when I tell them "no." She is always interfering like this. I cannot get my husband to rein her in. I feel just paralyzed. I had a long list of errands to run and I've just lost my focus. I just sit at my computer drafting e-mails that tell her off. I don't dare send any of them, they're so vicious. I just don't know what to do.
Therapist:	**What does your most adult self think you should do?**
Client:	I should probably just say "thanks but no thanks," and send back the tickets. I know I should set a boundary with her but I'm really afraid to do that.

Asking About the Client's Experience

Therapist:	**Is that fear connected to a negative belief about yourself?**

© Copyright 2009 by Shirley Jean Schmidt, MA, LPC. All rights reserved. Duplication in any form without permission is prohibited.

Client:	Yes. I don't have a right to stand up for myself.
Therapist:	**Would you like to process that today?**
Client:	That would be great.

Connecting to Resources

Therapist:	**Connect to your Resources. Tell me when you're connected.**
Client:	Okay.
Therapist:	**Good. Tell me when that's strengthened all the way?** *(Strengthened with ABS.)*
Client:	Okay.

Inviting Parts of Self Forward

Therapist:	**I'd like to invite, to approach the Resources, the part of self that believes "I don't have a right to stand up for myself". When you're ready, tell me what you notice.**
Client:	*(Starts to cry)* I see a little kid. She's very upset.
Therapist:	**May I speak with her?**
Client:	Yeah.
Therapist:	*(In a very soft and gentle voice)* **Hey little one. Thanks for coming. I'm really glad you're here. Can you tell me how old you are?**
Reactive part:	Thirteen.
Therapist:	**Okay, and what kind of mood are you in?**
Reactive part:	Sad... angry.
Therapist:	**I'm guessing you've been stuck in the past a long time. Is that right?**
Reactive part:	Yeah.
Therapist:	**How stuck are you, 0-10? If 10 is totally stuck and 0 is not stuck at all?**
Reactive part:	Nine.
Therapist:	**I'd like to help you get unstuck, and you can help. Are you interested?**
Reactive part:	Yeah.
Therapist:	**When you're ready, I'd like you to look to the right, where you will see appear the part or parts of self that you're reacting to. When you're ready, tell me what you notice.**

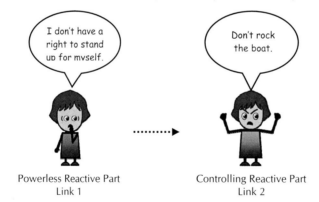

Powerless Reactive Part   Controlling Reactive Part
Link 1   Link 2

Encountering a Controlling Reactive Part

Reactive part:	She's warning me to keep quiet – says "Don't rock the boat."
Therapist:	**Okay. And what does she look like?**
CR part:	She looks like me in grammar school - the same haircut and dress I wore in the third grade.
Therapist:	**That would be about age eight?**
CR part:	Yeah.
Therapist:	**May I speak with this eight-year-old?**
CR part:	Yeah.
Therapist:	*(In a very soft and gentle voice)* **Hey little one. Thanks for coming. I'm really glad you're here. Can you tell me what kind of mood you're in?**
CR part:	I'm worried she's going to say something she shouldn't and upset mom.
Therapist:	**I see. That makes sense. I'm guessing you've been stuck in the past a long time. Is that right?**
CR part:	Yeah.
Therapist:	**How stuck are you, 0-10? If 10 is totally stuck and 0 is not stuck at all?**
CR part:	Ten.

© Copyright 2009 by Shirley Jean Schmidt, MA, LPC. All rights reserved. Duplication in any form without permission is prohibited.

Therapist:	**I'd like to help you get unstuck, and you can help. Are you interested?**
CR part:	Yeah.
Therapist:	**When you're ready, I'd like you to look to the right, where you will see appear the part or parts of self that you're reacting to. When you're ready, tell me what you notice.**

Finding the Presumptive Introject

CR part:	I see my mom. She's reading my diary. She sees where I wrote how mad I am at her for going through my clothes and papers, telling me what to wear, and generally invading my privacy. When she puts the diary down she's ice cold. She doesn't look at me or talk to me. She's really mad at me. I know I'm in serious trouble.

Getting and Rating the Presumptive Introject Message

Therapist:	**So is she conveying a message?**
CR part:	No. It's just stone cold silence.
Therapist:	**What non-verbal message does her silence seem to be conveying?**
CR part:	I'm a great mother to you. You can't see it because you're just spoiled and ungrateful. Shame on you.
Therapist:	**How disturbing is that message, 0-10?**
CR part:	Ten.

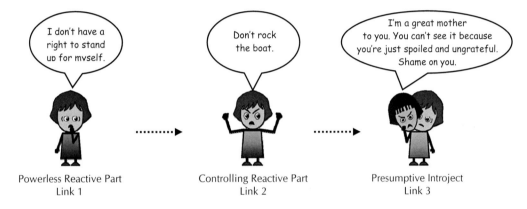

I don't have a right to stand up for myself.	Don't rock the boat.	I'm a great mother to you. You can't see it because you're just spoiled and ungrateful. Shame on you.
Powerless Reactive Part Link 1	Controlling Reactive Part Link 2	Presumptive Introject Link 3

Step 1: Permission to Speak to Child Behind Mask

Therapist:	**I'm guessing there's a little one behind that mom costume. Is that right?**
CR part:	Yeah. I think so.
Therapist:	**May I speak to the little one behind the costume?**
CR part:	Yeah.

Step 2. Welcoming the Child Behind the Mask

Therapist:	**Hey little one. Thanks for coming. I want you to know I see you, and I know that you're good. And I know the difference between you and this mom costume. What's it like to hear that?**
Child part:	Really? You see me?
Therapist:	**Yes I do. So do you like or need this mask? Does it serve a useful purpose?**
Child part:	It reminds me not to upset my mother. She doesn't like me when I upset her.

Found a Controlling Reactive Mimic

Therapist:	**I see what you mean. How old are you?**
Child part:	Nine.
Therapist:	**So nine-year-old, I'm guessing you've been stuck in the past a long time. Is that right?**
Child part:	Yeah.
Therapist:	**How stuck are you, 0-10?**
Child part:	Ten.
Therapist:	**I'd like to help you get unstuck, and you can help. Are you interested?**
Child part:	Yeah.
Therapist:	**When you're ready, I'd like you to look to the right, where you will see appear the part or parts of self that you're reacting to. When you're ready, tell me what you notice.**

© Copyright 2009 by Shirley Jean Schmidt, MA, LPC. All rights reserved. Duplication in any form without permission is prohibited.

Child part:	I see my mom. She's really mad. She's looking away. I told her I wanted to pick out my own clothes and she just shut down.
Therapist:	**So is she conveying a message?**
Reactive part:	No. She shut down.
Therapist:	**What non-verbal message does her body language convey?**
Child part:	You're spoiled and ungrateful. Shame on you.
Therapist:	**How disturbing is that message, 0-10?**
Child part:	Ten.

Powerless Reactive Part   Controlling Reactive Part   Reactive Mimic   Presumptive Introject
Link 1   Link 2   Link 3   Link 4

Step 1: Permission to Speak to Child Behind Mask

Therapist:	**I'm guessing there's a little one behind that mom costume. Is that right?**
Child part:	Yeah.
Therapist:	**May I speak to the little one behind the costume?**
Reactive part:	Yeah.

Step 2. Welcoming the Child Behind the Mask

Therapist:	**Hey little one. Thanks for coming. I want you to know I see you, and I know that you're good. And I know the difference between you and this mom costume. What's it like to hear that?**
Child part:	Wow. What a relief.
Therapist:	**Do you like or need this mask? Does it serve a useful purpose?**
Child part:	No. I hate it. Get it off me.

Step 3. Contrasting the True Nature of the Child with the Dysfunction of the Mask

Therapist:	**Let's talk about the ways you're different from this costume. Do you believe its okay for caregivers to shame children for age-appropriate requests?**
Child part:	No.
Therapist:	**Does the costume agree?**
Child part:	No.
Therapist:	**Do you believe caregivers should respect children's privacy and boundaries?**
Child part:	Yes.
Therapist:	**Does the costume agree?**
Child part:	No.
Therapist:	**Do you believe caregivers should manage their emotions around children?**
Child part:	Yes.
Therapist:	**Does the costume agree?**
Child part:	No.
Therapist:	**See how different you are from this costume?**
Child part:	Yes.
Therapist:	**You're nothing like it, are you?**
Child part:	No, I'm not.

Step 4. Getting the Child Part's Age

| Therapist: | **How old are you little one?** |
| Child part: | About 13. |

© Copyright 2009 by Shirley Jean Schmidt, MA, LPC. All rights reserved. Duplication in any form without permission is prohibited.

Step 5. Explaining the Illusion of Significance

Therapist:	**When you were about 13, interacting with your mom could be very stressful. She was inclined to intrude and invade your space and privacy, and shamed you for objecting. She managed her anger by completely shutting down. I want you to know I believe that's what happened, because you say that's what happened. Now while your mother was behaving this way, your brain was making a recording of her. Kind of like filming a home movie. That recording of mom behaving this way became encapsulated in this mom costume you're wearing. So the costume looks like your mom and sounds like your mom, but it's not your mom. It's just a recording of her behaving this way. Now every time this recording plays, it evokes some very painful emotions. Right?**
Child part:	Yeah.
Therapist:	**Those painful emotions create the illusion that this costume is real, important, and wounding, just like your mom was. But it's not real life. Now if I watch a scary movie I'm going to feel fear, right? But that doesn't mean I'm really in danger, does it? Because a movie is not real life. So just because you're having an emotional reaction, doesn't mean the costume is real. How does that sound?**
Child part:	Good.
Therapist:	**If you don't like a movie, you can turn it off. Right?**
Child part:	Yeah.
Therapist:	**Here's the good news. When you understand the truth about this mask – that it is about as real as a movie, you can turn it off. How does that sound?**
Child part:	Really good.

Step 6. Checking on the Appearance of the Mask

Therapist:	**So with all this new information, does the mask look any different now?**
Child part:	It looks like an empty, adult-size, Halloween costume. It's just draped over my arm.
Therapist:	**Wow. That's quite a change. See? That's proof that what I'm saying is true.**
Child part:	Yeah.

Step 7. Mini-Interventions Help Shift Dominance

Ask the Resources

Therapist:	**Ask the Resources if they believe the costume can hurt you now like mom hurt you back then?**
Child part:	They say "no," the costume is harmless.
Therapist:	**What's it like to hear that?**
Child part:	Very reassuring.

Adult Body Intervention

Therapist:	**So 13-year-old, do you understand you're in an adult body now?**
Child part:	Ummm. Yes, well, maybe.
Therapist:	**Take a look in this mirror. Is this what you expected to see?**
Child part:	(Looking in mirror) Well, not exactly.
Therapist:	**When you were 13, your parents were in charge of much of your life, weren't they? They owned the house and the car. They were in charge of the family checkbook. They made lots of decisions for you. They made up the rules you had to live by, and decided on your punishments if you broke their rules. You didn't have a lot of power, did you?**
Child part:	No I didn't.
Therapist:	**So now that you're in an adult body you have a lot more power, don't you? You own the house and car. You have control of the checkbook. You make up the rules of the house now, don't you?**
Child part:	Yes I do.
Therapist:	**What's it like to think about that?**
Child part:	Nice.

Checking Appearance of the Costume

Therapist:	**So 13-year-old, does the costume look any different now?**
Child part:	It about half the size, like a child-size Halloween costume.

Step 8. Assessing the Mask's Animation

Therapist:	**Very good. So if I were to poke it or shake it, would it have a response? Would it try to kick me, would it yell at me?**

© Copyright 2009 by Shirley Jean Schmidt, MA, LPC. All rights reserved. Duplication in any form without permission is prohibited.

Child part: It growls. It doesn't want to go away.

Step 7. Mini-Interventions Help Shift Dominance

Photo Not Dangerous

Therapist: **So 13-year-old, if I were to offer to give you to hold, either a rattlesnake or a photo of a rattlesnake, which would you choose?**
Child part: The photo.
Therapist: **Why's that?**
Child part: Because a photo can't bite me.
Therapist: **Okay. That makes sense. So is this costume more like a rattlesnake or a photo of a rattlesnake?**
Child part: More like a photo.
Therapist: **What's it like to consider that?**
Child part: I like it. It's stopped growling.

Checking Appearance of the Costume

Therapist: **Is there anything else about the costume's appearance that's changed?**
Child part: It's about the size of a handkerchief.

Step 8. Assessing the Mask's Animation

Therapist: **Okay, so now if I were to poke it or wiggle it, would it have a response?**
Child part: No. Nothing.
Therapist: **Has it lost all its animation?**
Child part: Yes.

Step 9. Highlighting the Child Part's Importance

Therapist: **Very good. So 13-year-old, who's in charge now, you or what's left of the costume?**
Child part: I am.
Therapist: **Who's alive and real now, you or what's left of the costume?**
Child part: I am.
Therapist: **Who matters now, you or what's left of the costume?**
Child part: I am.
Therapist: **Who has power now, you or what's left of the costume?**
Child part: I do.

Checking Appearance of the Costume

Therapist: **Is there anything else about the costume's appearance that's changed?**
Child part: It's the size of a postcard.
Therapist: **Does it have an image of your mom on it?**
Child part: It has her face in silhouette.

Step 7. Mini-Interventions Help Shift Dominance

Drawing on the Power of the Resources

Therapist: **So 13-year-old, let's tape the remains of the costume to the palm of your hand. Now play patty cake with the Nurturing Adult Self. When you're ready, tell me what you notice.**
Child part: The image disappears. It's just a white piece of paper.

Step 10. Pocketing the Remains

Therapist: **Great. Now would you have any aversion to putting what's left of this costume in a pocket?**
Child part: No.
Therapist: **So put it in your pocket. Pat on your pocket and say "I'm in charge now."**
Child part: I'm in charge now.
Therapist: **How does that feel?**
Child part: Great. Empowering.
Therapist: **Very good. Notice that good feeling. Take as long as you need to let it strengthen. Tell me when it's strengthened all the way.** (Strengthened with ABS.)
Child part: Okay. It's strengthened.

© Copyright 2009 by Shirley Jean Schmidt, MA, LPC. All rights reserved. Duplication in any form without permission is prohibited.

Step 11. Orienting the Child and Tucking In

Therapist: **So 13-year-old, I'd like to help you get totally unstuck from the remains of this costume, at the perfect time. I'm not sure when that will be, hopefully soon. In the meantime, let's check in with the nine-year-old reactive mimic that was wearing the mom costume conveying the message "I'm a great mother to you. You can't see it because you're just spoiled and ungrateful. Shame on you." How's the nine-year-old doing now?**

Client: She's smiling. She's holding the costume by her side.

Therapist: **Does it seem important now?**

Client: No.

Therapist: **She was stuck at a 10. How stuck does she seem now?**

Client: Maybe 1 or 2.

Therapist: **Great. Now let's check in with the 8-year-old third-grader, that was saying "Don't rock the boat." How's she doing now?**

Client: She looks more confident, more empowered.

Therapist: **She was stuck at a 10. How stuck does she seem now?**

Client: About a 2 or 3.

Therapist: **Great. Now let's check in with the 13-year-old reactive part that was feeling sad and angry. How's she doing now?**

Client: She looks happy and relieved.

Therapist: **She was stuck at a 9. How stuck does she seem now?**

Client: Not much. Maybe 0 or 1.

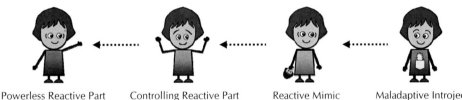

Powerless Reactive Part	Controlling Reactive Part	Reactive Mimic	Maladaptive Introject
Link 1	Link 2	Link 3	Link 4

Therapist: **Very good. So would the four of you like to get together to meet?**

Child parts: Yeah. Cool.

Therapist: **Okay. Come together. Tell me if that feels good.**

Child parts: Yeah.

Therapist: **Very good. Notice that good feeling. Take as long as you need to let it strengthen. Tell me when it's strengthened all the way.** (Strengthened with ABS.)

Child parts: Okay.

Therapist: **So girls, I'd like to help you get totally unstuck at the perfect time. I'm not sure when that will be, hopefully soon. In the meantime I'd like to invite you all to tuck in. Is there anything you'd like to say or ask before you tuck in?**

Child parts: Thank you.

Therapist: **You're welcome. Just find a nice, warm, safe place to tuck in to. You can tuck in with your Resources if you like. Just find a good safe place to wait until the next time you're needed.**

Step 12. Temporary Nature of the Shift

Therapist: **While this intervention has helped this little one get partly unstuck from the mask, we'll have to do the Needs Meeting Protocol later, to help her get totally unstuck. Until then, the mask could reanimate and start delivering the ugly message again. But even if that happens it's STILL harmless, and we can easily switch the dominance back again, in just a few minutes.**

Client: Okay.

Follow-up

Therapist: **When we started talking about your phone call this morning, you reported believing "I don't have a right to stand up for myself." How true does that belief feel now?**

Client: Not at all true.

Therapist: **The costume's message was "You're spoiled and ungrateful. Shame on you." How disturbing is that message now?**

Client: Not at all.

© Copyright 2009 by Shirley Jean Schmidt, MA, LPC. All rights reserved. Duplication in any form without permission is prohibited.

Therapist:	**When you think about the disturbing phone call you got from you mother-in-law this morning, is your reaction any different now?**
Client:	Yes. It still irks me that she made plans without consulting me. But I don't feel paralyzed anymore. I don't feel preoccupied or distracted by it. I can leave here and go run my errands.
Therapist:	**When you think about setting a boundary with your mother-in-law, is your reaction any different now?**
Client:	I can see my husband and I telling her we already have plans for Christmas but that she can take the kids to Hawaii at Spring Break. She might not want to hear that, but tough.

Chapter Summary
....

This chapter described the DNMS Switching the Dominance Protocol for helping maladaptive introjects to heal. A *paradigm shift* is a significant change from one worldview, or way of thinking, to another. This protocol aims for a paradigm shift. The shift occurs when a child part wearing a maladaptive introject mask learns the truth, that the mask is nothing but a harmless recording, that the painful restrictions of childhood are gone, that the freedoms of adulthood are here now, and that one or more loving adult Resource parts of self can meet needs now. This can calm internal conflicts, soothe painful emotions, and quiet negative self-talk. While this chapter focused on how this protocol can treat a simple symptom or problem, it also plays a significant role in selecting introjects for needs meeting work (page 94) and in handling certain types of processing blocks (page 158). The *Switching the Dominance Protocol Worksheet*, in Appendix E, can serve as a helpful guide while you're learning to apply the protocol.

Chapter 4 Notes
....

1. Please note, there is nothing special about telling a reactive part to look "to the right." You could just as well say "look up," "look around," "look to the left," or "look across the room."
2. Saying "I *see* you..." to a child part wearing an introject mask is a figure of speech – like saying "I *see* your point of view. I *see* your value." If you are uncomfortable with that language you can try saying, "I'm aware of you...."

© Copyright 2009 by Shirley Jean Schmidt, MA, LPC. All rights reserved. Duplication in any form without permission is prohibited.

Chapter 5

The Conference Room Protocol

Overview

In Chapter 4 you learned an ego state intervention that calms internal conflicts, soothes painful emotions, and quiets negative self-talk by switching the dominance of a *single* introject associated with a *simple* problem. The Conference Room Protocol involves switching the dominance of *multiple* introjects associated with a *complex* issue. It serves two purposes. (1) By itself it can provide noticeable symptom improvement, and (2) it can help single out the most important wounded child parts to heal with the Needs Meeting Protocol. The Conference Room Protocol is one of several parts in an overall healing cycle.

- In the first part of the cycle you'll guide your client to *identify a set of negative beliefs* associated with a target issue, such as a *specific current problem* or *old attachment wounds*. The DNMS Attachment Needs Ladder questionnaire can help your client identify attachment-wound beliefs.

- Next you'll invite, into an *imagined conference room*, all the reactive parts that hold this set of negative beliefs. Once in the conference room, you'll invite each reactive part, one at a time, to look across the table to see each maladaptive introject they are reacting to. As each introject is identified, you'll switch the dominance. This can result a notable diminishment of internal conflict. It also helps to prepare the introjects for the next healing intervention.

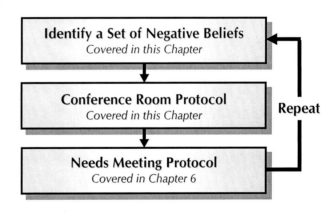

- Next you'll apply the Needs Meeting Protocol (Chapter 6) to help these introjects get totally unstuck. As the introjects get unstuck, the associated reactive parts will get unstuck too, and the negative beliefs the reactive parts had felt to be true, will no longer feel true. Once this protocol is complete, clients typically report a significant improvement in the unwanted behaviors, beliefs, and emotions associated with the targeted issue.

- Finally, you'll cycle through these protocols again, with another target issue (current problem or old attachment wound), until all treatment goals have been met.

A typical client/therapist dialogue is provided at the end of this chapter to illustrate the flow of these first two parts of this cycle. (A client/therapist dialogue of the Needs Meeting Protocol will be provided at the end of Chapter 6.) Forms and worksheets, which simplify the application of these steps, are provided in Appendix E. Look for the *Attachment Needs Ladder questionnaire*, the *Conference Room Map Template*, and the *Conference Room Protocol Worksheet*. This chapter describes the processing as it would proceed without complications. Instructions for handling blocks unique to this intervention are covered on pages 178-183 of Chapter 7.

© Copyright 2009 by Shirley Jean Schmidt, MA, LPC. All rights reserved. Duplication in any form without permission is prohibited.

Finding Negative Beliefs Associated with a Specific Current Problem

Current-problem processing should be considered for specific problems, such as complicated grief, poor money management, or unusual overreactions. It can also be helpful in addressing peak-performance issues (e.g. being a better athlete, actor, or salesman). Consider this option when a client is preoccupied with a specific current problem and needs some relief right away; when a moderate-to-high functioning client is seeking very brief therapy; when a client who has terminated therapy after resolving core issues, returns to address a new issue; or when a client's usual progress through a structured DNMS program is being interrupted by a distracting problem.

In Step 6 of the Conference Room Protocol (see page 90) you'll invite your client to get a mental picture of all the reactive parts, connected to the targeted problem, sitting down in a conference room. There are two ways to invite these reactive parts into the room: the *direct* approach and the *indirect* approach.

- **Direct approach:** To employ the direct approach you'll simply invite into the conference room all the reactive parts associated with a target problem.
- **Indirect approach:** To employ the indirect approach you'll elicit from your client a list of all the negative beliefs associated with the target problem; have her rate, from 0-10, how true each belief feels; then read the beliefs aloud as you invite into the conference room all the reactive parts that hold those beliefs.

The direct approach is recommended for those clients who are especially talkative, inarticulate, or have trouble focusing attention, as they can consume much session time struggling to articulate their negative beliefs.

After completing the Conference Room and Needs Meeting Protocols, you'll check on the processing outcome. If you employed the indirect approach, you'd invite the client to re-rate, from 0-10, how true each negative belief feels. Whether applying the direct or indirect approach, you'd ask the client to report on changes in his perception of the problem. Clients typically report that the targeted problem seems more resolved, and associated negative beliefs no longer feel true. When they return for the next session, they typically report a real improvement in the problem.

Finding Negative Beliefs Associated with Old Attachment Wounds

Attachment-wound processing should be considered for clients who have chronic feelings of inadequacy, poor ego strength, and/or dissociative symptoms stemming from a childhood with abusive, neglectful, or rejecting caregivers.

The Attachment Needs Ladder

The *Attachment Needs Ladder* is a DNMS questionnaire which consists of a list of negative beliefs clients might acquire in childhood if their attachment needs were not met well. It was developed from the assumption that the most efficient healing would occur if the most wounding caregiver/introject attachment messages were identified early in treatment, and processed in order of importance. The beliefs are compiled in four thematic sections – organized in order of importance, like rungs on a ladder. You'll guide your clients to rate, from 0-10, how true each belief feels. (10 is totally true.) Any rating above zero is considered an *endorsement*. The Rungs are summarized below. A copy of the questionnaire is provided in Appendix E, page 236.

Rung 1: Existence

Rung 1 can help you elicit a client's beliefs about self associated with issues of existence. Clients who felt unwanted, neglected, and rejected in childhood may endorse Rung 1 statements. Statements include:

- I don't exist.
- I shouldn't exist.
- It's not safe to exist.
- I don't deserve to exist.
- Shame on me for existing.
- I'm so alone, there's no point in existing.
- My existence is completely irrelevant.
- My existence is completely unimportant.
- My existence is completely unacceptable.

© Copyright 2009 by Shirley Jean Schmidt, MA, LPC. All rights reserved. Duplication in any form without permission is prohibited.

Rung 2: Basic Safety

Rung 2 can help you elicit a client's beliefs about self associated with issues of physical, sexual, and emotional safety. Clients who felt *physically and/or sexually abused* in childhood may endorse Rung 2A statements. Statements include:

- There is no safe place for me – physically and/or sexually.
- I am completely vulnerable – physically and/or sexually.
- Everyone is frightening – physically and/or sexually.
- Everyone is dangerous – physically and/or sexually.
- I don't deserve to be safe – physically and/or sexually.
- Everyone is out to physically and/or sexually hurt me.
- I must mistrust everyone to stay physically and/or sexually safe.
- I must hide to stay physically and/or sexually safe.
- I must be invisible to stay physically and/or sexually safe.
- I must be a pleaser or peacemaker to stay physically and/or sexually safe.
- I must be intimidating to stay physically and/or sexually safe.
- I must keep my guard up all the time to stay physically and/or sexually safe.
- I must be ready to threaten or attack all the time, to stay physically and/or sexually safe.

Clients who felt *emotionally unsafe* in childhood will endorse Rung 2B statements. Statements include:

- There is no safe place for me – emotionally.
- I am completely vulnerable – emotionally.
- Everyone is frightening – emotionally.
- Everyone is dangerous – emotionally.
- I don't deserve to be safe – emotionally.
- Everyone is out to emotionally hurt me.
- I must mistrust everyone to stay emotionally safe.
- I must hide to stay emotionally safe.
- I must be invisible to stay emotionally safe.
- I must be a pleaser or peacemaker to stay emotionally safe.
- I must be intimidating to stay emotionally safe.
- I must keep my guard up all the time to stay emotionally safe.
- I must be ready to threaten or attack all the time, to stay emotionally safe.

Rung 3: Sense of Self

Rung 3 can help you elicit a client's beliefs about self associated with issues of personal identity, differentiation with others, enmeshment, and personal boundaries. Clients who felt unsupported in developing a sense of *personal identity* in childhood may endorse Rung 3A statements. Statements include:

- I don't have a self.
- I shouldn't have a self.
- I don't deserve to have a self.
- Shame on me if I want a self.
- I must not be seen or heard.
- I must not grow.
- I must not individuate.
- I must not have needs.
- I don't matter.
- I must rely on others to tell me who I am.
- I must rely on others to tell me what I feel. (e.g. angry, sad, afraid)
- I must rely on others to tell me what I like. (e.g. red vs. blue)
- I must rely on others to tell me what to believe.
- It's acceptable for me to be an object, but not a person.

Clients who felt *boundary violations* in childhood may endorse Rung 3B statements. Statements include:

- I must let others smother or engulf me.
- I must not set or maintain interpersonal boundaries.
- I must do for others, even when it's not good for me.

Rung 4: Relationship to Others

Rung 4 can help you elicit a client's beliefs about how to relate to others. It can help reveal tendencies towards preoccupied and dismissive attachment styles. Clients with beliefs consistent with *preoccupied attachment* may endorse Rung 4A statements. Statements include:

- I must depend on others to feel secure.
- I must get lots of attention from others to feel secure.
- I must be emotionally close to others to feel secure.
- I cannot tolerate being alone.
- I cannot tolerate rejection.
- I cannot tolerate people leaving me.
- I cannot tolerate criticism.
- Others must meet my emotional needs, because I cannot.
- Others must comfort me when I'm feeling upset or insecure, because I cannot.

Clients who have beliefs consistent with either one or *both preoccupied and dismissive attachment* may endorse Rung 4B statements. Statements include:

- I am, and always will be, completely alone.
- People will accept me if I don't have needs.
- People will reject me if I have needs.
- People will inevitably ignore me.
- People will inevitably disappoint me.
- People will inevitably reject me.
- People will inevitably abandon me.

© Copyright 2009 by Shirley Jean Schmidt, MA, LPC. All rights reserved. Duplication in any form without permission is prohibited.

Clients with beliefs consistent with *dismissive attachment* may endorse Rung 4C statements. Statements include:

- I must rely solely on myself.
- I must not depend on others.
- I must not get emotionally close to others.
- I must not let others get emotionally close to me.
- I must not ask for comfort, advice, or help.

- I must not share my private thoughts/feelings.
- I must not show others how I feel deep down.
- I must comfort myself when I'm upset, because others cannot.
- I must meet my own emotional needs, because others cannot.

Administering the Attachment Needs Ladder

The Attachment Needs Ladder must be administered verbally. Most of the time you'll elicit ratings from just one Rung or Section at a time – getting ratings on a set of beliefs connected to a group of related ego states that you'll process together.

Use a Vulnerable-State-of-Mind Prompt

Because irrational statements, like "I don't deserve to exist," may feel untrue to a client's the most adult self, you must prompt your clients to rate each statement from a *vulnerable state of mind*. This should elicit ratings from wounded child parts. There are several ways you can do this.

- **Option 1:** Direct the client's attention to a *specific past vulnerability*. This could be any unresolved traumatic or wounding event. For example, you might ask something like:

    When you think about (your mother rejecting you in childhood), does the statement (I don't deserve to exist) feel true?

- **Option 2:** Direct the client's attention to a *specific recent vulnerability*. This could be any recent event that triggered an irrational, child-like response. For example, you might ask something like:

    When you think about (the irrational anger you felt towards your wife yesterday), does the statement (I don't deserve to exist) feel true?

- **Option 3:** Direct the client's attention to a *potential future vulnerability*. This could be any future event that is expected to trigger an irrational, child-like response. For example, you might ask something like:

    When you think about (how devastated you'll feel if you don't pass the bar exam), does the statement (I don't deserve to exist) feel true?

- **Option 4:** Ask the client whether *wounded child parts* believe a statement is true. This option should be reserved for clients with a heightened awareness of their wounded ego states. For example, you might ask something like:

    Are there any wounded child parts who believe the statement (I don't deserve to exist) is true?

    Or you might ask:

    When you think about (your rejecting mother), are there any wounded child parts who believe the statement (I don't deserve to exist) is true?

When selecting a prompt, consider the nature of the specific Rung or Section you are targeting, when prompting a vulnerable state of mind. For example you might prompt:

- Rung 1 with memories of childhood neglect or rejection.
- Rung 2A with memories of incest or domestic violence.
- Rung 3A with experiences of repressed self-expression.
- Rung 4A with current examples of being too needy.
- Rung 4C with current examples of social isolation.

Record the prompts used for each Rung or Section on the Attachment Needs Ladder. Later, when you ask for follow-up ratings, use those prompts again.

© Copyright 2009 by Shirley Jean Schmidt, MA, LPC. All rights reserved. Duplication in any form without permission is prohibited.

Getting the Ratings

When you ask whether a statement feels true, a client will answer "yes" or "no." If the client answers "yes," the statement might feel a *little* true, *somewhat* true, or *very* true. To find out *how true* it feels, ask:

> *How true does it feel (0-10) when it feels the most true?*

Record each rating on the questionnaire. Once a client has rated all the statements on a Rung or Section, ask if he has any *additional* negative beliefs related to that theme. If so, add them to the list, and record their ratings for each additional statement.

Rung 2A Processing Options

Give your clients two options for processing Rung 2A beliefs about physical and sexual safety.

- ***Process physical/sexual safety statements combined.*** When combining the themes, invite the client to rate the statements exactly as they are written on the Ladder. For example: *Everyone is out to physically and/or sexually hurt me,* and *I must hide to stay physically and/or sexually safe.* Then apply the Conference Room Protocol to all the physical/sexual safety statements endorsed, followed by the Needs Meeting Protocol.

- ***Process physical and sexual safety statements separately.*** Clients with a lot of physical and sexual trauma history may need Rung 2A administered twice – once focused only on physical safety, and once focused only on sexual safety. Let the client choose which to start with. If starting with physical safety, invite the client to rate all 13 Rung 2A statements, without the word *sexually*. For example: *Everyone is out to* <u>*physically*</u> *hurt me,* and *I must hide to stay* <u>*physically*</u> *safe.* After applying the Conference Room Protocol to all the physical safety statements endorsed, follow with the Needs Meeting Protocol. Then, to process sexual safety, invite the client to rate all 13 Rung 2A statements, without the word *physically*. For example: *Everyone is out to* <u>*sexually*</u> *hurt me,* and *I must hide to stay* <u>*sexually*</u> *safe.* Again apply the Conference Room Protocol to all the sexual safety statements endorsed, followed by the Needs Meeting Protocol.

Combining Rungs or Sections

Most of the time you'll elicit ratings from just one Rung or Section at a time, but occasionally it will be appropriate to combine statements from two Rungs or Sections. For example, if a client's only endorsement for Rung 1 is "It's not safe to exist," it may be appropriate to go ahead and elicit Rung 2A ratings, and process Rungs 1 and 2A statements together. Or, if a client only endorses two items on Rung 2A, it may be appropriate to go ahead and elicit Rung 2B ratings, and process Rungs 2A and 2B statements together. When in doubt about whether to proceed this way, ask the client what he would prefer to do. Combining Rungs and Sections can sometimes lead to more efficient processing, but some clients will become emotionally overwhelmed when confronted with processing more than a few statements at a time.

Follow-Up and Repeat

After completing the Conference Room and Needs Meeting Protocols on a Rung or Section, check on the outcome. Invite clients to re-rate the Attachment Needs Ladder statements that were initially endorsed. Clients typically report those negative beliefs no longer feel true. Then repeat this process for the next Rung or Section on the Ladder, until all four Rungs have been completed. For example, three to four months of processing might go like this:

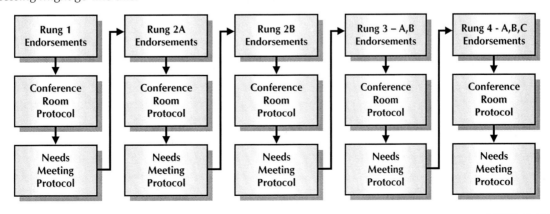

© Copyright 2009 by Shirley Jean Schmidt, MA, LPC. All rights reserved. Duplication in any form without permission is prohibited.

Conference Room Protocol

In 1991, George Fraser[1] introduced the *dissociative table technique* as a means for working with the alters of patients with dissociative identity disorder. He proposed inviting alters to an imagined meeting place (such as a table in a conference room), so they would be able to communicate more effectively with the therapist and with each other. The DNMS Conference Room Protocol borrows from Fraser's idea.

Providing the Client a Big Picture Overview

Before beginning the protocol, you'll provide your clients a general overview of the big picture. Start with a review of all the options and steps for selecting ego states for processing – including the options of processing a current problem or an attachment wound. Show clients the Attachment Needs Ladder, and invite them to casually note whether the statements seem familiar or evoke an emotional reaction. Clients who have a strong reaction to these statements should probably process attachment wounds. Tell clients who wish to process a current issue about the two ways to proceed: (1) the *indirect approach*, which involves listing all the negative beliefs associated with the problem, then inviting forward all the reactive parts that believe those statements; or (2) the *direct approach*, which involves simply inviting forward all the reactive parts connected to the problem.

You'll describe the Conference Room Protocol and Needs Meeting Protocol steps. You can explain the steps with visual aids, such as the Conference Room Map template, illustrations from this book, the Home Study Course Module 1 slide show,[2] the DNMS Flip Chart,[3] and/or drawings that you generate. Tell clients that once the needs meeting work is complete they'll be asked to re-rate the negative beliefs, and reassess their sense of the current issue. If the beliefs no longer feel true, and/or if the targeted issue feels largely resolved, processing would then continue with either the next Rung on the Attachment Needs Ladder, or another specific current problem. Explain that if a targeted issue did not feel fully resolved following the Needs Meeting Protocol, processing would focus on finding and healing any additional introjects connected to the issue.

Step 1: Preparing the Client the First Time

Step 1 applies only to first time clients. Just before starting this protocol for the first time, go over a few details, to reduce the possibility of misunderstandings confounding the process. Explain each of the following points:

- **Reactive Parts to Beliefs Ratio**

  Explain that you'll read aloud the list of negative beliefs as you invite all the reactive parts holding those beliefs into the conference room. There may or may not be one reactive part per belief. For example, there could be one reactive part holding four beliefs, or three reactive parts holding one belief.

- **Variations in How Reactive Parts Appear**

  Clients will usually get a mental picture of the reactive parts that appear in the conference room. Explain that there are different ways the parts might appear. For example, she might get a vivid picture, with an obvious number of reactive parts, and a clear sense of their ages and moods; or she might get a vague

© Copyright 2009 by Shirley Jean Schmidt, MA, LPC. All rights reserved. Duplication in any form without permission is prohibited.

picture, uncertainty about the number of parts, and no clear sense of their ages or moods. It's also possible that no reactive parts will appear at all. Encourage your client to accurately describe any mental picture that comes up – whether or not it makes sense.

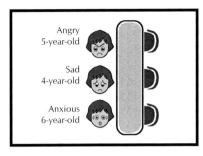  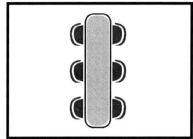

- ***Reactive Parts to Introjects Ratio***

  Explain that each reactive part will be asked to look across the table to see the introject she is reacting to. There may or may not be one introject per reactive part. For example, one reactive part might be reacting to three introjects. Likewise three reactive parts might be reacting to a single introject.

 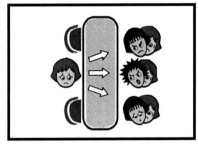 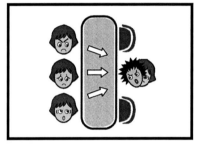

- ***A Reactive Part Appears Across the Table***

  Explain that sometimes another reactive part (instead of an introject) will appear across the table. Such a reactive part would be invited to sit on the other side with the other reactive parts, then look back across the table to see who she is reacting to.

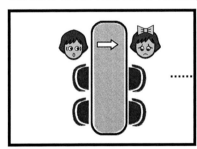 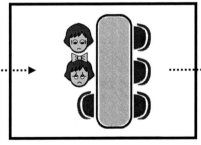 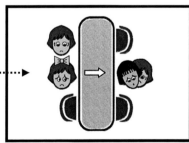

- ***Parts are Distinct and Separate***

  Sometimes clients new to the process get confused in the middle of the process, and erroneously assume that the reactive part looking across the table is the same part of self as the child part wearing the introject mask. This type of misunderstanding is more likely to happen when these two parts of self are the same age. This misunderstanding can create big processing problems if a reactive part answers protocol questions intended for a child part wearing an introject mask. Make a clear, color-coded drawing that clarifies this distinction to help clients see that these two parts of self are distinct and separate. (For example, you could draw the reactive parts in blue, the introject mask in red, and the child part wearing the mask in green.)

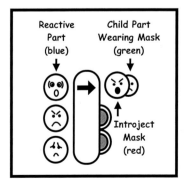

© Copyright 2009 by Shirley Jean Schmidt, MA, LPC. All rights reserved. Duplication in any form without permission is prohibited.

Step 2: Recording Information on the Conference Room Map

In Step 2 you'll start filling in the *Conference Room Map* template with the client's name, date, and issue or Rung. (See page 104 for an example of the completed map that goes with the sample dialogue provided in this chapter.) Throughout the Conference Room Protocol you'll be recording information on the map. You'll find a Conference Room Map template in Appendix E, page 240. Make copies of it to use in your sessions.

Step 3: Connecting to Resources

In Step 3 you'll invite your client to connect to her Resources. If a client is feeling disturbing emotions, after just rating the Attachment Needs Ladder statements, invite her to shift into a more neutral state of mind before trying to connect to Resources. Sometimes telling a few jokes can help. Then invite your client to connect to her Resources by saying something like:

> *Connect to your Resources. (Let me know if you need my help connecting.) Tell me when you're connected.*

Once your client reports she's connected, turn on ABS and say:

> *Let that get as strong as it wants to. Tell me when that's strengthened all the way.*

When your client says, "okay," turn ABS off.

Step 4: Picturing the Conference Room

In Step 4 you'll invite your client to begin picturing the conference room imagery. Say something like:

> *Picture a conference room with a table and chairs. Now picture the Resources in the conference room. Tell me when you've got the picture.*

Step 5: Checking for Processing Blocks

In Step 5 you'll check for unconscious blocks by asking your client something like:

> *When you think about beginning this conference room work with the child parts connected with (the target issue), for the purpose of identifying and working with the associated introjects, what do you notice in your body now?*

There are three possible body reactions. (1) The body might feel clear, indicating a readiness to begin; (2) the body might feel a little discomfort, indicating benign apprehension but no block; or (3) the body might feel uncomfortable or contracted, indicating a block. Any blocks revealed here must be addressed before proceeding. The most frequently used intervention for overcoming blocks at this point, is found on page 100 in this chapter. Instructions for handling all other processing complications and blocks are provided in Chapter 7.

Step 6: Inviting Parts into the Conference Room

In Step 6 you'll invite forward all the reactive parts that are associated with the target issue, with something like:

> *I'd like to invite into the conference room, to sit on one side of the table, all the reactive parts of self that are connected to (overspending). When you're ready, tell me what you notice.*   OR

> *I'd like to invite into the conference room, to sit on one side of the table, all the parts of self who believe the following statements.... (each negative belief is read aloud). When you're ready, tell me what you notice.*

© Copyright 2009 by Shirley Jean Schmidt, MA, LPC. All rights reserved. Duplication in any form without permission is prohibited.

Your client may give a precise description, like: "I see a baby, a toddler, and a four-year-old," or "I see a fearful child, an angry child, and a sad child." Or she may give a *vague* description, like: "There may be 3 or 4 present, but I can't see them clearly," or "There may be 20 or 30. They all look ghostly."

If your client provides any initial details, such as age or mood, about any of the reactive parts, record them on the Conference Room Map. If a client doesn't reveal much initially, expect to learn the details later in the protocol, when you begin to dialogue with specific reactive parts. Record the details whenever they are revealed.

Step 7: Engaging the Most Upset Reactive Part

In Step 7 you'll engage the most upset reactive part at the table in a dialogue. Record on the Conference Room Map, the key pieces of information you collect, along with a drawing of the reactive part's mood. Start by asking your client to identify the most upset reactive part at the table, with something like:

> *Which reactive part seems to be the most upset now?* OR *Which reactive part needs my attention first?*

Once your client has identified a specific reactive part, ask:

> *May I speak with this part?*

When permission is granted, begin your dialogue with that reactive part, with something like:

> *Welcome, I'm glad you're here.*

Then, if you don't yet know the reactive part's age, ask:

> *How old are you?*

And if you don't yet know the part's mood, ask:

> *What kind of mood are you in?*

Then say to the reactive part:

> *I'm guessing you've been stuck in the past a long time. Is that right?*

When the reactive part answers "yes," ask:

> *How stuck are you, 0-10, if 10 is totally stuck?*

When the reactive part answers with a rating, follow up with:

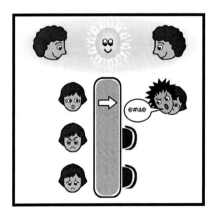

> *I'd like to help you get unstuck, and you can help me. When you're ready, take a look at that empty spot across the table from you. In a moment you'll see appear in that spot <u>the part (or parts) of self</u> that you're reacting to. When you're ready, tell me what you notice.*

If a reactive part is confused by the notion of seeing a part of self across the table, try rewording the instruction to:

> *In a moment you'll see appear in that spot <u>an image of the person or persons</u> that you've been reacting to. When you're ready, tell me what you notice.*

Step 8: Classifying the Part of Self that Appears Across the Table

In Step 7 the reactive part will usually report seeing a part of self appear across the table. Get a full description. Ask questions like:

> *Who does this part look like? What mood is this part in? Is this part conveying a message?*

© Copyright 2009 by Shirley Jean Schmidt, MA, LPC. All rights reserved. Duplication in any form without permission is prohibited.

- ### If the Part Appears Silent

  If a part appears *silent*, the message is non-verbal. To elicit the message ask something like:

  > *If this part's body language or facial expression could be translated into words, what would that message be?*

  For example, a reactive part saw his dad silently walking away. When asked for the message conveyed by dad's body language, the reactive part reported it was, "You're not important to me."

- ### If the Part Appears as a Metaphor

  If a part appears as a metaphor (e.g. rock, animal, monster, or witch), ask something like:

  > *Does (this metaphor) have a message for you?*

  If so, ask:

  > *Does this message remind you of someone?*

  For example, an aggressive dragon appeared, conveying the message, "Leave me alone or I'll burn you." The reactive part perceived the dragon as her mother. When a rock appeared conveying the message, "Leave me alone, don't hurt me," the client recognized it was another fearful reactive part. (See Chapter 4, page 66, for more information about parts appearing as metaphors.)

What Might Appear

There are several types and combinations of ego states that can appear across the table. Here they are:

1. **One Ego State Mimicking One Person:** One ego state might appear, literally or metaphorically, looking like a wounding role model (e.g. mother or father) conveying that role model's wounding message. This a *presumptive introject*, which means it is probably an introject, but it could also be a reactive mimic.

2. **One Ego State Mimicking More than One Person:** One ego state might appear, literally or metaphorically, looking like more than one wounding role model (e.g. mother and father). For example, a child part might be wearing (a) two masks conveying the messages of two different role models, (b) a composite mask that looks like several role models combined, conveying a combined message, or (c) one mask that looks like one role model that is conveying the message of several role models. Again any one of these would be a presumptive introject – probably an introject, but possibly a reactive mimic.

3. **Multiple Ego States Mimicking Others:** More than one ego state might appear looking literally or metaphorically like wounding role models (e.g. mother and father) conveying that role model's wounding messages. All of them would be presumptive introjects. They are probably all introjects , but one or more could also be a reactive mimic.

© Copyright 2009 by Shirley Jean Schmidt, MA, LPC. All rights reserved. Duplication in any form without permission is prohibited.

4. **A Child or Adult Part Issuing a Warning or Threat:** An ego state might appear looking literally or metaphorically like the client as a wounded child delivering a warning, threat, command, or admonition, such as "Keep quiet" or "Don't rock the boat." This would be a controlling reactive part.

5. **A Wounded Child or Adult Part with a Negative Behavior, Belief, or Emotion:** An ego state might appear looking literally or metaphorically like the client (often as a wounded child), either (a) engaging in a negative behavior, (b) stating a negative belief, and/or (c) feeling a painful emotion. Such ego states would be powerless reactive parts.

When a Classification is Difficult to Make

It'll usually be easy for you to tell whether a part that appears is a presumptive introject or a reactive part. But when the determination is difficult to make, ask the part something like:

Are you reacting to someone or mimicking someone?

If the answer is "reacting to someone," this is a reactive part. If the answer is "reacting and mimicking," this is probably a reactive mimic. If the answer is "mimicking," this is probably a maladaptive introject.

At this point in the Conference Room Protocol you only need to discern the presumptive introjects from the controlling and powerless reactive parts. Once you start switching the dominance of the presumptive introject (see Step 10 page 94) you'll discover whether the part is a maladaptive introject or reactive mimic.

Clues to Classifying Parts of Self

Clues That Differentiate Introjects & Reactive Parts	Powerless Reactive Part	Controlling Reactive Part	Controlling Reactive Mimic	Maladaptive Introject
Part (mask) looks like wounding role model.	No.	No.	Yes.	Yes.
Conveys wounding message (typically a "you" message).	No.	Yes – In reaction to a role model's message.	Yes –Mimicking a role model's message.	Yes –Mimicking a role model's message.
Reacting or mimicking?	Reacting.	Reacting.	Both.	Mimicking.
Mask (or costume) present.	Maybe.	Maybe.	Yes.	Yes.
Issues warnings, threats, commands, or admonitions.	No.	Yes.	Only if the wounding role model issued them.	Only if the wounding role model issued them.
Reveals behaviors, beliefs, or emotions suggestive of being wounded. ("I" statements).	Yes.	No.	No.	Not usually.
Mask is part of a valued coping strategy created by child part wearing it. *	If a mask is present – yes.	If a mask is present – yes.	Yes.*	No.*

*Assessed in Step 2 of the Switching the Dominance Protocol

© Copyright 2009 by Shirley Jean Schmidt, MA, LPC. All rights reserved. Duplication in any form without permission is prohibited.

When a Reactive Part Appears

If/when a powerless reactive part, a controlling reactive part, or a reactive mimic appear across the table, invite that part to sit with the other reactive parts on the other side of the table. Then say something like:

> *Welcome, I'm glad you're here. How old are you?* Then: *What kind of mood are you in?* Then: *I'm guessing you've been stuck in the past a long time. 0-10, how stuck are you?*

Record the answers on the Conference Room Map. Then say:

> *I'd like to help you get unstuck, and you can help me. When you're ready, take a look at that empty spot across the table from you. In a moment you'll see appear in that spot the part (or parts) of self that you're reacting to. When you're ready, tell me what you notice.*

Again determine whether the part that appears across the table is a reactive part or a presumptive introject. If a reactive part appears again, keep looking for the introject. Once a presumptive introject appears, proceed to Step 9.

Step 9: Collecting Information about the Presumptive Introject

In Step 9 you'll collect more information about the presumptive introject that has appeared across the table. Find out the name of the role model the mask is mimicking; the role model mask's verbal or non-verbal wounding message; the role model mask's mood; and a 0-10 rating of the level of disturbance evoked by the message. If a reactive part sees more than one role model appear across the table, find out if she's seeing *two separate* ego states (e.g. a mom introject and a dad introject) or, a single *combination* ego state (e.g. one part wearing two masks). Record all this information on your Conference Room Map template (page 240).

Make Sure the Wounding Message is Actually Wounding

An introject message should reveal one or more of the following:

- contempt for the client;
- a threat to emotional safety (such as threat of rejection, neglect, abandonment, or enmeshment);
- a threat of physical harm;
- an inappropriate assignment of responsibility;
- a person's negative belief about him or herself; and/or
- a faulty notion about the world.

Introjects can mirror wounding messages that were conveyed both verbally and non-verbally, and messages that were inferred from others' actions and inactions. Messages that were conveyed to the client verbally are usually the easiest for the client to talk about. The non-verbal and inferred messages are sometimes more difficult to articulate. When a client discloses a message that is neutrally worded or missing specificity, encourage elaboration. For example, a reactive part reported seeing her angry father saying "It's time to take out the trash." When asked for more details, the part revealed, her father meant it was time for her to leave – she was the trash. Suggestions for identifying and handling problematic introject messages are provided in Chapter 7, page 171.

Both the nature of the message and the level of disturbance evoked by the message should match the client's history. If they do not match, find out why. A mismatch may indicate a processing block or confusion that requires an intervention. Once all the details about a presumptive introject has been collected and recorded, proceed to Step 10.

Step 10: Switching the Dominance

In Step 10 you'll follow the Switching the Dominance Protocol steps, as described on pages 62-69 of Chapter 4. As soon as you start switching the dominance, you'll find out if the part is an introject or a reactive mimic when you ask the part wearing the mask if she likes or needs the mask, or if it serves a useful purpose.

© Copyright 2009 by Shirley Jean Schmidt, MA, LPC. All rights reserved. Duplication in any form without permission is prohibited.

If the part says something like, "Yes – the mask helps me, I need to keep it," it is a *reactive mimic*. Invite this part to move to the other side of the table, to sit with the other reactive parts, then repeat the Conference Room Protocol steps 7-10.

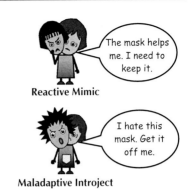

Reactive Mimic

But if the part says something like, "No – I hate this mask, get it off me," the *maladaptive introject* classification is confirmed, and you can continue switching the dominance.

Maladaptive Introject

Concluding the Switching the Dominance Protocol

When you get to the end of the Switching the Dominance Protocol, say to the child part with the pocketed mask:

> I'd like to help you get totally unstuck from the remains of the mask at the perfect time. I'm not sure when that will be – hopefully soon. In the meantime, let's check across the table and see how the (x-year-old reactive part) is doing.

Then say to the x-year-old reactive part something like:

> A few minutes ago, you reported feeling pretty stuck. Between 0-10, how stuck are you feeling right now?

Record this new rating on the Conference Room Map.

If the Reactive Part that Identified the Introject is Still Pretty Stuck

If this x-year-old reactive part reports feeling mostly unstuck, proceed to Step 11 below. But if she's stuck at a level 4 or higher, ask if she's reacting to yet another part of self. If she says "yes," say something like:

> When you're ready, look back across the table. In a moment you'll see appear another part of self that you're reacting to. When you're ready, tell me what you notice.

When the next part appears across the table, repeat Conference Room Protocol steps 8-10.

Step 11: Repeating Steps 7-10

In Step 11 you'll repeat Steps 7-10 with each reactive part at the table. Once you've finished working with all the reactive parts and introjects in the conference room, double check that all the reactive parts connected to the target issue are at the table.

- **Double-checking a List of Negative Beliefs**

  If you're working from a list of negative beliefs (e.g. Rung 3), you're going to re-read the list aloud to the client. First, say something like:

  > I'm going to re-read the list of beliefs you endorsed. Let me know if you feel we've identified all the reactive parts connected to these statements. If we've left anyone out, let me know, so we can bring them into the conference room now.

- **Double-checking a Specific Current Problem**

  If you're targeting a specific current problem (e.g. overspending), ask something like:

  > Are you aware of any additional reactive parts connected to your (overspending)?

If a client identifies one or more additional reactive parts, repeat Steps 7-10 with each new part. If a client believes that all the reactive parts connected to the targeted issue have been identified, and all the associated introjects have been processed, proceed to Step 12.

© Copyright 2009 by Shirley Jean Schmidt, MA, LPC. All rights reserved. Duplication in any form without permission is prohibited.

Step 12: Preparing for the Needs Meeting Protocol

Selecting Wounded Parts for Needs Meeting Processing

In Step 12 you'll prepare a client to begin the Needs Meeting Protocol. You'll invite the client to choose which introject(s) to process first. At the very least, one introject should be processed at a time, but the most efficient healing will occur when several are processed together. Group processing usually works very well, since all the introjects are related to a common theme. Reactive parts typically get totally unstuck automatically as the introjects they have been reacting to get unstuck – so including one or more of them in the needs meeting work is entirely optional. Say something like:

> Now we're ready to start the needs meeting work. There are (three) introjects and (three) reactive parts at the conference table. Ultimately we'll want to process all (three) introjects. We can work with one at a time, or we could work with several together. In addition, we can process one or more of the reactive parts along with the introjects, but they will likely get totally unstuck automatically as the introjects heal – so including them in the needs meeting work is optional. What do you think would be best?

Sometimes, when there are many introjects at the conference table, clients prefer to select a few at a time for needs meeting work. For example, by the end of the Rung 1 conference room work Jody had 8 reactive parts and 12 introjects at the table. She decided to do the needs meeting with the introjects only – a few at a time. The Needs Meeting Protocol was applied first to the five 5 conveying threatening messages, then to the 7 introjects conveying *rejecting* messages. After all 12 were unstuck, the Rung 1 statements no longer felt true.

Starting the Needs Meeting Protocol Immediately

If you're ready to begin the Needs Meeting Protocol immediately, you may need to first tuck in child parts that the client has chosen to exclude from the processing. Say to those parts, something like:

> Thanks to each of you for your hard work today. I'd like to invite each of you to find a nice warm safe cozy place to tuck in to. You can tuck in separately, each with your very own set of Resources, or tuck in as a group. Just find a good safe place to wait until the next time you're needed.

Then, say to the parts selected for needs meeting, something like:

> Let's take the table out of the room. Little ones, gather together in the center of the room, and let the Resources surround you.

- **Cloning Resources for Many Child Parts**

  When there are many child parts to process (e.g. 10 or more), a client might prefer to do the processing with more than three Resources. Fortunately, as discussed in Chapter 3 (page 47), the Resources can be cloned. Ask the client:

  > How many sets of Resources would the child parts like?

  When the client has provided a number (e.g. three sets of Resources) say something like:

  > Notice (three) sets of Resources surrounding the (12) little ones in the center of the room.

- **Checking for Processing Blocks**

  Check for processing blocks before starting the protocol. Ask something like:

  > When you think about beginning the Needs Meeting Protocol now, to help these little ones get totally unstuck, what do you notice in your body?

  There are three possible body reactions: (1) The body might feel clear, indicating a readiness to begin; (2) the body might feel a little discomfort, indicating benign apprehension but no block; or (3) the body might feel uncomfortable or contracted, indicating a block. Any blocks revealed here must be addressed before proceeding.

© Copyright 2009 by Shirley Jean Schmidt, MA, LPC. All rights reserved. Duplication in any form without permission is prohibited.

- *Starting the Needs Meeting Protocol*

   When you're ready to start the Needs Meeting Protocol, go to Step 4, Strengthening a Sense of Safety. Ask:

   > *Does it feel safe and comfortable with the Resources?*

   If the child parts answer "yes," strengthen the sense of safety with ABS.

Starting the Needs Meeting Protocol Later

If you plan to begin the Needs Meeting Protocol later (e.g. the next session), invite all the reactive parts and introjects to tuck in. But before they tuck in, you may wish to give them the option of meeting each other. You might say something like:

> *Would the (six) of you like to get together to meet? The Resources can serve you punch and cookies if you like.*

If they choose to meet, and the meeting feels good, strengthen the positive experience with ABS. When they are ready to tuck in say something like:

> *Thanks to each of you for your hard work today. In a few moments I'm going to invite you to tuck in. Is there anything you'd like to say or ask before you tuck in?*

After the child parts have responded, and you've addressed any concerns they raised, say:

> *When you're ready, find a nice warm safe cozy place to tuck in to. You can tuck in separately, each with your very own set of Resources, or tuck in as a group. Just find a good safe place to wait until the next time you're needed.*

Later, when you start the Needs Meeting Protocol, begin with Step 1, *Connecting to the Resources*.

Other Protocol Issues

This section briefly discusses some additional topics relevant to the Conference Room Protocol processing.

Target Flexibility

Even if a client has chosen to focus on healing attachment wounds with the Attachment Needs Ladder, you can offer some flexibility, week to week, in choosing what to work on. For example, if a client who is half way through the Attachment Needs Ladder and comes in one day completely distracted by an urgent current problem, she could opt to target that problem right away – either with just the Switching the Dominance Protocol, or in combination with the Needs Meeting Protocol. Once that work is complete, the Ladder work can be resumed. If a client has a specific, unresolved problem after completing all four Rungs of the Attachment Needs Ladder, that can still be targeted.

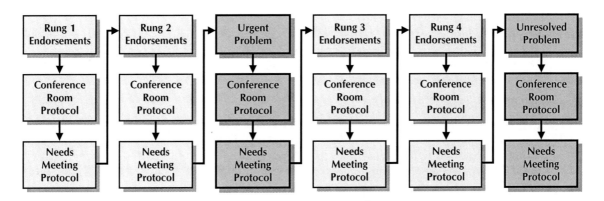

© Copyright 2009 by Shirley Jean Schmidt, MA, LPC. All rights reserved. Duplication in any form without permission is prohibited.

Reactive Parts Disappear in the Conference Room

Sometimes in Step 6, when reactive parts are invited into the conference room, a client reports many reactive parts show up. Later, after the dominance of an introject has been switched, the client reports fewer reactive parts are at the table. For example, at the start of the process Arlene reported that about 12 vague, ill-defined child parts had appeared into the conference room. She was unclear about their ages and moods, but was able to report that a fearful eight-year-old was the most upset. This reactive part looked across the table and saw a father introject. After the dominance of the father introject had been switched, Arlene reported just 9 reactive parts remained at the table. She reported that a sad ten-year-old was the most upset. This reactive part looks across the table and saw a mother introject. After the dominance of the mother introject had been switched, Arlene reported seeing only six reactive parts at the table. At first glance it appeared that some reactive parts had disappeared, but more likely they were consolidating, as each threatening introject mask message got silenced.

Adult Parts Appear in the Conference Room

Most DNMS processing involves wounded child parts, but some clients can legitimately have parts of self stuck in adulthood wounds too. Rebecca was in her 40s. She experienced physical abuse in childhood, and in a marriage she ended in her 30s. While working on Rung 2A, four reactive parts appeared in the conference room. One was a fearful 30-year-old. She looked across the table and saw an abusive ex-husband introject. Under the ex-husband costume was a 28-year-old part. This made sense in light of her history, so we proceeded with the processing as usual.

Many Reactive Parts Appear

Sometimes a client will report that an overwhelming number of reactive parts have responded to the invitation to take a seat in the conference room – too many to fit in the room. There are several ways to handle this. Discuss these options then let your client choose.

- **Enlarge the Conference Room:** *You* can invite the client to enlarge or modify the conference room to accommodate all the child parts, then proceed with the protocol as usual.
- **Invite One Reactive Part at a Time:** You can tuck in all but one reactive part – the one that is the most upset. Invite that most upset reactive part into the conference room, then proceed with the protocol as usual. When the dominance of the first introject has been switched, invite the next most upset child part into the room to identify the next introject. Proceed this way until all the reactive parts have been invited into the room, and the dominance of each associated introject has been switched. When there are many reactive parts, this may take several sessions to complete. This option is preferable for clients who are easily overwhelmed.

Working with an Overwhelming Number of Introjects

The Conference Room Protocol typically takes one or two sessions to complete. It usually reveals about two to five introjects connected to a target issue. Once the dominance of each has been switched, clients are invited to begin the Needs Meeting Protocol. They are given the option to do needs meeting with all the introjects at once, or a few at a time.

But sometimes the Conference Room Protocol unfolds slowly, over many sessions, revealing an overwhelming number of introjects. At such times a client might prefer to postpone completion of the Conference Room Protocol to apply the Needs Meeting Protocol to a selection of introjects. For example, say 20 reactive parts enter the conference room. The first four identify 12 introjects. After the dominance of each is switched, the client chooses to start the Needs Meeting Protocol with those 12 introjects. Once that work is complete, the Conference Room Protocol is resumed with the remaining 16 reactive parts.

© Copyright 2009 by Shirley Jean Schmidt, MA, LPC. All rights reserved. Duplication in any form without permission is prohibited.

Resuming the Conference Room Protocol

Sometimes the Conference Room Protocol takes more than one session to complete. In a follow-up session, review with the client what had occurred in the previous session. Here's a sample dialogue: "So Christi, last week you reported three reactive parts came into the conference room when I read your Rung 1 endorsements. One part was fearful, one was angry, and another was sad. I spoke to the fearful one and discovered she was age 8, and feeling stuck at about 9. She looked across the table and saw your angry father delivering the message, 'Since the day you were born you have completely ruined my life.' The father costume was being worn by a 2-year-old part. After we switched the dominance of the father introject, the fearful reactive part was feeling much less afraid, and much less stuck. Today we're going to address the two remaining reactive parts. How does that sound?"

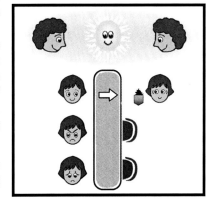

After this review, resume the Conference Room Protocol, starting with Step 3 - Connecting to Resources. There are two options for proceeding with the protocol from there.

- **Invite all the reactive parts back into the room.** Repeat the Step 6 invitation you used the first time, such as, "I'd like to invite into the conference room, to sit on one side of the table, all the reactive parts of self that are connected to (overspending). When you're ready, tell me what you notice." (In Missy's case, the fearful part, the angry part, and the sad part return to the conference room. The fearful part is still feeling better since the dominance of the introject was switched.) Typically the same reactive parts that appeared before will appear in the conference room again. Sometimes a reactive part that was addressed before does not reappear, because it no longer reacts to the invitation. Sometimes one or two additional reactive parts will appear. These anomalies are not a problem. But if a client reports that the reactive parts appearing on a second invitation, share nothing in common with the reactive parts that originally appeared, there may be a potential problem, confusion, or block which needs to be investigated.

- **Invite back only reactive parts that have not yet been addressed.** Start by reminding the client of the target issue, then read aloud any negative beliefs being processed. Check with the client that the reactive parts that were initially identified, are still connected to the target issue. Notice which of those reactive parts were not addressed in an earlier session. (In Christi's case, that would be the angry one and the sad one.) Then invite one or more of those reactive parts back into the conference room – depending on how many you expect you will have time to work with in that session. If in doubt, invite just the most upset reactive part into the room, find the associated introject, switch the dominance, then invite the next reactive part into the room. Repeat these steps until all the associated introjects have been identified and the dominance of each has been switched.

Starting the Needs Meeting Right Away After a Resumed Conference Room Protocol

Once you've completed the Conference Room Protocol you'll either tuck in all the parts with a plan to meet needs later, or you'll begin the Needs Meeting Protocol right away. If some of the associated child parts are not already in the conference room, you must take an *extra step* if you plan to start the Needs Meeting Protocol right away. For example, when processing Rung 2B, Randy took two sessions to complete the Conference Room Protocol. In session one he reported five reactive parts appeared in the conference room. Three of them identified three introjects, and the dominance of each was switched. At the end of session one, all eight child parts were tucked in. In session two, the remaining two reactive parts were invited back into the room. They identified two more introjects, and the dominance of both was switched. Randy was then ready to start the Needs Meeting Protocol. He opted to do the needs meeting with all five introjects. The two reactive parts that were in the conference room were tucked in. Then the three introjects that had been identified in session one were invited forward. Once all five introjects were gathered in the center of the conference room, and the Resources surrounded them. After checking for processing blocks, the Needs Meeting Protocol began, starting with Step 4.

© Copyright 2009 by Shirley Jean Schmidt, MA, LPC. All rights reserved. Duplication in any form without permission is prohibited.

So if a client opts to include in the needs meeting, parts of self that are not already in the conference room, you'll have to take an *extra step* and invite them to join the Resources. This brings all the relevant parts of self into the Healing Circle, ready to start the Needs Meeting Protocol.

Attachment Needs Ladder Follow-up Anomalies

After completing the Needs Meeting Protocol on a targeted issue (e.g. Rung 1), you will invite the client to re-rate the Attachment Needs Ladder statements. Clients typically report they are not-at-all true, but sometimes a client will report that one or more negative beliefs still feel a bit true. There are several possible reasons for this.

- It's possible that the needs meeting work just completed resolved one layer of a multilayered problem. By repeating the Conference Room Protocol on that Rung, additional related introjects will emerge to heal. Healing each layer will be necessary to get complete resolution of the problem.

- It's possible that a negative belief that still feels true will get fully resolved when the next Attachment Needs Ladder Rung is processed. For example, the Rung 1 belief "It's not safe to exist," may not completely resolve until the Rung 2A (physical and sexual safety) work is completed.

- It's possible that some of the processing occurred in the presence of an unexpressed processing block. To remedy this you'll need to find and clear the block; then repeat the portion of the Needs Meeting Protocol that was compromised by the block. The topic of overcoming processing blocks is addressed in Chapter 7.

Complications and Processing Blocks

The administration of the Attachment Needs Ladder and the execution of the Conference Room Protocol will not always unfold smoothly. Problems can arise at many points in the process, for example, while getting initial ratings on negative beliefs; while getting ready to invite reactive parts into the conference room; when reactive parts enter the conference room; and when reactive parts look across the table to see the introjects they are reacting to.

The most common block occurs just before inviting reactive parts into the conference room. In Step 5 you'll check for uncomfortable or contracted body sensations that indicate a processing block or concern. Clients often experience fear from reactive parts who expect to be threatened when introjects appear at the conference table. So if a client reports a disturbing a body sensation in Step 5, you can determine if this is the blocking concern by asking something like:

> *Would it help if we were to erect a protective glass wall across the middle of the conference room, so the reactive parts would be protected from any introject that shows up at the table? We could make it bullet-proof glass, or a one-way mirror.*

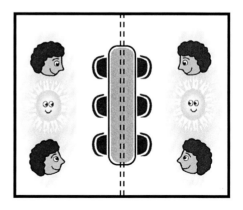

If the client likes the idea of a protective wall, say:

> *Good, picture that. Also picture two sets of Resources – one on each side of the table.*

Once the wall is in place, ask something like:

> *Now when you think about beginning this conference room work, with the child parts connected with (the target issue), what do you notice in your body?*

If a fear of threatening introjects was the sole concern, the body should feel clear, and you can proceed with the protocol. If a body disturbance remains, you'll need to find and clear the associated block. Detailed instructions for handling a number of Conference Room Protocol complications and processing blocks – large and small – are provided in Chapter 7, pages 180-183.

© Copyright 2009 by Shirley Jean Schmidt, MA, LPC. All rights reserved. Duplication in any form without permission is prohibited.

Typical Attachment Needs Ladder & Conference Room Protocol Session

The following is a typical client/therapist dialogue for administering the Attachment Needs Ladder followed by the Conference Room Protocol. A sample Conference Room Map is also provided. This will provide you an example of how to execute and transition between the following steps:

- Explaining the Attachment Needs Ladder Rating Process
- Getting Attachment Needs Ladder Ratings
- Step 1. Explaining the Process for the First Time
- Step 2. Recording Information on the Conference Room Map
- Step 3. Connecting to Resources
- Step 4. Picturing the Conference Room
- Step 5. Checking for Processing Blocks
- Step 6. Inviting Child Parts Into the Conference Room
- Step 7. Engaging the Most Upset Child Part
- Step 8. Classifying the Part of Self that Appears Across the Table
- Step 9. Collecting Information about the Presumptive Introject
- Step 10. Switching the Dominance
- Step 11. Repeating Steps 7-10
- Step 11. Checking that the Conference Room Work is Complete
- Step 12. Preparing for the Needs Meeting Protocol

Administering the Attachment Needs Ladder

Explaining the Attachment Needs Ladder Rating Process

Therapist:	**So Leslie, last week we talked about the Attachment Needs Ladder in general terms. Now we're going to start getting ratings on Rung 1. Some of the statements listed on Rung 1 may never feel true to you. Some may only feel true at times you feel especially vulnerable. When a statement does feel true, it might feel a little true, somewhat true, or very true. I'll be asking you whether each of the nine Rung 1 statements feel true when you think about growing up with your self-absorbed, neglectful parents. If you answer 'yes,' I'll ask you how true the statement feels when it feels the most true. Answer on a 1 to 10 scale, where 10 is totally true. Many of these statements may feel totally false to your most adult self. That's fine. But we're looking for ratings that reflect how wounded child parts feel. Any questions?**
Client:	No. I understand.

Getting Attachment Needs Ladder Ratings

Therapist:	**When you think about growing up with your self-absorbed, neglectful parents, does the statement, *I don't exist*, feel true?**
Client:	No.
Therapist:	**When you think about growing up with your self-absorbed, neglectful parents, does the statement, *I shouldn't exist*, feel true?**
Client:	Yes.
Therapist:	**How true does it feel when it feels the most true, 0-10?**
Client:	Seven.
Therapist:	**When you think about growing up with your self-absorbed, neglectful parents, does the statement, *It's not safe to exist*, feel true?**
Client:	Yes.
Therapist:	**How true does it feel when it feels the most true?**
Client:	Six.
Therapist:	**When you think about growing up with your self-absorbed, neglectful parents, does the statement, *I don't deserve to exist*, feel true?**

© Copyright 2009 by Shirley Jean Schmidt, MA, LPC. All rights reserved. Duplication in any form without permission is prohibited.

Client:	No.
Therapist:	When you think about growing up with your self-absorbed, neglectful parents, does the statement, *Shame on me for existing*, feel true?
Client:	No.
Therapist:	When you think about growing up with your self-absorbed, neglectful parents, does the statement, *I'm so alone, there's no point in existing*, feel true?
Client:	Yes.
Therapist:	How true does it feel when it feels the most true, 0-10?
Client:	Nine.
Therapist:	When you think about growing up with your self-absorbed, neglectful parents, does the statement, *My existence is completely irrelevant*, feel true?
Client:	No.
Therapist:	When you think about growing up with your self-absorbed, neglectful parents, does the statement, *My existence is completely unimportant*, feel true?
Client:	No.
Therapist:	When you think about growing up with your self-absorbed, neglectful parents, does the statement, *My existence is completely unacceptable*, feel true?
Client:	No.
Therapist:	Are there any other beliefs that you have about yourself, related to issues of existence?
Client:	Just one. It's No one wants me to exist.
Therapist:	And how true does that feel when it feels the most true?
Client:	Six.
Therapist:	Okay. Now we'll start the Conference Room Protocol.

The Conference Room Protocol

This Conference Room Protocol client/therapist dialogue demonstrates a typical session for processing Rung 1 attachment wounds. The Conference Room Map on page 104 has a record of all that transpired in the session.

Step 1: Explaining the Process for the First Time

Therapist:	Last week we talked about the Conference Room Protocol in general terms. Now that we're about to start it, I want to clarify a few details so we can avoid some potential confusions. You endorsed four Rung 1 statements. When I invite into the conference room all the parts of self that believe these four statements, any number of parts could appear. There could be one, four, or even 10 parts believing the four statements. So there will not necessarily be one reactive part per statement. When these parts appear in the conference room, you may get a vivid image, a vague image, or no image at all. Whatever image comes up is perfectly fine. Just describe it as best you can. Don't worry if it doesn't make sense. If it seems odd to us, we'll figure it out together. Okay?
Client:	Okay.
Therapist:	Once the reactive parts are in the conference room, we'll start by inviting the most upset part to look across the table, to see the part of self she's reacting to. When an image appears, just describe it as best you can, even if you don't understand it. Usually one introject will appear. But sometimes more than one will appear, or a part will appear as a metaphor. It's also possible that two or more reactive parts at the table will be reacting to the same introject. So there will not necessarily be one introject per reactive part.
Client:	Okay.
Therapist:	When an introject appears, I'll start by talking to the little Leslie wearing the introject costume. Some clients get confused at this point – especially if they don't yet see a part behind the costume. When they get confused, the reactive part might answer the questions I've directed to the part wearing the costume. Keep in mind that these parts of self are distinct and separate. It's imperative that the part wearing the costume answer the questions I direct to her. Does that make sense?

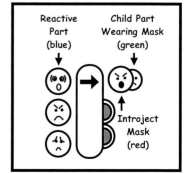

© Copyright 2009 by Shirley Jean Schmidt, MA, LPC. All rights reserved. Duplication in any form without permission is prohibited.

Client:	Yes.
Therapist:	**Great. Any questions?**
Client:	No.

Step 2: Recording Information on the Conference Room Map

Therapist:	*(Wrote the client's name, date, and target issue, on Conference Room Map template. See next page.)*

Step 3: Connecting to Resources

Therapist:	**Okay. Now, connect to your Resources. Tell me when you're connected.**
Client:	Okay.
Therapist:	*(Turned ABS on.)* **Good. Let that get as strong as it wants to. Tell me when it's strengthened all the way.**
Client:	Okay.

Step 4: Picturing the Conference Room

Therapist:	*(Turned ABS off.)* **Great. So now I'd like you to picture a conference room with a table and chairs. And picture the Resources in the conference room.**
Client:	Okay.

Step 5: Checking for Processing Blocks

Therapist:	**When you think about beginning this conference room work with the child parts connected with Rung 1, for the purpose of identifying and working with the associated introjects, what do you notice in your body now?**
Client:	I feel some tension in my stomach.
Therapist:	**If the tension could talk what would it say?**
Client:	Some part of me is afraid of this.
Therapist:	**I understand. Would it help if we were to erect a protective glass wall or one-way mirror across the middle of the conference room, so the reactive parts would be protected from any introject that shows up at the table? We could even make it bullet-proof glass if you like.**
Client:	That would be nice
Therapist:	**Good, picture that. Also picture two sets of Resources – one on each side of the table.**
Client:	That's much better.
Therapist:	**So now when you think about beginning this conference room work, with the child parts connected with Rung 1, what do you notice in your body?**
Client:	Nothing. It's clear.

Step 6: Inviting Child Parts into the Conference Room

Therapist:	**Now I'd like to invite into the conference room, to sit on one side of the table, all the parts of self who believe the following statements: I shouldn't exist; It's not safe to exist; I'm so alone, there's no point in existing; and No one wants me to exist. As I mentioned before, there may or may not be one child part per statement. When you're ready, tell me what you notice.**
Client:	I see a two-year-old, a five-year-old, and a seven-year-old. *(Recorded on Conference Room Map.)*

Step 7: Engaging the Most Upset Child Part

Therapist:	**Okay. Which one seems to be the most upset?**
Client:	The two-year-old.
Therapist:	**May I speak with her?**
Client:	Yes.
Therapist:	**Welcome, I'm so glad you're here. What kind of mood are you in?**
Reactive #1:	Afraid. *(Recorded on Conference Room Map.)*
Therapist:	**Afraid? Okay. So two-year-old, I'm guessing you've been stuck in the past a long time. Is that right?**

© Copyright 2009 by Shirley Jean Schmidt, MA, LPC. All rights reserved. Duplication in any form without permission is prohibited.

DNMS Conference Room Map

Client   Leslie Q.   Date Began   July 7

Rung or Current Problem   Rung 1

Age   2
Mood   afraid
Stuck now?   10
After SDP?   <1
After NMP? _____

Introject of   Dad   Part's age   2
Message   Get out of my way or I'll kill you.
_____
_____
_____
0-10, how disturbing is message now?   10   After NMP? _____
Dominance switched?   ❑ Partial _____   ☑ Complete   July 7
                               date   date

Age   5
Mood   angry
Stuck now?   9
After SDP?   2
After NMP? _____

Introject of   Mom reading a book   Part's age   4
Message   Leave me alone. My novel is more important
            than you or your needs. If you bother me
            I'll get angry and it will be your fault.
_____
0-10, how disturbing is message now?   10   After NMP? _____
Dominance switched?   ❑ Partial _____   ☑ Complete   July 7
                               date   date

Age   7
Mood   w/d
Stuck now?   10
After SDP?   0
After NMP? _____

Introject of _____ Part's age _____
Message _____
_____
_____
_____
0-10, how disturbing is message now? _____ After NMP? _____
Dominance switched?   ❑ Partial _____   ❑ Complete _____
                               date   date

Age   6
Mood   bossy
Stuck now?   10
After SDP?   0
After NMP? _____

Introject of   Mom & Dad screaming   Part's age   6
Message   You're very very bad. Keep it up and we'll
            send you to an orphanage.
_____
_____
0-10, how disturbing is message now?   10   After NMP? _____
Dominance switched?   ❑ Partial _____   ☑ Complete   July 7
                               date   date

Age _____
Mood _____
Stuck now? _____
After SDP? _____
After NMP? _____

Introject of _____ Part's age _____
Message _____
_____
_____
_____
0-10, how disturbing is message now? _____ After NMP? _____
Dominance switched?   ❑ Partial _____   ❑ Complete _____
                               date   date

There may not be a 1-to-1 correlation between *negative belief* and *reactive part* and *introject*. For example, 3 beliefs may be held by 1 reactive part; 1 reactive part may be reacting to 2 introjects; 2 reactive parts may be reacting to 1 introject. Use as much or as little of this template as needed. Use additional pages if needed.

Therapist:	**So how stuck are you, 0-10, if 10 is totally stuck?**
Reactive #1:	10. *(Recorded on Conference Room Map.)*
Therapist:	**10? Okay, thanks. Now I'd like to help you get unstuck, and you can help me. Okay? When you're ready, take a look at that empty spot across the table from you. In a moment you'll see appear in that spot the part (or parts) of self that you're reacting to. When you're ready, tell me what you notice.**

Step 8: Classifying the Part of Self that Appears Across the Table

Reactive #1:	I see a scary monster.
Therapist:	**Okay. Does this scary monster have a message for you?**
Reactive #1:	It's not saying anything.
Therapist:	**Okay. If the monster's scary expression could be translated into words, what would they be?**
Reactive #1:	"Get out of my way or I'll kill you."
Therapist:	**Oh, I see. Does this scary monster remind you of someone?**
Reactive #1:	My dad. *(This is a presumptive introject. All this information is recorded on Conference Room Map.)*

Step 9: Collecting Information about the Presumptive Introject

Therapist:	**Dad? Okay. From 0-10, how disturbing is your dad's message "Get out of my way or I'll kill you"?**
Child:	10. *(Recorded on Conference Room Map.)*

Step 10: Switching the Dominance   *Introject #1*

Therapist:	**Is there a little one behind this scary monster costume?**
Client:	Yes.
Therapist:	**May I speak to her?**
Client:	Yes.
Therapist:	*In a very gentle, loving voice:* **Hey little one, I want you to know I see you, and I know that you're good. And I know the difference between you and this costume. What's it like to hear that?**
Introject #1:	I didn't think anybody could see me.
Therapist:	**Well I can see you. Do you like or need this costume? Does it serve a useful purpose?**
Introject #1:	I don't like it.
Therapist:	**Okay. Now let's talk about the ways you're different from this costume. Do you believe caregivers should always treat children with respect?**
Introject #1:	Yes.
Therapist:	**Does the costume agree?**
Introject #1:	No.
Therapist:	**Do you believe caregivers should protect children from danger?**
Introject #1:	Yes.
Therapist:	**Does the costume agree?**
Introject #1:	No.
Therapist:	**Do you believe its okay for caregivers to threaten to kill children?**
Introject #1:	No.
Therapist:	**Does the costume believe that's okay?**
Introject #1:	Yes.
Therapist:	**Do you see how different you are from this costume?**
Introject #1:	Yes.
Therapist:	**You're nothing like it, are you?**
Introject #1:	No, I'm not.
Therapist:	**How old are you little one?**
Introject #1:	Two. *(Recorded on Conference Room Map.)*
Therapist:	**When you were two, your dad was real, his threats were real, and the wounds those threats inflicted were real. While your dad was behaving this way, your brain was making a recording of him; like filming a home movie. That recording has become encapsulated in this dad costume you're wearing. So the mask looks and sounds like your dad, but it's not your dad. It's just a**

© Copyright 2009 by Shirley Jean Schmidt, MA, LPC. All rights reserved. Duplication in any form without permission is prohibited.

recording of him behaving this way. But every time this costume gets triggered, it evokes some very painful emotions. Right?

Introject #1:   Yeah.

Therapist: That emotional reaction creates the illusion that the dad costume is real, important, and wounding, just like your dad was. Now watching a scary movie may make you feel afraid, but that doesn't mean you're really in danger, does it – because a movie isn't real life. And this mask isn't real life either. If you don't like a movie, you can turn it off. When you understand the truth – that this mask it is no more real than a movie, you can turn it off. How does that sound?

Introject #1:   Really?

Therapist: Yes, really! But don't take my word for it, ask the Resources if this costume is dangerous like dad was, and tell me what they say.

Introject #1:   They say "no."

Therapist: What's it like to hear that?

Introject #1:   That's a relief.

Therapist: So as you consider the truth about the costume, does it look any different now?

Introject #1:   It's smaller. It was huge, six feet tall and hairy. Now it's about three feet tall. It's more like a cloth costume on a hanger.

Therapist: See? It already appears less important. That's proof that what I'm saying is true. So, two-year-old, do you know you're in an adult body now?

Introject #1:   What?

Therapist: (Handed her a mirror.) Take a look in this mirror. Notice that adult face. Is this what you expected to see?

Introject #1:   No.

Therapist: As you look in the mirror, touch your nose. Notice that's your nose.

Introject #1:   Oh. Yeah.

Therapist: When you're two years old, who was in control of your life, you or your parents?

Introject #1:   My parents.

Therapist: They told you what to eat, what to wear, when to sleep. They were in control of who came in and out of the house. If there was someone dangerous in the house, you had no control over it at age two, did you?

Introject #1:   No.

Therapist: But now that you're in an adult body, you're in control of these things. You decide what to eat, where to go, and what people you're going to spend time with. If someone scary wanted to move in with you now, what would you say?

Introject #1:   No way!

Therapist: So with that in mind, does the costume look any different now?

Introject #1:   Now it just looks like strips of cloth on a hanger.

Therapist: If I were to shake what's left of the costume, what would happen? Would it say anything to me?

Introject #1:   No.

Therapist: So has it lost all its animation?

Introject #1:   Yeah. Cool.

Therapist: So little one – who's in charge now, you or what's left of this costume?

Introject #1:   I am!

Therapist: Who's alive and real, you or what's left of this costume?

Introject #1:   I am!

Therapist: Who's important now, you or what's left of this costume?

Introject #1:   I am!!

Therapist: Who has power now, you or what's left of this costume?

Introject #1:   I do!

Therapist: How big is the costume now?

Introject #1:   It's the size of a postage stamp.

Therapist: Is there any image of your dad on it?

Introject #1:   No. It's blank.

Therapist: Would you have any aversion to putting what's left of the costume it in your pocket?

© Copyright 2009 by Shirley Jean Schmidt, MA, LPC. All rights reserved. Duplication in any form without permission is prohibited.

Introject #1:	No.
Therapist:	**Good. Now put it in your pocket. Pat on your pocket and say "I'm in charge now."** *Pause* **Does that feel good?**
Introject #1:	Yes.
Therapist:	*(Turned ABS on.)* **Good. Notice that good feeling. Tell me when it's strengthened all the way.**
Introject #1:	Okay. *(Dominance completely switched – indicated on the Conference Room Map.)*
Therapist:	*(Turned ABS off.)* **So two-year-old, I'd like to help you get totally unstuck from what's left of this costume at the perfect time. I'm not sure when that will be, hopefully soon. But for now, let's check in across the table, to see how the other two-year-old is doing now.**
Introject #1:	Okay.
Therapist:	**So fearful two-year-old. Are you feeling any better now?**
Reactive #1:	Yes. A lot better.
Therapist:	**0-10, how stuck are you feeling now?**
Reactive #1:	Less than 1, almost zero.
Therapist:	**That sounds good. So I'd like the two of you to just hang out here a bit. I'll get back to you soon.**

Step 11: Repeating Steps 7-10

Repeating Step 7: Engaging the Most Upset Child Part

Therapist:	**Good. Now Leslie, which of the remaining two child parts seem the most upset now?**
Client:	The five-year-old.
Therapist:	**May I speak with her?**
Client:	Yes.
Therapist:	**Welcome, I'm so glad you're here. Can you tell me what kind of mood you're in?**
Reactive #2:	Angry. *(Recorded on Conference Room Map.)*
Therapist:	**Angry? Okay. So five-year-old, I'm guessing you've been stuck in the past a long time. Is that right?**
Reactive #2:	Yeah.
Therapist:	**So how stuck are you, 0-10, if 10 is totally stuck?**
Reactive #2:	9. *(Recorded on Conference Room Map.)*
Therapist:	**9? Okay, thanks. Now I'd like to help you get unstuck, and you can help me. When you're ready, take a look at that empty spot across the table from you. In a moment you'll see appear in that spot the part (or parts) of self that you're reacting to. When you're ready, tell me what you notice.**

Repeating Step 8: Classifying the Part of Self that Appears Across the Table

Reactive #2:	I see my mother reading a book.
Therapist:	**Okay. Is she conveying a message to you?**
Reactive #2:	Yes, "Leave me alone." *(This sounds like a presumptive introject. Mom reading a book is recorded on the Conference Room map. The message is not very specific. It needs to be clarified.)*

Repeating Step 9: Collecting Information about the Presumptive Introject

Therapist:	**Okay. And what does that mean about you? Is there an underlying message from mom?**
Reactive #2:	Her novel is more important than me – more important than my needs.
Therapist:	**Is there a penalty if you don't leave her alone.**
Reactive #2:	She'll get angry at me.
Therapist:	**Whose fault would it be if she gets angry at you?**
Reactive #2:	Of course it would be my fault.
Therapist:	**So as I understand it, your mother's message is: "Leave me alone. My novel is more important than you or your needs. If you bother me I'll get angry and it will be your fault."**
Reactive #2:	Yeah. That's it. *(Recorded on Conference Room Map.)*
Therapist:	**So from 0-10, how disturbing is this message now?**
Reactive #2:	10. *(Recorded on Conference Room Map.)*

© Copyright 2009 by Shirley Jean Schmidt, MA, LPC. All rights reserved. Duplication in any form without permission is prohibited.

Repeating Step 10: Switching the Dominance   *Introject #2*

Therapist:	**Is there a little one behind this mother costume?**
Client:	Yes.
Therapist:	**May I speak to her?**
Client:	Yes.
Therapist:	*In a very gentle, loving voice:* **Hey little one, I want you to know I see you, and I know that you're good. And I know the difference between you and this costume. What's it like to hear that?**
Introject #2:	It's a relief.
Therapist:	**Is there anything about this costume that you like or need? Does it serve a useful purpose?**
Introject #2:	No. I hate it.
Therapist:	**So let's talk about the ways you're different from this costume. Do you believe caregivers should always treat children with respect?**
Introject #2:	Yes.
Therapist:	**Does the costume agree?**
Introject #2:	No.
Therapist:	**Do you believe caregivers should make their children's needs a high priority?**
Introject #2:	Yes.
Therapist:	**Does the costume agree?**
Introject #2:	No.
Therapist:	**Do you believe caregivers should manage their emotions around children?**
Introject #2:	Yes.
Therapist:	**Does the costume agree?**
Introject #2:	No.
Therapist:	**See how different you are from this costume?**
Introject #2:	Yes.
Therapist:	**You're nothing like it, are you?**
Introject #2:	No, I'm not.
Therapist:	**How old are you little one?**
Introject #2:	Four. *(Recorded on Conference Room Map.)*
Therapist:	**When you were four, your mother was real, the rejecting way she treated you was real, and the wounds she inflicted were real. While your mother was behaving this way, your brain was making a recording of her; like filming a home movie. That recording became encapsulated in the costume you're wearing. So the mask looks and sounds like your mother, but it's not your mother. It's just a recording of her behaving this way. But every time this recording plays, it evokes some very painful emotions. Right?**
Introject #2:	Right.
Therapist:	**That emotional reaction creates the illusion that the costume is real, important, and wounding, just like your mother was. But it's no more real than a movie is real. If you don't like a movie you're watching, you can turn it off, right? When you understand the truth – that this mask it is about as real as a movie, you'll be able to turn it off. How does that sound?**
Introject #2:	That sounds great.
Therapist:	**So as you consider what I'm saying, does the costume look any different now?**
Introject #2:	It looks like a life-size cardboard cut-out of my mom reading a book.
Therapist:	**Wow. That's a big change. That's proof that what I'm saying is true.**
Introject #2:	Yeah.
Therapist:	**So ask the Resources about this costume – what do they say? Do they think it's important?**
Introject #2:	They say it's nothing really - nothing important.
Therapist:	**What's it like to hear that?**
Introject #2:	I like it.
Therapist:	**So four-year-old. Do you know you're in an adult body now?**
Introject #2:	Ummmm..... yeah.
Therapist:	*(Handed her a mirror.)* **Look in this mirror. Is this what you expected to see?**
Introject #2:	Ummmm..... no.

© Copyright 2009 by Shirley Jean Schmidt, MA, LPC. All rights reserved. Duplication in any form without permission is prohibited.

Therapist:	This is good news. At four years old your parents were in total control of your life, weren't they?
Introject #2:	Yeah.
Therapist:	They told you what to eat, when to eat, what to wear, when to sleep. They were in control of who came to the house and who you spent time with. They controlled everything didn't they?
Introject #2:	Ummmm..... yeah.
Therapist:	But now that you're in an adult body, you make those decisions. You decide what to eat, when to eat it, what to wear, when to sleep. You decide who to spend time with, and who to stay away from. What's it like to think about that?
Introject #2:	I like it.
Therapist:	So I wonder, with that in mind, does the mask look any different now?
Introject #2:	It looks like cardboard square with a picture of her reading a book. It's about a foot square.
Therapist:	So if I were to poke at this cardboard square, what would happen? Would it say anything to me?
Introject #2:	It wouldn't say anything.
Therapist:	So has it lost all its animation?
Introject #2:	Yeah. It's just cardboard.
Therapist:	So who's important now, you or what's left of the costume?
Introject #2:	I'm important.
Therapist:	Who matters now, you or what's left of the costume?
Introject #2:	I matter.
Therapist:	Who's alive and real, you or what's left of the costume?
Introject #2:	I am.
Therapist:	And who has power now, you or what's left of the costume?
Introject #2:	I do.
Therapist:	Does the mask look any different now?
Introject #2:	It looks like postcard.
Therapist:	Does it have an image of your mother on it?
Introject #2:	No. It's blank.
Therapist:	Would you have any aversion to putting what's left of the costume in your pocket now?
Introject #2:	No.
Therapist:	Good. Now put it in your pocket, pat on your pocket and say "I'm in charge now." *Pause* Does that feel good?
Introject #2:	Yes.
Therapist:	*(Turned ABS on.)* Good. Notice that good feeling. Tell me when it's strengthened all the way.
Introject #2:	Okay. *(Dominance completely switched – indicated on the Conference Room Map.)*
Therapist:	*(Turned ABS off.)* So little one. I'd like to help you get totally unstuck from what's left of this costume at the perfect time. I'm not sure when that will be, hopefully soon. But for now, let's check in across the table, to see how the five-year-old is doing now.
Introject #2:	Okay.
Therapist:	So five-year-old. How are you doing? You were feeling pretty stuck when we started. 0-10, how stuck are you feeling now?
Reactive #2:	Much better – maybe a 2.
Therapist:	That sounds much better. So I'd like the two of you to just hang out here a bit. I'll get back to you soon.

Step 11: Repeating Steps 7-10

Repeating Step 7: Engaging the Most Upset Child Part

Therapist:	So we have one reactive part left here. May I speak with the seven-year-old?
Client:	Yes.
Therapist:	Welcome, I'm glad you're here. What kind of mood are you in?
Reactive #3:	Withdrawn. *(Recorded on Conference Room Map.)*
Therapist:	Withdrawn? Okay. So seven-year-old, I'm guessing you've been stuck in the past a long time. Is that right?
Reactive #3:	Yeah.

© Copyright 2009 by Shirley Jean Schmidt, MA, LPC. All rights reserved. Duplication in any form without permission is prohibited.

Therapist:	**So how stuck do you feel, 0-10, if 10 is totally stuck?**
Reactive #3:	10. *(Recorded on Conference Room Map.)*
Therapist:	**10? Okay, thanks. Now I'd like to help you get unstuck, and you can help me. When you're ready, take a look at that empty spot across the table from you. In a moment you'll see appear in that spot the part (or parts) of self that you're reacting to. When you're ready, tell me what you notice.**

Repeating Step 8: Classifying the Part of Self that Appears Across the Table

Reactive #3:	I see a girl screaming at me.
Therapist:	**Okay. Is she conveying a message to you?**
Reactive #3:	Yes. "Just stop it! Don't move. Don't speak."
Therapist:	**May I speak to her?**
Client:	Yes.
Therapist:	**Hey little one. Thanks for coming. Tell me why you're screaming this.**
Reactive #4:	I'm trying to keep the others in line. They can make a lot of trouble. Someone has to rein them in.
Therapist:	**So it sounds like you're trying to keep the other parts in line to protect them from something threatening. Is that right?**
Reactive #4:	Yeah. *(This is a controlling reactive part.)*
Therapist:	**That makes a lot of sense to me. I'd like to invite you to take a seat on the other side of the table. You can sit next to the seven-year-old. Tell me when you're settled there.** *(Recorded on Conference Room Map.)*
Reactive #4:	Okay.
Therapist:	**So little one. How old are you?**
Reactive #4:	Six. *(Recorded on Conference Room Map.)*
Therapist:	**It sounds like you're in a bossy mood. Is that right?**
Reactive #4:	Yeah, that's me – bossy. *(Recorded on Conference Room Map.)*
Therapist:	**Okay. So six-year-old, I'm guessing you've been stuck in the past a long time. Is that right?**
Reactive #4:	Yeah.
Therapist:	**So how stuck are you, 0-10, if 10 is totally stuck?**
Reactive #4:	10. *(Recorded on Conference Room Map.)*
Therapist:	**10? Okay, thanks. Now I'd like to help you get unstuck, and you can help me. When you're ready, take a look at that empty spot across the table from you. In a moment you'll see appear in that spot the part (or parts) of self that you're reacting to. When you're ready, tell me what you notice.**
Reactive #4:	I see my mom and dad screaming.
Therapist:	**What are they saying?**
Reactive #4:	"You're very, very bad. Keep it up and we'll send you to an orphanage." *(This is a presumptive introject. All this information is recorded on Conference Room Map.)*

Repeating Step 9: Collecting Information about the Presumptive Introject

Therapist:	**So from 0-10, how disturbing is this message?**
Client:	10. *(Recorded on Conference Room Map.)*
Therapist:	**So are you seeing two separate parts of self – a mom part and dad part? Or is this one mom/dad part?**
Client:	It seems to be one part wearing a mom mask and a dad mask.

Repeating Step 10: Switching the Dominance   Introject #3

Therapist:	**May I speak to her?**
Client:	Yes.
Therapist:	**Hey little one, I want you to know I see you, and I know that you're good. And I know the difference between you and these mom and dad masks. What's it like to hear that?**
Introject #3:	What a relief.
Therapist:	**Do you like or need these masks? Do they serve a useful purpose?**
Introject #3:	No. They're icky.
Therapist:	**Let's talk about the ways you're different from these masks. Do you believe caregivers should always treat children with respect?**
Introject #3:	Yes.

© Copyright 2009 by Shirley Jean Schmidt, MA, LPC. All rights reserved. Duplication in any form without permission is prohibited.

Therapist:	**Do the masks agree?**
Introject #3:	No.
Therapist:	**Do you believe caregivers should manage their emotions around children?**
Introject #3:	Yes.
Therapist:	**Do the masks agree?**
Introject #3:	No.
Therapist:	**Do you believe its okay for caregivers to threaten children with abandonment?**
Introject #3:	No.
Therapist:	**Do the masks agree?**
Introject #3:	No.
Therapist:	**See how different you are from these masks?**
Introject #3:	Yes.
Therapist:	**You're nothing like them, are you?**
Introject #3:	No, I'm not.
Therapist:	**How old are you little one?**
Introject #3:	Six. *(Recorded on Conference Room Map.)*
Therapist:	**When you were six, your mom and dad screamed real threats of abandonment at you. That was a very real and very wounding experience, wasn't it? While they were behaving this way, your brain was making a recording of them; like filming a home movie. That recording became encapsulated in these mom and dad masks that you've been wearing. So while the masks look and sound like your mom and dad, they're really just a recording of them behaving this way. But every time this recording of them plays, it evokes some very painful emotions. Right?**
Introject #3:	Yeah.
Therapist:	**That emotional reaction can create the illusion that these masks are real, important, and threatening, just like your parents were. Actually the masks are no more threatening than a scary movie. The good news is, if you don't like the mom and dad movie, you can turn it off. How does that sound?**
Introject #3:	Sounds great.
Therapist:	**So as you think about what I'm saying, do the masks look any different now?**
Introject #3:	They're a little smaller, but I still don't like them.
Therapist:	**So ask the Resources if these masks are a real threat like your parents were. Tell me what they say?**
Introject #3:	They say they're harmless.
Therapist:	**What's it like to hear that?**
Introject #3:	Really good.
Therapist:	**So six-year-old... do you know you're in an adult body now?**
Introject #3:	What?
Therapist:	*(Handed her a mirror.)* **Take a look in this mirror. Is this what you expected to see?**
Introject #3:	No. That's weird.
Therapist:	**At age 6, you didn't have much power, did you? Your parents owned the house, the car the checkbook... they bought the groceries, cooked the meals, and made up the rules. They were in total control of your life, weren't they?**
Introject #3:	Yeah.
Therapist:	**But now that you're in an adult body, you own your own house, car, and checkbook. You buy your own groceries and cook your own meals. You call the shots now, don't you?**
Introject #3:	Yeah.
Therapist:	**What's it like to think about that?**
Introject #3:	Amazing. I like it.
Therapist:	**So do the masks look any different now?**
Introject #3:	There's just one mask now. Their images have blended together. It looks like a single angry blob.
Therapist:	**If I were to shake it or wiggle it. Would it do anything or say anything?**
Introject #3:	It would hiss at you.
Therapist:	**So let's say I have over here, a scorpion and a photo of a scorpion, and I'm going to ask you to hold one or the other. Which one will you want to hold?**
Introject #3:	The photo.
Therapist:	**Why?**

© Copyright 2009 by Shirley Jean Schmidt, MA, LPC. All rights reserved. Duplication in any form without permission is prohibited.

Introject #3:	Because the photo can't hurt me.
Therapist:	**Exactly. Is this mask more like a scorpion or more like a photo of a scorpion?**
Introject #3:	It's more like a photo. Oh, I get it. It's harmless.
Therapist:	**So does the mask look any different now?**
Introject #3:	It looks like a rubber super ball.
Therapist:	**So if were to poke at the ball, would it say anything to me?**
Introject #3:	Of course not, it's just a ball.
Therapist:	**Has it lost all its animation?**
Introject #3:	Yes. It's just a ball now.
Therapist:	**So who's in charge now, you or what's left of this mask?**
Introject #3:	I am!
Therapist:	**Who's alive and real, you or what's left of this mask?**
Introject #3:	I am!
Therapist:	**Who's important now, you or what's left of this mask?**
Introject #3:	I am!
Therapist:	**Who has power now, you or what's left of this mask?**
Introject #3:	I do!
Therapist:	**How big is the mask now?**
Introject #3:	It's the size of a rubber eraser on the end of a pencil.
Therapist:	**Would you have any aversion to putting what's left of the mask in your pocket?**
Introject #3:	No.
Therapist:	**Good. Now put it in your pocket, pat on your pocket and say "I'm in charge now."** *Pause* **Does that feel good?**
Introject #3:	Yes.
Therapist:	*(Turned ABS on.)* **Good. Notice that good feeling. Tell me when it's strengthened all the way.**
Introject #3:	Okay. *(Dominance completely switched – indicated on the Conference Room Map.)*
Therapist:	*(Turned ABS off.)* **So six-year-old. I'd like to help you get totally unstuck from what's left of this mask at the perfect time. I'm not sure when that will be, hopefully soon. But for now, let's check in across the table, to see how the bossy six-year-old is doing.**
Introject #3:	Okay.
Therapist:	**So six-year-old. How are you doing? You were feeling pretty stuck when we started. 0-10, how stuck are you feeling now?**
Reactive #4:	Not at all stuck
Therapist:	**That sounds great. And seven-year-old... you were needing to withdraw. How are you doing now?**
Reactive #3:	Much better, thank you.
Therapist:	**0-10, how stuck are you feeling now?**
Reactive #3:	Zero.
Therapist:	**That's good to hear. So I'd like the three of you to just hang out here a bit. I'll get back to you soon.**

Step 11: Checking that the Conference Room Work is Complete

Therapist:	**So Leslie, I'm going to re-read the list of Rung 1 beliefs that you endorsed. Let me know if you feel we've identified all the reactive parts connected to these statements. If we've left anyone out, let me know, so we can bring them into the conference room now. I shouldn't exist; It's not safe to exist; I'm so alone, there's no point in existing; and No one wants me to exist.**
Client:	They feel pretty neutral right now. I think we've got them all.

Step 12: Preparing for the Needs Meeting Protocol

Therapist:	**So we're out of time today, but next week we can start the needs meeting work. There are 3 introjects and 4 reactive parts at the conference table. Ultimately we'll want to process all 3 introjects. We can work with one at a time, or we could work with several together. In addition, we can process one or more of the reactive parts along with the introjects, but they will likely get totally unstuck automatically as the introjects heal – so including them in the needs meeting work is optional. What do you think would be best?**

© Copyright 2009 by Shirley Jean Schmidt, MA, LPC. All rights reserved. Duplication in any form without permission is prohibited.

Client:	Let's just do the three introjects.
Therapist:	**Okay. We can start with that next time if you like. There are seven child parts at the conference table right now. So little ones, would the seven of you like to get together to meet? We can move the table out of the way.**
Child Parts:	That would be nice.
Therapist:	**So when you're ready, come together. The Resources can put out some punch and cookies if you like. Let me know if that feels good.**
Child Parts:	Yeah.
Therapist:	*(Turned ABS on.)* **Notice that good feeling. Tell me when it's strengthened all the way.**
Child Parts:	Okay.
Therapist:	*(Turned ABS off.)* **I'd like to thank each of you for your hard work today. In a few moments I'm going to invite you to tuck in. Is there anything you'd like to say or ask before you tuck in?**
Child Parts:	Will the costumes get big and scary again?
Therapist:	**This intervention has helped you get partly unstuck from the costumes, but we'll have to do the Needs Meeting Protocol later, to get you totally unstuck. Until then, one or more costumes could reanimate and start delivering their ugly message again. But even if that happens, it's STILL a harmless illusion, and we can easily switch the dominance back again, in just a few minutes.**
Child Parts:	Okay.
Therapist:	**So girls when you're ready, find a nice warm safe cozy place to tuck in to. You can tuck in separately, each with your very own set of Resources, or tuck in as a group. Just find a good safe place to wait until the next time you're needed.**

Chapter Summary

This chapter provided instructional details for guiding reactive parts to identify the maladaptive introjects most responsible for a target issue – either a specific current problem or old attachment wounds. Once these introjects have been found, and the dominance of each has been switched, they can be selected for needs meeting processing. The next chapter will describe the Needs Meeting Protocol, which helps these ego states completely heal. Forms and worksheets, which can simplify the application and mastery of these steps, are provided in Appendix E. Look for the *Attachment Needs Ladder questionnaire*, the *Conference Room Map Template*, and the *Conference Room Protocol Worksheet*.

Chapter 5 Notes and References

1. Fraser, G.A. (1991). The dissociative table technique: A strategy for working with ego states in dissociative disorders and ego-state therapy. *DISSOCIATION, 4,* 205-213.
2. The DNMS Home Study Course was released in 2008. It is a 7-module Course which teaches psychotherapists how to competently execute each DNMS protocol. Each Course module consists of a narrated slide show and an illustrated study guide. The slide shows explain key concepts with animated illustrations. Review questions are provided throughout the slide shows to check comprehension of the material. Modules 3-7 include recordings of real sessions, to demonstrate specific protocols. The slide shows are provided on a single DVD (or 7 CDs) which will play on most Windows-based and Macintosh computers. The study guides provide an outline of all the material covered in the slide shows. The Module 2-7 study guides include study questions and answers. You can see what the Home Study Course slide shows are like by watching a 25-min Introduction to the DNMS slide show. For more information about the Course, go to Appendix F, page 256, or go to www.dnmsinstitute.com/dnmscourse.html. To see the 25-min Introduction to the DNMS slide show go to www.dnmsinstitute.com/ dnmsintro.html.
3. The DNMS Flip Chart provides an easy way to explain the DNMS to clients and colleagues. It is a 75-page "slide show" that: introduces the DNMS; explains *parts of self*; explains neural integration; explains alternating bilateral stimulation; describes the Resources and Healing Circle; describes reactive parts and introjects; explains the Switching the Dominance Protocol; describes the Conference Room Protocol with text and pictures; and describes the Needs Meeting Protocol with pictures. The Flip Chart includes lots of pictures to illustrate complex concepts. The chart is provided in a 3-ring binder so you can add your own pages or tabs, or move pages around. For more information about the Flip Chart, go to Appendix F, page 255, or go to www.dnmsinstitute.com/flipchart.html.

© Copyright 2009 by Shirley Jean Schmidt, MA, LPC. All rights reserved. Duplication in any form without permission is prohibited.

Chapter 6
The Needs Meeting Protocol

Overview

The Needs Meeting Protocol covered in this chapter is one of several elements of an overall healing cycle. In the first part of the cycle you'll guide a client to identify a set of *negative beliefs* associated with a target issue. In the second part you'll call forward, into an imagined *conference room*, all the reactive parts that hold this set of negative beliefs. You'll invite each one to look across the conference table to see each of the maladaptive introjects they're reacting to, so you can switch the dominance of each introject. And in the third part you'll apply the *Needs Meeting Protocol* to help these introjects get totally unstuck. Once you've completed these three, you'll repeat the cycle with another targeted issue, until all treatment goals have been met.

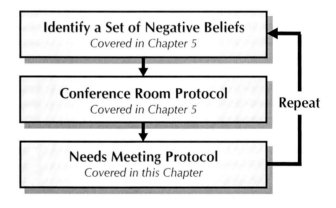

The DNMS model is based on the assumption that children grow and develop in stages, and that each developmental stage involves a set of needs that should be met by parents or caregivers. Caregivers can fail to meet developmental needs by acts of commission, such as verbal, physical, or sexual abuse, and/or acts of omission, such as misattunement, neglect, and abandonment. The degree to which developmental needs – particularly emotional needs – were not adequately met, is the degree to which parts of self may be stuck in childhood, and stuck in the emotional wounds of the past.

The Needs Meeting Protocol aims to heal such wounds by remediating the unmet developmental needs. The process starts by inviting all the child parts selected by the client (at the end of the Conference Room Protocol) for needs meeting work, into the Healing Circle, where the Resources can meet their developmental needs, help them process through painful emotions, and establish an emotional bond. As the Resources meet these needs, the old emotional wounds begin to heal. As the child parts get unstuck from the past, the unwanted behaviors, beliefs, and emotions associated with a targeted issue abate.

A typical client/therapist dialogue is provided at the end of this chapter to illustrate the flow of this protocol. Forms and worksheets, which simplify the application of this protocol, are provided in Appendix E. Look for the *Needs Meeting Protocol Session Notes* form and the *Needs Meeting Protocol Worksheet*. This chapter describes the Needs Meeting Protocol as it would proceed with no complications. Instructions for handling blocks unique to this intervention are covered on pages 184-192 of Chapter 7.

© Copyright 2009 by Shirley Jean Schmidt, MA, LPC. All rights reserved. Duplication in any form without permission is prohibited.

The Needs Meeting Protocol

This protocol consists of a series of steps for guiding selected child parts to directly and indirectly disclose their unmet needs, so the DNMS Resources can meet those needs. Each protocol step approaches this task from a different angle, so nothing is missed. The aim is to be very thorough so complete healing is accomplished.

Preparing First Time Clients

Clients who are doing the protocol for the first time should be informed about a few items at the outset.

- **Prepare Clients to Disclose Blocks**

  Prepare your clients to disclose processing blocks as soon as they arise. This is the same information you provided just before starting the Resource Development Protocol. It's so important you'll want to inform clients about this at least twice. Say something like:

  > Sometimes during this protocol, concerns or fears about the processing will arise. Unconscious fears can be expressed by the sudden arrival of a body disturbance such as unpleasant sensations, dissociation, distracting thoughts, numbness, or sleepiness. That may or may not happen to you, but if it does, please tell me about it, even if it doesn't seem important. You're welcome to have concerns or fears – just let me know if they come up. I'll want to address them right away.

- **Prepare Clients to Process in Present Time**

  It's very important for the child parts getting their needs met inside the Healing Circle to understand that the Resources are meeting their needs in present time, and not in their troubled past. To make sure the processing unfolds this way, prepare clients in advance, to process in present time. Say something like:

  > During this protocol, the Resources will be meeting needs in present time – in (2009). Please let me know, if at any point, your mental pictures suggest the Resources are meeting needs in the past, rather than in present time, for example, if you picture the Resources meeting needs in your childhood home. We want to make sure that the child parts are getting their needs met in the Healing Circle now, because the Resources can't change the past.

- **Prepare Clients to Process Emotions with a Sensorimotor Activity**

  Step 8 of this protocol is for processing the child parts' painful emotions. Sometimes during this step you'll want to invite the child part to process escalating emotions with a sensorimotor activity. It is helpful to brief clients on this technique before starting the protocol, so when you need to use it, you don't have to interrupt the processing to explain it. Say something like:

  > At some point during this protocol, painful emotions will likely come up. One of the options for processing emotions gets the body involved with a sensorimotor activity. I suggest doing this by (punching on this pillow). This intervention is based on the idea that a child being physically or emotionally wounded has an urge to fight or flee. When fighting back is forbidden, or physically impossible, the urge gets submerged in the body – often for years. (Punching the pillow) helps get your body involved in the emotion processing. It helps the physical and emotional tension to finally be expressed and resolved. When we get to a point in the protocol that it might help to use this, I'll ask you if you want to try it. I'm just letting you know about it now, so I don't have to interrupt the processing to tell you about it later.

  This topic will be discussed in more detail in the Step 8 description.

© Copyright 2009 by Shirley Jean Schmidt, MA, LPC. All rights reserved. Duplication in any form without permission is prohibited.

■ *Prepare Clients to Engage in Authentic Processing*

Sometimes clients engage in superficial processing. This is more likely to happen with clients who don't understand the process well, who are afraid of "doing it wrong," or who tend to be highly defended. As the protocol unfolds, they seem to move through the steps but they're not really fully engaged. For example, when a client is not sure how to answer a question he may give an answer he thinks is "correct," rather than saying "I don't know." Or a client's adult self might answer questions intended for wounded child parts. Clients will only benefit from the process if they are authentically engaged in it. To reduce the possibility of inauthentic processing, say something like:

> I'll be asking a lot of questions as we go through the protocol. Most of them will be addressed to the (three) child parts we'll be working with. It's very important that each question is answered honestly and authentically. If I ask a question you cannot answer, just tell me you don't know the answer. For example, if I ask what a child part looks like, and you can't see the part, don't tell me what you think it should look like, tell me you can't see it. It's important for the child parts to personally feel the Resources meeting their needs. Let me know if they don't. If we engage in a protocol step that you don't like, or if you start to feel uncomfortable, please tell me. As soon as I know about a processing problem I can take steps to fix it.

Step 1: Connecting to Resources   ABS On

In Step 1 you'll invite your client to connect to her Resources by saying something like:

> Connect to your Resources. (Let me know if you need my help connecting.) Tell me when you're connected.

Once your client reports she's connected, turn on ABS and say:

> Let that get as strong as it wants to. Tell me when that's strengthened all the way.

When your client says, "okay," turn ABS off.

Healing Circle

Step 2: Checking for Processing Blocks   ABS Off

To check for unconscious blocks, ask the client something like:

> When you think about beginning the needs meeting work now, with (the Rung 1 introjects), what do you notice in your body?

There are three possible body reactions: (1) The body might feel clear, indicating a readiness to begin, (2) the body might feel a little discomfort, indicating benign apprehension but no block, or (3) the body might feel uncomfortable or contracted, indicating a block. Any blocks revealed here must be addressed before proceeding. Information about identifying and clearing processing blocks are discussed in Chapter 7.

Step 3: Inviting the Child Parts into the Healing Circle   ABS Off

Step 3 is a two-part process. Child parts are invited to approach the Resources. Then, if the Resources seem safe, they are invited into the Healing Circle. A little delay in bringing child parts in to the Circle provides an opportunity for them to voice any concerns about the Resources, so they can be handled in advance of the processing – although sometimes child parts automatically appear in the circle as soon as they are invited forward. Invite the introjects forward first, followed by reactive parts.

© Copyright 2009 by Shirley Jean Schmidt, MA, LPC. All rights reserved. Duplication in any form without permission is prohibited.

- ***Inviting the Selected Introjects***

    Before inviting the selected introjects forward, say something like:

    > *By the time we had finished switching the dominance of these introjects, all the masks were pocketed. When I invite them forward today, the masks might still be pocketed, they might be a little bigger than before, or they might be big again – completely reanimated. As each introject comes forward, tell me what you notice.*

    Invite one at a time with something like:

    > *I'd like to invite, to approach the Resources, the (<u>x-year-old</u>) we worked with (<u>last week</u>), the one that was mirroring your (<u>wounding role model</u>), delivering the message, ("<u>You're not good enough</u>"). When you're ready, tell me what you notice.*

    When the part appears, ask the client:

    > *What do you notice? Is the mask still in the pocket?*

    Regardless the answer given, speak with the child part with the costume by saying:

    > *Hey little one. Thanks for coming. Take a look at the Resources. Do they look safe to you?*

    If the answer is "yes," ask:

    > *Would you like to get up close... right in between them?*

    If the answer is "yes," say:

    > *Good. Move in close. Tell me when you're there.*

    Once inside the circle ask:

    > *Does it feel safe here?*

    If the answer is "yes," say:

    > *Good. (Just hang out here. I'll be back with you in a moment.)*

    Once all the introjects are in the Healing Circle, begin inviting any selected reactive parts forward. If none were selected for processing, go to Step 4.

- ***Inviting the Selected Reactive Parts***

    If you invite selected reactive parts, invite them all at once, by age and mood. For example:

    > *I'd like to invite, to approach the Resources, (<u>the sad two-year-old, the anxious four-year-old, and the angry ten-year-old</u>).*

    When they all come forward ask:

    > *Do the Resources look safe? Would you like to get up close... right in between them?*

    When they answer "yes," say:

    > *Good. Move in close. Tell me when you're there.*

    Once inside the Circle ask:

    > *Does it feel safe here?*

    If it feels safe to them, proceed to Step 4.

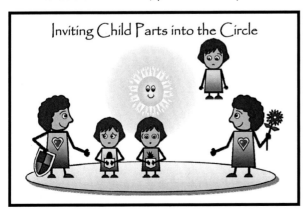

Inviting Child Parts into the Circle

Strengthening the Sense of Safety

© Copyright 2009 by Shirley Jean Schmidt, MA, LPC. All rights reserved. Duplication in any form without permission is prohibited.

Step 4: Strengthening the Sense of Safety   ABS On

Once all the selected introjects and reactive parts are inside the Healing Circle, use ABS to strengthen the sense of safety and comfort. Turn on ABS and say to the child parts:

> *Notice the sense of safety and comfort here. Let it get as strong as it wants to. Tell me when it's strengthened all the way.*

When they say "okay," turn ABS off.

Step 5: Asking for a Generalization Effect   ABS Off

Role models can deliver wounding messages over many developmental stages, not just the stages represented by the ages of the child parts in the circle. For that reason, just before the needs meeting begins, invite the brain to generalize the effects of the work. Ask something like:

> *I'm guessing these wounding messages were delivered over many developmental stages, not just (ages x-y). Is that right?*

When the client agrees, say:

> *Brain, please allow all the work we do today with the (x-y-year-olds) to apply to all the developmental stages affected by these messages from (the wounding role models)."*

Step 6: Explaining the Process   ABS Off

This step orients the child parts to the processing. Say something like:

> *So little ones, I'm guessing you've been stuck in the past for a long time. Does that sound right to you?*

When they agree say:

> *If it were possible to get unstuck, would that interest you?*

When they answer "yes," say:

> *Notice the Resources. Notice they're real, notice they're here for you, and notice they can help you get unstuck because they can meet needs for you now that were not met well in the past. Think back to being (ages x-y). Think about needs you had at that time that were met well... and needs that were not met well... and when you're ready, tell me what you need most, right now.*

The child parts usually answer with a need, like: "to be loved," "to be validated," or "to be seen and heard."

Step 7: Meeting Needs   ABS On

In Step 7 you'll follow-up Step 6 with a question like:

> *Can the Resources (give you all the unconditional love you need), right now?*

When the child parts acknowledge that the Resources can meet the need, start ABS and say something like:

> *Good. Notice that. Let it get as strong as it wants to. Tell me when it's strengthened all the way.*

When the child parts say it has strengthened, say:

> *Good. And what else do you need?*

Repeat this cycle of questioning awhile.

© Copyright 2009 by Shirley Jean Schmidt, MA, LPC. All rights reserved. Duplication in any form without permission is prohibited.

Here are examples of typical needs child parts express and helpful follow-up questioning:

When child parts express a need...	Follow up with...
To be loved.	Can the Resources give you all the unconditional love you need now?
To be encouraged.	Can the Resources encourage you now?
To be safe.	Can the Resources keep you safe now?
To have my own opinions.	In the Resource's care can you have and express your own opinions?
Parents who are logical and rational.	Are the Resources logical and rational?
Privacy.	Can the Resources give you age-appropriate privacy now?
To be accepted.	Can the Resources accept you unconditionally now?
To be comforted when I'm upset.	Will the Resources comfort you when you're upset?
Positive attention.	Can the Resources give you the positive attention you need now?

Suggest Needs When Child Parts Don't Know What They Need

If the child parts don't know what they need, or if they can only list a few items, ask about some possibilities. For clues about what they need, refer to the target issue negative beliefs and introject messages. You can also refer to the table in Appendix B, page 210, with a list of typical needs from five stages of development from conception to age 18. For example, you might ask the child parts:

Do you need caregivers who can manage their own emotions well?

If they answer "yes," ask:

Can the Resources manage their own emotions well?

If they answer "yes," start ABS and say something like:

Good. Notice that. Let it get as strong as it wants to. Tell me when it's strengthened all the way.

Here are examples of typical needs you might ask about and helpful follow-up questioning if the child parts answer "yes":

If the child parts answer "yes" to...	Follow up with...
Do you need caregivers who can manage their emotions?	Can the Resources manage their emotions?
Do you need caregivers who can see reality clearly?	Can the Resources see reality clearly?
Do you need caregivers who provide loving corrections?	Can the Resources provide loving corrections?
Do you need warmth and affection?	Can the Resources give you warmth and affection now?
Do you need caregivers who understand you?	Can the Resources understand you?
Do you need caregivers who are good at listening?	Are the Resources good at listening?
Do you need caregivers who can attune to you?	Can the Resources attune to you now?
Do you need age-appropriate guidance?	Can the Resources give you age-appropriate guidance?

Plan to leave ABS on through Step 17.

© Copyright 2009 by Shirley Jean Schmidt, MA, LPC. All rights reserved. Duplication in any form without permission is prohibited.

Checking for Processing Problems

After meeting a few needs in Step 7, you may want to check to make sure the processing is flowing well, especially if you're working with a client who is new to the protocol.

■ ***Checking for Present-time Processing***

It is sometimes helpful to verify that the child parts are experiencing the needs meeting by the Resources as a present-time activity. Say something like:

Does it seem like the Resources are meeting the child parts' needs in present time?

If not, use the interventions provided on page 186, in the section titled *Child Parts are Fixated on the Past.*

■ ***Checking for Vague Processing***

Vague mental pictures are often a sign of blocked processing. So ask the client:

How's the processing going? Do the Resources and child parts seem more vivid or more vague?

If the answer is "more vague," consider that there may be a problem. It may help to ask:

If the Resources could meet the needs of these child parts now, is there something you'd lose or something bad that would happen?

If you discover a processing complication or block, clear it before continuing. If no blocks are found, continue with the protocol, but check in with the client again later. The pictures should become more vivid, as the process unfolds.

Preparing for Emotion Processing

After you've met about 10-15 needs, begin preparations for the Step 8 emotion processing. Ask the child parts:

Do you need caregivers who want you to feel and express the full range of emotions?

If they answer "yes," ask:

Do the Resources want you to feel and express the full range of emotions?

If they answer "yes," say:

Good. Notice that. Tell me when it's strengthened all the way.

When the child part's say "okay," ask:

Do you need caregivers who can help you process through painful emotions, like anger or grief?

If they answer "yes," ask:

Can the Resources help you process through painful emotions?

If they answer "yes," say:

Good. Notice that. Tell me when it's strengthened all the way.

Checking on Changes in Appearance

After the Resources have met these last two needs (above), ask the client:

As you picture these little ones now, is there anything different about their appearance? Have the masks (or costumes) changed? Are there any remains left in the pockets? AND What do you notice in your body now?

Clients typically report that the child parts appear happier, masks/costumes that are either smaller or gone, and a body that feels relaxed and calm. When a client reports something like this, a *substantial shift* has occurred. That's your cue to proceed to Step 8. But if the child parts appear serious or gloomy, or if the masks/costumes appear exactly the same size, meet more needs in Step 7 until a substantial shift is reported.

If a client reports a body disturbance, there may be a processing block. Determine the nature or source of the discomfort by asking:

If the (body disturbance) could talk, what would it say?

© Copyright 2009 by Shirley Jean Schmidt, MA, LPC. All rights reserved. Duplication in any form without permission is prohibited.

If the disturbance is connected to a painful emotion that the child parts are ready to process (e.g. anger or grief), proceed to Step 8. If the disturbance is due to a processing block, clear it – then, ask again about body sensations. The body disturbance should disappear once the block has been cleared. When the block has cleared, determine whether the child parts need more needs met in Step 7, or whether they're ready to process emotions in Step 8.

Step 8: Processing Painful Emotions   ABS On

In Step 8 you'll help the wounded parts express and release painful emotions that have been held in the body for years. This processing is focused specifically on working through the anger and grief that developed in reaction to others' wounding messages and behaviors. Other kinds of emotions, like disappointment, frustration, or fear, which are processed differently, are discussed in the *Other Protocol Issues* section below.

Some child parts will process through emotions with tears, growls, facial expressions, or body language that clearly communicates their feelings. Others will process with little or no outward expression. It appears the painful emotions will process through, whether or not they are outwardly expressed. Start Step 8 by asking:

> *Your experiences with your (wounding role models) were pretty upsetting, weren't they? I wonder if you might have some unresolved painful emotions connected to those experiences – maybe anger or grief.*

If the child parts are in doubt, read aloud the wounding introject messages. Most of the time child parts will admit to having unresolved emotions to process. When they do, ask:

> *Would you like to process those emotions now?*

- If the child parts respond with a "yes," ask:

  > *Which emotion would you like to process first – anger or grief?*

- If the child parts report a fear of contacting painful emotions, say:

  > *I understand you're afraid of contacting these emotions. I know a way we can process them without you having to fully feel them. You won't even have to cry. It's very gentle. It involves the Resources meeting more needs. Let's give it a try. If you don't like it, we can stop. Which emotion would you like to explore first – anger or grief?*

- If the child parts report their access to painful emotions is blocked, say:

  > *I understand that you have some unresolved grief or anger to process, but access to these emotions is blocked. We can actually process them in a way that does not require you to fully access them. Which emotion would you like to explore first – anger or grief?*

- If the child parts deny having unresolved emotions to process, respond with:

  > *I understand your grief and anger may be completely resolved and you have nothing left to process through, but I'd like to pursue this a little bit, just in case there might be something left to work through. If you did have some unresolved emotions buried, which would you want to explore first – anger or grief?*

Once the child parts have answered with either "anger" or "grief," begin emotion processing with the first of the three major DNMS emotion-processing modes. If the child parts are unwilling to discuss or explore the possibility of processing emotions, look for and clear the associated block, then return to Step 8.

Three DNMS Emotion Processing Modes

The DNMS offers three different emotion processing modes. They include: *Processing Emotions by Meeting Needs, Processing Emotions with the Loving Support of Resources,* and *Processing Emotions with a Sensorimotor Activity*. Each tool solves a different problem. *Processing Emotions by Meeting Needs* is the primary tool used because it is gentle and effective, even when clients have fear of emotional overwhelm, have blocked access to emotions, or deny unresolved emotions are present. The other two can be used as well, if and when they are needed. Each one is described below.

© Copyright 2009 by Shirley Jean Schmidt, MA, LPC. All rights reserved. Duplication in any form without permission is prohibited.

1. *Processing Emotions by Meeting Needs*

To process emotions by meeting needs, ask the child parts:

> *So little ones, <u>if you could feel</u> the (<u>anger</u>) completely and fully in your body now, <u>how intense would it be</u>, from 0-10, where 10 is the most intense you could imagine and 0 is none at all?"*

When they answer with a rating (e.g. 8), ask:

> *Which of your (<u>wounding role models'</u>) behaviors are most connected to that (<u>8</u>)?*

From the behavior disclosed, figure out the associated need (e.g. safety). Then ask something like:

> *Can the Resources (<u>keep you safe</u>) now?*

When the child parts say "yes," say:

> *Good. Notice that. Tell me when it's strengthened all the way.*

Then ask again:

> *So little ones, <u>if you could feel</u> the (<u>anger</u>) completely and fully in your body now, <u>how intense would it be</u>, 0-10?*

The rating will typically be 1 to 3 points lower. When they answer with a rating (e.g. 5), ask:

> *Which of your (<u>wounding role models'</u>) behaviors are most connected to that (<u>5</u>)?*

From the behavior disclosed, figure out another unmet need (e.g. validation). Then ask something like:

> *Can the Resources (<u>validate you</u>) now?*

When the child parts say "yes," say:

> *Good. Notice that. Tell me when it's strengthened all the way.*

Here are some typical wounding behaviors and logical follow-up questions:

If the child parts disclose...	Follow up with...
My parents neglected me.	Can the Resources tend to your needs well now?
Mom was over-protective.	Can the Resources appropriately protect you now?
Dad would lapse into rages.	Can the Resources manage their emotions well?
Mom expected me to meet her needs.	Can the Resources meet their own needs?
Dad loved his beer more than me.	Do the Resources love you more than anything else?
When I was upset, mom told me to "get over it."	Can the Resources comfort you when you're upset?
Dad told me I had to become a doctor like him.	Can the Resources allow you to develop *your* interests?
Mom was intrusive and engulfing.	Will the Resources give you the space you need now?

You'll repeat this questioning again and again with the first emotion (e.g. anger). Each time a need is identified and met, the intensity rating will drop a little, until it finally reaches 0. You'll repeat the steps with the second emotion (e.g. grief), until it also reaches 0. Clients usually process anger and grief separately, but sometimes clients will spontaneously combine them.

2. *Processing Emotions with the Loving Support of the Resources*

Sometimes while processing painful emotions, the child parts might burst into tears, saying something like: "It was just so bad," or "I thought the abuse would never end." This is a cue to direct their attention to the loving support of the Resources. Respond with something like:

> *Do the Resources understand (<u>just how bad it was</u>)?*

When the child parts say "yes," say:

> *Notice the Resources completely understand what you're feeling. They totally support you and honor your emotions. Express them any way you need to.*

As the processing unfolds, softly add:

> *Feel the Resources' compassion, empathy, and support... Notice they completely understand... Just let it heal...*

© Copyright 2009 by Shirley Jean Schmidt, MA, LPC. All rights reserved. Duplication in any form without permission is prohibited.

This keeps the child parts aware of the support, empathy, compassion, and non-judgmental understanding provided freely by the Resources now. After processing this way for awhile say:

> *When you're ready, tell me what you notice.*   Or ask: *Does this seem to be processing through?*

If the child parts report that the processing is still underway, encourage them to continue noticing the Resources' empathy and support. If this processing feels complete, return to *Processing Emotions by Meeting Needs*. If the disturbance is escalating, ask if adding a sensorimotor activity would help.

3. *Processing Emotions with a Sensorimotor Activity*

ABS On

TASPER

A sensorimotor activity incorporates the muscles of the body in the processing of emotion, such as when a client pushes on the therapist's hands, twists a towel, or hits a pillow while expressing anger or grief. A *TASPER* (acronym for Therapist's Aid for Sensorimotor Processing for Emotional Release) provides the sensorimotor activity of choice for many DNMS therapists. It consists of two 14″ padded bars connected at the ends by two ropes. Clients can pull on the top bar with their hands while pushing on the bottom bar with their feet. This engages both arm and leg muscles. For more information go to Appendix F, page 255, or go to www. dnmsinstitute.com/tasper.html.

When a child is physically or emotionally wounded, the body has an urge to fight or flee. When doing so is forbidden, or physically impossible, the urge to physically react gets submerged in the body – often for years. According to Peter Levine and Pat Ogden, a sensorimotor activity can help a client shift from helpless victim mode to a sense of empowerment.[1] This intervention provides a means for that physical or emotional tension to finally be expressed. By combining a sensorimotor activity with the loving support of the Resources, clients with both overwhelming and buried emotions are often able to resolve them relatively quickly.

If, in the course of Step 8, it seems the child parts need a more physical way to process disturbing emotions, ask something like:

> *Would you be interested in (pulling on the TASPER) right now? It may help these emotions process through more quickly and thoroughly.*

If they are agreeable, begin the process by saying:

> *Notice your connection to the Resources. Think about those things your (wounding role model) did to make you (angry), and when you're ready, (pull).*

As the child parts are pulling, softly add:

> *Feel the Resources' compassion, empathy, and support... Notice they completely understand... Just let it heal...*

After awhile say:

> *When you're ready, tell me what you notice.*   Or ask: *Does this seem to be processing through?*

If this processing is still underway, encourage the child parts to continue noticing the Resources' empathy and support. When the processing feels complete, or if it's not processing through, return to *Processing Emotions by Meeting Needs*

It's best to introduce new clients to the sensorimotor concept before starting the first needs meeting session, so they understand it in advance. That way you won't have to interrupt the processing flow to explain this basic information.

Verifying Processing Completion with a Sensorimotor Activity

ABS On

A sensorimotor activity can also be used to verify that processing is complete. When the child parts rate the intensity of both the anger and grief as 0, say something like:

© Copyright 2009 by Shirley Jean Schmidt, MA, LPC. All rights reserved. Duplication in any form without permission is prohibited.

Would you be willing to check for completeness by (pulling on the TASPER)? If the emotion has completely resolved, you should know right away because it will feel good to pull. If there are any unresolved emotions left, pulling should bring them to the surface so we can finish them off. How does that sound?

Child parts are usually very agreeable to this. Once the client is holding the (*TASPER*) and is ready to start, say:

Notice your connection to the Resources. Think about those things your (<u>wounding role models</u>) did to make you sad and angry, and when you're ready, (<u>pull</u>).

As the child parts pull, say:

And if there is anything you wished you could have said to your (<u>wounding role models</u>) then, but knew you couldn't, you can say it out loud now.

They may say something like: "Mom how dare you ignore my needs. How dare you make me take care of you. You're the parent, not me – but you make me mother you. I needed you to take care of me, but you made me take care of you. What are you thinking?!" It's best if these expressions are the *exact words* the client had an urge to use in childhood. For example, saying "I hate you Mom," would be more effective than saying, "I hated you then Mom," or "I hated Mom." The combination of verbal expression, physical exertion, ABS, and the loving support of the Resources in present time, can help the painful emotions process through quickly.

Occasionally at this point in the protocol, a client may report that the emotion intensity has reduced significantly, but not quite to 0. When this happens, ask something like:

Is this as low as the intensity is going to get for now?

If the client answers "no," continue with Step 8. If the client answers "yes," proceed to Step 9. The remaining emotions will usually process through all the way at some point in the steps that follow.

Checking on Changes in Appearance

Next check on changes in the appearance of the child parts and body sensations by asking something like:

As you picture these little ones now, is there anything different about their appearance? Have the masks/costumes changed? Are they still in the pockets? What do you notice in your body now?

Clients typically report that the child parts are much happier and all the costumes are gone. The body usually feels quite relaxed.

Step 9: Bonding With the Resources   (ABS On)

Many therapists have promoted the idea of establishing a loving bond between a caring adult self and child parts of self.[2] In Step 9 you'll further strengthen the emotional connection between the child parts and each individual Resource, and with the Resources as a group. Say to the child parts:

So little ones, look into the eyes of the Nurturing Adult Self and tell me what you see.

© Copyright 2009 by Shirley Jean Schmidt, MA, LPC. All rights reserved. Duplication in any form without permission is prohibited.

They will typically answer with something like: "Love, caring, kindness." Then say:

> *And notice that as you're looking into (her) eyes, (she's) looking in your eyes, seeing straight into your hearts. Do you feel a bond forming?*

If the child parts answer "yes," say:

> *Good. Notice that bond. Take as long as you need to let it strengthen. Tell me when it's strengthened all the way.*

Repeat this with the Protective Adult Self and the Spiritual Core Self.

Strengthen a Group Bond

To strengthen a group bond, add up all the Resources and child parts in the circle, then say:

> *Notice the (six) of you together. Do you feel a group bond?*

If the child parts answer "yes," say:

> *Good. Notice that. Tell me when it's strengthened all the way.*

Explain What a Bond Means

It is not uncommon for child parts to not know what a bond means. To explain what the bond means, say:

> *I'd like to explain what a bond means. It means when you hurt, the Resources hurt. They don't want to hurt and they don't want you to hurt, so they're going to do whatever they have to, as quickly as they can, to help you feel better. How does that sound?*

When they express a favorable response, say:

> *Think about that. Tell me when it's strengthened all the way.*

Forming a Bond with Nurturing Adult Self

Forming a Bond with Protective Adult Self

Step 10: Heightening Awareness of the Adult Body   (ABS On)

In Step 10 you'll apply the Adult Body Intervention. This heightens the child parts' awareness of being in an adult body. The introjects already experienced this intervention once during the Switching the Dominance Protocol. This step reinforces it. As before, ask the child parts:

> *Do you know you're in an adult body now?*

Whether their answer is "yes" or "no," follow up with:

> *Look at your hands.   OR   Look in this mirror.*

Then ask:

> *Is this adult body what you expected to see?*

It may help to add:

> *Now wiggle your fingers. Notice those are your fingers.   OR*
> *Now touch your nose. Notice that's your nose.*

© Copyright 2009 by Shirley Jean Schmidt, MA, LPC. All rights reserved. Duplication in any form without permission is prohibited.

▪ ***Child Parts Say They <u>Didn't Expect</u> to See an Adult Body***

Often child parts say they didn't expect to see adult hands or an adult face in the mirror. When this happens, contrast the downside of being in a child body with the upside of being in an adult body. Tailor the contrast to elements that are relevant to the child parts' ages and issues. For example, you might say something like:

> *As a child your parents were in total control of your life, weren't they? They told you what to eat, when to eat, what to wear, when to sleep. They were in control of who came to the house and who you spent time with. They made up the rules and punished you if you broke the rules. The younger you were, the more control they had. Right?*

When the child parts are in agreement follow-up with something like:

> *But now that you're in an adult body, you make those decisions. You decide what to eat, when to eat it, what to wear, when to sleep. You decide who to spend time with, and who to stay away from. You make up the rules now, right? What's it like to think about that?*

▪ ***Child Parts Say They <u>Did Expect</u> to See an Adult Body***

Occasionally child parts say they expected to see an adult body. When this happens, ask:

> *Tell me how being in an adult body now, better than being in a child body at (<u>age x</u>)?*

The answer allows you to verify that they do indeed know what the benefits are. If they are only partially aware of the benefits, you can elaborate on the rest, or invite the Resources to explain it to them. As the child parts articulate the benefits they are aware of, it heightens their awareness of their personal power.

Strengthening Awareness of the Adult Body

Whether the child parts already knew, or are just now learning about the adult body, follow up by saying:

> *So little ones, I want you to think about the good news of being in an adult body now. Take as long as you need to let it strengthen. Tell me when it's strengthened all the way.*

Step 11: Checking In   ABS On

In Step 11 you'll ask about the child parts' subjective sense of how unstuck they are, with something like:

> *So little ones, I'm guessing when we started you felt pretty stuck. How stuck do you feel now? Somewhat stuck, somewhat unstuck, mostly unstuck, or totally unstuck?*

The most common responses are "mostly unstuck" and "totally unstuck." If the child parts give any other answer, you may be processing over a block. Sometimes the child parts' positive perception of how unstuck they are can be distorted by the "feel-good" experience of being connected to loving Resources. This common problem is remedied in Steps 12-15. So if the child parts report they are totally unstuck, say:

> *I hear you believe you're totally unstuck. In fact you may be. But I have a few more steps to take you through. If you're totally unstuck they'll go very quickly, but if you're still a little stuck, we'll catch it and clear it. How does that sound?*

Child parts are typically agreeable to this.

Step 12: Returning to the Wounding Experiences   ABS On

Steps 12 through 15 are similar to Peter Levine's technique of "pendulating" between comfort and trauma when processing through disturbing memories.[3] In Step 12 you'll identify any remaining disturbance. When using this protocol the first time, start with a brief explanation. In subsequent work, this explanation may or may not be necessary. Say something like:

> *Now little ones, so far everything we've done has been in the presence of the Resources. To find out if there's any remaining disturbance I'll be asking you to disconnect from the Resources*

© Copyright 2009 by Shirley Jean Schmidt, MA, LPC. All rights reserved. Duplication in any form without permission is prohibited.

for just a moment, so you can revisit (those wounding experiences) from the past – just as they were back then, without your Resources present for support. You'll do this for just a moment, long enough to tell me how much disturbance comes up, then you'll come right back to the Resources. Are you okay with that?

- **If the child parts are okay with this, say:**

   Good. Now little ones, disconnect from the Resources for just a moment and, when you're ready, bring your attention back to (those wounding experiences) from (ages x-y), remembering them just the way they were back then, when you didn't have Resources present for support. How much disturbance comes up now, from 0-10, where 0 is none and 10 is the worst disturbance you can imagine?

- **If the child parts are not okay with this, say:**

   Okay. So we can do this in a way that's comfortable for you, without leaving the company of the Resources. Now little ones, if you were to bring your attention back to (those wounding experiences) from (ages x-y), remembering them just the way they were back then, when you didn't have Resources present for support, and if you could feel the disturbance completely and fully in your body now, how intense would it be, from 0-10, where 0 is none and 10 is the worst disturbance you can imagine?

The child parts will give you a 0-10 rating.

- If the rating is 0 proceed to Step 15, unless it is coming from child parts that expressed an aversion to disconnecting from the Resources. Such an aversion is a sign of being stuck. A rating of 0 is a sign of being unstuck. This mixed message signals there's a processing block to find and clear.
- If the rating is above 0, (e.g. 3) ask:

   Which of the (wounding role models') behaviors is most connected to that (3)?

Child parts will answer with something like: "Mom invalidated everything I did."

Step 13: Returning to the Care of the Resources   ABS On

In Step 13 you'll figure out the unmet need, from the role model behaviors reported. Then say something like:

   So little ones, bring your attention back to the Resources. Can the Resources (validate you) now?

When the child parts say "yes," say:

   Good. Notice that. Tell me when that's strengthened all the way.

Here are some sample wounding behaviors and helpful follow-up questions:

If the child parts disclose...	Follow up with...
My father ignored me.	Can the Resources give you all the attention you need now?
My brother abused me.	Can the Resources protect you from abusive people now?
My mother humiliated me.	Will the Resources always treat you with respect?
My parents over-protected me.	Can the Resources grant you age-appropriate autonomy?
My parents never listened to me.	Will the Resources listen to you now?
My mom expected me to meet her needs.	Can the Resources meet their own needs?

Step 14: Repeating Steps 12 & 13   ABS On

In Step 14 you'll repeat Steps 12 and 13, to take the disturbance level to zero. Start with something like:

   Good. Now little ones, once again disconnect from the Resources, and when you're ready, revisit (those wounding experiences) from (ages x-y). Remembering them just the way they were back then, when you didn't have Resources present for support, 0-10, how much disturbance comes up now?

© Copyright 2009 by Shirley Jean Schmidt, MA, LPC. All rights reserved. Duplication in any form without permission is prohibited.

OR:

> *Good. Now little ones, if you were to revisit (those wounding experiences) from (ages x-y), remembering them just the way they were back then, when you didn't have Resources present for support, and if you could feel the disturbance completely and fully in your body, 0-10, how intense would it be now?*

The intensity rating typically drops a little after each additional need is met. When the rating drops to 0 proceed to Step 15, but as long as the rating is above 0 follow up with:

> *Which of the (wounding role model) behaviors is most connected to that (1-10 rating)?*

Again, from the behavior reported figure out another unmet need (e.g. to be heard). Then say something like:

> *So little ones, bring your attention back to the Resources. Can the Resources (hear you) now?*

When the child parts say "yes," say:

> *Good. Notice that. Tell me when that's strengthened all the way.*

© Copyright 2009 by Shirley Jean Schmidt, MA, LPC. All rights reserved. Duplication in any form without permission is prohibited.

Shifting Attention Back and Forth

Step 15: Shifting Attention Back and Forth

ABS On

When the wounds are truly healed, the body should feel at peace, whether the child parts are revisiting the wounding events from the past, or being in the Resources' care now. In Step 15 you'll assess protocol progress and help any remaining unresolved hurt process through. This step is analogous to holding an 85% brightness-rated paper, next to a 98% brightness-rated paper. When contrasted to the brighter paper, the lower-rated paper is obviously not as bright as it could be. In this step any remaining disturbances will be noticed, no matter how slight. Say to the child parts:

Okay little ones, now shift your attention back and forth between (those wounding experiences) from the past when you had no Resources for support, and the Resources' care now... back and forth, and back and forth... and when you're ready, tell me what you notice.

Their reply should tell you whether any disturbance remains.

If the child parts say something like...	This suggests...	Follow up with...
- The picture is fading; - The image is getting smaller; - It doesn't seem important now; or - Now it feels no different from being in the Resources' care.	No disturbance remains.	*Are you saying there is absolutely no disturbance in your body when you revisit (those wounding experiences)?* *(Ignore any unrelated physical pain.)*
- It's a little yucky; - It feels creepy; - I really don't like it; or - I don't want to go back.	Some disturbance remains.	*Keep shifting attention back and forth. The remaining disturbance will either go away, or it won't go away. When you're ready, tell me which is happening.*
- I can now shut the door on my past; - I can finally walk away from it; - I prefer being with the Resources; or - I'm not going to let it bother me anymore.	They may be dismissive of some remaining disturbance.	*It sounds like you still have some aversion to revisiting (the wounding experiences). Keep shifting your attention back and forth. That remaining aversion will either go away, or it won't go away. When you are ready, tell me which is happening.*
- Now I can go there and not get hurt because I have my Resources to support and protect me; or - My Resources provide a protective bubble for me now, so these people can't hurt me anymore.	They are using the Resources to insulate themselves from the remaining disturbance.	*The fact that you believe you need the protection tells me that you haven't processed this disturbance all the way through yet. How much disturbance would you feel if you didn't have their protection and support right now?*

© Copyright 2009 by Shirley Jean Schmidt, MA, LPC. All rights reserved. Duplication in any form without permission is prohibited.

If the child parts report that absolutely no disturbance comes up, proceed to Step 16. But, if the child parts report any disturbance or aversion remains, even if it's just a teeny tiny bit, ask:

> *Of your (<u>wounding role models'</u>) behaviors, which is most connected to the disturbance that remains?*

From the behavior reported figure out another unmet need (e.g. attunement). Then say something like:

> *So little ones, bring your attention back to the Resources. Can the Resources (<u>attune to you</u>) now?*

When the child parts say "yes," say:

> *Good. Notice that. Tell me when that's strengthened all the way.*

Once the need is met, invite the child parts again to shift attention back and forth. Stay with Step 15 until the child parts report absolutely no body disturbance comes up when they revisit the old wounding experiences.

Step 16: Checking In   ABS On

In Step 16 you'll assess four criteria that signal the child parts' healing is complete. The child parts are most likely totally unstuck if: (1) they report feeling totally unstuck; (2) they look happy and are ready to engage in age-appropriate play and exploration; (3) the masks/costumes are gone; and (4) the body feels completely clear of disturbing emotions.

- ***Child Parts' Report of Feeling Unstuck***

  Ask the child parts:

  > *So little ones, are you feeling mostly unstuck or totally unstuck now?*

  The usual answer is "totally unstuck."

- ***Clients' Report of How the Child Parts Appear***

  Ask the client:

  > *As you picture these little ones now, is there anything different about their appearance? Is there anything left of the masks or costumes?*

  The masks or costumes are usually completely gone. The child parts typically appear happy, confident, unburdened, smiling, playing, and exploring. If words like *playing* and *exploring* are not part of the description, ask the client:

  > *If we were to take the child parts out to a playground, which would they prefer to do, play on the swings and jungle-gym, or sit at the picnic table with the Resources?*

  Clients typically report the child parts want to engage in age-appropriate play or exploration. Child parts that got stuck at an especially young age, such as infancy, would most likely to want to hang out with the Resources – and that would be age-appropriate.

- ***Clients' Report on How the Body Feels***

  Finally ask the client:

  > *What do you notice in your body now?*

  The body typically feels calm and clear.

If all four criteria are met, and the healing appears to be complete, proceed to Step 17. If not, find out why. The possible reasons for a problem here are discussed on page 189 of Chapter 7.

Step 17: Strengthening a Positive Belief   ABS On

In Step 16 you'll invite the child parts to strengthen a positive belief about self. Start by asking:

> *So little ones, when you think about what we've done today – what you've learned and how you've grown – what positive belief do you know to be true about you now?*

© Copyright 2009 by Shirley Jean Schmidt, MA, LPC. All rights reserved. Duplication in any form without permission is prohibited.

Encourage positively-worded statements such as those that start with "I am...," "I can...," "I deserve...," or "I'm now able to...." For example, "I'm lovable," "I'm safe now," "I can express myself," and "I deserve good things." Once a belief is disclosed, ask:

How true does that feel, 0-10, where 10 is totally true?

The rating should be around 9 or 10. Then say:

Good. Think about these words. Tell me when they've strengthened all the way.

Step 18: Tucking In the Child Parts   ABS Off

In Step 18 you'll turn ABS off, and *tuck in* the child parts. Tucking in puts them in a non-active state, so the clients' most adult self can take over executive functioning. Say something like:

So little ones, I want to thank you for all your hard work today. You've been very courageous and have done a marvelous job of working through this old stuff. It sounds like you're totally unstuck. If it turns out you're not, or if you need additional help, I'll be happy to help you in a future session. In a few moments I'm going to invite you to tuck in. Is there anything you'd like to say or ask before you tuck in?

After acknowledging any comments, or answering any questions, say:

Now find a nice, warm, cozy, safe place to tuck into. You can tuck in with your Resources if you like. Just find a good safe place to wait until the next time you're needed.

Step 19: Counting Up   ABS Off

In Step 19 you'll notice whether your client is having difficulty reorienting to present time. If so, you'll want to encourage the process by asking:

Would you like for me to count up from 1-5?

If the client says "yes," say:

One, coming up slowly. Two, a little more alert, and little more awake. Three, notice your body in the chair, notice your hands... your feet... your breath. Prepare to open your eyes. Four, letting your eyes open. Notice colors... notice sounds... notice your body in the chair... feeling a little more awake, a little more alert...   Once eye contact is made, add: *...and five, completely and totally awake and alert.*

If counting up is not sufficient to bring a client into the present moment, invite her to engage in a sensorimotor activity (e.g. pulling on the TASPER) as she looks into your smiling eyes. Say to the client:

Now bring your body completely and fully back into this room, back into this chair, back into the present moment.

This combination of words and sensorimotor activity can be very effective at grounding a disoriented client.

© Copyright 2009 by Shirley Jean Schmidt, MA, LPC. All rights reserved. Duplication in any form without permission is prohibited.

Step 20: Checking on the Outcome

ABS Off

In Step 20 you'll check to verify that the protocol has successfully accomplished the desired outcome.

- **■ *Ask Client to Re-Rate Wounding Introject Messages***

  Start by referring to the Conference Room Map. Ask the client to re-rate, from 0-10, the level of disturbance evoked by each of the wounding introject messages on the map that were processed in this protocol. Clients typically report that the messages no longer evoke a disturbance.

- **■ *Ask Client to Re-Rate How Stuck the Reactive Parts Are***

  Ask the client to re-rate, from 0-10, how stuck the associated reactive parts are (if they did not just complete this protocol). Limit this questioning to those reactive parts that correspond to the introjects that just completed this protocol. Clients typically report that these reactive parts are no longer stuck.

- **■ *Ask Client to Re-Rate the Initial List of Negative Beliefs***

  If your target issue was a Rung or Section of the Attachment Needs Ladder, ask the client to re-rate, from 0-10, how true the targeted beliefs feel now. Use the same past, present, or future vulnerable-event prompt you used initially, when asking for the new ratings. If your target issue was a specific current problem, and if the client had initially provided and rated a list of beliefs connected to the problem, ask the client to re-rate each statement now. Clients typically re-rate their initial negative beliefs a 0 (not at all true).

- **■ *Ask Client to Report Changes in Perception of the Problem***

  If your target issue was from the Attachment Needs Ladder, ask the client to report on any perceptions of desirable changes in associated behaviors, beliefs, or emotions – that correspond directly to the Rung that was processed. (For example, after processing Rung 3, you might ask if the client now feels differently about developing and expressing her own opinions.) Clients typically report noticeable improvement in those symptoms clearly connected to a Rung just processed. If your target issue was a specific current problem, ask the client to report on any changes in perception of that problem. Clients typically report seeing the situation from an adult perspective rather than their usual wounded-child perspective.

Other Protocol Issues

Orienting Clients to the Needs Meeting Protocol

The best time to orient first-time clients to the Needs Meeting Protocol steps is while you're introducing the Attachment Needs Ladder and Conference Room Protocol. You can explain the protocol steps with visual aids, such as illustrations from this book, the Home Study Course Module 1 slide show,[4] the DNMS Flip Chart,[5] and/or drawings that you generate. See Appendix F for more information about these visual aids.

Strengthening Positives with Alternating Bilateral Stimulation (ABS)

If you're applying tactile or aural ABS electronically (with a TheraTapper or headphones), leave it on continuously from Step 7 through Step 18. If a block comes up, turn ABS off until the block has been cleared. If a client does not like ABS you can leave it out, but give the client enough time to let items strengthen, just as you would if you were using ABS.

- **■ *When the Client Takes a Long Time to Strengthen an Item***

  It usually takes about 5-60 seconds for an item to "strengthen all the way." If a client takes much longer than this, check in to make sure the client has not checked out. Gently ask:

  Is that still strengthening?

© Copyright 2009 by Shirley Jean Schmidt, MA, LPC.　All rights reserved.　Duplication in any form without permission is prohibited.

- ***When the Client Takes Very Little Time to Strengthen an Item***

  If a client takes less than five seconds to strengthen an item, find out why. Ask:

  What was happening in the (five) seconds it took to strengthen that? How did you determine this had strengthened all the way?

  If the answer suggests a processing block, clear it. If the client is confused about the process, provide the needed clarifications. Otherwise, encourage the client to let items strengthen a little longer.

- ***Shortening the Strengthening Instruction***

  When you're first strengthening items in Step 7 say to the client:

  Good. Notice that. Let it get as strong as it wants to. Tell me when it's strengthened all the way.

  You may shorten this as the child parts get accustomed to the process.

  You can shorten it to: *Good. Notice that. Tell me when it's strengthened all the way.*
  Then to: *Tell me when it's strengthened all the way.*
  Then to just: *Notice that.*

Dialogue Between Child Parts and the Resources

Sometimes during the protocol, child parts need reassurance, validation, or new information – help that can be provided by the therapist, the Resources, or both. When such help comes from loving, attuned Resources it is usually more valuable and more credible, and will lead to a better resolution. So whenever feasible, direct child parts to the Resources for answers and encouragement. Supplement any Resource responses which seem incomplete. When you do provide information, it may help to follow it with:

But don't take my word for it, ask the Resources. Do they agree with me?

Child Parts Report Needs in the Negative

To the question, "And what else do you need?" child parts may answer in the negative, with something like, "I need a father who *won't* sexually abuse me," "I need my mom to *not* scream at me," or "I need my parents to *not* get drunk and fight." These answers contain valuable clues about what is needed from the Resources now, but it is not sufficient to just ask the child parts to notice that the Resources: "would *not* sexually abuse you,' "would *not* scream at you," or "would *not* get drunk and fight."

It is better to identify the positive behavior that was missing, then ask if the Resources can engage in that behavior now. For example you might ask questions like: "Can you count on the Resources to honor your boundaries?" "Will the Resources treat you with respect at all times, no matter what kind of mood you're in or they're in?" or "Can the Resources settle conflicts well, without alcohol?"

Processing Other Painful Emotions

Step 8 is focused primarily on processing anger and grief that is a reaction to others' wounding messages and behaviors. But other emotions can also come up at any point in the protocol – emotions such as fear, confusion, doubt, disappointment, guilt, regret, and frustration. Fear is handled by saying something like:

Notice you're safe and protected with the Resources now... take as long as you need to let that strengthen. Tell me when that's strengthened all the way.

Most other emotions can be handled by saying something like:

It makes perfect sense that you'd be feeling (confusion, doubt, regret, etc.) now, considering what's happened to you in the past. Notice the Resources completely understand why you feel this way.... Feel their empathy and compassion..... Feel that love.... Notice their support.

This should help the emotion resolve enough to resume the protocol step you were on.

© Copyright 2009 by Shirley Jean Schmidt, MA, LPC. All rights reserved. Duplication in any form without permission is prohibited.

Painful Emotions Arise Early in Step 7

If painful emotions, such as sadness, anger, or fear come up early in Step 7, ask:

> *What did your caregivers do that makes you so (angry) now?*

Figure out the associated unmet need (e.g. comfort, safety, or love) then ask, for example:

> *Can the Resources (<u>comfort you</u>) now?*

When they say "yes," invite the child parts to notice the Resources comforting them now. If anger or grief comes up late in Step 7, after 15 or more needs have been met, it may be time go directly to Step 8.

Needing Parents to Meet a Need

Sometimes when asked, "And what else do you need?" child parts simply state a need. For example they may say, "I need protection." But sometimes they say they need a parent to meet a need. For example they may say, "I need my parents to protect me." Ask them if the Resources can meet that need now. For example, "Can the Resources protect you now?" When they say "yes," invite them to notice the Resources protecting them now. As the Resources meet the need, the fact that it was not met by a particular parent usually becomes less important.

Child Parts "Need" a Positive Trait

Sometimes when asked, "And what else do you need?" the child parts name a positive trait, such as "self-esteem," "confidence," or "courage." You have two options for handling this:

- ***Restate the question:***

  > *What else did you need from your parents that they didn't provide?*

- ***Ask for more information:***

  > *What would you need caregivers to do for you, to help you develop (<u>confidence</u>)?*

  If the answer is, for example, "encouragement," then ask:

  > *Can the Resources (<u>encourage</u>) you now?*

  When they say "yes," say:

  > *Good. Notice that. Tell me when that's strengthened all the way.*

If the Resources Had Been Your Parents Then...

Usually child parts list general needs, like "unconditional love," "nurturing," or "protection." But sometimes they will express a specific need related to a specific experience. For example, child parts may say something like, "I needed my father to let me go to my Senior Prom," "I needed my mother to drive me to school to protect me from Buster, the neighbor's Pit Bull," "I needed my parents to punish my brothers when they pushed me off the roof." The intervention to address this has two parts. First, ask the child parts:

> *If the Resources had been your parents then, would they have (<u>responded appropriately</u>)?*

For example you might need to say, "If the Resources had been your parents then, would they have let you go to the Senior Prom?" or "If the Resources had been your parents then, would they have driven you to school?" When the child parts respond with a "yes," let that strengthen all the way. Then, for part two say:

> *Can the Resources (<u>take appropriate action</u>) now?*

For example you might need to say, "Are the Resources supportive of your social life now?" or "Can the Resources protect you from imminent dangers now?" When the child parts respond with a "yes," let that strengthen all the way.

© Copyright 2009 by Shirley Jean Schmidt, MA, LPC. All rights reserved. Duplication in any form without permission is prohibited.

Getting the Strongest Positive Belief

In Step 17 you'll ask the child parts to express a positive belief about self that feels true, now that they are totally unstuck. Sometimes the child parts disclose positive beliefs about others, such as, "The Resources love me," or "The world is not so dangerous." Ask if a more self-referential version of this is true. "Are you saying you believe, '*I'm* lovable'?" or "Are you saying you believe, '*I'm* safe now'?"

Sometimes the child parts disclose positive beliefs that are irrational or untrue, such as "Nothing can hurt me now." When this happens, encourage construction of a realistic statement like, "There are many things I can do now to protect myself." If child parts have difficulty articulating a belief, look at the original introject messages for ideas. For example you could say something like:

> *Your (mom's) message was ('You have no value.') Do you believe ('I have value') now? OR*
> *Your (dad's) message was ('You're powerless.') Do you believe ('I have power') now?*

Interruption While Tucking In Child Parts

Step 18 involves tucking in the child parts at the end of the processing. Just before tucking them in, ask:

> *Is there anything you'd like to say or ask before you tuck in?*

Most of the time the child parts will say "thank you," or nothing at all. Sometimes the child parts will ask a question about the future. Occasionally, a client who does not understand that the question was addressed *only* to the child parts, will launch into a new topic – interrupting Step 18. When this occurs, ask the client:

> *Is that question (or comment) coming from the child parts I'm about to tuck in?*

If not, invite the client to hold the question (or comment) for a moment. Again ask the child parts if they have anything to say or ask before they tuck in. Once they are tucked in, invite the client to express what's on her mind.

Closing an Unfinished Protocol

It is not always possible to finish the entire Needs Meeting Protocol in a single session. Before closing down an incomplete session, ask for and strengthen a positive belief; tuck in the child parts; then count up (if necessary).

Getting the Best Positive Belief

Since the protocol is not yet finished, the child parts are still partially stuck. Positive beliefs like, "I'm safe now" or "I'm lovable," may only feel partially true. Look for and strengthen positive work-in-progress beliefs that feel very true or totally true. These may be statements that start with words like: "I'm beginning to...," "I'm learning to...," or "I'm becoming...." For example: "I'm beginning to understand I'm okay after all," "I'm learning that I may be lovable," or "I'm becoming a stronger person."

Tucking In Child Parts

Tuck in the child parts with something like this:

> *So little ones, I want to thank you for all your hard work today. You've been very courageous and have done a marvelous job of working through this old stuff. I understand we have more work to do to get you totally unstuck. I promise to help you with that in a future session. In a few moments I'm going to invite you to tuck in. Is there anything you'd like to say or ask before you tuck in?*

Once they have expressed their thoughts, say:

> *Good, now find a nice, warm, cozy, safe place to tuck into. You can tuck in with your Resources if you like. Just find a good safe place to wait until the next time you're needed.*

© Copyright 2009 by Shirley Jean Schmidt, MA, LPC. All rights reserved. Duplication in any form without permission is prohibited.

Resuming an Unfinished Protocol

When you close down an unfinished Needs Meeting Protocol in one session, you'll need to resume it in a follow-up session. Resume unfinished needs meeting work by starting with Steps 1-5 of the protocol. When you get to Step 6, you'll need to modify it a bit. You'll say:

> *When you were here last time we talked about how you were stuck in the past and wanted to get unstuck. Do you still want to get unstuck?*

When the child parts say "yes," say:

> *I explained that the Resources could help you get unstuck by meeting needs for you now. Think back to being (ages x-y). Think about needs you had at that time that were met well... and needs that were not met well... and when you're ready, tell me what you need most, right now.*

If your previous session ended in Step 7, simply resume that step, and follow the protocol to the end. If your previous session had ended in Steps 8-15, and if the child parts appear confident and the costumes are gone, meet one or two needs in Step 7. Then say:

> *So little ones, in our last session we had completed (the emotion processing step). Are you ready to go forward (to the bonding step), or should we go back to (the meeting needs or processing emotion step)?"*

But if the previous session had ended in Steps 8-15, the child parts now appear in a somber, anxious, or angry mood, meet a lot of needs in Step 7 before moving on.

Complications and Processing Blocks

The application of the Needs Meeting Protocol will not always unfold smoothly. Problems can arise at many points in the process, for example, while inviting child parts into the Healing Circle, while meeting needs, while processing painful emotions, while strengthening an emotional bond, and while reporting levels of remaining disturbance. Furthermore, global complications can interfere with processing, for example, when a client will not honestly disclose what is transpiring during the processing, or when child parts are expecting the Resources to rescue them from a past traumatic event. Complications can occur when a client has a misunderstanding about the processing; an introject blocking processing: or when a therapist is confused or makes an error. Pages 184-192 of Chapter 7 explore many of the complications and blocks that are unique to the Needs Meeting Protocol, offering suggestions for handling them.

Typical Needs Meeting Protocol Session

The following is a typical client/therapist dialogue for applying the Needs Meeting Protocol. It follows the typical client/therapist dialogue from Chapter 5, pages 102-113. This will provide you an example of how to execute and transition between the following steps:

- Preparing First Time Clients
- Step 1: Connecting to Resources
- Step 2. Checking for Processing Blocks
- Step 3. Inviting the Child Parts into the Healing Circle
- Step 4. Strengthening the Sense of Safety
- Step 5. Asking for a Generalization Effect
- Step 6. Explaining the Process
- Step 7. Meeting Needs
- Step 8. Processing Painful Emotions
- Step 9. Bonding With the Resources
- Step 10.   Heightening Awareness of the Adult Body

© Copyright 2009 by Shirley Jean Schmidt, MA, LPC. All rights reserved. Duplication in any form without permission is prohibited.

- Step 11.   Checking In
- Step 12.   Returning to the Wounding Experiences
- Step 13.   Returning to the Care of the Resources
- Step 14.   Repeating Steps 12 & 13
- Step 15.   Shifting Attention Back and Forth
- Step 16.   Checking In
- Step 17.   Strengthening a Positive Belief
- Step 18.   Tucking In the Child Parts
- Step 19.   Counting Up
- Step 20.   Checking on the Outcome

Preparing First Time Clients   *ABS Off*

Therapist: This is our first needs meeting session, so there are a few things I want to explain up front. The first item is something we talked about just before you established the Resources. I want to remind you of this again… Sometimes during this protocol, concerns or fears about the processing will arise. Unconscious fears can be expressed by the sudden arrival of a body disturbance such as unpleasant sensations, dissociation, distracting thoughts, numbness, or sleepiness. That may or may not happen to you, but if it does, please tell me about it, even if it doesn't seem important. You're welcome to have concerns or fears – just let me know if they come up. I'll want to address them right away.

Client: Okay.

Therapist: During this protocol, the Resources will be meeting needs in present time – in 2009. Please let me know, if at any point, your mental pictures suggest the Resources are meeting needs in the past, rather than in present time. For example, if you picture the Resources meeting needs in your childhood home. Okay?

Client: Okay.

Therapist: At some point during this protocol painful emotions will likely come up. One of the options for processing emotions gets the body involved with a sensorimotor activity. I suggest doing this with a TASPER. The word TASPER is an acronym for *Therapist's Aid for Sensorimotor Processing for Emotional Release*. As you can see, it has two bars. You can pull on one while you push on the other. This intervention is based on the idea that a child being physically or emotionally wounded has an urge to fight or flee. When doing so is forbidden, or physically impossible, the urge gets submerged in the body – often for years. The TASPER helps get your body involved in the emotion processing. It helps the physical and emotional tension to finally be expressed and resolved. When we get to a point in the protocol that it might help to use this, I'll ask you if you want to try it. I'm just letting you know about it now, so I don't have to interrupt the processing to tell you about it later. Any questions?

Client: No. I understand.

Therapist: I'll be asking a lot of questions as we go through the protocol. Most of them will be addressed to the three child parts we'll be working with. It's very important that each question is answered honestly and authentically. If I ask a question you cannot answer, just tell me you don't know the answer. For example, if I ask what a child part looks like, and you can't see the part, don't tell me what you think it *should* look like, tell me that you can't see it. It's important for the child parts to personally feel the Resources meeting their needs. Let me know if they don't. If we engage in a protocol step that you don't like, or if you start to feel uncomfortable, please tell me. As soon as I know about a processing problem I can take steps to fix it.

Client: I'm afraid I won't do it right.

Therapist: The only way you can do it wrong, is if you don't tell me about what you're really experiencing. I'll be making decisions throughout the protocol about what to ask the child parts, and what interventions to apply, based on what I know about how the child parts are doing. If I don't know what's really going on, I may well take them in the wrong direction without knowing it. So if there's something odd occurring, or if you get confused, please tell me. Together we'll be able to figure it all out and make the protocol work.

Client: Okay. I understand.

Step 1. Connecting to Resources   *ABS On*

Therapist: **Okay. Think about your Resources. Let me know if you need my help connecting to them. Tell me when you're connected.**

© Copyright 2009 by Shirley Jean Schmidt, MA, LPC. All rights reserved. Duplication in any form without permission is prohibited.

Child parts:	I'm connected.
Therapist:	**Good. Let that get as strong as it wants to. Tell me when it's strengthened all the way.**
Client:	Okay.

Step 2. Checking for Processing Blocks   *ABS Off*

| Therapist: | **When you think about doing needs meeting work today with the three Rung 1 introjects, what do you notice in your body?** |
| Client: | Nothing. It's clear. |

Step 3. Inviting the Child Parts into the Healing Circle   *ABS Off*

Therapist:	**By the time we had finished switching the dominance of these three introjects, all the masks were pocketed. When I invite them forward today, the masks might still be pocketed, they might be a little bigger than before, or they might be big again – completely reanimated. As each introject comes forward, tell me what you notice.**
Client:	Okay.
Therapist:	**Good. Now, I'd like to invite, to approach the Resources, the <u>two-year-old</u> we worked with last week... the one that was mirroring your dad, delivering his message, "Get out of my way or I'll kill you." When you're ready, tell me what you notice.**
Client:	I see the two-year-old.
Therapist:	**How does this part appear? Is the mask still in the pocket?**
Client:	She's in a serious mood. I don't see the mask.
Therapist:	**Have her check the pocket.**
Client:	It's in there.
Therapist:	*(To the child part...)* **Hey there little one. Thanks for coming. Take a look at the Resources. Do they look safe to you?**
Child part:	Yes.
Therapist:	**Would you like to get up close... right in between them?**
Child part:	Okay.
Therapist:	**Good. Move in close. Get right in between them.** *Pause* **Does it feel safe here?**
Child part:	Yes.
Therapist:	**Good. Just hang out here. I'll be back with you in a moment.** *(To the client...)* **Now I'd like to invite, to approach the Resources, the <u>four-year-old</u> we worked with last week... the one that was mirroring your mom reading a book, conveying her message, "Leave me alone. My novel is more important than you or your needs. If you bother me I'll get angry and it will be your fault." When you're ready, tell me what you notice.**
Client:	Here she comes. She's holding a book with mom's face on it.
Therapist:	*(To the child part...)* **Hey little one. Thanks for coming. Take a look at the Resources. Do they look safe to you?**
Client:	Sure.
Therapist:	**Would you like to get up close... right in between them?**
Child part:	Okay.
Therapist:	**Good. Move in close. Get right in between them.** *Pause* **Does it feel safe here?**
Child part:	Yeah.
Therapist:	**Good. Just hang out here. I'll be back with you in a moment.** *(To the client...)* **Now I'd like to invite, to approach the Resources, the <u>six-year-old</u> we worked with last week... the one that was mirroring your mom and dad delivering their message, "You're very, very bad. Keep it up and we'll send you to an orphanage." When you're ready, tell me what you notice.**
Client:	She's happy to see the Resources. She's already in the Circle.
Therapist:	**Is the mask still in the pocket?**
Client:	Yes.

© Copyright 2009 by Shirley Jean Schmidt, MA, LPC. All rights reserved. Duplication in any form without permission is prohibited.

Step 4. Strengthening the Sense of Safety   *ABS On*

Therapist: So little ones, notice the sense of safety and comfort here with the Resources. Let it get as strong as it wants to. Tell me when it's strengthened all the way.

Child Parts: Okay.

Step 5. Asking for a Generalization Effect   *ABS Off*

Therapist: So I'm guessing these messages from mom and dad were delivered over many developmental stages, not just ages two, four, and six. Is that right?

Client: Right.

Therapist: So brain, please allow all the work we do today with the two, four, and six-year-olds, to apply to all the other developmental stages affected by these messages from mom and dad.

Client: Sounds good.

Step 6. Explaining the Process   *ABS Off*

Therapist: So girls, I'm guessing you've been stuck in the past a long time. Is that right?

Child Parts: Yes.

Therapist: **If it were possible to get unstuck, would that interest you?**

Child Parts: Yes.

Therapist: **Notice these Resources. Notice they're real, notice they're here for you. Notice they can help you get unstuck because they can meet needs for you now that were not met well in the past. Think about being ages two through six. Think about needs you had at that time that were met well... and needs that were not met well... and when you're ready, tell me what you need most, right now.**

Child Parts: I need my parents to want me.

Step 7. Meeting Needs   *ABS On*

Therapist: **Do the Resources want you now?**

Child Parts: Yes.

Therapist: **Good. Notice that. Let that get as strong as it wants to. Tell me when it's strengthened all the way.**

Child Parts: Okay.

Therapist: **Good. And what else do you need?**

Child Parts: *(Starts to cry.)* I need them to love me.

Therapist: **Do the Resources love you now?**

Child parts: Yeah.

Therapist: **Good. Notice that. Tell me when it's strengthened all the way.**

Child parts: Okay.

Therapist: **Good. And what else do you need?**

Child parts: I need parents who aren't angry all the time.

Therapist: **Are the Resources angry all the time?**

Child parts: No.

Therapist: **Can they manage their emotions well?**

Child parts: Yes.

Therapist: **Good. Notice that.**

Child parts: Okay.

Therapist: **Good. And what else do you need?**

Child parts: I want to be important to them.

Therapist: **Are you important to the Resources now?**

Child parts: Yes.

Therapist: **Good. Notice that.**

Child parts: Okay.

Therapist: **Good. And what else do you need?**

© Copyright 2009 by Shirley Jean Schmidt, MA, LPC. All rights reserved. Duplication in any form without permission is prohibited.

Child Parts:	I need to feel safe. My dad had a temper. Whenever he'd get mad he'd hit me.
Therapist:	**Are you safe and protected in the care of the Resources now?**
Child Parts:	Yes.
Therapist:	**Good. Notice that. Tell me when it's strengthened all the way.**
Child Parts:	Okay.
Therapist:	**Good. And what else do you need?**
Child parts:	They keep changing the rules. They're never consistent.
Therapist:	**Are the Resources consistent and predictable now?**
Child parts:	Yes.
Therapist:	**Good. Notice that.**
Child parts:	Okay.
Therapist:	**Good. And what else do you need?**
Child Parts:	I need my dad not to hit me every time I do something he doesn't like.
Therapist:	**Will the Resources treat you with respect, no matter what kind of mood you're in or they're in?**
Child Parts:	Yes.
Therapist:	**Good. Notice that.**
Child Parts:	Okay.
Therapist:	**Good. And what else do you need?**
Child Parts:	I need my dad to leave me alone.
Therapist:	**Say more about that.**
Child Parts:	Whenever my dad was around me he was verbally abusive. I just wanted him to leave me alone.
Therapist:	**Do you need kind caregivers who can give you positive attention? Caregivers who are fun to be around?**
Child Parts:	That would be nice.
Therapist:	**Can the Resources give you positive attention now? Are they fun to be around?**
Child parts:	Yeah.
Therapist:	**Good. Notice that.**
Child parts:	Okay.
Therapist:	**Good. And what else do you need?**
Child Parts:	I need to be good so they won't punish me.
Therapist:	**Let me ask that another way. What did you need your parents to do that they didn't do?**
Child Parts:	Be fair with me.
Therapist:	**Do the Resources know the difference between behaviors that require a correction or punishment from those that don't?**
Child parts:	Yeah.
Therapist:	**Good. Notice that.**
Child parts:	Okay.
Therapist:	**And can they provide fair and loving correction when a correction is appropriate?**
Child parts:	Uh-huh.
Therapist:	**Good. Notice that.**
Child parts:	Okay.
Therapist:	**Good. And what else do you need?**
Child parts:	I don't know.
Therapist:	**Do you need caregivers who put your needs above their wants?**
Child parts:	Yes.
Therapist:	**Can the Resources put your needs above their wants?**
Child parts:	Yes.
Therapist:	**Good. Notice that.**
Child parts:	Okay.
Therapist:	**Do you need caregivers who are mature, responsible, grown-ups?**
Child parts:	Definitely!
Therapist:	**Are the Resources mature, responsible, grown-ups?**
Child parts:	Yes.

© Copyright 2009 by Shirley Jean Schmidt, MA, LPC. All rights reserved. Duplication in any form without permission is prohibited.

Therapist:	**Good. Notice that.**
Child parts:	Okay.
Therapist:	**Do you need caregivers who will make a loving connection with you?**
Child parts:	Yes.
Therapist:	**Are the Resources here to make a loving connection with you now?**
Child parts:	Yes.
Therapist:	**Good. Notice that. Take as long as you need to let that strengthen.**
Child parts:	Okay.
Therapist:	**Do you need caregivers who are attuned to you? That means they can sense what you need by your body language, and then respond appropriately.**
Child parts:	That would be nice
Therapist:	**Are the Resources attuned to you now?**
Child parts:	Yes.
Therapist:	**Good. Notice that.**
Child parts:	Okay.
Therapist:	**Do you need caregivers who are nurturing and caring?**
Child parts:	Oh yeah.
Therapist:	**Are the Resources nurturing and caring?**
Child parts:	Yes.
Therapist:	**Good. Notice that.**
Child parts:	Okay.
Therapist:	**Do you need caregivers who want to help you grow to meet your full potential?**
Child parts:	Definitely!
Therapist:	**Are the Resources here to help you grow to meet your full potential?**
Child parts:	Yes.
Therapist:	**Good. Notice that.**
Child parts:	Okay.
Therapist:	**Do you need caregivers who want you to feel and express the full range of emotions?**
Child parts:	What a strange idea. I like it.
Therapist:	**Can the Resources give you permission to feel and express your emotions now?**
Child parts:	Yes.
Therapist:	**Good. Notice that.**
Child parts:	Okay.
Therapist:	**Do you need caregivers who can help you process painful emotions, like anger or grief?**
Child parts:	Yeah!
Therapist:	**Can the Resources help you process through painful emotions?**
Child parts:	Yes.
Therapist:	**Good. Notice that.**
Child parts:	Okay.
Therapist:	**Leslie, as you picture these little ones now, is there anything different about their appearance?**
Client:	They're more relaxed. Smiling. Really happy to be with the Resources.
Therapist:	**How big are the masks now?**
Client:	I only see the four-year-old's book – actually it's more like a single page now. Mom's face is not on the page now.
Therapist:	**Have the two-year-old and six-year-old check their pockets.**
Client:	There are a few specks of dust left. That's all.
Therapist:	**Good. And Leslie, what do you notice in your body now?**
Client:	I feel relaxed.

Step 8. *Processing Painful Emotions* *ABS On*

Therapist:	**So girls, when you think about these messages delivered by your mom and dad, do any strong emotions come up now - maybe anger or grief?**

© Copyright 2009 by Shirley Jean Schmidt, MA, LPC. All rights reserved. Duplication in any form without permission is prohibited.

Child parts:	No. I think it's all gone.
Therapist:	**Okay. You may be right. Close your eyes and listen, while I read you their messages. "Get out of my way or I'll kill you." "Leave me alone. My novel is more important than you or your needs. If you bother me I'll get angry and it will be your fault." "You're very, very bad. Keep it up and we'll send you to an orphanage." Does that bring up any emotion now?**
Child parts:	Yes. But I don't want to feel it. It's too much.
Therapist:	**I understand you're afraid of contacting these emotions. I know a way we can process them without you having to fully feel them. You won't even have to cry. It's very gentle. It involves the Resources meeting more needs. Let's give it a try. If you don't like it, we can stop. Which emotion would you like to explore first – anger or grief?**
Child parts:	Anger.
Therapist:	**Okay. So little ones, <u>if you could</u> feel the anger completely and fully in your body now, how intense <u>would it be</u>, from 0-10, where 10 is the most intense you could imagine and 0 is none at all?**
Child parts:	Nine.
Therapist:	**Which of your parents' behaviors are most connected with that nine?**
Child parts:	They were always yelling at me. I was always in trouble for something.
Therapist:	**Do the Resources treat you with respect now?**
Child parts:	Yes.
Therapist:	**Good. Notice that.**
Child parts:	Okay.
Therapist:	**Do the Resources know which behaviors need a correction and which ones don't?**
Child parts:	Yes.
Therapist:	**And when a correction is needed, can they do it lovingly – with great respect for you?**
Child parts:	Yes.
Therapist:	**Good. Notice that.**
Child parts:	Okay.
Therapist:	**Good. So little ones, <u>if you could</u> feel the anger completely and fully in your body now, how intense <u>would it be</u>, 0-10?**
Child parts:	Seven.
Therapist:	**Which of your parents' behaviors is most connected to the seven?**
Child parts:	They expect me to do things I'm too little to do, then punish me when I do them wrong.
Therapist:	**Can the Resources give you age-appropriate responsibilities?**
Child parts:	Yes.
Therapist:	**Can the Resources provide age-appropriate guidance and encouragement for carrying out those responsibilities?**
Child parts:	Yes.
Therapist:	**Good. Notice that.**
Child parts:	Okay.
Therapist:	**And can the Resources praise you when you master those responsibilities?**
Child parts:	Yes.
Therapist:	**Good. Notice that.**
Child parts:	Okay.
Therapist:	**Good. So little ones, <u>if you could</u> feel the anger completely and fully in your body now, how intense <u>would it be</u>?**
Child parts:	Four.
Therapist:	**Which of your parents' behaviors is most connected to the four?**
Child parts:	They're always making their bad mood my fault. I get blamed for everything that's wrong with them.
Therapist:	**Can the Resources take responsibility for their own behavior and emotions?**
Child parts:	Yes.
Therapist:	**Good. Notice that.**
Child parts:	Okay.
Therapist:	**Can the Resources see reality clearly and respond to reality appropriately?**
Child parts:	Yes.

© Copyright 2009 by Shirley Jean Schmidt, MA, LPC. All rights reserved. Duplication in any form without permission is prohibited.

Therapist:	**Good. Notice that.**
Child parts:	Okay.
Therapist:	**Good. So little ones, <u>if you could</u> feel the anger completely and fully in your body now, how intense <u>would it be</u>?**
Child parts:	Zero.
Therapist:	**Good. So little ones, <u>if you could</u> feel the grief completely and fully in your body now, how intense <u>would it be</u>, from 0-10?**
Child parts:	Nine.
Therapist:	**Which of your parents' behaviors is most connected to the nine?**
Child parts:	They had me, but they didn't want me.
Therapist:	**Do the Resources want you now?**
Child parts:	Yes.
Therapist:	**Good. Notice that. Take as long as you need to let that strengthen.**
Child parts:	It's just so painful. It's like I didn't belong anywhere. Not with them – not with anybody.
Therapist:	**Do the Resources understand just how difficult it was for you to grow up with rejecting parents.**
Child parts:	Yes.
Therapist:	**Good. Notice the Resources completely understand what you're feeling. Notice they totally support you and honor your emotions. Just express your feelings any way you need to.**
Child parts:	*(Started sobbing.)*
Therapist:	**The Resources completely understand. Notice they're here for you.**
Child parts:	*(More sobbing.)*
Therapist:	**That's good... just let it heal.**
Child parts:	*(Less sobbing.)*
Therapist:	**That's good... feel their support. Feel their empathy.**
Child parts:	*(Stopped sobbing.)*
Child parts:	*(After a minute...)* It's better now.
Therapist:	**Good. So, little ones, <u>if you could</u> feel the grief completely and fully in your body now, how intense <u>would it be</u>, 0-10?**
Child parts:	Six.
Therapist:	**Which of your parents' behaviors is most connected to the six?**
Child parts:	There was no unconditional love. What little affection they gave me was based on my being compliant and sweet.
Therapist:	**Do the Resources love you unconditionally now?**
Child parts:	Yes.
Therapist:	**Will they love you even if you misbehave, talk back, or spill Kool-Aid?**
Child parts:	Yes.
Therapist:	**Good. Notice that. Take as long as you need to let that strengthen.**
Child parts:	Okay. That feels good.
Therapist:	**So, girls, <u>if you could</u> feel the grief completely and fully in your body now, how intense <u>would it be</u>?**
Child parts:	Five.
Therapist:	**Which of your parents' behaviors is most connected to the five?**
Child parts:	In public my mom acted like she was such a great mother. Her church friends told me how lucky I was that she was my mom. No one could see how awful she really was.
Therapist:	**Do the Resources understand how awful she was?**
Child parts:	Yes.
Therapist:	**Can they provide you all the validation you need now?**
Child parts:	Yes.
Therapist:	**Good. Notice that. Take as long as you need to let that strengthen.**
Child parts:	Okay. That's good.
Therapist:	**So, girls, <u>if you could</u> feel the grief completely and fully in your body now, how intense <u>would it be</u>?**
Child parts:	Three.
Therapist:	**Which of your parents' behaviors is most connected to the three?**

© Copyright 2009 by Shirley Jean Schmidt, MA, LPC. All rights reserved. Duplication in any form without permission is prohibited.

Child parts:	When they got really mad at me, they would threaten to put me in an orphanage. They said I was just so awful that they were saints to put up with me.
Therapist:	**Would the Resources ever threaten you like that?**
Child parts:	No.
Therapist:	**Do they understand how horrible it was to hear that from them?**
Child parts:	Yes.
Therapist:	**Good. Notice that. Take as long as you need to let that strengthen.**
Child parts:	Okay.
Therapist:	**Can the Resources enjoy and appreciate you – even when you might be frustrating?**
Child parts:	Yes.
Therapist:	**Good. Notice that.**
Child parts:	Okay.
Therapist:	**So, girls, <u>if you could</u> feel the grief completely and fully in your body now, how intense <u>would it be</u>?**
Child parts:	Zero.
Therapist:	**Good. I hear you feel the anger and grief have completely resolved. So girls, would you be willing to check for completeness by pulling on the TASPER? If the emotion has completely resolved, you should know right away because it will feel good to pull. If there are any unresolved emotions left, pulling should bring them to the surface so we can finish them off. How does that sound?**
Child parts:	Okay. *(Picked up the TASPER.)*
Therapist:	**Good. Notice your connection to the Resources. Think about those things your parents did to make you sad and angry... and when you're ready, pull.**
Child parts:	*(Face got red and a few tears fell while pulling.)*
Therapist:	**And if there is anything you wished you could have said to your parents then, but knew you couldn't, you can say it out loud now.**
Child parts:	*(Started sobbing.)*
Therapist:	**That's good... just let it heal.**
Child parts:	*(To parents...)* Why did you have me if you didn't want me?!!
Therapist:	**The Resources completely understand. Notice they're here for you.**
Child parts:	*(More sobbing.)*
Therapist:	**That's good... feel their support. Feel their empathy.**
Child parts:	*(To parents...)* Why don't you care?
Therapist:	**Feel that loving connection to your Resources.**
Child parts:	*(Tears stopped. Face returned to normal color.)*
Therapist:	**That's good. Notice it healing.**
Child parts:	Whew. I'm done. It's all clear. *(Put the TASPER down.)*
Therapist:	**Wonderful! So Leslie, when you picture the little ones now, how do they appear? Do you notice anything different?**
Client:	Yeah! They're happy. Standing straight. Feeling strong. They love being with the Resources.
Therapist:	**And the masks?**
Client:	All gone. The page with mom's face is gone. The pockets are empty.
Therapist:	**Great. Leslie, what do you notice in your body now?**
Client:	My body feels greatly relieved. Tension I was holding for years is gone now.

Step 9. *Bonding With the Resources*   *ABS On*

Therapist:	**So girls, look into the eyes of the Nurturing Adult Self and tell me what you see?**
Child parts:	Love, caring, and warmth.
Therapist:	**And notice that as you're looking in her eyes, she's looking in your eyes, seeing straight into your hearts. Do you feel a bond forming?**
Child parts:	Yes.
Therapist:	**Good. Notice that bond. Let it get as strong as it wants to. Tell me when it's strengthened all the way.**
Child parts:	Okay.
Therapist:	**Okay. Now look into the eyes of the Protective Adult Self. What do you see in these eyes?**

© Copyright 2009 by Shirley Jean Schmidt, MA, LPC. All rights reserved. Duplication in any form without permission is prohibited.

Child parts:	I see fierce protection and love.
Therapist:	**Is there a bond here too?**
Child parts:	Yes.
Therapist:	**Good. Notice that bond. Tell me when it's strengthened all the way.**
Child parts:	Okay.
Therapist:	**Okay. Now look into the eyes of the Spiritual Core Self and tell me what you see?**
Child parts:	Sweet, gentle love.
Therapist:	**Is there a bond here too?**
Child parts:	Yes.
Therapist:	**Good. Notice that bond. Tell me when it's strengthened all the way.**
Child parts:	Okay.
Therapist:	**Now notice the six of you together. Do you feel a group bond?**
Child parts:	Yes.
Therapist:	**Good. Notice that group bond. Tell me when it's strengthened all the way.**
Child parts:	Okay.
Therapist:	**So girls, I'd like to explain what a bond means. This means when you hurt, the Resources hurt. They don't want to hurt and they don't want you to hurt, so they're going to do whatever they have to, as quickly as they can, to help you feel better. How does that sound?**
Child parts:	That sounds great!
Therapist:	**Good. Think about that. Tell me when it's strengthened all the way.**
Child parts:	Okay.

Step 10. *Heightening Awareness of the Adult Body*   ***ABS On***

Therapist:	**So little ones, do you know you're in an adult body now?**
Child parts:	Uh...yes.
Therapist:	**Okay. Take a moment and look in this mirror. Is that what you expected to see?**
Child parts:	Oh... right.
Therapist:	**Touch your nose. Notice – that's <u>your</u> nose!**
Child parts:	Hmmmm.
Therapist:	**How is being in an adult body now better than being in a child body back then?**
Child parts:	I'm grown up now.
Therapist:	**Right. And when you were little your parents were in total control of your life, weren't they?**
Child parts:	Pretty much, yeah.
Therapist:	**They told you what to eat, when to eat it, what to wear, when to sleep. They were in control of who came to the house and who you spent time with. They made up the rules and they doled out the punishments. Right?**
Child parts:	Yeah.
Therapist:	**But now that you're in an adult body, you make all those decisions. Now you have your own job, checkbook, car, and telephone. In this adult body you can protect yourself in many ways that you couldn't when you were small. What's it like to think about that?**
Child parts:	Ahhhh... right. I like that.
Therapist:	**Think about the good news of being in an adult body now. Take as long as you need to let it strengthen. Tell me when it's strengthened all the way.**

Step 11. *Checking In*   ***ABS On***

Therapist:	**So girls, I'm guessing when we started you felt pretty stuck. How stuck do you feel now? Somewhat stuck, somewhat unstuck, mostly unstuck, or totally unstuck?**
Child parts:	Totally unstuck.
Therapist:	**I hear you believe you're totally unstuck. In fact you may be. But I have a few more steps to take you through. If you're totally unstuck they will go very quickly. If there is a little stuck left, we'll catch it and clear it. How does that sound?**
Child parts:	That's fine.

© Copyright 2009 by Shirley Jean Schmidt, MA, LPC. All rights reserved. Duplication in any form without permission is prohibited.

Step 12. *Returning to the Wounding Experiences*   *ABS On*

Therapist: Now girls, so far everything we've done has been in the presence of the Resources. To find out if there's any remaining disturbance I'll be asking you to disconnect from the Resources for just a moment, so you can revisit those past wounding experiences with your parents – just as they were back then, without your Resources present for support. You'll do this for just a moment, long enough for you to tell me how much disturbance comes up, then you'll come right back to the Resources. Are you okay with that?

Child parts: Ummmm. Sure.

Therapist: Good. Now girls, disconnect from the Resources for just a moment and, when you're ready, bring your attention back to those wounding experiences with your parents, from ages two through six, remembering them just the way they were back then, when you didn't have Resources present for support. How much disturbance comes up now, from 0-10, where 0 is none and 10 is the worst disturbance you can imagine?

Child parts: Four.

Therapist: **Which of your parents' behaviors is most connected with that four?"**

Child parts: They rejected, threatened, and abused me.

Step 13. *Returning to the Care of the Resources*   *ABS On*

Therapist: **Now bring your attention back to the Resources. Do the Resources love and appreciate you now?**
Child parts: Yes.
Therapist: **Good. Think about that. Tell me when it's strengthened all the way.**
Child parts: Okay.
Therapist: **Will the Resources always treat you with respect?**
Child parts: Yes.
Therapist: **Good. Think about that. Tell me when it's strengthened all the way.**
Child parts: Okay.

Step 14. *Repeating Steps 12 & 13*   *ABS On*

Therapist: **Good. Now little ones, once again disconnect from the Resources, and when you're ready, revisit those wounding experiences with your parents, from ages two through six. Remembering them just the way they were back then, when you didn't have Resources present for support, 0-10, how much disturbance comes up now?**

Child parts: Two.

Therapist: **Which of your parents' behaviors is most associated with that two?**

Child parts: When my grandmother died my parents had to leave town for the funeral. They called a sitter service and left me at home for about a week with a lady they didn't even know. She had her boyfriend over every day. They sat around drinking and smooching. Sometimes they would leave me in the house alone and go out. Sometimes he would fondle me. I had no idea if they were coming back or when. They did not call to check on me while they were gone.

Therapist: **If the Resources had been your parents then, would they have wanted to take you along on their trip?**
Child parts: Yes.
Therapist: **If there was no way they could take you, would they have left you with someone they knew could take good care of you?**
Child parts: Yes.
Therapist: **Would they have called you every day while they were gone to send their love?**
Child parts: Yes.
Therapist: **Good. Notice that. Tell me when that's strengthened all the way.**
Child parts: Okay.
Therapist: **And now, can you trust the Resources will maintain a close loving connection to you all the time – no matter what?**
Child parts: Yes.
Therapist: **Good. So girls once again disconnect from the Resources, and when you're ready revisit those wounding experiences with your parents, from ages two through six. Remembering them just the**

© Copyright 2009 by Shirley Jean Schmidt, MA, LPC. All rights reserved. Duplication in any form without permission is prohibited.

way they were back then, when you didn't have Resources present for support, how much disturbance comes up now?

Child parts: Zero.

Step 15. *Shifting Attention Back and Forth*   *ABS On*

Therapist: **Okay little ones, now shift your attention back and forth between those wounding experiences from the past when you had no Resources for support, and the Resources' care now... back and forth, and back and forth... and when you're ready, tell me what you notice.**

Child parts: I prefer the Resources.

Therapist: **Sounds like there may be just a little disturbance left.**

Child parts: Just a little.

Therapist: **Keep shifting attention back and forth. The remaining disturbance will either go away, or it won't go away. When you're ready, tell me which is happening.**

Child parts: The picture of them has faded quite a bit. It's hard to hold on to now. It doesn't seem at all important.

Therapist: **Are you saying there is <u>absolutely no disturbance</u> in your body when you revisit your parents' care?**

Child parts: Yes. It's absolutely all clear.

Step 16. *Checking In*   *ABS On*

Therapist: **So little ones, the last time I asked how unstuck you were, you said "totally." Are you still feeling totally unstuck?**

Child parts: Yes, even more totally!

Therapist: **Leslie, as you picture the little ones now, is there anything different about their appearance?**

Client: They are playing in the grass. Having a great time. *(Remains of the masks disappeared in Step 8.)*

Therapist: **Good. And Leslie, what do you notice in your body now?**

Client: My body is relaxed. I feel fabulous.

Step 17. *Strengthening a Positive Belief*   *ABS On*

Therapist: **So girls, when you think about what we've done today – what you've learned and how you've grown – what positive belief do you know to be true about you now?**

Client: I have a right to be here. I'm important.

Therapist: **Great. Think about all these wonderful statements, "I have a right to be here. I'm important." How true do they feel now?**

Client: Totally true.

Therapist: **Good. Think about these words. Tell me when they've strengthened all the way.**

Client: Okay.

Step 18. *Tucking In the Child Parts*   *ABS Off*

Therapist: **So girls, I want to thank you for all your hard work today. You've been very courageous and have done a marvelous job of working through this old stuff. It sounds like you're totally unstuck. If it turns out you're not, or if you need additional help, I'll be happy to help you in a future session. In a few moments I'm going to invite you to tuck in. Is there anything you'd like to say or ask before you tuck in?**

Child parts: Thank you.

Therapist: **You're welcome. Now find a nice, warm, cozy, safe place to tuck into. You can tuck in with your Resources if you like. Just find a good safe place to wait until the next time you're needed.**

Client: They're all tucked in.

Step 19. *Counting Up*   *ABS Off*

Therapist: **Would you like me to count you up from 1-5?**

Client: No. I'm good.

© Copyright 2009 by Shirley Jean Schmidt, MA, LPC. All rights reserved. Duplication in any form without permission is prohibited.

Step 20.   Checking on the Outcome   ***ABS Off***

Therapist:	Let's come back to the Conference Room Map and check on a few numbers. Right now, 0-10, how disturbing is your dad's message "Get out of my way or I'll kill you"?
Client:	Zero.
Therapist:	Right now, 0-10, how disturbing is your mom's message "Leave me alone. My novel is more important than you or your needs. If you bother me I'll get angry and it will be your fault?"
Client:	Zero.
Therapist:	Right now, 0-10, how disturbing is your parents' message "You're very, very bad. Keep it up and we'll send you to an orphanage?"
Client:	Zero.
Therapist:	In the beginning you had identified four reactive parts that believed the four Rung 1 statements. The first one was a fearful two-year-old reacting to the message, "Get out of my way or I'll kill you." How stuck is this fearful two-year-old now, 0-10?
Client:	Not at all stuck. Zero.
Therapist:	The second reactive part was an angry five-year-old reacting to mom's message, "Leave me alone. My novel is more important than you or your needs. If you bother me I'll get angry and it will be your fault." How stuck is this five-year-old now, 0-10?
Client:	Zero.
Therapist:	The third reactive part was a withdrawn seven-year-old who was reacting to a bossy six-year-old. The six-year-old was reacting to your parents' message, "You're very, very bad. Keep it up and we'll send you to an orphanage." How stuck are the six and seven-year-olds now?
Client:	Zero and zero.
Therapist:	Let's take a look at the Rung 1 statements you endorsed. How true does the statement, "I shouldn't exist," feel now, 0-10?
Client:	Zero.
Therapist:	How true does the statement, "It's not safe to exist," feel now?
Client:	Zero.
Therapist:	How true does the statement, "I'm so alone, there's no point in existing," feel now?
Client:	Zero.
Therapist:	How true does the statement, "No one wants me to exist," feel now?
Client:	Zero.

ANL Statements Endorsed	Before	After
2. I shouldn't exist	7	0
3. It's not safe to exist,	6	0
6. I'm so alone, there's no point in existing	9	0
10. No one wants me to exist.	6	0

Therapist:	In your first session we discussed your inability to trust others, especially your boyfriend. A year ago when he proposed marriage, it was very hard for you to believe he wanted to marry you. You said you just couldn't believe that he really loved you or wanted you, or that if you married him if he would really stay around. When you think about that proposal now, do you have a different reaction?
Client:	I used to get a huge knot in my stomach at the thought of getting married. My parents were never happy with each other and fought all the time. I'm sure that's part of it. But mostly I've just never been able to believe anyone would want me. Now when I think about his proposal I don't get the knot. It makes me smile a little. I'm not sure I should do it, but this idea isn't so frightening right now.
Therapist:	**Is there anything else you want to say about this experience?**
Client:	I feel lighter. Like a huge weight has been lifted. I think it's really okay for me to be here. That's so different. Thanks.
Therapist:	**You're welcome.**

© Copyright 2009 by Shirley Jean Schmidt, MA, LPC. All rights reserved. Duplication in any form without permission is prohibited.

DNMS Needs Meeting Protocol: Session Notes

Client: **Leslie Q.** CR Map Date(s): **July 7** NMP Date(s): **July 14**

Introjects: **2-yr-old dad IJ; 4-yr-old mom IJ; 6-yr-old mom/dad IJ**

Reactive Parts (optional): **None selected**

NEEDS MEETING: *Blacken the □ below next to each need met in Step 7*

■ ○ △ Safety/Protection	□ ○ △ Peaceful environment	**Caregivers who...**
■ ○ ▲ To be wanted/valued	□ ○ △ Safe environment	■ ○ △ can manage their own emotions
■ ● △ Respect	□ ○ △ Age-appro. boundaries	□ ○ △ can meet their own needs
■ ○ △ Attunement	□ ● △ Age-appro. responsibility	■ ○ △ put your needs above their wants
■ ○ ▲ Unconditional love	□ ○ △ Age-appro. freedoms	■ ○ ▲ are nurturing, caring, loving
□ ○ △ Unconditional accept.	□ ● △ Age-appro. expectations	□ ○ △ are consistently respectful
■ ○ △ Loving connection	□ ○ △ Age-appro. guidance	■ ○ △ are good at listening
□ ○ ▲ Understanding	□ ○ △ Age-appro. privacy	■ ○ △ are mature, respons, grown-ups
□ ○ △ Empathy/compassion	□ ○ △ Age-appro. supervision	□ ● △ take respons. for their behavior
□ ○ △ Warmth/affection	**Permission/encouragement to...**	□ ● △ see reality clearly
■ ○ △ Positive attention	□ ○ △ develop autonomy	□ ● △ respond to reality appropriately
□ ○ △ Support	□ ○ △ develop/express a self	■ ○ △ will help you meet your potential
□ ● △ Praise	□ ○ △ express opinions	■ ● △ know which behaviors need
□ ○ △ Reassurance	□ ○ △ take age-appro. risks	correction and which don't
□ ● △ Encouragement	□ ○ △ learn from mistakes	■ ● △ provide loving correction when
□ ○ ▲ Validation	□ ○ △ enjoy life	correction is needed
□ ○ △ _____	□ ○ △ _____	■ ○ △ fun to be around.
□ ○ △ _____	□ ○ △ _____	■ ○ △ are happy I'm here.
□ ○ △ _____	□ ○ △ _____	■ ○ △ consider me important.
□ ○ △ _____	□ ○ △ _____	□ ○ △ _____
□ ○ △ _____	□ ○ △ _____	□ ○ △ _____

Before processing emotions...

■ ○ △ Do you need caregivers who want you to feel and express the full range of emotions?

■ ○ △ Do you need caregivers who can help you process through painful emotions, like anger or grief?

APPEARANCE: More relaxed. Smiling. Masks: 4-yo's looks like a page, others are specks.   BODY: Relaxed

---

PROCESSING EMOTIONS: *Blacken ○ above for each anger need met; Blacken △ above for each grief need met*

ANGER level: **9, 7, 4, 0**	***GRIEF/SADNESS*** level: **9, 6, 5, 3, 0**
Processed anger with Resources' support:	Processed grief with Resources' support:
○ *with* or ○ *without* a sensorimotor activity	△ *with* or ▲ *without* a sensorimotor activity

■ Anger and grief processing tested for completeness with a sensorimotor activity.

APPEARANCE: Happy. Standing straight. Feeling strong. Love being with Rs. Masks gone.   BODY: Relieved.

BONDING: ■ NAS   ■ PAS   ■ SCS   ■ Group   ■ Explanation

ADULT BODY: □ Knew about adult body   ■ Resources explained adult body   ■ Therapist explained adult body

---

BLOCKS

Block #:	Details: _____	Block #:	Details: _____
Step #:	_____	Step #:	_____
	_____		_____
□ Misunderstanding	_____	□ Misunderstanding	_____
□ Reactive Part		□ Reactive Part	
□ Maladaptive Introject		□ Maladaptive Introject	

© Copyright 2009 by Shirley Jean Schmidt, MA, LPC. All rights reserved. Duplication in any form without permission is prohibited.

CHECKING IN: ☐ Somewhat stuck   ☐ Somewhat unstuck   ☐ Mostly unstuck   ■ Totally unstuck

PENDULATING: *Blacken the ☐ below next to each need met in Steps 12-15.*

Steps 12-14 disturbance level changes ___**4, 2, 0**___

Step 15:   ■ All body sensations gone   ☐ Met more needs before body sensations gone

☐ Safety/Protection	☐ Peaceful environment	***Caregivers who...***
☐ To be wanted/valued	☐ Safe environment	☐ can manage their own emotions
■ Respect	☐ Age-appropriate boundaries	☐ can meet their own needs
☐ Attunement	☐ Age-appropriate responsibility	☐ put your needs above their wants
☐ Unconditional love	☐ Age-appropriate freedoms	☐ are nurturing, caring, loving
☐ Unconditional acceptance	☐ Age-appropriate expectations	☐ are consistently respectful
■ Loving connection	☐ Age-appropriate guidance	☐ are good at listening
☐ Understanding	☐ Age-appropriate privacy	☐ are mature, responsible grown-ups
☐ Empathy/compassion	☐ Age-appropriate supervision	☐ take responsibility for their behavior
☐ Warmth/affection	***Permission/encouragement to...***	☐ see reality clearly
☐ Positive attention	☐ develop autonomy	☐ respond to reality appropriately
☐ Support	☐ develop/express a self	☐ will help you meet your potential
☐ Praise	☐ express opinions	☐ know which behaviors need a
☐ Reassurance	☐ take age-appropriate risks	correction and which don't
☐ Encouragement	☐ learn from mistakes	☐ provide loving correction when
☐ Validation	☐ enjoy life	correction is needed
☐ _____	☐ _____	■ *love and appreciate her.*
☐ _____	☐ _____	■ *want her to exist.*
☐ _____	☐ _____	■ *are thrilled she exists.*
☐ _____	☐ _____	☐ _____

CHECKING IN: ☐ Mostly unstuck   ■ Totally unstuck   ■ Child parts playing   ■ Mask/costumes gone   ■ Body clear

POSITIVE BELIEF: I have a right to be here. I'm important.   How True, 0-10?   10

TUCKING IN: ■ Completed NMP on: July 14   **COUNTED UP:**   ■ Yes   ☐ No

CHECKING ON OUTCOME:

■ How disturbing are the introject messages now? _____ All zeros. _____

■ Unless just processed, how stuck are the reactive parts now? _____ All zeros. _____

■ Re-rate negative beliefs: _____ All zeros. _____

■ Status of unwanted behavior, beliefs, or emotions: __ "Now when I think about his proposal I don't get the knot." __

BLOCKS	Block #: ____ Details: _____	Block #: ____ Details: _____
	Step #: _____	Step #: _____
	☐ Misunder-standing _____	☐ Misunder-standing _____
	☐ Reactive Part _____	☐ Reactive Part _____
	☐ Maladaptive Introject _____	☐ Maladaptive Introject _____

UNFINISHED PROTOCOL	Date: ____ How True, 0-10? ____ ☐ Tucked in Positive Belief: _____	Date: ____ How True, 0-10? ____ ☐ Tucked in Positive Belief: _____
	Date: ____ How True, 0-10? ____ ☐ Tucked in Positive Belief: _____	Date: ____ How True, 0-10? ____ ☐ Tucked in Positive Belief: _____

© Copyright 2009 by Shirley Jean Schmidt, MA, LPC. All rights reserved. Duplication in any form without permission is prohibited.

Chapter Summary

This chapter provided instructional details for executing the Needs Meeting Protocol. This protocol is designed to help heal the maladaptive introjects most responsible for a target issue – whether a specific current problem or old attachment wounds. Clients report that healing such introjects diminishes unwanted behaviors, beliefs, and emotions.

Chapter 6 Notes and References

1. Levine, P. (1997). *Waking the tiger: Healing trauma.* Berkeley, CA: North Atlantic Books.
    Ogden, P., Minton, K. & Pain, C. (2006). *Trauma and the body: A sensorimotor approach to psychotherapy.* New York: Norton.
2. Napier, N. (1990). *Recreating your self: Building self-esteem through imaging and self-hypnosis.* New York: Norton.
    Paulsen, S. (2000). *EMDR and the Divided Self: EMDR and ego state therapy for non-dissociative and dissociative clients.* All-day workshop in San Antonio, Texas, April, 2000.
    Steele, A. (2001). *Introduction to imaginal nurturing with EMDR in the treatment of adult clients with insecure attachment.* Presentation at 2001 EMDRAC Conference in Vancouver, BC.
    Watkins, J. G., & Watkins, H. H. (1997). *Ego states: Theory and therapy.* New York: Norton.
3. Poole Heller, D. (2001). *Crash course: A self-healing guide to auto accident trauma and recovery.* North Atlantic Books.
4. The DNMS Home Study Course was released in 2008. It is a 7-module Course which teaches psychotherapists how to competently execute each DNMS protocol. Each Course module consists of a narrated slide show and an illustrated study guide. The slide shows explain key concepts with animated illustrations. Review questions are provided throughout the slide shows to check comprehension of the material. Modules 3-7 include recordings of real sessions, to demonstrate specific protocols. The slide shows are provided on a single DVD (or 7 CDs) which will play on most Windows-based and Macintosh computers. The study guides provide an outline of all the material covered in the slide shows. The Module 2-7 study guides include study questions and answers. You can see what the Home Study Course slide shows are like by watching a 25-min Introduction to the DNMS slide show. For more information about the Course, go to Appendix F, page 256, or go to www.dnmsinstitute.com/dnmscourse.html. To see the 25-min Introduction to the DNMS slide show go to www.dnmsinstitute.com/ dnmsintro.html.
5. The DNMS Flip Chart provides an easy way to explain the DNMS to clients and colleagues. It is a 75-page "slide show" that: introduces the DNMS; explains *parts of self*; explains neural integration; explains alternating bilateral stimulation; describes the Resources and Healing Circle; describes reactive parts and introjects; explains the Switching the Dominance Protocol; describes the Conference Room Protocol with text and pictures; and describes the Needs Meeting Protocol with pictures. The Flip Chart includes lots of pictures to illustrate complex concepts. The chart is provided in a 3-ring binder so you can add your own pages or tabs, or move pages around. For more information about the Flip Chart, go to Appendix F, page 255, or go to www.dnmsinstitute.com/flipchart.html.

© Copyright 2009 by Shirley Jean Schmidt, MA, LPC. All rights reserved. Duplication in any form without permission is prohibited.

Chapter 7
Complications & Blocks

Overview

A processing *complication* is anything that happens during a DNMS protocol that suggests the processing might not end with the expected or desired outcome. Complications can be caused by client confusion, therapist confusion, case complexity, or ego states deliberately interfering with the processing. A deliberate interference is called a processing *block*.

In the DNMS, all processing blocks are welcome! Blocks can arise at many points in this model. They always arise for a reason – to solve a perceived problem. Clearing blocks does not just make way for DNMS work, it is DNMS work. Blocks can provide valuable information about a client's internal world. The process of clearing blocks helps wounded child parts at moments they feel especially vulnerable. This can be reassuring and ego strengthening. Blocks are not impediments; they are prime opportunities to help clients heal.

DNMS protocols carried out over unexpressed or unresolved blocks will be ineffective, and the benefits expected will not be achieved. Clients who process over blocks may become disinterested in continuing the DNMS or may simply avoid DNMS processing. That's why DNMS blocks should be identified early and addressed right away. That will lead to more efficient and effective processing.

That is why the importance of mastering the art of working through blocks cannot be overstated. For many clinicians, it is the most challenging aspect of the DNMS because the solutions are not always obvious. Expect this part of the model to take time to master. Give yourself permission to make mistakes as you learn. Internalizing all the information provided here may seem like a daunting challenge, but you can do it if you persevere. Eventually it will all come together.

This chapter will teach you some general principles for overcoming blocks that can come up during any DNMS protocol, in a section titled *General Complications*. This section covers:
*   real and perceived problems with the Resources,
*   misunderstandings about the protocol process or outcome, and
*   blocking maladaptive introjects that attempt to sabotage protocol progress.

This chapter will then cover complications unique to each DNMS protocol and procedure, in sections titled:
*   Resource Development Protocol Complications,
*   Switching the Dominance Protocol Complications,
*   Attachment Needs Ladder Complications,
*   Conference Room Protocol Complications, and
*   Needs Meeting Protocol Complications.

© Copyright 2009 by Shirley Jean Schmidt, MA, LPC. All rights reserved. Duplication in any form without permission is prohibited.

Inviting Clients to Disclose Processing Blocks

You'll want to encourage your DNMS clients to express their processing fears and concerns as soon as they arise. Sometimes clients are *consciously aware* of concerns and can easily articulate them. For example a client might say outright, "I'm afraid I'll do it wrong." But often fears are just outside of conscious awareness. Unconscious concerns are often expressed by a physical or cognitive disturbance. For example, a client's suddenly elevated heart rate might be an expression of a fear of "doing it wrong."

Orienting New Clients to Processing Blocks

As discussed in Chapters 3 and 6, you'll tell new clients that unconscious concerns and fears about the processing can be subtly expressed in the body. You'll encourage them to notice and disclose any physical or cognitive disturbances that arise during a protocol. Just before beginning the Resource Development and Needs Meeting Protocols, you'll say something like:

> *Sometimes during a DNMS protocol, concerns or fears about the processing will arise. Unconscious fears can be expressed by the sudden arrival of a body disturbance such as unpleasant sensations, dissociation, distracting thoughts, numbness, or sleepiness. That may or may not happen to you, but if it does, please tell me about it, even if it doesn't seem important. You're welcome to have concerns or fears – just let me know if they come up. I'll want to address them right away.*

Checking for Blocks Before Starting Each Protocol

In addition, you'll check for blocks just before starting (or resuming) each DNMS protocol. To check for blocks *you could ask*:

> *Do you have any fears or concerns about doing this protocol?*

Unfortunately, the answer to this would only illuminate concerns that are within conscious awareness. *Instead ask*:

> *When you think about beginning this (protocol) now, to (meet the protocol objective), what do you notice in your body?*

The sudden arrival of a body disturbance suggests the presence of an unconscious fear or concern. For example, a client suddenly becomes sleepy at the though of beginning the Needs Meeting Protocol. A disclosure like this gives you an opportunity to identify and address the associated concern before beginning the protocol. Handling blocks before beginning a protocol will usually ensure processing gets off to a good start, but additional blocks could also arise during the protocol.

Sudden Versus Preexisting Body Disturbance

It is necessary to distinguish a *sudden disturbance* from a *preexisting disturbance* that is unrelated to the processing. For example, a client who is experiencing jet lag, may report sleepiness arising during a protocol that is solely related to sleep deprivation, having nothing to do with the processing. And a client recovering from back surgery might report his back aches at the idea of starting a protocol. If the pain intensity was the same as it was before the session, it probably has nothing to do with starting the protocol.

But sometimes a preexisting disturbance will *suddenly increase* in intensity, either before or during a protocol. That increase in disturbance may be evidence of a processing concern. If in doubt you can ask:

> *Did this (backache) just now suddenly get worse? Is it directly related to (doing this protocol)?*

Another approach is to find out how the body reacts when you say:

> *We're not going to do (this protocol) today. How does your body react to that news?*

If the disturbance is related to a processing concern, the body will instantly feel a sense of relief. That's your cue to identify and address the concern. But if a disturbance is unrelated to the protocol, the body will either register a disappointment at not starting it, or nothing at all. That's your cue to proceed with the protocol.

© Copyright 2009 by Shirley Jean Schmidt, MA, LPC. All rights reserved. Duplication in any form without permission is prohibited.

General Complications

Misunderstandings and maladaptive introjects can complicate or block processing in every DNMS protocol and procedure. This section focuses on how to identify and handle such blocks.

Blocks from Simple Misunderstandings

Simple misunderstandings are *faulty assumptions* about the processing that stop it from moving forward. They can be held by adult parts and/or wounded child parts. The more irrational a faulty assumption is, the more likely it is held by a wounded child part. Some misunderstandings can come up during any DNMS protocol, while some are unique to one protocol or another. For example:

- A belief like, "If I heal my childhood wounds, my abusive parents are off the hook," could come up during any one of the protocols.
- A belief like, "I'm afraid if I establish a Protective Adult Self she'll be overprotective like my father was," would only come up during the Resource Development Protocol.
- A belief like, "The child parts will not be safe if the perpetrator introjects are allowed into the conference room," would only come up during the Conference Room Protocol.
- A belief like, "I can't process painful emotions without becoming overwhelmed," would only come up during the Needs Meeting Protocol.

Blocks from Maladaptive Introjects

Maladaptive introjects can block processing *directly* and *indirectly*. A client's statement like, "I hear my mom saying, 'You're not allowed to ask for what you need,'" suggests a maladaptive introject is directly blocking the processing with this wounding message.

**Introject *directly* blocking
processing with a wounding message**

A negative belief like, "I'm not allowed to ask for what I need," coming from a reactive part, suggests a maladaptive introject is indirectly blocking the processing. That means that, while the client may initially be aware of just a reactive part in the foreground, an introject is blocking processing from the background.

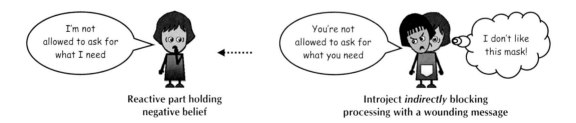

**Reactive part holding
negative belief**   **Introject *indirectly* blocking
processing with a wounding message**

Blocks from Both Misunderstandings and Maladaptive Introjects

Some blocks are due to both misunderstandings and maladaptive introjects. For example, consider a statement like: "If I admit to having adult skills, I'm bragging. Bragging is bad and will be punished." This contains the faulty assumption that acknowledging adult skills is bragging. It also contains an inappropriate threat to safety suggestive of a parental introject conveying a message like: "If you brag you're bad and I'll punish you."

© Copyright 2009 by Shirley Jean Schmidt, MA, LPC. All rights reserved. Duplication in any form without permission is prohibited.

The Overcoming Processing Blocks Flowchart

The *Overcoming Processing Blocks Flowchart* (page 156) summarizes all the steps involved in overcoming blocks from these two sources. The steps include: (a) eliciting a concern at the root of the block, (b) classifying the elicited concern, (c) applying the appropriate interventions for handling misunderstandings and blocking introjects, and (d) verifying that all blocks have been cleared. The next eight pages will tell you how to apply these steps.

Eliciting the Concern

This section focuses on several options for eliciting a concern at the root of a block. You'll start with a simple inquiry. (See the first box on the flowchart.) When your client reports evidence of a processing block, such as the sudden arrival of a headache, ask:

> If the (headache) could talk, what would it say?   OR   Why does this (headache) need to be here right now? How does it help? What problem does it solve?

Often clients can readily reveal the concern. For example a client might respond with: "I'm afraid if I connect to a Nurturing Adult Self, I'll have to martyr myself to care for everyone else." But sometimes clients respond with an "I don't know," or functional equivalent, like "Ouch." So if a client cannot readily articulate a concern, you'll need to probe for it. Five different ways to probe are listed below. If one method does not succeed, try another. (See the second box on the flowchart.)

1. **Ask "What would you lose...?"**

   One popular way to elicit a concern is to inquire about any problem that would result if the processing began or continued. Ask something like:

   > If you were to successfully (complete this protocol), what would you lose or what bad thing would happen?

   The answer to this could reveal: (a) a misunderstanding, such as "I'm afraid if I connect to the Resources I'll have to act like a grown-up all the time;" (b) a blocking introject such as, "I hear my mother telling me to get off my high horse;" or (c) both, such as, "If I bring all three Resources together I'll be too powerful, and I'll get in trouble."

2. **Look for Blocking Caregiver Introjects**

   If you suspect a childhood caregiver introject is blocking the processing, you can look for it directly by asking something like:

   > If the wounding (parents) of your childhood were sitting here right now, commenting on your interest in (beginning/completing this protocol), what would they say to you?

   The answer might reveal a parental introject conveying a wounding message (such as, "You don't deserve to be nurtured," or "Shame on you for being so needy.") which could clearly inhibit the successful completion of a protocol.

   Sometimes parents who were unsupportive in a client's childhood, are supportive in adulthood. When this is the case, it is imperative that clients envision their *unsupportive childhood caregivers* commenting on the therapy – because those parental introjects can block processing.

3. **Check the Status of the Resources**

   If a client is fearful of connecting to Resources, or is perceiving real or imagined problems with existing Resources, ask something like:

   > Are you concerned that the Resources are not (or won't be) competent caregivers?

   If a client has fears about establishing Resources, the answer to this might reveal misunderstandings about their nature, such as: "If I connect to Resources they'll be intrusive like my parents were," or "Caregivers cannot be trusted." If Resources have been established the answer to this might reveal real or imagined problems with them. This topic is discussed in detail below, on page 163, in the section titled, *Complications with the Resources.*

© Copyright 2009 by Shirley Jean Schmidt, MA, LPC. All rights reserved. Duplication in any form without permission is prohibited.

Overcoming Processing Blocks Flowchart

Begin this flowchart if a client reports an unpleasant body sensation, dissociation, distracting thoughts, numbness, sleepiness, or some other complaint suggestive of a processing block, just before beginning or during a DNMS protocol. If ABS is on, turn it off.

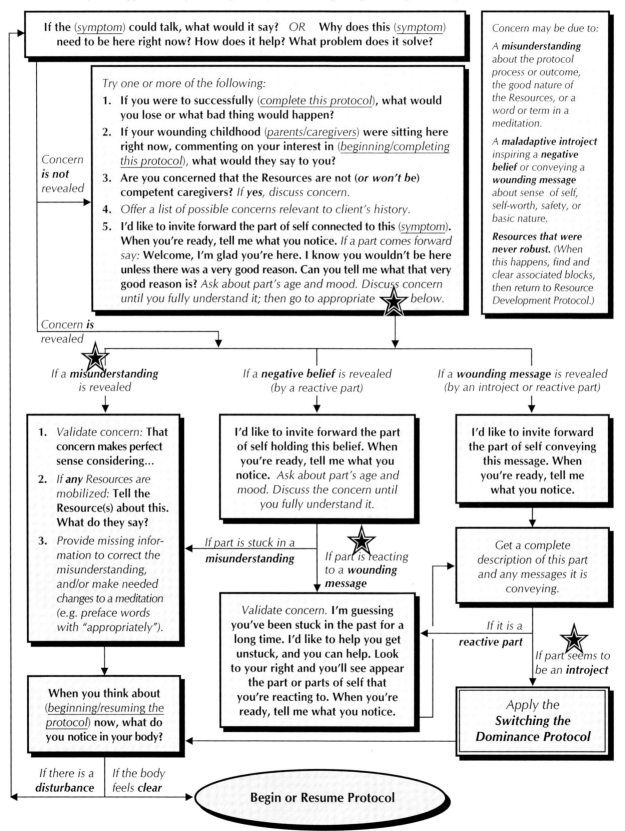

If the (symptom) could talk, what would it say? *OR* **Why does this (symptom) need to be here right now? How does it help? What problem does it solve?**

Concern may be due to:

A ***misunderstanding*** about the protocol process or outcome, the good nature of the Resources, or a word or term in a meditation.

A ***maladaptive introject*** inspiring a ***negative belief*** or conveying a ***wounding message*** about sense of self, self-worth, safety, or basic nature.

Resources that were never robust. *(When this happens, find and clear associated blocks, then return to Resource Development Protocol.)*

Concern **is not** revealed

Try one or more of the following:

1. **If you were to successfully (complete this protocol), what would you lose or what bad thing would happen?**

2. **If your wounding childhood (parents/caregivers) were sitting here right now, commenting on your interest in (beginning/completing this protocol), what would they say to you?**

3. **Are you concerned that the Resources are not (or won't be) competent caregivers?** *If yes, discuss concern.*

4. *Offer a list of possible concerns relevant to client's history.*

5. **I'd like to invite forward the part of self connected to this (symptom). When you're ready, tell me what you notice.** *If a part comes forward say:* **Welcome, I'm glad you're here. I know you wouldn't be here unless there was a very good reason. Can you tell me what that very good reason is?** *Ask about part's age and mood. Discuss concern until you fully understand it; then go to appropriate ★ below.*

Concern **is** revealed

If a ***misunderstanding*** is revealed

If a ***negative belief*** is revealed (by a reactive part)

If a ***wounding message*** is revealed (by an introject or reactive part)

1. *Validate concern:* **That concern makes perfect sense considering...**

2. *If **any** Resources are mobilized:* **Tell the Resource(s) about this. What do they say?**

3. *Provide missing information to correct the misunderstanding, and/or make needed changes to a meditation (e.g. preface words with "appropriately").*

I'd like to invite forward the part of self holding this belief. When you're ready, tell me what you notice. *Ask about part's age and mood. Discuss the concern until you fully understand it.*

I'd like to invite forward the part of self conveying this message. When you're ready, tell me what you notice.

*If part is stuck in a **misunderstanding***

*If part is reacting to a **wounding message***

Get a complete description of this part and any messages it is conveying.

Validate concern. **I'm guessing you've been stuck in the past for a long time. I'd like to help you get unstuck, and you can help. Look to your right and you'll see appear the part or parts of self that you're reacting to. When you're ready, tell me what you notice.**

*If it is a **reactive part***

*If part seems to be an **introject***

When you think about (beginning/resuming the protocol) now, what do you notice in your body?

Apply the ***Switching the Dominance Protocol***

*If there is a **disturbance*** | *If the body feels **clear***

Begin or Resume Protocol

© Copyright 2009 by Shirley Jean Schmidt, MA, LPC. All rights reserved. Duplication in any form without permission is prohibited.

4. Offer a List of Blocks

Offer the client a list of possible blocks to consider. You can refer the client to the list of typical misunderstandings from Appendix D, page 253, or list a few plausible blocks, considering the client's history. For example, you might ask a client resistant to connecting to a NAS something like:

> *If you successfully connected to a Nurturing Adult Self would that be the same as being disloyal to your mother? ...abandoning your mother? ...discounting her positive qualities?*

Very often, just considering several wrong items will help a client to articulate the real concern.

5. Speak to the Concerned Child Part Directly

The interventions listed above guide the client to name a fear or concern. When a client has trouble articulating it, it may help to go directly to the source, by saying something like:

> *I'd like to invite forward the part of self connected to this (*<u>symptom</u>*). When you're ready, tell me what you notice.*

If a part comes forward say:

> *Welcome, I'm glad you're here. I know you wouldn't be here unless there was a very good reason. Can you tell me what that very good reason is?*

Ask about part's age and mood. Discuss the concern until you fully understand it. (See section titled *Two Paths to Resolving Blocks*, on page 162.) If no part comes forward, consider that the client's symptom may not be related to a processing block.

Classifying the Concern

The type of concern expressed dictates the intervention needed, therefore, you'll need to determine whether a block is due to a simple misunderstanding, a maladaptive introject, or both; or whether the Resources never were robust. (See the upper right-hand sidebar on the Overcoming Processing Blocks Flowchart.)

Identifying Misunderstandings

Simple misunderstandings are *faulty assumptions*, usually about the protocol process or outcome, the good nature of the Resources, or words/terms in a meditation. Here are some examples:

- Misunderstandings about *protocol process* include beliefs like: "I can't connect to a Spiritual Core Self, because I don't believe in God," and "I'll become overwhelmed if I try to process my anger."
- Misunderstandings about *protocol outcome* include beliefs like: "If my child parts heal they won't be safe," and "If I connect to Resources I'll have to be perfect all the time."
- Misunderstandings about the *good nature of the Resources* include beliefs like: "The Resources expect me to meet their needs," and "If I connect to Resources they'll impose their agenda on me."
- Misunderstandings about the *words/terms in a meditation* include beliefs like: "I can never be good with boundaries," and "If I'm a nurturing person, people will take unfair advantage of me."

Identifying Blocking Introjects

When a concern is due to a maladaptive introject, a client will report holding a negative belief or hearing a wounding message about *sense of self, self-worth, safety, or basic nature*. For example:

- *Negative beliefs* include statements like: "I'm not allowed to grow up," and "I don't deserve nurturing."
- *Wounding messages* include statements like: "Shut up or I'll hurt you," and "Don't grow up."

Identifying Resources that are Not Robust

If the Resources are not robust, the Switching the Dominance, Conference Room, or Needs Meeting Protocol may stall. You'll most likely discover this when a client is processing with the Resources for the first time. If a client reveals the Resources are not robust, find out why, clear all the associated blocks, then repeat the Resource Development Protocol. Once the client finally has robust Resources, repeat the protocol that stalled.

© Copyright 2009 by Shirley Jean Schmidt, MA, LPC. All rights reserved. Duplication in any form without permission is prohibited.

Handling Misunderstandings

Simple misunderstandings about a protocol process or outcome, the good nature of the Resources, or a word in a meditation can usually be quickly handled with corrective information provided by you and/or the Resources. Faulty assumptions about the Resources may be better handled by the Resources, while faulty assumptions about the protocol process are better handled by you. (See the third box from the top, on the left-hand side of the Overcoming Processing Blocks Flowchart.)

To handle a misunderstanding, start with a validation that shows you understand the source of the stated concern. For example when a child part says, in the middle of the Needs Meeting Protocol, something like: "If I bond with the Resources they'll eventually abandon me," respond with something like:

> That concern makes perfect sense considering (how your mother abandoned you).

Then, if appropriate, direct the child part's attention to the Resources for the needed corrective information. Say:

> Tell the Resource(s) (you expect they'll eventually abandon you). What do they say?

After a brief conversation with the Resources, the child part would likely say something like: "The Resources say they'd never abandon me. They're devoted to me." A supportive response like this is often enough to resolve the concern, but sometimes you'll have to add a little more to it. For example, you could add:

> Each Resource is a mature, adult part of you that cares for and cherishes (your pet Fluffy). Would these Resources ever abandon Fluffy?

When the part answers "no," say:

> Then they most certainly wouldn't abandon you!

Corrective information that comes from the Resources is generally easier for wounded parts to integrate, so encourage their input whenever feasible. But some corrective information must come from you – particularly when there are concerns and misperceptions about what a protocol step will involve. For example, my client Pamela was afraid of becoming overwhelmed while processing painful emotions. I explained how the Needs Meeting Protocol was designed for processing emotions in a way that was not overwhelming, and that processing painful emotions in the presence of the Resources can make it much easier to tolerate. The information about the protocol design was information I had to provide. But after providing the information about better tolerating the emotion processing with the Resources' support, I added:

> But don't take my word for it, ask the Resources about this. Do they agree?

Pamela said the Resource's did agree with me, and felt reassured by this. She was then able to engage in the emotion processing without becoming overwhelmed.

See Appendix B, Section 7, page 211, for a three-page list of typical misunderstandings that block processing and suggestions for correcting them.

Handling Blocking Introjects

Introjects that block processing are handled with the Switching the Dominance Protocol (as described on page 62). While an introject mask's message might complicate protocol processing, the child part wearing the mask wants the processing to happen. As switching the dominance illuminates the mask's illusion of significance, the mask loses its power to interfere with the processing. That allows the good true nature of the child part to shine.

The biggest challenge to clearing these types of blocks is getting to the introject at the root of the block. Sometimes these introjects are easy to access. Sometimes they are elusive. If you follow the steps laid out below, you should be able to identify blocking introjects, so you can switch the dominance, no matter how elusive they are.

As mentioned earlier, maladaptive introjects can block processing *directly* and *indirectly*. There are three types of reactive parts, so there are four ways this can play out. This example illustrates the possibilities: After two needs were met in Step 7 of the Needs Meeting Protocol, Mary reported getting a headache. The therapist asked her, "If the headache could talk, what would it say?"

© Copyright 2009 by Shirley Jean Schmidt, MA, LPC. All rights reserved. Duplication in any form without permission is prohibited.

1. Direct Block with a Wounding Message

Mary reported that her sudden-onset headache said, "Shut up or I'll hurt you!" This *wounding message* was blocking processing. It was coming from a maladaptive introject that was *directly* influencing the processing.

Maladaptive introject is directly blocking
processing with a wounding message

2. Indirect Block A

Mary reported that her sudden-onset headache said, "If I don't shut up I'll be hurt." This statement was a *negative belief* held by a *powerless reactive part*. It was perpetuated by a maladaptive introject that was indirectly blocking processing in the background, with the wounding message, "Shut up or I'll hurt you!"

Powerless reactive part is conveying a negative
belief in reaction to the introject's message

Maladaptive introject is blocking
processing in the background

3. Indirect Block B

Mary reported that her sudden-onset headache said, "You'd better shut up!" This statement was a *wounding message* conveyed by a *controlling reactive part*. It was perpetuated by a maladaptive introject that was indirectly blocking processing in the background, with the wounding message, "Shut up or I'll hurt you!"

Controlling reactive part is conveying a wounding
message in reaction to the introject's message

Maladaptive introject is blocking
processing in the background

4. Indirect Block C

Mary reported that her sudden-onset headache said, "Shut up or I'll hurt you!" At first this *wounding message* appeared to be coming from an introject directly blocking the processing, but in Step 2 of the Switching the Dominance Protocol, the part wearing the introject mask disclosed she needed the mask for protection. So in reality, this wounding message was being conveyed by a *controlling reactive mimic*. The mimic's message was perpetuated by a maladaptive introject that was indirectly blocking processing in the background, with the same wounding message, "Shut up or I'll hurt you!"

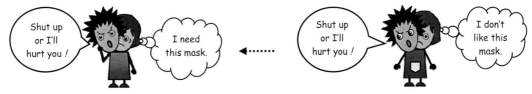

Controlling reactive mimic is conveying a wounding
message in reaction to the introject's message

Maladaptive introject is blocking
processing in the background

© Copyright 2009 by Shirley Jean Schmidt, MA, LPC. All rights reserved. Duplication in any form without permission is prohibited.

This table provides a quick summary description of these parts of self. Chapter 2 provides a complete description.

Clues to Classifying Parts of Self

Clues That Differentiate Introjects & Reactive Parts	Powerless Reactive Part	Controlling Reactive Part	Controlling Reactive Mimic	Maladaptive Introject
Part (mask) looks like wounding role model.	No.	No.	Yes.	Yes.
Conveys wounding message (typically a "you" message).	No.	Yes – In reaction to a role model's message.	Yes –Mimicking a role model's message.	Yes –Mimicking a role model's message.
Reacting or mimicking?	Reacting.	Reacting.	Both.	Mimicking.
Mask (or costume) present.	Maybe.	Maybe.	Yes.	Yes.
Issues warnings, threats, commands, or admonitions.	No.	Yes.	Only if the wounding role model issued them.	Only if the wounding role model issued them.
Reveals behaviors, beliefs, or emotions suggestive of being wounded. ("I" statements).	Yes.	No.	No.	Not usually.
Mask is part of a valued coping strategy created by child part wearing it. *	If a mask is present – yes.	If a mask is present – yes.	Yes.*	No.*

*Assessed in Step 2 of the **Switching the Dominance Protocol**

Handling a Blocking Introject – Starting with a Negative Belief

When a client like Mary reports a body disturbance (like a headache) connected to a negative belief, invite the part holding that belief by saying something like:

> I'd like to invite forward the part of self that believes ("If I don't shut up I'll be hurt"). When you're ready, tell me what you notice.

When the part comes forward, ask about age and mood. Discuss the concern until you fully understand it. Understanding the concern helps you apply the appropriate intervention. You'd intervene in different ways, for example, if a child part was afraid of being hurt by the Resources, by her childhood caregivers, or by her elderly parents now. (See the two center boxes in the bottom half of the Overcoming Processing Blocks Flowchart.)

If this questioning uncovers a misunderstanding, such as a belief that the Resources might inflict harm, address it with the needed clarification (as described in section above). But if the child part's negative belief seems to be prompted by a maladaptive introject conveying a threatening message in the background, validate the concern, then say:

> I'm guessing you've been stuck in the past for a long time. I'd like to help you get unstuck, and you can help. Look to your right and you'll see appear the part or parts of self that you're reacting to. When you're ready, tell me what you notice.

When the next part of self comes forward get a complete description of it and any messages it is conveying. (See the three lower right-hand boxes in the bottom half of the Overcoming Processing Blocks Flowchart.) Determine whether the part that appears is (a) another powerless reactive part expressing another negative belief; (b) a controlling reactive part or reactive mimic conveying a wounding message, or (c) the presumptive maladaptive introject at the source of the block. If it appears to be another reactive part, keep looking for the introject.

For example, Mary's therapist invited forward the part that believes "If I don't shut up, I'll be hurt." A fearful four-year-old appeared. This was a powerless reactive part fearful of being punished by her dad (from childhood). The therapist invited her to look to the right. She saw a bossy five-year-old part conveying the message, "You'd better shut up." This was a controlling reactive part because the message was a command,

© Copyright 2009 by Shirley Jean Schmidt, MA, LPC. All rights reserved. Duplication in any form without permission is prohibited.

delivered by a child, intended to control the fearful four-year-old. The therapist invited this controlling reactive part to look to the right. She saw a child part wearing a Dad mask conveying the message, "Shut up or I'll hurt you." The therapist began switch the dominance. In Step 2 she determined it was an introject because the child part wearing the mask said it served no useful purpose. Once the dominance was completely switched the headache was gone and the client felt free to continue with the protocol.

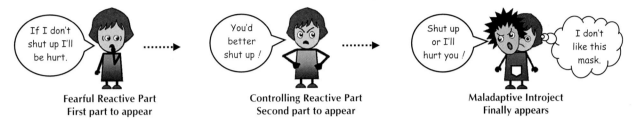

If I don't shut up I'll be hurt.	You'd better shut up!	Shut up or I'll hurt you! — I don't like this mask.
Fearful Reactive Part First part to appear	**Controlling Reactive Part** Second part to appear	**Maladaptive Introject** Finally appears

Handling a Blocking Introject – Starting with a Wounding Message

When a client like Mary reports a body disturbance (like a headache) connected to a wounding message, invite the part forward by saying something like:

> *I'd like to invite forward the part of self conveying the message ("You'd better shut up"). When you're ready, tell me what you notice.*

There are three types of ego states that can deliver the types of wounding messages that can block processing. They include: maladaptive introjects, controlling reactive parts, and controlling reactive mimics. So when a part comes forward, get a full description. (See the three right-hand side boxes in the bottom half of the Overcoming Processing Blocks Flowchart.) As best you can, determine which type of part has come forward. If the part appears to be an introject, begin switching the dominance. It the part is clearly a reactive part, say:

> *I'm guessing you've been stuck in the past for a long time. I'd like to help you get unstuck, and you can help. Look to your right and you'll see the part or parts of self that you're reacting to. When you're ready, tell me what you notice.*

When another part comes forward, get a full description. You'll cycle through these steps as often as necessary. You might encounter several reactive parts before the introject you're looking for appears.

For example, Mary's therapist invited forward the part of self conveying the message "You'd better shut up!" A bossy five-year-old part appeared. This was a controlling reactive part. The therapist invited this part to look to the right. She saw a child part wearing a Dad mask conveying the message, "Shut up or I'll hurt you." This was presumed to be an introject. The therapist began to switch the dominance, but soon learned that the part of self wearing the mask needed it for protection. This reactive mimic was invited to look to the right. She saw another child part wearing a Dad mask, conveying the same message, "Shut up or I'll hurt you." This was presumed to be an introject. The therapist began to switch the dominance, and determined it was an introject because the child part wearing the mask said it served no useful purpose. Once the dominance was completely switched the headache was gone and the client felt free to continue with the protocol.

You'd better shut up!	Shut up or I'll hurt you!	Shut up or I'll hurt you! — I don't like this mask.
Controlling Reactive Part First part to appear	**Reactive Mimic** Second part to appear	**Maladaptive Introject** Finally appears

Verifying All Blocks Have Been Cleared

Sometimes there are several blocks to clear before a client is ready to start or resume a protocol. After clearing a misunderstanding or an introject block, ask the client:

> *When you think about (beginning/resuming the protocol) now, what do you notice in your body?*

© Copyright 2009 by Shirley Jean Schmidt, MA, LPC. All rights reserved. Duplication in any form without permission is prohibited.

If the body is clear, the client is probably ready to begin or resume the protocol. If the old symptom is still present, or if a new symptom has appeared, return to the top of the flowchart to look for and clear the additional disturbance. (See the last box on the bottom left corner of the Overcoming Processing Blocks Flowchart.)

If you had encountered one or more reactive parts on your way to finding a blocking introject, check in with them when the Switching the Dominance Protocol is complete. They will probably all feel much better.

But if any of the reactive parts are still feeling distressed, look for any additional introjects they may be reacting to. Switch the dominance of any additional introjects you find. When the dominance of all the associated introjects has been switched, all the reactive parts should feel much better. Then ask the above question again, to verify all blocks are cleared.

Two Paths to Resolving Blocks

There are two paths you can take to resolve a block. When you take *Path 1* you'll start by eliciting the blocking concern from the client, then you'll classify the concern (misunderstanding versus introject), then you'll invite forward the part of self connected to the concern, then apply the needed intervention. When you take *Path 2* you'll start by inviting forward the child part connected to the symptom, then you'll elicit the concern from that child part, then you'll classify the concern or part, then apply the needed intervention.

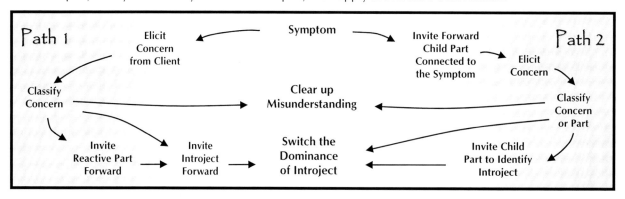

Path 1 is usually the best starting point for two reasons. (1) Typically clients can easily articulate their concerns, and (2) many misunderstandings are the adult client's confusion about the process or outcome.

Path 2 can help when a client has trouble articulating a concern. Simply invite forward the child part connected to the symptom. Once forward, the part can often express the associated misunderstanding, negative belief, or wounding message quite easily. (See option 5, in the *Eliciting the Concern* section on page 157.) The Overcoming Processing Blocks Flowchart illustrates Path 2 with four little stars. When following Path 2, apply the appropriate intervention depending on the type of concern revealed by the child part. For example, when a part has a misunderstanding, provide the needed corrective information; when a part seems to be reacting to a wounding message, invite it to look to the right to identify the introject; and when a part seems to be an introject, start the Switching the Dominance Protocol.

Applying the Adult Body Intervention

Sometimes child parts holding misunderstandings are so stuck in the past, they have trouble believing or integrating new corrective information. Sometimes child parts that are reacting to maladaptive introjects are so stuck in the past they have trouble expressing their concerns or looking to the right to see the introject

© Copyright 2009 by Shirley Jean Schmidt, MA, LPC. All rights reserved. Duplication in any form without permission is prohibited.

they're reacting to. Whenever this happens you can inform the child parts that they are in an adult body now. Apply the Adult Body intervention described on page 65. In addition, invite them to notice the loving support and protection that the Resources can provide them now.

Complications with the Resources

This section covers Resource complications that can arise during a DNMS protocol (e.g. the Switching the Dominance, Conference Room, or Needs Meeting Protocols). (The *Resource Development Protocol Complications* section, on page 166, will focus on problems that can arise before, during, and immediately after a client completes a Resource development meditation.)

The success of DNMS processing depends on robust Resources engaging in supportive interactions with receptive wounded child parts. The processing will fail if the Resources are not robust or if the interactions are not effectively supportive. Several clues can signal a problem. For example, a client or child parts might report reluctance to engage in or return to DNMS processing; trouble connecting to or visualizing the Resources; Resources that seem incompetent or untrustworthy; Resources that seem unable to meet their needs; Resources that seem unsafe or threatening; or a NAS or PAS that now looks like someone else.

Problems can arise when the Resources are not robust; but they can also arise when wounded child parts cause problems or just perceive problems with Resources that are perfectly fine. For example: child parts can block access to robust Resources; child parts can stand in for the Resources; and child parts can project their wounding caregivers onto the Resources.

The Resources are not robust.

Access to robust Resources is blocked.

Child parts are standing in for the Resources.

Child part projects wounding caregivers onto robust Resources.

Option 3 in the section titled, *Eliciting the Concern* (page 155), involves checking the status of established Resources. If you suspect one of these problems occurring with the Resources, ask the client something like:

Are you concerned that the Resources are not strong enough or competent enough caregivers?

© Copyright 2009 by Shirley Jean Schmidt, MA, LPC. All rights reserved. Duplication in any form without permission is prohibited.

If the answer is "yes," find out why the Resources seemed sufficiently capable at the conclusion of the Resource Development Protocol, but are not perceived that way now. While both new and seasoned DNMS clients can perceive problems with their Resources, this is most likely to occur when new clients are "road-testing" their Resources in a DNMS protocol for the first time.

Diagnosing Resource Complications

Your first step will be to determine whether wounded child parts are causing problems or just perceiving problems with Resources that are *robust*, or whether the Resources are *not robust*. Here are two methods which can help you diagnose a problem.

Check the Resources' Energy Glow

Check on the energy glow around the Resources. If the energy seems "clean" the Resources are probably robust. If the energy seems "dirty" they may or may not be robust. Ask something like:

> *Notice the energy radiating from the Resources. Does that energy seem clean or dirty?*

If the energy seems "dirty," ask:

> *Do they look exactly like the Resources you described (two weeks ago) when you pictured yourself nurturing and protecting (your cherished loved one)? Were they radiating dirty energy then too?*

If they were always radiating "dirty energy," they never were robust. If the appearance of the Resources has changed since completing the Resource Development Protocol, it is possible that robust Resources were once established, but (for some reason) they are not currently present.

Apply the TV Metaphor

To find out if child parts are distorting the appearance of robust Resources, apply the TV metaphor. Say:

> *If I'm not able to see a clear picture on my TV, it might be that the set is bad, or it might be that something is obstructing the view. For example, if cheesecloth is draped over a perfectly good TV, the picture will appear fuzzy. Does it seem more like something is distorting perfectly good Resources, or does it seem more like the Resources are not okay?*

If a client reports perceiving that something is distorting perfectly good Resources, they are probably robust. If a client reports nothing is distorting the perception of the Resources, and they do not seem solid or trustworthy, they are probably not robust.

Addressing Resource Complications

Once you know whether or not the Resources are robust, you can begin an intervention.

Resources Were Not Robust from the Beginning

If you determine that a client's Resources were not robust from the beginning, find out what went wrong with the original Resource development steps. You'll probably find that either the client was unprepared to establish Resources, or that there were unexpressed confusions, misunderstandings, or maladaptive introjects complicating the process. If a client was unprepared to connect to Resources, figure out what preparations are needed for it to be successful. Handle any associated misunderstandings and blocking introjects with the interventions listed above (pages 158-162), then start the Resource Development Protocol again, with a keen awareness of any additional blocks arising. The section below, titled *Resource Development Protocol Complications* (pages 166-171), provides lots of information about complications unique to this protocol.

© Copyright 2009 by Shirley Jean Schmidt, MA, LPC. All rights reserved. Duplication in any form without permission is prohibited.

Child Parts are Causing/Perceiving Problems with Robust Resources

If you determine that child parts are causing or perceiving problems with robust Resources, you'll need to find out why. Listed below are some common examples of this, with suggestions for illuminating the underlying concerns. The interventions listed below will point to blocks that need to be cleared. Once cleared, the robust Resources will be free to come forward.

- *Problems Making Contact with the Resources*

  Sometimes clients have problems making contact with the Resources. They may report that the Resources (a) fail to show up, (b) show up then disappear, (c) appear then become vague, (d) flicker in and out, or (e) seem very far away. This can happen when a client is connecting to the Resources before a protocol begins, or somewhere in the middle of a protocol.

  - **A Part is Not Ready to Start a Protocol:** A part of self that is not ready to start a protocol may interfere with a client's efforts to connect to the Resources just before a protocol begins. Use the Overcoming Processing Blocks Flowchart to identify and handle the part's concern. It may help to start by asking:

    If you were to begin the (Needs Meeting Protocol) now, what would you lose or what bad thing might happen?

  - **A Part Wants to Stop a Protocol in Progress:** A part of self that *wants* to stop a protocol in progress may interfere with a client connection to his Resources as the protocol unfolds. When this happens, direct the client's attention to the exact moment the connection to the Resources changed, then ask about why the change occurred right then. For example, when you ask why the Resources started to fade out in the middle of the Needs Meeting Protocol, you may find out it happened just as the emotion processing began. Use the Overcoming Processing Blocks Flowchart to identify and handle the part's concern. It may help to start with a carefully tailored question like:

    If you were to (fully engage in the emotion processing) now, what would you lose or what bad thing might happen?

  - **Stuck in the Past:** Sometimes the Resources will appear distant or vague when child parts are feeling especially *stuck in the past* – at a time when there were no Resources present for support. Reminding (or informing) the child parts that they are in an adult body now, for example in 2009, may be enough to bring them back in contact with robust Resources in present time. (The *Adult Body Intervention* is described on page 65. Also see the *Child Parts are Fixated on the Past* intervention, page 186.)[1]

- *The Appearance of the Resources Has Changed Over Time*

  At the successful conclusion of the Resource Development Protocol, a robust Nurturing and Protective Adult Self will look like the adult client in an ordinary, familiar experience of caring for a cherished loved one. There is clearly a problem when clients later report that the Resources appear (a) insecure or unsupportive, (b) like someone else, (c) like the client as a child, or (d) like the client in some unusual attire (e.g. wearing a superman costume or angel wings). When this happens, remind them of how these Resources originally appeared – when they were able to competently care for a cherished loved one. Say something like:

  So the appearance of your Nurturing and Protective Adult Self has changed. When you put your original mental picture of them, next to this new mental picture, which feels more empowering?

  If a client reports the original mental picture feels more empowering, and can comfortably return to that picture, the problem may be solved. But if a client is no longer comfortable with the original mental picture, follow the Overcoming Processing Blocks Flowchart to find and clear the associated blocks. It may help to start with the question:

  If you were to comfortably picture your Nurturing Adult Self as who you are caring for your cherished loved one, what would you lose or what bad thing might happen?

- *The Positive Attitude of the Resources Has Changed Over Time*

  At the successful conclusion of the Resource Development Protocol, clients experience their Resources as nurturing, protective, and attuned. But child parts can later project a wounding caregiver's negative attitude onto the Resources, inaccurately perceiving them to be incompetent, untrustworthy, indifferent, rejecting,

© Copyright 2009 by Shirley Jean Schmidt, MA, LPC. All rights reserved. Duplication in any form without permission is prohibited.

enmeshing, threatening, or unable to meet needs. For example, a child part might confess, "I know the Resources will reject me because my parents rejected me." Here are three ways to remedy such projections.

- **Compare Attitudes:** Compare the Resources' attitude to the wounding caregiver attitude by reminding the client of how supportive he is with his cherished loved one. Ask something like:

    Would you ever treat your (cherished love one) *the way your* (wounding caregiver) *treated you in childhood?*

    When the client answers, "Of course not," say:

    Remember, the Nurturing and Protective Adult Self Resources are you, in your most adult self, caring for your (cherished love one).

    This reminder is often all that is needed to stop the projection.

- **Compare Energy Glows:** Compare the Resources' energy glow to the wounding caregiver's energy glow by saying:

    Notice the energy radiating from the Resources. Does that energy seem clean or dirty?

    If the child parts answer "clean," ask:

    Was the energy radiating from your (parents) *clean or dirty?*

    If the child parts say "dirty," ask:

    Do you now see that the Resources are very different from your (parents)?

    If the child parts answer "yes," ask:

    Do the Resources seem nurturing and protective now?

    This comparison is often all that is needed to stop the projection.

- **Hypothetical Childhood Scenario:** Invite the child parts to *test the Resources* in a hypothetical childhood scenario. For example you might say something like:

    Let's say you're four years old eating a grape Popsicle on the floor while you watch Saturday morning cartoons. Your golden retriever suddenly rushes into the room and startles you. You shriek – which wakes up your parents. They come into the room and see you crying over a puddle of grape Popsicle melting into the carpet. What would your childhood parents have done next? What would the Resources have done if they'd been your parents?

    If the Resources are robust, the child parts will report them handling your scenario with respect and compassion. As child parts see the Resources responding appropriately, the projection will stop.

Resource Development Protocol Complications

While the section above covered Resource complications that can come up during a DNMS protocol, this section covers complications that can arise as you guide clients to establish robust Resources.

Complications can occur at many points in the Resource Development Protocol, for example, while discussing caregiving experiences; discussing the 24 caregiver skills; guiding clients in a Resource meditation; strengthening a Resource after a meditation; asking for a mental picture; and forming a Healing Circle of Resources. Some complications are minor and can be overcome easily by simply educating a client more about the processing – for example, clearing up a confusion about what the word *attunement* means. Some are based on misunderstandings about the outcome of the processing. Some are due to processing fears rooted in wounding messages and threats received in childhood and conveyed now by maladaptive introjects.

Clients are more likely to complete the Resource Development Protocol easily in one to three sessions, with minimal complications, if they (a) had at least one relationship in childhood with a loving, attuned role model or caregiver, and/or (b) have had at least one relationship in adulthood in which they were lovingly, attuned to a cherished loved one (person or animal). Those clients without one or more of these relationships are more likely to encounter processing blocks.

© Copyright 2009 by Shirley Jean Schmidt, MA, LPC. All rights reserved. Duplication in any form without permission is prohibited.

Problems Discussing Caregiving Experiences

Before connecting to the Nurturing and Protective Adult Self, you'll ask your client to recall and discuss a meaningful experience of being in a competent, adult caregiver role with a cherished loved one. For example, a client might discuss an experience of protecting her grandchild, or nurturing the first-graders she teaches. These experiences will serve as anchors for strengthening a connection to the two adult Resources. Several problems can arise at this step. For example, a client might recall *childhood* caregiving experiences, a client might focus on caregiving *incompetencies*, or a client might *deny* competent caregiving experiences.

Client Recalls Childhood Caregiving Experiences

When asked to recall an experience of caring for a cherished loved one, Ben recalled that at age 10 he stopped his father from hitting his little brother, then comforted his upset brother. Childhood memories like this are not good anchors for connecting to adult Resources, because such experiences are often associated with many unmet developmental needs. For example, children who are not getting good care from their parents may be ill equipped to provide good care to others (such as neglected siblings), and children often resent being trapped in such caregiver roles. When clients recall such childhood experiences, redirect them to their adulthood experiences of competent caregiving. When Ben was encouraged to focus on his adulthood caregiving, he was able to recall many experiences of competently caring for his two young nephews.

The only exception to this rule applies when you're working with young clients, who simply don't have adulthood experiences to draw on. Invite such clients to reflect on childhood experiences that were not connected to unmet needs. For example, 16-year-old Emily's fond experiences of competently babysitting her neighbors' children could serve as positive anchors, but her memories of nurturing her devastated mother after a messy divorce, could not.

Client Over-Focuses on Caregiving Incompetencies

When asked to recall an experience of competently caring for a cherished loved one, some clients feel compelled to focus on their caregiving failures. When this happens acknowledge the failures, then encourage them to talk about *at least one* positive caregiving experience they can feel good about.

It may help to focus clients like this on *recently acquired* caregiver skills. For example, Judy regretted being a neglectful parent when she raised her six children, but could acknowledge being a good caregiver to her infant granddaughter. It may help to focus them on *selectively applied* caregiver skills. For example, Miranda felt inadequate to care for children, but could acknowledge skill and passion in caring for her Persian cats

Caregiving decisions and actions can come from both *wounded child ego states* and *healthy adult ego states*. A wounded child self is more likely to caretake out of an irrational sense of fear, anger, or powerlessness, while a healthy adult self is more likely to see reality clearly, and nurture and protect appropriately. Therefore it may help to focus these clients on caregiving they've accomplished while in a *competent adult state of mind*. For example, Miranda reported she does not take such good care of her cats when she's depressed, but can readily admit to taking very good care of them when she's feeling confident and grown-up.

Client Denies Competent Caregiving Experiences

Some clients will simply categorically *deny* having any competent caregiving experiences. This can happen when the experiences are difficult for a client to recognize or recall; when a client has an aversion to admitting his strengths; or when there are no such caregiving experiences in his history. What you know about a client's relationship history will provide clues about such a denial.

If a client has *difficulty recognizing and recalling caregiver experiences* they may need only to be reminded of them. For example: Arthur, a client with no children and no interest in children, needed to be reminded of his loving, attuned connection to his German Shepherd; and Donna needed to be reminded that years ago, as a camp counselor, she made a loving, attuned connection with a troubled 12-year-old.

If a client has *an aversion to admitting caregiver strengths* they know they have, they probably have blocks that need to be cleared. For example, Bonnie had a reluctance to say out loud, "I'm good at nurturing my

© Copyright 2009 by Shirley Jean Schmidt, MA, LPC. All rights reserved. Duplication in any form without permission is prohibited.

dog." Such an aversion may be related to a misunderstanding and/or maladaptive introjects. For example, Bonnie believed that saying something positive about her self was bragging, and that bragging was bad and deserved to be punished. It helped her to hear that the expression of healthy self esteem is not the same as self-absorbed bragging. It was also necessary to identify and switch the dominance of two parental introjects that threatened to punish her when she spoke positively of herself.

Some clients have actually had *no experiences being in a caregiver role*. This can happen because they're young, have had limited life experiences, or have an aversion to relationships.

- When this is due to *youth or limited life circumstances*, you'll want to find out if the client has a caregiver *potential* that is ready to be expressed. Invite your client to imagine being in a caregiver role - for example, nurturing a sick puppy, or being a loving aunt/uncle to a future niece or nephew. If the client can get a felt sense of being a good future caregiver, proceed with the protocol.

- When this is due to a general *aversion to relationships*, the client must face the aversion and move beyond it. Encourage these clients to experiment with being in a real caregiver role. For example, encourage them to adopt a pet, or become a tutor, mentor, or Big Brother. My client Vicki has a significant aversion to relationships, but she was able to adopt a dog that she "fell in love with." In her caregiving relationship with her dog she has discovered she has the potential to express each of the 24 caregiver traits on the NAS & PAS skills list.

Problems Discussing Specific Items on the Caregiver Skills List

Once a client has identified a special time of competently caring for a cherished loved one, you'll show him the list of 24 caregiver skills and traits. If that special time was a good example of being a competent caregiver, he will likely recognize that each skill on the list was active in that experience. Just to be sure, you'll ask the client if he sees any items on the list that are/were *absent* in that relationship or event. If a client indicates a particular skill is/was absent, probe for more information. The probe could reveal a client's confusion about the definition of a skill or confusion about the requirement of consistency with a skill. Sometimes a particular skill is not endorsed because it is considered irrelevant to the event in question.

Confusion about the Definition of a Skill

Even though the list of skills you'll give a client includes their definitions, some clients overlay private definitions that take precedence. These private definitions can prevent them from endorsing a skill. Here are some examples:

- A client who was parentified as a child might say something like, "I don't want to connect to a Nurturing Self, because people take unfair advantage of me when I nurture them." She has confused having an ability to nurture, with having her nurturing skills exploited. To correct this perception, you'd want to explain that a skillful Nurturing Adult Self would be able to nurture appropriately while maintaining good boundaries.

- A client who grew up with over-protective parents might say something like, "I don't want to connect to a Protective Self, because people who are protective are up-tight and restrictive." He has confused being appropriately protective with being overly protective. To correct this perception, you'd want to explain that a skillful Protective Adult Self would be able to be appropriately protective while being lovingly attuned.

- A client who grew up with an enmeshing mother might say something like, "I wouldn't want to be open, because everyone would know what I'm thinking and feeling." She has confused the word "open," which means "being open-minded and receptive" with exposing all personal thoughts and feelings. To correct this perception, you'd want to explain that a skillful Nurturing or Protective Adult Self would be able to be appropriately open-minded and receptive while maintaining good boundaries.

Confusion about the Requirement of Consistency with a Given Skill

When looking at the list of skills, clients often erroneously assume that they must exhibit a given skill *all the time* before they can endorse it. Encourage your clients to recall experiences expressing the given skill – even if they are rare events. If a client has expressed a skill even once, it can be expressed again.

- One client looked at the list and said, "I'm not good with boundaries. When I baby sit my toddler grandson I let him snack as much as he wants." But, when asked if she would let him play in the street,

© Copyright 2009 by Shirley Jean Schmidt, MA, LPC. All rights reserved. Duplication in any form without permission is prohibited.

stay up past his bedtime, or hit his little sister, she said "never." She endorsed "good with boundaries" because she could exhibit this skill with some of her grandson's behaviors.

- Another looked at the list and said, "I'm usually very impatient with my daughter." When asked to describe times he was patient with his daughter, he could recall several good examples, especially times he was parenting from his most adult self. He could endorse "patient" because he could see he could exhibit this skill when he was being a skillful parent.

Absent Skills Considered Irrelevant To the Special Event

Sometimes a client indicates a particular skill on the list was not present at the time of the special event, because it was not relevant to the event. For example, Lisa recalled lovingly reading to her niece as she put her to bed. She acknowledged accessing all the skills on the list except courage, which was not needed at the time. There are two ways I could have responded to this. I could have asked if she would have been able to *access courage if it had been needed*, for example if the house had suddenly caught on fire. If she answered "yes," I could say that suggests she could be courageous with her niece, when courage was needed. Or I could have asked her if she could *recall some other experience* of being courageous, with her niece or with another a loved one. If so, the two experiences combined demonstrate she has all the skills.

Problems with the Mental Pictures

The mental picture a client reports at the very end of each Resource meditation, can provide a lot of information about the outcome of a meditation. For example, a mental picture of a Resource that looks alive, confident, benevolent, and powerful indicates protocol success, while a Resource that looks impotent or ominous indicates a problem. Any indication of a problem merits further investigation. The Overcoming Processing Blocks Flowchart can be a helpful problem-solving guide. Other common problems that can arise with the mental pictures of each of the three Resources, and of the Healing Circle, are discussed here.

Mental Pictures of the Nurturing and Protective Adult Self

Clients are encouraged to picture their adult Resources as themselves, competently caring for their cherished loved one, in a nurturing role, and in a protective role. When pictured in an ordinary, familiar experience, the adult Resources are extremely believable to wounded child parts. That makes them especially effective internal caregivers.

Sometimes clients report a Nurturing or Protective Adult Self that looks like someone or something else, for example, a shaman, a warrior, an angel, an animal, a favorite aunt, a tree, and so on. This is called a *Not-Self Resource.* While clients may legitimately benefit from a Not-Self Resource, for the purposes of executing the DNMS protocols, a Nurturing or Protective Adult Self who looks and feels like self are by far the best, because they look and feel real. Clinical experience of doing the DNMS with both types of Resources had led me to conclude that clients will get the greatest processing benefit from a NAS and PAS that look and feel like self.

If a client describes a mental picture of a Not-Self Resource, you'll need to follow-up. Invite the client to hold his mental picture of his Not-Self Resource next to his mental picture of who he is caring for a cherished loved one. To the client who has pictured his Protective Adult Self as a Samurai warrior, you might say something like:

> *Hold this picture of you as a (Samurai warrior), next to a picture of you (pulling your son from the edge of the cliff). Which image feels the most comfortable and powerful in the body?*

Clients will often concede that the picture of self is preferable, because it feels more real, and will gladly associate that mental picture of self with that Resource.

Occasionally a client will feel uncomfortable picturing a Resource as self – preferring a Not-Self Resource instead. An aversion to picturing an Adult Resource as self indicates one or more processing blocks coming from misunderstandings, and/or blocking introjects. You should be able to handle the aversion by following the Overcoming Processing Blocks Flowchart.

For example, before the NAS meditation Connie offered several examples of being good at caring for her dog. At the end of the meditation she pictured her Nurturing Adult Self as her loving, attuned granny. When asked

© Copyright 2009 by Shirley Jean Schmidt, MA, LPC. All rights reserved. Duplication in any form without permission is prohibited.

which picture felt the most comfortable or powerful, the picture of herself caring for her dog or the picture of her loving granny, she answered, "the granny picture." When asked why she preferred to picture her NAS as her granny, she replied she believed her granny was a better caregiver than she could ever be. She also admitted hearing her father's voice telling her she was worthless. Her belief that she must picture her Nurturing Adult Self as granny, because granny was a better caregiver, was a misunderstanding. The sound of her father telling her she was worthless, was coming from a maladaptive introject. After both of these blocks were successfully handled, Connie could comfortably picture her Nurturing Adult Self as herself.

Mental Picture of the Spiritual Core Self

The Spiritual Core Self is often described in terms of light and energy, such as a ball or column of light, a luminous body, a ray of sunlight, or a wave of loving energy. This type of description indicates the client has connected with her spiritual or soul dimension. Those who report a mental picture that is far away from this description need to be nudged in the right direction. Here are some examples of nudging:

- One client reported seeing his Spiritual Core Self as himself on the top of a mountain, fully connected with the nature around him. I asked him to picture himself on the mountain, without a body. He reported seeing himself a luminous wave of energy – which he recognized instantly as his Spiritual Core.

- Another reported seeing her Spiritual Core Self as Jesus. I asked her to put a hand on the part of her body that feels Jesus' love the most. She put her hand on her heart. I asked her to close her eyes and get in touch with the part of self that resonates with Jesus' love the most. Then I asked her to picture that part of self without her body. She described it as a glowing ball of light – which she knew was her Spiritual Core.

- Another reported her Spiritual Core Self looked like a happy and free spirited two-year-old. When I asked if the two-year-old had any unmet needs, she said, "No." I asked her to reflect on her peak spiritual near-death experience and contrast her picture of her Spiritual Core Self as a two-year-old, with a picture of her Spiritual Core Self as a ball of loving energy and light. After a few minutes the client said the ball of light felt more powerful, and more like the Spiritual Core Self she had connected to in her near-death experience.

Mental Picture of the Healing Circle

Ordinarily, when clients bring all three Resources together to form a Healing Circle, they picture three individual Resources standing together. Occasionally a client will report seeing all three Resources merge into a single Resource. Ordinarily this would not matter, but it is not ideal for DNMS interventions. The Healing Circle is a special place where wounded child parts will get their needs met. These child parts seem to benefit greatly from having three separate Resource caregivers in distinct roles because it provides a greater sense of containment and community. Because of this, doing DNMS processing with a single merged Resource is discouraged. If a client reports seeing all three Resources merge into one big Resource, invite him to separate the Resources when it comes time for healing interventions.

Difficulty Visualizing the Resources

At the conclusion of each Resource meditation, clients are usually able to report a clear mental picture of a Resource, and of all three together as a team. There are three exceptions.

- Those who do not visualize anything well – not their home, car, or loved ones – will have difficulty visualizing the Resources and other parts of self. These clients may be able to proceed with the DNMS by relying on their felt sense of parts of self.

- Those who can visualize mental pictures may not be able to see a robust Resource well because of a block. This is analogous to a cheese cloth draped over a TV. The picture appears blurry because of the cloth, but there's nothing wrong with the set. Before the client can establish a clear mental picture, you'll have to identify and clear all the associated processing blocks.

- Those who can visualize mental pictures may not be able to see a Resource well because it is not robust. This can happen when a client goes through the Resource Development Protocol over an unexpressed processing block. The solution is to identify and clear all blocks then do the Resource meditation again.

© Copyright 2009 by Shirley Jean Schmidt, MA, LPC. All rights reserved. Duplication in any form without permission is prohibited.

Provisional Resources

Robust Resources can play an important role in helping a client work through processing blocks. So what can you do if the blocks arise before a single DNMS Resource has officially been established? What can you do if a client has blocks to connecting to DNMS Resources? Answer: You can guide him to connect to a Provisional Resource. A Provisional Resource is a temporary helper – any entity, real or imagined, self or not-self, that a client perceives as supportive and kind. It is usually easy for a client to connect to a Provisional Resource. There is no official, structured protocol for connecting clients to a Provisional Resource, but here are some guidelines about how to proceed.

- You can invite clients to talk about perceptions of feeling supported by someone real or imagined. This could be someone they know (e.g. a mentor), a pet (e.g. Fluffy); a deceased loved one (e.g. great grand-mother), a spirit guide (e.g. an angel), a fictional character (e.g. June Cleaver), a mystical archetype (e.g. Earth Goddess), or a religious figure (e.g. Jesus). For example, my client Sally described how she felt supported by a guardian angel throughout her troubled childhood. When she felt sleepy during the NAS meditation, we discovered a wounded child part fearful that connecting to a Nurturing Adult Self meant being disloyal to her mother. I invited this child part to discuss this fear with her guardian angel. The angel told her she had a right to grow to meet her full potential, whether that felt loyal or disloyal to her mother. The reassurance and support from her guardian angel helped us clear the block.

- You can invite clients to talk about personal experiences of nurturing someone. For example, my client Alice had a two-year-old niece, whom she treasured. She was able to care for her niece, from her most adult self, with all the skills common to a competent caregiver. Just before beginning the SCS meditation, Alice reported getting a headache. This was connected to a maladaptive introject of her abusive minister father. I began to switch the dominance of this introject. When I needed a Resource to provide validation and support I called upon her *Aunt Alice* ego state. Her Aunt Alice ego state provided the help the child part needed to fully understand the father costume was not a real threat. Once the dominance of this introject was switched she was able to connect with her Spiritual Core Self.

- Sometimes at the conclusion of the NAS and PAS meditation, a client will prefer to picture her Nurturing or Protective Adult Self as something other than self. If this *not-self image* is positive and supportive, this *Not-Self Resource* can serve as a Provisional Resource. For example, my client Lucy reported that the idea of picturing her Protective Adult Self as herself, caring for her three dogs, evoked intense discomfort. Instead she preferred to picture it as a strong and vigilant Lioness. The Lioness served as a helpful Provisional Resource as we addressed and cleared each block related to her aversion to picturing her Protective Adult Self as self.

Switching the Dominance Protocol Complications

Complications can occur at many points in the Switching the Dominance Protocol, for example, while eliciting an introject's wounding message; while trying to contact the child part wearing the mask; while talking to the child part wearing the mask; while contrasting the child's good true nature with the mask's wounding nature; and while checking on the appearance of the mask. Likewise, misunderstandings can arise at any step, and blocking introjects can intrude at any step. This section will prepare you to successfully identify and handle a variety of complications.

Problematic Introject Messages

The Switching the Dominance Protocol may not go well if there are problems with the way the introject message is worded. A wounding caregiver message must include one or more of the following:
- Contempt for the client.
- A threat to emotional safety (such as threat of rejection, neglect, abandonment, or enmeshment).
- A threat of physical harm.

© Copyright 2009 by Shirley Jean Schmidt, MA, LPC. All rights reserved. Duplication in any form without permission is prohibited.

- An inappropriate assignment of responsibility.
- A caregiver's negative belief about him or herself.
- A faulty notion about the world.

A well-worded message will evoke disturbing emotions, be stated in the client's own words, and make sense in the context of the client's history. Examples of well-worded, wounding introject messages include: "You're a lazy, no-good tramp," "Get out of my sight or I'll kill you," "You shouldn't have been born," "If I get mad and hit you, it'll be your fault for being so bad," "We women are helpless," and "The world is a dangerous place."

Sometimes there are problems with an introject message a client reports. For example, a client may report that the introject that has appeared is not conveying a message; a client may report a message that does not match the introjected person's wounding nature; or a client might report a neutral or poorly worded message. Each of these problems is discussed below.

The Introject is Apparently Not Conveying a Message

Sometimes a client reports that an introject is silent, or is not conveying any message at all. An introject, by definition, is conveying someone else's wounding message, even if the message is non-verbal. To get to the non-verbal message ask a question like:

> *What message does the mask's mood or facial expression convey? What message does the costume's mood or body language convey? What message does the silence convey?*

The Introject "Message" Does Not Match the Caregiver

Sometimes a client gets confused and reports an introject statement that is not actually a caregiver's message. For example, Eddie reported an angry father introject appeared conveying the message *"I can't do anything right."* That made no sense, given that his father was a hostile narcissist. This was actually a negative belief held by a reactive part. The hostile father introject message was, *"You can't do anything right."*

Neutrally-Worded Introject Message

Sometimes a client reports an introject message that is neutrally worded, such as, "I'm busy," "Clean your room," or "My world is upside down." This may be a sign that the real wounding message was conveyed non-verbally. For example, Debbie's father verbally said, "I'm busy," but non-verbally said, "Don't bother me with your problems. Your needs aren't important to me." When an introject message sounds neutral, ask questions like:

> *Is there an underlying message here? What does that message mean about you? What message does the caregiver's facial expression or body language convey?*

Introject Message Missing an "Or Else"

Sometimes a client reports an introject message that is a thinly veiled threat that is missing an "or else." For example, Brenda's father introject appeared conveying the message, "You'd better watch it, young lady." This could have been an intimidating threat or it could have been a helpful warning about an impending danger. You'll want to make thinly veiled threats explicit. To do that, ask questions like:

> *What does ('watch it') mean? What would happen if you didn't ('watch it')?*

When asked to elaborate, Brenda revealed that her father did not verbalize any more than that, but that she watched him viciously beat her older siblings when they disobeyed or annoyed him. She understood it to mean, "You'd better watch it, young lady, or I'll beat you into submission. I have all the power – you have none."

Introject Message Missing an Assignment of Fault

Sometimes a client reports an introject message that is missing an assignment of fault. For example, a client might report a father introject message like, "If you make me mad I'll hit you," or a mother introject message like, "Don't leave or I'll feel lonely." It may help to follow up with a question like:

> *Is it your fault if (your dad hits you)?   OR   Is it your fault if (your mom feels lonely)?*

If the wounding caregivers held the client responsible for their behaviors or emotions, the introject messages might be more like: "*It's your fault* if I get mad and hit you," or "Don't leave. If I feel lonely *it's your fault.*"

© Copyright 2009 by Shirley Jean Schmidt, MA, LPC. All rights reserved. Duplication in any form without permission is prohibited.

If Processing Stalls

Sometimes processing stalls in the middle of the protocol, for no apparent reason. For example, the child part reports the mask does not change in size, or seems very uncomfortable with the idea of the mask changing or going away. When this happens, ask the child part wearing the mask:

> *If this mask got small enough, and felt harmless enough, to put in your pocket, is there something you'd lose or something bad that would happen?*

- **Misunderstanding:** The child part's answer may reveal a misunderstanding, such as: "If I heal I'll lose a familiar sense of identity," or "If the mask goes away I'll lose my connection to my mother." Clear such a block by providing the relevant missing information. (See page 158.)

Processing is Blocked		Processing Block Cleared
I'll lose a familiar sense of identity	Provide the relevant missing information	I can develop a new sense of identity.
Child part has a misunderstanding		Child part has a new understanding

- **Introject is blocking the processing:** The child part's answer may reveal an introject is blocking the processing. For example, a statement like "If this mother mask gets small, I'll betray my father's dying wish that I devote myself to caring for my mother," suggests there may be a father introject interfering with switching the dominance of the mother introject. <u>Invite the child part to look to the right to see the part of self that she's reacting to.</u> Locate and switch the dominance of the blocking introject (page 158), then come back to the child part that stalled out in the middle of the protocol. If this was the only block you'll be able to finish switching the dominance.

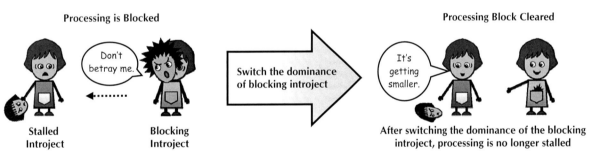

Processing is Blocked		Processing Block Cleared
Don't betray me.	Switch the dominance of blocking introject	It's getting smaller.
Stalled Introject Blocking Introject		After switching the dominance of the blocking introject, processing is no longer stalled

- **The "introject" is actually a reactive mimic:** The child part's answer may reveal that the part is actually a reactive mimic, not an introject after all. For example, a child part might say something like, "I need this mask. It protects me. If I give it up I'll be defenseless and exposed." When this happens, you'll need to keep looking for the introject at the root of the issue you're processing. <u>Invite the reactive mimic to look to the right to see the part of self that she's reacting to.</u> Locate and switch the dominance of the target introject. If this was the only introject the reactive mimic was reacting to, afterwards she'll feel great relief, and the reactive mask will appear inanimate and irrelevant.

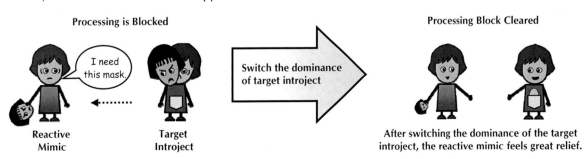

Processing is Blocked		Processing Block Cleared
I need this mask.	Switch the dominance of target introject	
Reactive Mimic Target Introject		After switching the dominance of the target introject, the reactive mimic feels great relief.

© Copyright 2009 by Shirley Jean Schmidt, MA, LPC. All rights reserved. Duplication in any form without permission is prohibited.

A Reactive Part Answers the Questions

All the Switching the Dominance Protocol questions are only intended for the child part wearing the introject mask. Sometimes a child part's answers to these questions seem strange or out of context. This can happen when the questions are being answered by a child part *reacting* to the mask instead of the one *wearing* it. This is most likely to happen when a client who's new to the DNMS is confused about the different parts of self.

This one or this one?

Reactive Part   Introject

To clarify what is occurring, draw a picture of the introject and the child part reacting to it. Then, ask the client to point out which one is answering your questions. After you clear up the confusion, you should be able to successfully resume the protocol.

On rare occasions a reactive part that's trying to sabotage the processing will answer the questions to disrupt the processing. To stop the sabotage, welcome the reactive part. Invite him to look to the right to identify the introject that has inspired his sabotaging behavior. Once you've identified the introject, switch the dominance. That should end the sabotage. You should then be able to resume the protocol with the first introject.

Enmeshment Reversal

The *Enmeshment Reversal* is a simple intervention based on the idea that a client who was enmeshed with a childhood caregiver might have a child part enmeshed with an introject mask. This may become evident when a client reports no sense of a child part wearing an introject mask, or reports a child part fears she won't exist without the introject mask. The Enmeshment Reversal helps the child part see she is actually a separate person from the caregiver.

For example, Carmen, who grew up enmeshed with her mother, had a four-year-old child part wearing a mother introject costume. As the Switching the Dominance Protocol unfolded, the child part worried, as the costume got smaller, that she too would disappear. The following information turned her around:

> At age 4 you were about 3 feet tall and your mother was 6 feet tall. You drank milk. She drank coffee. You wore tennis shoes. She wore high heels. You watched Sesame St. She watched the news. You read picture books, she read the newspaper. She drove a car, you rode a tricycle. Do you see how you were a completely separate person from your mother?

Some child parts will say with amazement: "I had no idea." "This is totally new to me." As the child becomes aware of the enmeshment with the caregiver, the enmeshment with the introject mask softens and the child part may be observed behind the mask or the child part may feel free to separate from the mask.

Problems Finding the Child Part Wearing the Mask (In Step 1)

You'll start Step 1 of the Switching the Dominance Protocol by asking if there's a little one behind the introject mask. Clients will usually say "yes." Then you'll ask permission to speak to the part. Sometimes a client will tell you she doesn't see a child part, or there is no child part wearing the mask; or permission to speak to the child part will not be granted. Instructions for handling each of these are provided here.

Client Reports There Does Not Appear to be a Child Part Wearing the Mask

Just because a client doesn't see a part there, doesn't mean there isn't one. That's because the dominance of a mask can eclipse awareness of the part of self wearing it. To get around this, say something like:

> So I understand you're not aware of a child part wearing this costume. I'm going to speak as if there is a part there. If she's there she'll hear me and respond. If not, you'll get a sense that I'm not making contact. Either one is fine – just tell me what you notice.

© Copyright 2009 by Shirley Jean Schmidt, MA, LPC. All rights reserved. Duplication in any form without permission is prohibited.

Then, speak directly to the part wearing the mask. Say:

> *Hey little one, I'm very glad you're here. I want you to know I see you and I know that you're good. What's it like to hear that?*

Usually the client will report you've made contact with the child part, who will then respond to your question. If this does not establish that contact, you'll need to find out why. There are several reasons why this might happen.

- The part might be a *reactive part*, not a maladaptive introject. To check, ask the part:

  > *Are you reacting to someone or mimicking someone?*

- There could be a *processing block*. To find out if there are any blocks to root out and clear, ask:

  > *If there were a child behind the mask, and if I were to talk with (her), is there something you'd lose or something bad that would happen?*

- If the client had been *enmeshed* with a childhood caregiver, the child part wearing the mask might be enmeshed with the mask the way the client was enmeshed with the caregiver. The remedy for this is the *Enmeshment Reversal* intervention described above.

Permission to Talk to the Child Part Wearing the Mask is Denied

On rare occasions the mask or the client denies permission to speak to the child wearing the mask. This will usually happen when some part of self is afraid that your message to the child part will be shaming or invalidating. To remedy this misperception, say:

> *If I could speak to the child, this is what I'd say... Hey little one, I want you to know I see you and I know that you're good. And I know the difference between you and this angry mom mask. What's it like to hear that?*

These kind words will usually resolve the fear of making contact, and open the dialogue with the child part.

Access to the Child Part Wearing the Mask is Deliberately Blocked

On very rare occasions a mask will block access to the child part wearing it. Here are two responses to that:

- Check to see if this is a *reactive mimic* holding onto a mask it needs for safety and protection. Ask the part:

  > *Are you reacting to someone or mimicking someone?*

- Check for a *processing block*. Ask the client:

  > *If I were to talk with the child part wearing this mask, is there something you'd lose or something bad that would happen?*

- If this is clearly not a reactive mimic, it may simply be that the mask is very dominant. With the assumption that it is just an illusion, say to the mask something like:

  > *Well, you're not real, so I'm going to speak to the child anyway.*[2]

  Then go on to Step 2, "Hey little one I want you to know I see you and I know that you're good...."

When a Child Part under the Mask is Also Reacting to It (In Step 1)

Sometimes a client reports an introject appears looking like a cover or container metaphor, such as a box, a blanket, or a jail. In Step 1, when you make contact with the child part wearing the introject costume, you might find yourself speaking with an upset reactive part covered by the costume, *and* reacting to it.

For example, Annie's five-year-old upset reactive part looked to the right to see who she was reacting to. She saw a blanket conveying message, "I'm going to smoother you." She reported this was her mother's non-verbal message. When I asked "Is there a little one wearing this blanket?" she described a very *upset, fearful* four-year-old being smothered by it. This child part's emotional state revealed she was *reacting to be smothered by the costume*. So even though the four-year-old was technically *wearing it*, she was not the child part component of the introject. I invited the four-year-old to tuck in, then asked Annie about the possibility of a child part that took on the mom costume because of the firing of mirror neurons. She was able to contact a three-year-old

© Copyright 2009 by Shirley Jean Schmidt, MA, LPC. All rights reserved. Duplication in any form without permission is prohibited.

embedded in the blanket, who felt relatively emotionless. After we switched the dominance of this introject, the four-year-old and five-year-old reactive parts felt substantially safer.

Differentiating Reactive Mimics and Introjects (In Step 2)

The Switching the Dominance protocol helps *maladaptive introjects* heal. It is not fruitful to do it with reactive mimics because the introjects they're reacting to will just continue to provoke problems. Unfortunately these two types of ego states can be difficult to tell apart. So you must always be mindful to check, and if necessary recheck, to be sure you're applying the protocol to the introject at a problem's source. The protocol has a built-in introject check. In Step 2 you'll begin with a welcoming dialogue with the child part wearing the presumptive introject mask. Then, to verify the part is actually and introject, you'll ask:

> *Do you like or need this mask? Does it serve a useful purpose?*

And, when necessary, you can add:

> *If the mask were to suddenly disappear, would that be a good thing or a bad thing?*

The child parts' response to these questions will usually reveal whether she's a reactive mimic or an introject. But sometimes a child part cannot give a single clear answer about the usefulness of the mask, and/or an interest in keeping the mask. A child part may give you statements that suggest the part is an introject, and statements that suggest the part is a reactive mimic. It clearly cannot be both. Here are three options for how to proceed when you're just not sure.

- The first option applies primarily to clients who were enmeshed in childhood with the caregiver the mask is mirroring. If a child part does not know she is separate from the caregiver, she may not know she can exist separate from the caregiver mask. Apply the *Enmeshment Reversal* mentioned above. Afterwards, the child part may be able to make a clear statement like: "I don't like this mask, get it off me."

- Another option is to ask the child part to look to the right, to see who she is reacting to – with the knowledge that if this child part is actually an introject, nothing will appear. You might say to the child part:

> *In a moment I'm going to ask you to look to the right to see the part or parts of self that you're reacting to. If you're reacting to another part, you'll see that part appear. If you're not reacting to another part, you'll see nothing appear. So when you're ready look to your right... and tell me what you see.*

- A final option is to proceed with the Switching the Dominance Protocol with the knowledge that, if this is a reactive mimic, it will become clear later, when the child part resists changes to the mask.

Problems Contrasting the Child's Good True Nature with the Mask (In Step 3)

In Step 3 you'll ask a series of questions to contrast the good true nature of the child wearing the mask, with the wounding nature of the mask. This could include a question to the child part like:

> *Do you believe caregivers should (<u>always treat children with respect</u>)?*

In a typical exchange the child part will answer "yes." You'd then ask if the mask agrees. The child part would say the mask does not agree. You'd do this about three times before pointing out to the child part how different she is from the mask she's been wearing. But occasionally child parts will give an unexpected response to one of these questions. Three such responses are described here.

"I Don't Know"

To a question like, "Do you believe caregivers should always treat children with respect?" the child parts may answer, "I don't know." Respond to this with something like:

> *Do the <u>Resources believe</u> caregivers should always treat children with respect?*

© Copyright 2009 by Shirley Jean Schmidt, MA, LPC. All rights reserved. Duplication in any form without permission is prohibited.

The child part will probably say the Resources believe that positive statement about caregivers. You can then ask if the mask agrees. It will probably not agree. You can use these types of interactions to help the child part see she is different from the mask. [3]

The Mask Agrees

Sometimes when asked, "Does the mask agree?" the child part will answer "yes" instead of "no." When this happens, find out why she believes the mask agrees. The child part will probably say the caregiver *sometimes* acted in agreement with the statement, or *always* acted in agreement with the statement.

- *Caregiver <u>Sometimes</u> Acted in Agreement with the Statement*

    If a child part says the caregiver *sometimes* acted in agreement with a statement he's probably referring to behaviors *unrelated* to the mask message. For example, when switching the dominance of a mother mask conveying the message, "Your needs are not important," the therapist asked, "Do you believe caregivers should consider children's needs to be important?" The child part said "yes." When asked if the mask agreed, he said "yes." When asked to clarify, he explained that his mother *could* attend to his needs – sometimes quite effectively – but usually ignored them by drinking too much.

    To handle this discrepancy, you'd explain to the child part that the mask only represents one wounding aspect of the caregiver. For example you might say:

    > This mask does not represent every aspect of your (mother). Those kinder aspects of her are recorded elsewhere in the brain. This (mother) mask, delivering the message ("<u>Your needs are not important</u>,") is a record of just those times (<u>she did not attend to your needs</u>). With that in mind, does the mask agree with you that (<u>children's needs are very important</u>)?

    Given this clarification, the child part is now likely to report that the mask does not agree with the statement.

- *Caregiver <u>Always</u> Acted in Agreement with the Statement*

    If a child part says the caregiver *always* acted in agreement with the statement, the question was probably not appropriately tailored to the mask's message. For example, when switching the dominance of a father mask conveying the message, "You may not grow up and leave home," the therapist asked, "Do you believe caregivers should be protective of children?" The child part said "yes." When asked if the mask agreed, she said "yes." When asked to clarify, she explained that her father was *overprotective* and would not let her go to slumber parties or school dances, and would not let her drive.

    You can avoid this problem by focusing on questions that highlight *areas of clear disagreement* with the wounding message. For the overprotective, father-introject message in this example, three better questions would be: "Do you believe caregivers should help children grow to meet their full potential?", "Do you believe caregivers should honor a child's need for age-appropriate freedoms?" and "Do you believe caregivers should encourage a child's expression of age-appropriate autonomy?" The child part will likely say "yes," to each of these, and report that the father mask does not agree.

The Mask Moves Away or Disappears Prematurely (In Step 6)

Throughout the protocol you'll check on changes in the appearance of the mask (Step 6). Occasionally a child part will report that the introject mask has disappeared or moved away.

- If a mask disappears, it could indicate very effective processing – particularly if it's reported late in the protocol. But if it's reported right after you've explain the illusion of significance (Step 5), it could indicate a processing block or confusion, especially if the client is highly defended, highly dissociated, or new to the DNMS. (Sometimes clients new to the DNMS do not fully understand the process, and will report a mask has disappeared because they think it's supposed to disappear.) If you suspect the disappearance of a mask is a defensive maneuver, ask the child part:

    > If the mask were to reappear what would you lose or what bad thing would happen?

    The answer may reveal misunderstandings or blocking introjects that need to be handled. If the answer does not reveal a block, it may be a sign of unusually fast and effective processing.

© Copyright 2009 by Shirley Jean Schmidt, MA, LPC. All rights reserved. Duplication in any form without permission is prohibited.

- If a mask moves away, it's often a sign that the child part wants distance from it, because of an aversion to it. When this happens, invite the child part to bring it back in close. Then continue to explain that the mask is not a threat, and can do no real harm.

Fear that Losing Interest in the Mask Means Losing Interest in the Caregiver (Step 10)

In Step 10 you'll invite the child part to put the remains of the mask in a pocket. Sometimes a child part will worry that losing interest in the mask will mean losing interest in the caregiver. While this could come up during any protocol step, it will most likely come up in Step 10. This occurs most often with clients who felt enmeshed with, or responsible for, the caregiver in childhood. You'll want to help the child part see that her relationship with the caregiver is completely independent of reactions to the mask. Such an explanation might sound something like this:

> Remember now, this mask is not your mother – it's just a recording of the way she behaved many years ago. You'll continue to have a relationship with your 60-year-old mother who lives in Springfield. Your interactions with her will sometimes be pleasant and sometimes be unpleasant, but they have nothing whatsoever to do with what's left of this mask. How does that sound?

Such an explanation will usually be reassuring, leading to a comfortable pocketing of the mask.

Attachment Needs Ladder Complications

When administering the Attachment Needs Ladder, both initially and at follow-up, clients will sometimes offer 0-10 ratings that seem unusually high or unusually low, in light of their history, presenting problems, or the processing they have completed. When this happens, further investigation is required. The following two sections explore this problem.

Initial Rating Complications

This section focuses on the problems that can arise when a client *initially* rates a set of Attachment Needs Ladder statements (e.g. Rung 1). If a client gives a particular statement an oddly high or low rating, ask something like:

> What were you thinking when you rated this statement (a zero)?

The answer should help you determine whether or not the odd rating accurately reflected the client's emotional wounds. There are several ways clients can fail to give accurate ratings. Each is described below.

Rating a Statement from a Rational State of Mind

Before you invite a client to rate a statement, you'll want to preface your question with a prompt that increases the likelihood a rating will reflect the views of wounded child parts. If you forget this step, if the prompt you're using isn't matched well to the statement, or if the client is highly defended, it's possible she'll rate items from a rational, adult state of mind, rather than a wounded child state of mind. For example, LeAnn, a successful engineer, felt rejected throughout her childhood by both parents. When getting Rung 1 ratings I used the prompt, "When you think about growing up with your rejecting parents, does the statement, (*I shouldn't exist*), feel true?" She gave unusually low ratings to each of the Rung 1 statements, with most rated at zero. When I asked her what she was thinking when she rated the statements so low, she said she knew intellectually that the statements were largely untrue. I reminded her that, while her intellectual point of view had value, it was irrelevant to these ratings. I invited her to rate the statements again. This time I changed the prompt. I asked, "When you think about growing up with your rejecting parents, are there any wounded child parts that believe the statement, (*I shouldn't exist*), is true?" This change bypassed her intellectual defenses, and she was able to give much higher ratings.

© Copyright 2009 by Shirley Jean Schmidt, MA, LPC. All rights reserved. Duplication in any form without permission is prohibited.

Confusion about a Statement

Sometimes clients get confused about what they're rating. For example, Carrie, who grew up with constant verbal abuse, but no physical abuse, gave a rating of 8 to the Rung 2A statement "I must hide to stay physically safe." When I asked what she was thinking when she rated the statement an 8, she reported recalling the many times she would hide under her bed to avoid her mother's verbal assaults. I reminded her that Rung 2A was only about *physical safety*, and that the statement, "I must hide to stay *emotionally* safe," would get rated in Rung 2B. With that in mind she changed her rating from 8 to 2. She later rated "I must hide to stay *emotionally* safe," an 8.

Privately Changing a Statement

Sometimes clients will privately change the wording of a statement. For example, Lucy rated the Rung 2B statement "I must depend on others to feel secure," a 10. This rating seemed unusually high considering she was highly independent. When I asked her what she was thinking when she rated this statement a 10, she talked about the workers she supervises. She said her job security depends on how much they produce. She had privately changed the statement to "I must depend on others for *my job to be secure*." I asked her to think about how the Ladder statement applied in a context other than supervising her workers, for example in her relationships with family and friends. She acknowledged that she isolates herself socially, and feels more secure and in control when she relies largely on herself. She changed her rating from 10 to 2.

Underrating a Statement in the Context of Supportive Resources

Sometimes clients let their awareness of loving, supportive Resources mask accurate ratings, by confusing the temporary feel-good state the Resources can evoke, with permanent trait change. For example, Nancy, who was regularly molested by her father in childhood, gave the Rung 2A statements about physical and sexual safety, ratings of 0. When I asked her what she was thinking when she rated this statement a 0, she said, "I know I'm safe now because I have the Resources to protect me." When asked to re-rate each item as if the Resources were *not* there to protect her, her ratings ranged from 6-9. These higher ratings reflected the degree to which the sexual trauma was yet unresolved.

Reluctance to Admit a Negative Statement Feels True

Some clients are inclined to downplay their negative feelings – reluctant or embarrassed to admit a negative statement sometimes feels true. For example, Vicki was almost always smiling and cheerful. While growing up, her mother never validated her feelings, never truly soothed her when she was upset. Instead she taught Vicki to look happy and act friendly, no matter how she felt inside. Vicki had great difficulty rating the Rung 1 statements. She resisted my references to her mother being invalidating, as a prompt to help her answer from a wounded state of mind. Vicki defended her mother, saying she was doing what she thought was best. This launched a series of interventions to clear a number of blocks prohibiting her from expressing her true feelings. Once all the blocks were cleared, she was able to comfortably rate the Rung 1 statements.

Follow-up Rating Complications

Once the Needs Meeting Protocol is complete, clients are asked to re-rate the Attachment Needs Ladder statements they had initially endorsed. Clients will typically re-rate those beliefs as 0 (not at all true). But occasionally a client will re-rate items above 0. The following three possibilities can account for this.

Confusion about a Statement

A higher-than-expected follow-up rating might be a sign that a client is confused about the statement being rated. For example, Marci initially rated the Rung 2A statement, "Everyone in dangerous – physically and/or sexually," a 10. After the Needs Meeting Protocol she re-rated it a 1. When asked what she was thinking when she rated this a 1, she replied that there are a lot of sexual predators in the world. I agreed with her, then I pointed out that the statement was "Everyone is dangerous," not "There are some dangerous people in the world." She laughed and said, "Oh right. When I gave it a 1, I was thinking 10% of people are dangerous." She said no part of her believed that everyone was dangerous, and changed her rating from 1 to 0.

© Copyright 2009 by Shirley Jean Schmidt, MA, LPC. All rights reserved. Duplication in any form without permission is prohibited.

Deeper Layer to Process

If a client has several layers of wounds, the deeper layers become exposed once the top layer has been processed. Higher-than-expected follow-up ratings may be evidence of additional maladaptive introjects operating at a deeper level. Repeat the Conference Room Protocol with reactive parts associated with the statements re-rated above 0. This should reveal the additional introjects. Once the second layer of introjects has completed the Needs Meeting Protocol, the second round of follow-up ratings will likely be 0.

There's a simple way you can increase the probability of addressing all the layers the first time through the Conference Room and Needs Meeting Protocol. After switching the dominance of all the identified introjects in the conference room, be sure to follow the Step 11 instruction (page 95) to double check that all the reactive parts connected to the target issue, are at the table. In Step 11 you'll say to the client something like:

> I'm going to re-read the list of negative beliefs. Let me know if you feel we've identified all the reactive parts connected to these statements. If we've left anyone out, let me know, so we can bring them into the conference room now.

When you re-read a list of negative beliefs a client may sense more associated reactive parts to process. When this happens, invite the additional reactive parts into the conference room, then identify and switch the dominance of the additional associated introjects. This double-check increases the probability that all the associated introjects will be identified and handled in the Conference Room Protocol, so they can all be included in the needs meeting processing.

Incomplete Processing

Incomplete processing can lead to higher-than-expected follow-up ratings. It can occur when a client inaccurately reports on protocol progress, or fails to disclose evidence of processing blocks. It can also occur when a therapist skips a step, rushes over a step, or fails to successfully resolve a processing block. This is discussed in more detail in the section titled, *Incomplete Processing*, on page 190.

Conference Room Protocol Complications

Complications can occur with the Conference Room Protocol while getting ready to invite reactive parts into the conference room; when reactive parts enter the conference room; and when reactive parts look across the table to see the introjects they are reacting to. This section will prepare you to successfully handle these complications.

Erecting a Glass Wall (In Step 5)

In Step 5 of the Conference Room Protocol you'll check for uncomfortable or contracted body sensations that indicate a processing block or concern. The most common concern is the fear held by the reactive parts who expect to be threatened when introjects appear at the conference table.

If a body sensation is reported, determine if this is the concern, by asking something like:

> Would it help if we were to erect a protective glass wall or one-way mirror across the middle of the conference room, so the reactive parts would be protected from any introject that shows up at the table?

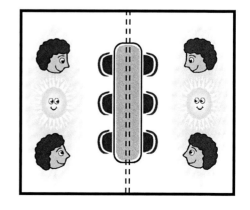

If the client likes the idea of a wall, say:

> Good, picture that. Also picture two sets of Resources – one on each side of the table.

Once the wall is in place, ask something like:

> Now when you think about beginning this conference room work, with the child parts connected with (the target issue), what do you notice in your body?

© Copyright 2009 by Shirley Jean Schmidt, MA, LPC. All rights reserved. Duplication in any form without permission is prohibited.

If erecting a wall does not calm the body, there is some other concern. Use the Overcoming Processing Blocks Flowchart to identify and handle concern. It may help to start with the question:

If the reactive parts connected to (the target issue) appeared in the conference room now, to identify the introjects they're reacting to, what would you lose or what bad thing might happen?

Once all concerns have been addressed, and the body feels comfortable, begin the protocol.

No Reactive Parts Enter the Conference Room (In Step 6)

In Step 6 of the Conference Room Protocol you'll invite into the room all the reactive parts connected to the target issue. Sometimes following the invitation, no reactive parts appear. One of these three problems listed below will usually account for this.

Reactive Parts are Present but Invisible

A client reports nothing appears because the reactive part(s) that have shown up are invisible. To check for invisible reactive parts ask:

Do you have a sense of reactive parts present in the room? Perhaps hidden or invisible?

If the answer is "yes," say to the invisible reactive parts:

Feel free to stay invisible as long as that helps you feel safe.

Then proceed with the protocol. Once all the associated introjects have been identified, and the dominance of each has been switched, the reactive part will become visible.

Reactive Parts are Fearful of Introjects

Sometimes reactive parts fail to appear because they expect to be threatened or harassed by the introjects that will appear across the table. To assess for this, ask something like:

Would these reactive parts feel comfortable coming forward if there were a glass wall across the table, protecting them from any introjects that appear?

If the answer is "yes," have the client picture the wall (as described above), then ask:

Now does it feel safe enough for the reactive parts to come forward?

If the answer is "yes," re-invite the reactive parts into the room. If the answer is "no," look for processing blocks.

There is a Processing Block

Sometimes an unexpressed concern may be blocking the process. Use the Overcoming Processing Blocks Flowchart to identify and handle such blocks. It may help to start with the question:

If the reactive parts connected to (the target issue) were to appear in the conference room now, what would you lose or what bad thing might happen?

Once all the concerns have been addressed, re-invite the reactive parts into the room.

Very Fearful Reactive Parts Appear (In Step 6)

Sometimes a client will appear visibly frightened as reactive parts enter the conference room. This is most likely to happen with highly dissociative clients who were severely traumatized in childhood. It happens when reactive parts are very fearful of encountering the introjects they'll be asked to identify. Here are three ways to help these child parts feel safer. Use one or all of these interventions.

Erect a Glass Wall

Ask the reactive parts about erecting a protective glass wall across the center of the room (as described on page 180 above). This can have a remarkably calming effect.

© Copyright 2009 by Shirley Jean Schmidt, MA, LPC. All rights reserved. Duplication in any form without permission is prohibited.

Resources Provide Protection

Direct the reactive parts to notice that the Resources are there to comfort and reassure them. Say something like:

> Hey little one(s), notice the Resources can sit right next to you. They are here to protect you. And notice, when you look across the table now, you'll see another set of Resources right next to the empty chair in front of you. So if anything shows up in that chair that might want to hurt you, the Resources on both sides of the table will protect you. How does that sound?

This will usually have an immediate calming effect.

Educate the Fearful Part

Explain to a fearful reactive part, basic information about the true nature of the introject mask that will be appearing across the table. A fearful reactive part can feel reassured when she learns that the mask is harmless, and the child part wearing it is precious and good. You could say something like:

> It sounds as if you're afraid that, if the part of self that you're reacting to appears across the table, it's going to hurt you. Is that right? I have some good news for you. That part of self is not a real threat, even though it might look and sound threatening. What you're afraid of is actually just a costume – a recording of a threatening person from your past. Watching a scary movie can make you feel fear, even though it doesn't put you in danger, right? A costume that appears across the table is about as dangerous as a scary movie – not dangerous at all. There is an innocent and wonderful child part wearing that costume. I want to work with her to help her see that she has power, and that the costume she's wearing has none. How does that sound?

This usually has an immediate calming effect.

Confident Parts Appear (In Step 6)

Sometimes, when wounded child parts are expected to appear in the conference room, confident and healthy parts appear instead. For example, after the therapist has invited forward the parts of self that believe, "I don't deserve to exist," "It's not safe to exist," and "My existence is completely irrelevant," a confident adult self appears. Several things can account for this. They are discussed below.

The Client May Be Confused

Clients who are doing this protocol for the first time are sometimes confused about the process. When this happens invite the client to talk about how long he has held these negative beliefs. As the client recalls they formed during wounding experiences in childhood, he's more likely to contact the associated reactive parts.

The Client May Be Highly Defended

Clients who are highly defended may not want wounded parts of self to appear. Use the Overcoming Processing Blocks Flowchart to identify and handle the concern about this. It may help to start with the question:

> If the wounded reactive parts connected to (the target issue) appeared in the conference room now, what would you lose or what bad thing might happen?

Once all the concerns have been addressed, re-invite the reactive parts into the room, and see if the client is now able to allow vulnerable child parts to sit at the table.

The "Confidence" May Be a Costume

Reactive parts will sometimes appear wearing costumes that conceal feelings like fear, insecurity, and anger. When such a reactive part enters the conference room, a client may describe the costume – unaware of the part of self wearing it. Some reactive part costumes exude confidence. For example, Ted was a timid, mild-mannered, 60-year-old accountant. He reported that one of the reactive parts that entered the conference room was a confident, cocky, tattooed, 30-year-old biker, wearing leather and chains. Because the client has never behaved or dressed this way, I asked if this biker persona is a costume. Ted confirmed that it was. He said at age 10, when he was a shy, insecure boy, he adopted the biker persona to create the illusion of confidence.

© Copyright 2009 by Shirley Jean Schmidt, MA, LPC. All rights reserved. Duplication in any form without permission is prohibited.

When the ten-year-old child part wearing a biker costume looked across the conference table, he saw his childhood bullies teasing him for being "girly."

No Part Appears Across the Table (In Step 8)

In Step 8 of the Conference Room Protocol you'll classify the part of self that appears across the table. Usually the part that appears is obviously an introject, but on rare occasions a client reports that nothing appears across the table. There are several reasons this might happen. Each is described below.

The "Nothing" Might Be an Introject Mask

Often when a reactive part sees nothing appear across the conference table, the "nothing" is an introject mask mirroring a caregiver who should have been physically or emotionally present, but wasn't. To verify this, ask something like:

> *Is there a little one wearing a "nothing" costume? OR Is the "nothing" conveying a message that reminds you of someone?*

A "yes" answer to either of these suggest the "nothing" may be an introject mask being worn by a child part.

The "Nothing" Might Indicate No Part is Appearing

Sometimes a child part reports seeing nothing across the table, because nothing has appeared. Several problems can account for this.

- ### *The Client May Be Confused*

   Clients who are doing this protocol for the first time sometimes get confused when looking for parts of self. If a client expresses confusion about seeing a part of self across the table, try changing the wording of the instruction from:

   > *In a moment you'll see appear in that spot, the <u>part of self</u> that you're reacting to...*

   To something like:

   > *In a moment you'll see appear in that spot, an <u>image of the person</u> you're reacting to....*

- ### *Reactive Parts are Fearful*

   Sometimes a reactive part is so fearful of what might appear across the table that nothing will appear. This is most likely to happen with highly dissociative clients who felt threatened in childhood. When you reassure and calm the reactive part he will be able to see a part of self appear across the table. The three solutions (listed above) for calming fearful reactive parts can solve this problem too. They include: (a) erecting a glass wall, (b) bringing in the Resources to reassure the child part, and (c) informing the child part that the introject that is about to appear is actually harmless.

- ### *Error in the Conference Room Set-Up*

   If the part of self looking across the table is not actually a wounded reactive part, she will not see anything appear. This might happen if a current problem being targeted is not related to irrational negative beliefs or unmet childhood needs. For example, Sally reported hearing credible rumors about layoffs at work. Her fear about losing her job was completely rational. The therapist *erroneously* invited into the conference room all the parts of self fearful of being laid off. One adult part showed up. When the adult part looked across the table, she saw nothing – because the threat was not internal, it was external. In contrast, Sally's co-worker Bob held irrational beliefs about losing his job. He disclosed a list of the associated negative beliefs like, "No one else would ever want to hire me," "I cannot tolerate rejection," and "If I lose my job that's proof that I have no value." When the therapist invited into the conference room the parts of self holding these beliefs, a fearful eight-year-old and a sad six-year-old appeared. When the fearful one looked across the table he saw a part of self mirroring a rejecting mom. This is the way this process is designed to work.

© Copyright 2009 by Shirley Jean Schmidt, MA, LPC. All rights reserved. Duplication in any form without permission is prohibited.

Needs Meeting Protocol Complications

Complications can occur at many points in the Needs Meeting Protocol, for example, while inviting child parts into the Healing Circle; while meeting needs, while processing painful emotions; while strengthening an emotional bond; and while reporting levels of remaining disturbance. This section will prepare you to successfully handle a variety of needs meeting complications.

Fear of Losing a Familiar Sense of Identity

A fear of losing a familiar sense of identity can block processing at any point in the protocol. For some clients, being a victim, being lonely, or being depressed is (comfortably) familiar, while being confident is not. The idea of changing drastically can be scary. This concern is often difficult for clients to articulate. It may not be revealed until you ask something like:

> Are you afraid of losing a familiar sense of identity?

When clients acknowledge this fear, reassure them by saying something like:

> That concern makes perfect sense. The good news is you'll never be without a sense of identity. While you maintain your old familiar negative identity, based on (feeling depressed), the Resources will help create a new one, based on self-esteem and self-confidence. Anything of value from your old sense of identity will be integrated into your new identity. Once your new identity is strong enough, everything about your old identity that no longer helps you will be naturally and automatically discarded. How does that sound?

This usually resolves the fear.

Unclear Replies Require Further Investigation

As you proceed through the protocol it is important to stay attuned to the child parts' communications. Sometimes a reply to a question like, "What else do you need?" will be unclear. You'll want to catch that, and elicit a clarification. The better you understand what the child parts say they need, the better equipped you'll be to provide the best possible response. Here are some examples of unclear replies.

- **Example 1:** To the question, "And what else do you need?" child parts say they need "patience." Taken at face value, this translates to "we need to be more patient." But often what child parts are thinking is, "we need patient caregivers." Ask for clarification. If they mean "we need patient caregivers," say "Can the Resources be patient with you now?" If they mean "we need to be more patient," ask, "What would you need caregivers to do for you, to help you develop more patience?" Their answer will tell you a need that the Resources can meet.

- **Example 2:** To the question, "Which of your parents' behaviors are most associated with that (rating of) 9?" the child parts say "They would never leave me alone." A first impulse might be to ask, "Can the Resources leave you alone now?" But this may not be a helpful response. You'd first want to know if this is the complaint of a teen part that was not given age-appropriate privacy; or of a five-year-old part that was smothered; or of a ten-year-old part that was constantly verbally abused. The appropriate response depends on this context. For example it might be: "Can the Resources grant you age-appropriate privacy?" "Can the Resources encourage you to develop age-appropriate autonomy?" "Can the Resources respect your boundaries?" or "Are the Resources good company now – comfortable to be around?"

- **Example 3:** To the question, "And what else do you need?" the child parts say they need "parents who don't play games." Before responding, find out what this metaphor means to the child parts. For example if "playing games" means "being deceptive," respond with, "Can the Resources be honest with you now?" If it means "being manipulative" respond with, "Can the Resources be *open and straight* with you now?"

© Copyright 2009 by Shirley Jean Schmidt, MA, LPC. All rights reserved. Duplication in any form without permission is prohibited.

- **Example 4:** To the question, "And what else do you need?" the child parts say they need "to be forgiven for being bad." Before you ask, "Can the Resources forgive you for being bad?" you'll want to ask about what "being bad" means to them. For example, they might believe that any behavior that was irritating to, inconvenient to, or punished by a parent was "bad," even those that were normal and age-appropriate. More than *forgiveness*, the child parts may need caregivers who understand normal child development, and who can manage stress well.

Aversive Reactions to the Processing

Sometimes child parts will have an aversive reaction to the processing itself. For example they might be confused by an outpouring of love and compassion from the Resources; or have an urge to hide when a specific need is being met; or be fearful about bonding with the Resources. When this happens, invite the child parts to notice that the Resources love and support them while they feel that aversion. Say something like:

> *It makes perfect sense that you'd (be confused by the Resources' unconditional love) now. Notice that the Resources completely understand why you're feeling that way. They're here to support you while you to hold on to your (confusion) as long as you need to. Meanwhile, the Resources are here to love you, care for you, and keep you safe. Just feel their empathy and support.*

Strengthen this with ABS. Usually within a few minutes the aversive reaction will diminish, and the child parts will be ready to resume the processing steps. If not, there may be blocks (caused by misunderstandings or introjects) to find and clear with the Overcoming Processing Blocks Flowchart.

Premature Empathy or Forgiveness for Wounding Role Models

The term *premature empathy* refers to a sudden preoccupation with compassion for the unresolved issues of a wounding role model, sufficient to block processing. The term *premature forgiveness* refers to a sudden preoccupation with forgiving wounding role models, sufficient to block processing. Such reactions will typically arise early in the processing, or in the middle of some painful processing. They are a problem because they can dull awareness of unmet needs and unprocessed emotions. For example, during anger processing the child parts abruptly said: "Now I understand that mother did the best she could, given that she was so wounded by her mother. I can forgive her now. I feel better. The anger level is now 0." If their empathy and forgiveness is premature, the anger level is not really 0. You'd need to intervene with something like:

> *So little ones, I'm so glad you're able to feel (empathy/forgiveness) for your (mother). It shows you have a greater level of maturity. But I'm concerned that if you focus too much on that right now it might prevent you from processing your (anger) all the way through. So I'd like to encourage you to set this empathy aside for a while, perhaps in a box on a shelf, where it can be retrieved later. When the needs meeting work is complete, you'll be able to experience this empathy and forgiveness completely and fully without any mixed feelings, confusion, or internal conflict at all. How does that sound?*

Once the child parts set premature empathy or forgiveness aside, they can engage in more authentic processing. For example, if they'd reported, before putting the empathy aside, that the anger level had dropped to 0, after putting the empathy aside, they'd rate it much higher than 0.

Wishful Thinking

Wishful thinking is a pain-avoidant strategy employed to shut down disturbing feelings. It can come up in Step 8 (emotion processing) and Step 12 (returning to wounding experiences) when child parts are asked to report the 0-10 disturbance levels associated with wounding role model behaviors. Normally, as each associated need gets met by the Resources, the wounding behaviors feel gradually less disturbing to recall. But sometimes mental pictures of wounding experiences are suddenly replaced by images of positive experiences that never happened.

© Copyright 2009 by Shirley Jean Schmidt, MA, LPC. All rights reserved. Duplication in any form without permission is prohibited.

For example, the child parts say, "Finally my mom and dad have stopped fighting. They're happy and smiling now. We're going out for ice cream. The disturbance is gone." To handle this, say something like:

> To get totally unstuck you'll have to picture your (parents) as they really were – both the good and the bad. When this is totally resolved you'll be able to recall their wounding behavior as something unfortunate from the past, but it will no longer evoke disturbing emotions. But to accomplish this, you must be totally honest with yourself about what happened.

This should resolve the problem, but if the child parts continue to resort to wishful thinking, or any other pain-avoidant strategies, look for and clear the associated processing blocks.

Child Parts are Fixated on the Past

Sometimes the child parts' present-tense wording suggests they may be *fixated on the past*, and do not know a trauma is long over. For example they may say: "Dad keeps coming in the bathroom while I'm showering," "Mother is threatening to send me to an orphanage," or "Uncle Joe comes over every day to molest me." Address this by heightening the child parts' awareness of being in an adult body now. (See instructions for the Adult Body Intervention on page 65.) This intervention can be applied at any time during the protocol, as necessary, to bring child parts into present time.

Child parts sometimes word needs in a way that suggests they believe the Resources can intervene now to change events that ended years ago. For example, to the question, "And what else do you need?" the child parts may say things like: "I need the Resources to stop Uncle Joe from molesting me," or "I need the Resources to get my mother to stop hitting me." Correct their misperception with the following explanation as you make the drawing below:

> When you were (ages 4-6) some terrible things happened, and you've been stuck there ever since. It's like you put on a backpack with rocks in it, and you've been wearing that backpack for years. The Resources cannot go back in time with you to change what happened then, but now that you're in an adult body they can meet needs for you now that were not met back then. When enough needs get met, you'll be able to put down the backpack, and move into the future without it – no longer stuck in the past. How does that sound?

This perspective is usually a great comfort to the wounded child parts. Strengthen that sense of comfort with ABS.

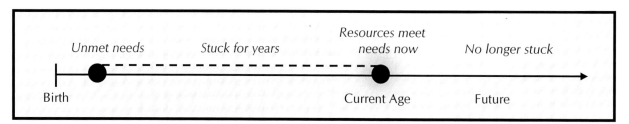

An Upset Adult Self Interrupts the Processing

Sometimes the painful emotions of an adult part of self arise and interrupt the needs meeting work. For example, an adult self may become overcome with grief for the child parts' wounds, may feel guilty about her failings as a mother, or may experience a surge of anger at a perpetrator. A client might say something like, "I'm so mad at my father. If he hadn't destroyed my self-esteem I'd have gone to college. I really wanted to be an architect." Or "Because my mother put up with so much abuse from my father, I've been afraid to get married. Now it's too late for me to have children." If you suspect an adult part is interrupting the needs meeting work, ask:

> Is this concern held by the child parts in the circle or by an adult part of self?

If the client affirms this is an adult part's reaction, say:

> I understand this is very upsetting to you. The Resources would like to help you with that at the perfect time. Would you be willing to step aside for now so we can continue working

© Copyright 2009 by Shirley Jean Schmidt, MA, LPC. All rights reserved. Duplication in any form without permission is prohibited.

with the little ones? Before we close the session, we can take a few minutes to let the Resources soothe your upset. How does that sound?

Upset adult parts are usually willing to step aside. Later, when you get to the end of the protocol, you'll ask the client if that upset adult part still needs to be comforted by the Resources. Most of the time clients feel so good, they decline an additional intervention. But if an intervention is requested, either in the middle or the end of the protocol, say to the overwhelmed adult part:

Picture your very own set of Resources – here just for you. When you're ready, move up close – get right in between them. Notice how safe it is here. Tell the Resources about your concern. Notice they completely understand why this is upsetting you.... Feel that love.... Feel their empathy and compassion.... Express yourself however you need to.... Notice their support.

If you apply this in the middle of the protocol, return to working with the wounded child parts as soon as the adult part feels sufficiently soothed.

Problem Making an Initial Connection with the Resources (In Step 1)

In Step 1 you'll invite the client to connect to the Resources. Sometimes child parts, fearful of beginning the protocol, will make it difficult for the connection to happen. A client might say something like, "I see the Resources, but I can't get close to them," or "I see them, but they look fuzzy, not clear like before."

If this problem is the expression of a processing block, delivering the following system-wide announcement should help:

If any part has a concern about the needs meeting work we're about to start, I'm very interested in hearing from you. In just a moment, I'll be inviting you to express your concerns, but I'd like to bring the Resources forward first. If you will allow the Resources to come forward and be strengthened, I promise we won't begin the protocol until all your concerns and fears have been addressed.

If the client still has difficulty connecting to the Resources, use the Overcoming Processing Blocks Flowchart to identify and handle the child parts' concern. It may help to start with the question:

If you could connect to the Resources now, is there something you'd lose or something bad that would happen?

If this is the client's first time with the Needs Meeting Protocol, it's possible the Resources are not robust enough for the task. When this is the case, you'll have to find out why, handle the concern, and then return to the Resource Development Protocol.

Needs Meeting Complication (In Step 7)

Sometimes in Step 7 child parts *express doubt* that the Resources can meet a specific need (e.g. protection). There are two ways to handle this. You can have the child parts ask the Resources directly whether they are able to meet the need, by saying something like:

Ask the Resources if they (can protect you) now. What do they say?

Or you can remind the child parts that the Resources are able to meet that need for a special loved one. If the doubt persists, the Resources may not be robust enough, or there may be a processing block to address.

Emotion-Processing Complications (In Step 8)

Step 8 is a series of steps for processing through painful emotions. Expect that there will almost always be some painful emotions to process – even if the child parts deny having unresolved anger or grief to process. If the usual steps for working through emotions are unsuccessful, or if the client refuses to process emotions, look for faulty beliefs complicating the process, such as the following:

© Copyright 2009 by Shirley Jean Schmidt, MA, LPC. All rights reserved. Duplication in any form without permission is prohibited.

- **Anger is a Bad Emotion:** Some clients believe there are good emotions and bad emotions – and that bad emotions, like anger, must be avoided. Explain that emotions are not good or bad, they are comfortable and uncomfortable, pleasant and unpleasant. When managed appropriately, every emotion can serve a valuable purpose – even anger. For example, in adulthood, appropriate anger about being mistreated at work may provide the needed motivation to get a new job in a supportive environment.

- **Only Bad People Express Anger:** Some clients associate all anger with mean people victimizing others. Explain that healthy people can express anger in healthy ways – with skill and respect for others. For example, a wife who is angry at her husband can express her upset in a normal tone of voice, using respectful language, like "I understand you're tired when you come home from work, and you just want to relax, but I really need your help cleaning up after dinner and getting the kids to bed. Will you help me come up with a plan for dividing the evening chores fairly?"

- **If I Express My Anger I'll be Disloyal:** Some clients grew up with parents who conveyed the message that any negative emotions a child expressed towards them or about them was a sign of being ungrateful or disloyal. These clients may have trouble acknowledging unexpressed and unresolved anger or grief from unmet childhood needs. It may be sufficient to explain that the expression of anger about wounding parental behaviors is natural and appropriate – whether or not the parents agree. It may also be necessary to find and switch the dominance of the parental introject conveying a disloyalty message.

Bonding Complications (In Step 9)

In Step 9 you'll strengthen an emotional bond between the child parts and the Resources. Several complications can arise during the bonding step.

Aversion to Bonding with the Resources

An aversion to bonding with the Resources is usually associated with childhood experiences of being engulfed or smothered by parents, or being drawn into intimate encounters that ended in betrayal. When this happens, say to the child parts something like:

> It makes perfect sense that you'd have an aversion to bonding with the Resources now, considering (how engulfing your mother was in childhood). Notice that the Resources completely understand why you're feeling this way now. They're here to support you. Hold on to your aversion as long as you need to. Meanwhile, they'll be here to love you, care for you, and keep you safe. Just feel their empathy and support.

A compassionate, understanding response from the Resources is the polar opposite response from the intrusive/betraying childhood role model. It sends the child parts a compelling non-verbal message about boundaries, safety, and respect. If this intervention is not enough, it may also help to engage the child parts in a conversation with the Resources about what bonding means. In some cases it may also be necessary to find and switch the dominance of introjects conveying messages about engulfment or betrayal.

Aversion to "Hurting the Resources"

Sometimes child parts express an aversion to the Step 9 statement "…when you hurt, the Resources hurt." This aversion is often associated with childhood experiences of being shamed or punished by parents for "making them hurt." Any one or all of the following four interventions should help resolve this aversion:

- Have the child parts ask the Resources if they are okay with hurting when they hurt. When the Resources say something like "yes, the hurting is part of the valued bond," the aversion may soften.

- Ask the child parts if they would feel distressed seeing their favorite kitten or puppy hurt, and if so, would that be okay? The child parts may then see it is a normal appropriate reaction.

- Help the child parts understand that the hurt experienced in *empathy* for a loved one is a good hurt.

- Tell the child parts that parents who cannot manage emotions well are more likely to shame or punish a child for "making them hurt." In contrast, the Resources can manage emotions quite well.

© Copyright 2009 by Shirley Jean Schmidt, MA, LPC. All rights reserved. Duplication in any form without permission is prohibited.

End of Protocol Complications (In Step 16)

In Step 16 you'll check on the four criteria that signal the healing is complete. They include: (1) child parts reporting feeling totally unstuck; (2) child parts appearing happy and confident – engaged in age-appropriate play or exploration; (3) costumes that are completely gone; and (4) a body that feels completely clear of disturbing emotions. Usually these criteria are met by this point in the protocol, but sometimes they are not. Directions for handling some of the Step 16 problems are discussed here. A few more are discussed in the *Incomplete Processing* section on page 190.

Not Quite Totally Unstuck and/or A Just Little Body Disturbance Present

Sometimes the child parts will report feeling *mostly unstuck,* or the client will report a little body disturbance remains. At first glance it looks like a case of incomplete processing, and in fact it might be. But it's also possible that a part of self from outside the circle is imposing itself on the process, or that a child part inside the circle just has a misunderstanding that needs to be cleared. Begin by asking something like:

> *Is this (little body disturbance) connected to one or more of the child parts inside the circle, or to a part of self outside the circle?*

The intervention you'll want to use will depend on the answer to this question.

- **Complication Coming from Outside the Circle:** If the answer to this question reveals a part of self outside the circle is creating a disturbance, invite that part forward and ask about its concerns. Then, apply the appropriate intervention from the Overcoming Processing Blocks Flowchart. Once this extra part's concern has been addressed, the child parts inside the circle should feel totally unstuck, and/or the client should notice the little bit of disturbance is gone.

- **Complication Coming from Inside the Circle:** If the answer to the above question reveals that one or more parts of self inside the circle are creating a disturbance, invite them to talk about their concerns. They may reveal misunderstandings about becoming totally unstuck. For example, child parts might believe that becoming unstuck means losing a familiar sense of identity, or dismantling needed protective boundaries. Clear up any misunderstandings revealed here. Once the concern has been addressed, the child parts should feel totally unstuck, and/or the client should notice the little bit of disturbance is gone.

Child Parts Cling to the Resources

Clinical experience has led me to conclude that when child parts are totally unstuck and well bonded with competent Resources they'll naturally want to engage in age-appropriate play and exploration. In Step 16 you'll invite the client to describe how the child parts appear. If they are not clearly playing or exploring, you'll set up a scenario to test them. You'll ask:

> *If we were to take the child parts out to a playground, which would they prefer to do, play on the swings and jungle-gym, or sit at the picnic table with the Resources?*

It may be age-appropriate for very young or adult-age parts to hang out with the Resources, but other child parts should want to go play. If they'd rather cling to the Resources instead, find out why. Here are two possible explanations:

- **Misunderstandings about the Resources:** The child parts may have misunderstandings about the Resources. To find out, ask them:

> *If you were to let go of the Resources and go play, is there something you'd lose or something bad that would happen?*

Their answer may reveal parental behaviors projected on the Resources. For example, they might say, "If we go play we can't care for the Resources," "If we go play they will judge us harshly," or "If we go play they will leave and never return." Clear up any misunderstandings revealed here.

- **Resource Substitution:** The client may have privately replaced real, robust Adult Resources that looked like self, with fantasy ones that look like someone else – real or fictional. This can happen when a client believes imaginary Resources can provide better care to child parts than their most nurturing and protective

© Copyright 2009 by Shirley Jean Schmidt, MA, LPC. All rights reserved. Duplication in any form without permission is prohibited.

adult self. If you suspect this has happened, follow the Overcoming Processing Blocks Flowchart to find and clear the associated blocks. It may help to start with the question:

> *If you were to comfortably picture your Nurturing Adult Self as who you are caring for your cherished loved one, what would you lose or what bad thing might happen?*

If the entire Needs Meeting Protocol was completed with substitute Resources, you may need to go back over some of the protocol steps, once you have real, robust Adult Resources back in place.

A Bit of Mask or Costume Remains

If the child parts are totally unstuck, there will not be a shred or molecule of a mask or costume left. If there is something left, ask:

> *If the mask or costume were to completely vanish, is there something you'd lose or something bad that would happen?*

The answer to this may reveal misunderstanding that can easily be cleared. After clearing the block, the mask or costume should be gone. Sometimes just making the client aware that a mask or costume is still present helps it disappear. If not, there may be more needs to meet.

Incomplete Processing

In Step 16 you'll check on the four signs that the child parts' healing is complete. In Step 20 you'll check for signs that the client has benefited from work. If the processing was incomplete, in Step 16 the child parts may still feel a little stuck, some shreds of masks may remain, the child parts might not feel completely comfortable going off to play, and the body might feel a little bit of disturbance; and in Step 20, one or more associated introject messages may still be disturbing; one or more associated reactive parts may still feel stuck; an associated negative belief (e.g. from the Attachment Needs Ladder) may still feel true; or a targeted problem may not feel notably better. This section discusses several ways that incomplete needs meeting processing can account for these atypical outcomes.

Processing was Inauthentic

In order to be effective, the processing must be real and authentic. To check for inauthentic processing, ask something like:

> *Has the processing we've been doing felt real or contrived? Were you answering the questions easily and honestly, or were you struggling to 'figure out the right answers'?*

If the client admits the answers were contrived, look for the source of the problem. Here are three possibilities.

- **The client was confused:** If the client was confused by the protocol, unsure how to react to the questions, find and clarify each confusion.

- **The Resources were not robust:** If the Resources were not robust enough to meet the needs of the child parts, return to the Resource Development Protocol. Clear blocks and misunderstandings, so robust Resources can be mobilized.

- **There were unexpressed processing blocks:** If you suspect misunderstandings or introjects were driving the inauthentic processing, follow the Overcoming Processing Blocks Flowchart to find and clear the associated blocks. It may help to start with the question:

> *If you were to experience real and authentic protocol processing, is there something you'd lose or something bad that would happen?*

Once the source of the problem has been identified and resolved, repeat the Needs Meeting Protocol.

Painful Emotions Were Not Fully Processed

The Step 16 and 20 goals will not be met if painful emotions are not processed all the way through.

- **Step 16 Check:** To check for unprocessed emotions in Step 16, ask the child parts:

> *Do you have any anger or grief that did not get processed all the way through?*

© Copyright 2009 by Shirley Jean Schmidt, MA, LPC. All rights reserved. Duplication in any form without permission is prohibited.

If the child parts answer "yes," follow the Step 8 instructions to process through the unresolved emotions. If this was the only problem, then the four Step 16 criteria should be met as soon as all the emotions have processed through.

- **Step 20 Check:** To check for unprocessed emotions in Step 20, ask the client:

    Is it possible we did not process through all the anger and grief?

    If the client answers "yes," invite the child parts back into the Healing Circle, then follow the Step 8 instructions to process through the unresolved emotions. Once complete, tuck them back in. If this was the only problem, then the client's answers to the Step 20 outcome questions should indicate the processing is complete.

Client Inaccurately Reported Protocol Progress

Sometimes you will not get completely accurate and honest reports about protocol progress. For example, child parts might *report* feeling *totally unstuck* when they really feel *mostly unstuck*; child parts might report painful emotions were fully resolved when they were not; a client might report the body feels clear and calm, when it does not, or a client might say the child parts appear happy and confident, when they really appear somber, serious, or sad.

A reluctance to give accurate and honest answers throughout the protocol indicates a serious problem. If you suspect this has happened, follow the Overcoming Processing Blocks Flowchart to find and clear the associated blocks. It may help to start with the question:

If you were to accurately disclose everything occurring throughout the protocol, is there something you'd lose or something bad that would happen?

Once the client feels free to be honest and accurate, repeat the protocol.

Client Failed to Disclose a Processing Block

A client may fail to disclose evidence of a processing block, such as the sudden arrival of a headache, sleepiness, or distracting thoughts. This failure can occur when a client is unaware of the evidence of the block, or when a client deliberately chooses to keep such evidence secret. Some clients believe that if they ignore a block it will go away – but usually it just renders the processing useless. If, in Step 16 or 20, you suspect a client may have failed to disclose evidence of a processing block, ask:

Did any strange or uncomfortable sensations suddenly arise during this processing? For example, did you experience a headache, sleepiness, confusion, tension, or nausea that you didn't mention?

If the client reveals a block did come up, find out what it was about, and why it was not disclosed. Reiterate the importance of disclosing blocks as soon as they arise. After you clear the block, you may need to repeat each protocol step that was influenced by the block.

Rushing Through or Skipping Steps

Some therapists will rush through or skip a step when the significance of the step is not well understood, or when a client compels them to rush. For example:

- **Example 1:** When the child parts report in Step 11, that they are totally unstuck, a naive therapist might choose to skip Steps 12-15, assuming that the processing is complete.

- **Example 2:** Clients who are uncomfortable with the emotion processing step (Step 8) may insist there is little or nothing to process, when there actually is. A therapist who takes them at their word, without some investigation, is likely to skip the needed emotion processing.

- **Example 3:** In Step 15, child parts are asked to report what they notice when they shift attention back and forth between their wounding experiences of the past and the Resources' care now. Sometimes their reaction to the past is not well articulated. A reaction like: "I can shut the door on the past now," could mean "It's completely resolved" or "I can shut out the little disturbance remaining." A therapist who fails to notice and investigate such ambiguous wording may end this step prematurely.

© Copyright 2009 by Shirley Jean Schmidt, MA, LPC. All rights reserved. Duplication in any form without permission is prohibited.

Failure to Completely Clear a Processing Block

A block may not get completely addressed or cleared if you fail to verify a block has been cleared; if you fail to follow-up on subtle cues which suggest a block has not been fully cleared; or if a client discounts the symptoms of the block and convinces you to do likewise. Here are examples of how this can happen.

- *Example 1:* In Step 8 a client reported a sudden headache. When the therapist learned the headache was connected to the belief "only mean people express anger," she explained that, by processing emotions by meeting needs, the child parts would not need to express their anger. When the client was glad to hear this, the therapist assumed the block was completely clear and continued with Step 8. But because she didn't also ask about the status of the headache, she couldn't really know whether the block had been fully cleared. There was a possibility that she was continuing the processing over an unresolved block.

- *Example 2:* In Step 9 the therapist told the child parts that a bond means "...when you hurt the Resources hurt." The child parts expressed a fear that the Resources (like the parents) could not tolerate feeling hurt. The therapist assured them that the Resources could feel appropriate empathy for them, then asked, "What's it like to hear that?" The child parts answer with a cautious "okay." The therapist assumed that "okay" meant the issue was settled, and proceeded with the protocol. However, if she had also asked, "Why did you say, 'okay' instead of 'great,' she might have learned that the child parts had never heard of "appropriate empathy" and did not know what that meant.

- *Example 3:* In the middle of Step 7 the client suddenly appeared sleepy. The therapist asked, "If the sleepiness could talk, what would it say?" The client said she often feels sleepy right after lunch and insisted they proceed with the protocol. The therapist agreed. If the sleepiness was connected to a block that the client was avoiding, the subsequent processing would be incomplete.

Chapter Summary

This chapter provided a comprehensive layout of the many complications that can arise in each of the DNMS protocols. It provided general guidance for handling blocks due to the misunderstandings and maladaptive introjects that can intrude across the board – in any protocol. It provided suggestions for how to troubleshoot complications with the Resources – including how to determine which complications are due to problem Resources, and which are due to child part's misperceptions of problem Resources. Specific instructions were provided for dealing with problems unique to the Resource Development Protocol, the Switching the Dominance Protocol, the Attachment Needs Ladder questionnaire, the Conference Room Protocol, and the Needs Meeting Protocol.

Chapter Notes and References

[1] Intervention idea submitted by Joan Bacon in 2008.
[2] Intervention idea submitted by Richard Holcomb in 2006.
[3] Intervention idea submitted by Richard Holcomb in 2006.

© Copyright 2009 by Shirley Jean Schmidt, MA, LPC. All rights reserved. Duplication in any form without permission is prohibited.

Epilogue

After the DNMS

Clients can experience a remarkable transformation as their developmental needs are met and their internal conflicts fade away. As the healing unfolds they are able to see reality more clearly. This enables clients to better evaluate and handle current stressors. For example, some clients discover that clearing away parents' internalized wounding messages gives them hope for healing a troubled marriage. Others discover the power of setting boundaries and end abusive relationships. Some discover they can finally repair breaks with estranged family members. Some become more successful at work, or find the courage to attend college. Some begin to care for their bodies with nourishing food and exercise. Those who are raising children find they are better able to competently parent them. (See the Introduction, page vii, for several success stories.)

While not all problems come from unmet developmental needs, healing developmental wounds and quieting internal conflicts can reveal other sources of a problem. For example, a client who was sexually abused by a mentor for years as a young adult began therapy to treat a resistance to intimacy with her husband. After the DNMS resolved the sexual trauma wounds, she could clearly see a portion of the resistance was a reaction to his unfriendly behavior. Before the DNMS she assumed all the resistance was related to the sexual abuse. Another client began therapy to treat chronic depression. The processing healed many introjects associated with a childhood replete with parental abuse and rejection. Upon terminating therapy the painful memories were no longer disturbing. When she found herself depressed again, she was diagnosed with hypoglycemia. As long as her depression seemed solely related to her history, she could not see the portion of it that had a medical cause.

After You Finish this Book

Reading this book and practicing the DNMS with the help of worksheets from Appendix E, is the logical and necessary starting point for learning the DNMS. A few more options can help you master the DNMS.

- **E-Mail Community**

  Although the book is written to include just about everything you'd need to know to get started with the model, sometimes unexpected things will arise in practice that are not covered in the book. The DNMS listserv is an e-mail community where DNMS professionals can post questions, share insights, and get help from experienced clinicians. The list is carefully moderated, so it only contains posts relevant to all list members. I personally answer most questions posted to the list. The list is free, but only open to licensed psychotherapists who have purchased the book. To enroll, go to **www.dnmsinstitute.com/list.html**.

- **Study Groups**

  Participating in a local DNMS study group is a great way to hone your DNMS skills. To find out about study groups in your area, or to start a group, post a study group query on the DNMS listserv.

- **DNMS Home Study Course**

  The Home Study Course is a convenient, comfortable and economical alternative to attending a two or three-day workshop. It consists of seven modules. Each provides a narrated slide show and an illustrated study guide. Each slide show explains key concepts with animated illustrations. Review questions are provided throughout the slide shows, so you can check your comprehension of the material. Modules 3-7 demonstrate the key protocols with recordings of real sessions. Each study guide provides an illustrated outline of all the material covered in the slide shows. The Module 2-7 study guides include long lists of study questions and answers. For more information about the Course, go to page 256 of this book, or go to **www.dnmsinstitute.com/dnmscourse.html**.

© Copyright 2009 by Shirley Jean Schmidt, MA, LPC. All rights reserved. Duplication in any form without permission is prohibited.

- ### *Use the DNMS Handouts, Forms, and Worksheets*

  Appendices D & E provide client handouts, protocol worksheets, and protocol forms. The handouts in Appendix D can be used to inform clients about the model. The Protocol forms and worksheets in Appendix E can make it easier for you to learn and execute the protocols. You can also download these materials at **www.dnmsinstitute.com/doc/dnmstherapistworksheets.pdf**. This pdf file provides a convenient means for printing the documents. (You can print as many copies as you need for your personal practice, but you may not distribute copies to others.)

- ### *Live Workshops and Telecourses*

  A variety of workshops will be offered, including basic workshops to introduce the model and advanced workshops and telecourses for therapists who are using the model. Workshops can also be provided "on request," for example, if a group of practitioners in an area would like to have a presentation focused on a particular topic. For more information about scheduled workshops, go to **www.dnmsinstitute.com**.

- ### *DNMS Certification*

  A therapist certified in the DNMS has completed the Home Study Course and demonstrated skill and competence with the model. A certification candidate will submit taped DNMS sessions to a skilled DNMS clinician for review and subsequent consultation. For more information about becoming a Certified DNMS therapist, go to **www.dnmsinstitute.com/dnmscertification.html**.

- ### *Professional Consultation*

  One-on-one and group case consultation is available from myself and Certified DNMS therapists. Consultation can be in person, on the phone, or via internet video conferencing. For more information about getting consultation, go to **www.dnmsinstitute.com/consultation.html**.

- ### *Be a DNMS Client*

  Being on the receiving end of the DNMS can teach you a lot about the process. To find a DNMS therapist, go to **www.dnmsinstitute.com/findatherapist.html**. I personally work with a lot of out-of-town therapists, in weekend intensives, and via internet video conferencing.

- ### *Research*

  As of the writing of this book, two DNMS case-study articles have been published in peer-reviewed journals. (See the abstracts on page 195.) While they both support the assertion that the DNMS is effective, they do not meet the criteria for empirical research. Until that research has been completed, the DNMS cannot be called an *evidence-based therapy*. The DNMS Institute encourages clinical research facilities and graduate students to conduct such rigorous research. We also encourage private practice clinicians to write up case study reports for publication. The more the DNMS appears in the literature, the more clinicians and public will come to know its value in healing trauma and attachment wounds.

Best of luck to you as you learn and master the DNMS. I welcome your e-mail contact at **sjs@dnmsinstitute.com**.

© Copyright 2009 by Shirley Jean Schmidt, MA, LPC. All rights reserved. Duplication in any form without permission is prohibited.

Appendix A:
Glossary

Alternating bilateral stimulation (ABS): Side-to-side eye movements, alternating bilateral auditory, or alternating bilateral tactile stimulation. Used to enhance processing and strengthen positive DNMS experiences.

Attachment Needs Ladder: A questionnaire that helps clients articulate negative attachment beliefs.

Attachment wounds: The emotional wounds sustained in childhood with caregivers' day-to-day failures to meet attachment needs by being chronically disrespectful, rejecting, neglectful, enmeshing, or unsupportive.

Blank slate: Mirror neurons that are ready to mirror and mimic someone. Embodies a person's true nature – to be in respectful harmony with self and others.

Block: A fear or concern that interrupts processing. Usually due to a misunderstanding or blocking introject.

Checking in: Asking the client and child parts to report on progress made towards the goal of getting unstuck, during the course of the Needs Meeting Protocol.

Conference Room Map: A document that keeps track of the reactive parts, introjects, and wounding messages that are identified during the Conference Room Protocol.

Conference Room Protocol: A protocol that facilitates a group reactive parts, connected to a common theme, to identify, one at a time, the maladaptive introjects they are reacting to. The dominance of each introject is switched. Introjects from the conference room are selected for the Needs Meeting Protocol.

Counting up: A technique used at the end of the Needs Meeting Protocol to help a client awaken from a light trance.

Developmental needs: The specific needs that primary caregivers must meet in order to maximize the expression of a child's physical, intellectual, behavioral, emotional, and social potential.

Developmental stages: For DNMS purposes, a developmental stage is defined as a span of time relevant to a baby's, child's, or adolescent's physical, intellectual, social, and emotional maturation.

Double bind: A lose-lose proposition. Given two choices, whatever decision is made will have an unpleasant outcome.

Ego state: An engrained state of mind with a point of view; a part of self.

Ego state therapy: A type of psychotherapy based on the premise that different personality parts or ego states can have different views of reality. The aim is to help individual ego states heal and increase healthy communication and cooperation between ego states.

Embodied simulation: Refers to the way mirror neurons can automatically and unconsciously create an internalized representation of someone – not the result of a willed or conscious cognitive effort. Embodied simulation influences the way we model others. (As opposed to *standard simulation*.)

Emotional overreaction: Any emotional response considered excessive for the triggering event.

Engrained: A state of mind that is experienced repeatedly, or experienced during a single traumatic event, can become engrained in a single neural network, or ego state, which can be reactivated at a later time.

Enmeshment Reversal: An intervention for handling a Switching the Dominance Protocol complication based on the idea that a client who was enmeshed with a childhood caregiver might have a child part that is enmeshed with an introject mask. The intervention helps a child part see she was actually a separate person from the caregiver.

Healing Circle: A loving, nurturing, protective container for healing wounded child parts. It consists of the three internal Resources (a Spiritual Core Self, Nurturing Adult Self, and Protective Adult Self) working as a team. The Healing Circle is the cornerstone of the DNMS. Child parts get unstuck from the past as needs get met by the Resources in the Healing Circle.

Integration: In the DNMS, it is process of connecting child parts that are stuck in the past (isolated neural network) with a client's Resources (adaptive neural network). This leads to communication and cooperation between ego states.

Introject: A part of self that has unconsciously internalized a significant role model's behaviors, ideas, values, or points of view as the result of the firing of mirror neurons. See *embodied simulation*.

    Adaptive introject: A part of self that mimics a respectful, healthy, adaptive role model.

    Maladaptive introject: A part of self that mimics a wounding role model. It is comprised of two parts: (1) a mask or costume that mirrors a wounding role model, and (2) a silent, numb, innocent, virtually invisible part of self wearing the mask or costume.

© Copyright 2009 by Shirley Jean Schmidt, MA, LPC. All rights reserved. Duplication in any form without permission is prohibited.

Mask/costume: A mental representation of a wounding role model that integrates superficially, because the behavior of the role model it does not match the person's good true nature (to be in respectful harmony with self and others). It's like a child who is reluctantly wearing a (metaphorical) mask/costume that mimics a role model's wounding behaviors and words.

Mirror neurons: Neurons that fire while observing someone else. The firing of mirror neurons appears to influence the learning of new behaviors and the embodied simulation of people who are observed.

Needs Meeting Protocol: A protocol that facilitates communications between wounded child parts (usually maladaptive introjects) and the Resources. As the Resources meet their developmental needs, process strong emotions, and make an emotional bond, the child parts get totally unstuck from the past and fully integrated with the clients' most adult self ego states.

Negative belief: An irrational, untrue, or over-generalized belief about self, relationships, or the world.

Neural network: A network of individual neurons with recorded information, such as that held in a *state of mind*. Under certain conditions a state of mind can become engrained in a complex neural network – an ego state or part of self.

Neural pathway: A structure of the brain; a channel for the flow of information between neural networks.

Nurturing Adult Self (NAS): An internal nurturing Resource; a part of self that can competently nurture a loved one.

Pendulating: A technique for moving back and forth between disturbing memories and the comfort of the Resources to ensure processing gets completed. (Steps 12-15 of the Needs Meeting Protocol.)

Protective Adult Self (PAS): An internal protective Resource; a part of self that can competently protect a loved one.

Reactive part: A wounded part of self that formed in reaction to a trauma, or to the wounding behavior of another.

Resources: Three healthy parts of self – a Nurturing Adult Self, a Protective Adult Self, and a Spiritual Core Self, which together form a Healing Circle.

Resource Development Protocol: Special DNMS meditations used to connect clients to their Nurturing Adult Self, Protective Adult Self, and Spiritual Core Self.

Role model: A person who has significantly influenced a client's life – for better or worse. Childhood role models may include parents, grandparents, siblings, neighbors, teachers and ministers. Adulthood role models may include people like spouses, supervisors, and friends. The significant influence may include positive actions, such as loving support, protection, and guidance; or negative actions, such as abuse, neglect, betrayal and assault.

Self-regulation: A person's ability to modulate their emotional states; the ability to self-soothe.

Self-system: Refers to a person's ego states and the relationships between them.

Sensorimotor activity: A physical activity that a client engages in, while processing through painful emotions.

Spiritual Core Self (SCS): An internal Resource that is a client's essence or core of goodness; soul.

Standard simulation: Refers to the way we can explicitly simulate (or mimic) another's internal state, by consciously and deliberately taking on their perspective. Involves introspection. (As opposed to *embodied simulation*.)

State of mind: The emotions, body sensations, beliefs, and behaviors evoked by the environment at a given moment in time. Under certain conditions a state of mind can become engrained in a complex neural network called an ego state.

Stuck: Behaviors, beliefs, or emotions connected to unresolved wounds from the past can get triggered today.

Switching the Dominance Protocol: A protocol for helping maladaptive introjects heal. It switches the dominance from the mask to the child beneath the mask. As a result, the mask and its wounding message becoming unimportant.

System-wide announcement: Messages a therapist directs to the entire self-system to educate, calm, or reassure child parts.

TASPER: Acronym for *Therapist's Aid for Sensorimotor Processing for Emotional Release*, a devise for helping the client engage in sensorimotor activity. Consists of two solid soft-grip 14" bars connected at the ends by two ropes. Clients can pull on the top bar with their hands while pushing on the bottom bar with their feet. This engages both arm and leg muscles.

TheraTapper: A device for delivering tactile alternating bilateral stimulation. Consists of a small control box attached by six-foot wires to two handheld pulsers with small, enclosed motors which vibrate in an alternating fashion.

Trauma: A single, highly disturbing event that produces acute distress.

Trauma wound: The unresolved emotional pain associated with a trauma (from childhood or adulthood).

True nature: Desire to be in respectful harmony with self and others.

Tucking in: A process for putting a child part into a non-active state.

Unstuck: The resolving of painful, negative experiences, such as trauma, abuse, neglect, or unmet needs that occurs during the DNMS as the Resources help wounded parts of self heal.

© Copyright 2009 by Shirley Jean Schmidt, MA, LPC. All rights reserved. Duplication in any form without permission is prohibited.

Appendix B:

Additional Background Material

Section 1: DNMS Journal Article Abstracts

Both articles are available on-line at www.dnmsinstitute.com.

Developmental Needs Meeting Strategy: A New Treatment Approach Applied to Dissociative Identity Disorder

Shirley Jean Schmidt, MA, LPC
Private practice

Published in the *Journal of Trauma & Dissociation*
December 2004, Volume 5, Issue 4, pages 55-78.
The *Journal of Trauma & Dissociation* is published by Haworth Press, Inc.
10 Alice St., Binghamton, NY 13904 www.HaworthPress.com

This article describes the use of the Developmental Needs Meeting Strategy (DNMS) for the treatment of dissociative identity disorder (DID). The DNMS is an ego state therapy which guides a client's own internal resources to meet developmental needs that were not met in childhood. After 17 months of DNMS treatment a client with DID reported a near total elimination in frequency and severity of symptoms of depression, anxiety and suicidal thoughts, her Trauma Symptom Inventory scores indicated no trauma-related symptoms, and her Multidimensional Inventory of Dissociation scores indicated she no longer met the diagnostic criteria for DID. She was functioning well without any medication. Further research concerning this treatment strategy is warranted.

The Developmental Needs Meeting Strategy: Eight Case Studies

Shirley Jean Schmidt, MA, LPC, Private Practice and
Arthur Hernandez, PhD, University of Texas at San Antonio

Published in the March 2007 issue of *Traumatology*, Volume 13, Issue 1, pages 27-48
Traumatology is an on-line journal published by Sage Publications
2455 Teller Road, Thousand Oaks, CA 91320 http://www.sagepub.com/

This study investigates the merits of the Developmental Needs Meeting Strategy (DNMS), a relatively new ego state therapy. The DNMS is based on the assumption that many presenting problems are due to wounded ego states stuck in childhood because of unmet developmental needs. DNMS protocols endeavor to identify and heal the wounded child parts most responsible for a presenting problem. When internal Resource ego states, which serve as competent caregivers, meet the wounded ego states' developmental needs, the wounded ego states become unstuck and heal. Eight participants were recruited from the private practice caseloads of 3 DNMS therapists. All participants reported significant improvement in the targeted problems, with gains maintained at follow-up. These findings suggest that the DNMS has therapeutic potential.

© Copyright 2009 by Shirley Jean Schmidt, MA, LPC. All rights reserved. Duplication in any form without permission is prohibited.

Section 2: Maslow Pyramid & Maslow/Erikson Chart

Maslow's Hierarchy of Needs[1]

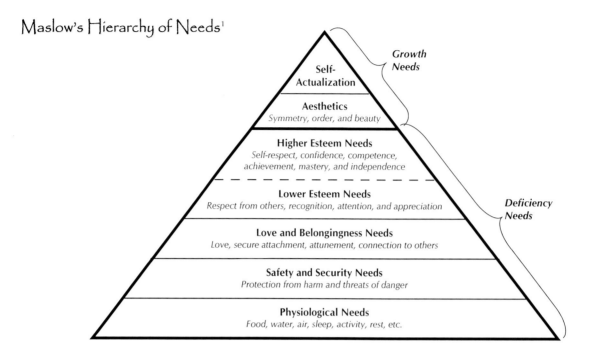

Integration of Erikson's[2] Developmental Stages with Maslow's Needs

Erikson's First 5 Developmental Stages	Key Features	Maslow's Needs *A developmental perspective*	Virtues Achieved When Needs are Met
Stage 1: **Trust vs Mistrust** Infant, Ages 0-1	Baby ready to trust that mom will feed, protect comfort & bond	Physiological needs Safety needs Belongingness needs	Trust, hope, faith, an ability to mistrust
Stage 2: **Autonomy vs Shame & Self Doubt** Toddler, Ages 2-3	Child ready to develop a sense of self control, safe differentiation, and independence	Physiological needs Safety needs Belongingness needs Lower Esteem needs	Determination, willpower, sense of self control & of being separate from mom
Stage 3: **Initiative vs Guilt** Preschool, Ages 3-6	Child ready to take initiative, make things, and compete.	Physiological needs Safety needs Belongingness needs Lower Esteem needs	Purpose, initiative, courage, capacity for action while knowing limits
Stage 4: **Industry vs Inferiority** School-age, Ages 7-12 or so	Child ready to learn, master new things, & develop competencies	Physiological needs Safety needs Belongingness needs Lower Esteem needs Higher Esteem needs	Sense of industry, mastery and competence
Stage 5: **Ego-identity vs Role-confusion** Adolescent, Ages 12-18 or so	Adolescent ready to find a sense of identity & begin making educational & occupational decisions	Physiological needs Safety needs Belongingness needs Lower/Higher Esteem needs Aesthetic needs	Identity, fidelity, loyalty, willing to accept and contribute to society despite its imperfections

1.   Maslow, A.H. (1968). *Toward a Psychology of Being*. D. Van Nostrand Company
2.   Erikson, E.H. (1950). *Childhood and Society*. New York: Norton.

© Copyright 2009 by Shirley Jean Schmidt, MA, LPC. All rights reserved. Duplication in any form without permission is prohibited.

Section 3: Background Material on Attachment

Attachment Theory

The DNMS is designed to heal attachment wounds. This section provides an overview of some attachment theory basics and the neurobiology of attachment. It is intended to give DNMS therapists a fuller appreciation of what the DNMS endeavors to accomplish in healing clients with who suffer with attachment wounds.

The Attachment System

According to John Bowlby,[1] an inborn *attachment system* has emerged in humans over the course of evolution. This system provides the instinctive motivation for a child to *seek proximity* to a caregiver who will provide a safe, *secure base* from which to learn and grow. A child naturally anticipates that a caregiver will provide a *safe haven* and a source of comfort in times of distress. This attachment system increases the likelihood that young children, who cannot care for themselves, will survive and eventually reproduce.

The attachment system motivates a child to bid for a caregiver's attention, reassurance, comfort, and protection with *attachment behaviors*. For example, a baby may cry, reach out, or cling to her mother; a toddler may follow mother or climb on her lap; a five-year-old may make contact with mother by catching her eye or calling out for a vocal response. These behaviors are designed to elicit a caregiver response that reassures the child she is loved and safe. An appropriate caregiver answer to such bids might include holding, rocking, or stroking the child; or making vocal or eye contact. The child will return to sleep, play, or exploration once she feels sufficiently reassured.[2] This helps the child develop an enduring emotional bond with the caregiver.[3]

Attunement

According to Allan Schore,[4] caregiver *attunement* conveys to an infant that she is loved, seen, heard, and understood. It occurs during intense moments of non-verbal communication between an infant and caregiver when their states of mind are aligned (e.g. gazing, smiling, and laughing together). They communicate their affect to each other, via facial expression, vocalizations, body gestures, and eye contact. An attuned caregiver will sense what the infant wants and needs from behavioral cues – whether obvious (crying, clinging, reaching) or subtle (looking away, becoming numb), and will respond appropriately to those cues. This includes engaging when the infant wants connection, and disengaging when the infant wants distance. During affect attunement the infant and caregiver communicate their internal emotional states externally. For example, they smile and laugh at each other. *Alignment*, a component of attunement, occurs when one person alters her state of mind to approximate the state of mind of the other. This can be a one-way or two-way process. For example, a mother preparing an excited child for bed calms the child down more easily if she first aligns with the child's excited state, then brings the child down to a calmer state.[5]

Mental Models

Mental models are summations or generalized representations of repeated experiences.[6] They guide a person to unconsciously interpret present experiences and anticipate future ones. The mental models a child creates over the first two years of life are significant, because they form the basis for assumptions about self, relationships, and the world that can last a lifetime. A baby who is skillfully cared for and comforted by loving, attuned caregivers will learn to expect care and comfort in the future. As the baby gets what she expects, over time the mental model of a predictable world with safety and connection is strengthened.[7]

Within an intimate, attuned, interpersonal relationship, a young *child's immature brain uses the mature functions of a caretaker's brain to organize its own processes*.[8] Loving, sensitive caregivers will amplify a child's positive states and modulate the negative states. When this is experienced repeatedly, the child can construct a mental model for managing her own emotions. As a child's needs for love, safety, comfort, and connection are consistently met throughout childhood, she will grow into an adult who can feel secure in herself and securely attach to others.

© Copyright 2009 by Shirley Jean Schmidt, MA, LPC. All rights reserved. Duplication in any form without permission is prohibited.

In contrast, a baby who is subjected to abuse, rejection, neglect, or enmeshment in the care of unskillful caregivers will learn to anticipate more of the same. As this baby continues to get what she expects (e.g. abuse or neglect), her mental model of an unsafe or insecure world is strengthened. Even if this child is later moved to a loving home, those mental models formed in the early years will continue to contribute to her assumptions about self, relationships, and the world and to her interpretations of new experiences. If a child is consistently led to expect mistreatment or rejection throughout childhood, she will grow into an adult who will not be able to feel secure in herself, or to securely attach to others.

Internalized Representations of Caregivers and Self-Regulation

Children develop internalized representations of their significant caregivers.[9] This works to a child's advantage when *skillful caregivers* are able to manage and regulate her emotions well. By providing an internalized sense of a *secure base* and a *safe haven*, these internalized caregivers can *facilitate the self-regulation of emotions*. For example: Each time a young girl suffers minor injuries playing in the yard, her mother comforts her with a smile, a hug, and a band-aid. Mother tells her, "It may hurt for a while, but you're going to be okay." At age 15, she suffers her first romantic loss when her boyfriend breaks up with her. As she grieves the loss, her internalized mother reassures her with, "It's going to hurt for a while, but you're going to be okay." As children learn to manage their emotions they are able to individuate and mature in healthy ways. (In the DNMS model, internalized representations of skillful caregivers are referred to as *Adaptive Introjects*.)

In contrast, internalization of caregivers works to a child's disadvantage when *unskillful caregivers* are unable to manage and regulate emotions well. Such internalized caregivers can *perpetuate the dysregulation of emotions* by either generating, or failing to soothe, insecurity and anxiety. This dysregulation will impair a child's development of normal behaviors, such as play, exploration, and social interactions. (In the DNMS model, internalized representations of unskillful caregivers are referred to as *Maladaptive Introjects*.)

Attachment Styles

Individuals can form secure or insecure styles of attachment depending on their interactions with their primary caregivers.

- ### Secure Attachment

  Children develop secure attachments to caregivers who rate high in maternal sensitivity[10], respond promptly to distress,[11] provide moderate stimulation,[12] are non-intrusive,[13] interact with synchrony,[14] and are warm, involved, and responsive.[15] Caregivers of secure infants interact positively, are rarely over-arousing, and are able to stabilize a child's disorganized emotional responses. These caregivers remain calm and secure in stressful situations, and regard their child's negative emotions as meaningful and not threatening.[16]

  The benefits of a secure attachment last a lifetime. Securely attached infants trust they will be soothed when upset, so they readily engage in play and exploration. Securely attached preschool children have been observed to be more ego-resilient and independent, demonstrating higher self-esteem than insecure children. They have friends, social skills, and empathy for peers in distress.[17] Securely attached adults are able to understand themselves and others; recognize their own internal conflicts; and realize why their parents behaved as they did.[18] Mary Main observed that securely attached adults, when asked to discuss childhood experiences (including painful interactions with parents), were able to discuss their experiences coherently, accept their parents' failings, show compassion, value attachment, demonstrate a strong personal identity, display ease with their personal imperfections, accept personal responsibility, and see reality clearly.[19]

  A secure attachment to loving, attuned caregivers is the most important of all childhood needs. Children who grow up feeling securely attached to consistently loving, attuned caregivers become well-adjusted adults with the ability to form secure attachments and regulate their own emotions, and hold a positive outlook on self and world.[20]

- ### Insecure Attachment

  A child will form an *insecure or anxious attachment* to caregivers who are not able to provide a secure base or a safe haven. Ainsworth *et al.* observed two types of insecure attachments in children: *avoidant* and *ambivalent*.[21] Avoidantly attached children tend to enter adulthood with a *dismissing* state of mind

© Copyright 2009 by Shirley Jean Schmidt, MA, LPC. All rights reserved. Duplication in any form without permission is prohibited.

with respect to attachment, while ambivalently attached children tend to enter adulthood with a *preoccupied* state of mind with respect to attachment.[22]

- Avoidant/Dismissing Attachment

  A child will develop an avoidant attachment to *rejecting caregivers*. Caregiver behaviors that predict an avoidant attachment include withdrawing, hesitating, wincing, and arching away from the child. These caregivers actively block awareness of a child's attachment behaviors (e.g. crying, reaching). They are averse to physical and emotional interactions with the child. Children will experience such withdrawals as an assault on their safe haven. These caregivers are reluctant to organize the child's attention or behavior, or modulate her emotions. They are unwilling to provide comfort, whether the child's distress is aroused by environmental upsets or by the caregiver's behavior.[23]

  The avoidant toddlers exhibit little interest in adults attempting to attract their attention or little motivation to maintain contact. They appear undisturbed by a caregiver's departure, and indifferent about the caregiver's return. While avoidant children feel angry that proximity to the caregiver is restricted or blocked, they will not openly express their distress. Children may respond with rejecting behaviors, such as not looking at the caregiver, or avoiding the caregiver entirely. They have learned to expect the caregiver will not provide comfort. Main and Stadtman believe that avoidance is a mechanism to "modulate the painful and vacillating emotion aroused by the historically rejecting mother."[24] Alan Sroufe observed three types of avoidant preschoolers: (1) the lying bullies who blame others; (2) the shy, spacey, loners who appear emotionally flat; and (3) the obviously disturbed daydreamers with repetitive tics, who show little interest in their environment. The avoidant children were observed to be sullen and oppositional, often preying on other children.[25] They were disliked by their peers and described by preschool teachers as dishonest and mean. While they normally exhibited negative, attention-seeking, dependent behaviors, they would withdraw if injured or disappointed. Adults who had an avoidant attachment style in childhood are said to have a *dismissing state of mind with respect to attachment* in adulthood.[26] Main observed that these adults, when asked to discuss childhood experiences (including painful interactions with parents), tend to idealize one or both parents, fail to support idealized characterizations with meaningful examples, show contempt for attachment figures or attachment related experiences, and describe themselves positively, as strong, independent, and normal. They minimize their negative childhood attachment experiences by reporting they had little or no negative impact; by insisting they were character-building experiences; by suggesting everyone has these experiences; and/or by summarizing a negative story with a positive spin. They are not able to talk about or express feelings of vulnerability. Many are unable or unwilling to answer questions about attachment experiences from childhood.

  Children who grow up with an avoidant attachment to caregivers become adults who are dismissive of emotional connections and attachments, and who manage distress by ignoring painful realities and repressing unpleasant emotions.

- Ambivalent/Preoccupied Attachment

  A child will develop an ambivalent attachment to *intrusive/engulfing caregivers*. Caregiver behaviors that predict an ambivalent attachment (sometimes called *resistant* attachment) include routinely subjecting the child to high-intensity emotional stimulation, while ignoring the child's bids for stimulation reduction (e.g. crying, looking away). These caregivers are emotionally insensitive, haphazard, and unpredictable – emotionally available sometimes but not always. Even when they are present, the child cannot be sure her signals and communications will be handled by the caregiver appropriately. Because these caregivers are not attuned or sensitive to a child's cues, they overwhelm the child with stimulation. This interferes with the child's ability to assimilate new experiences. These caregivers are ineffective at setting boundaries and limits, at reducing feelings of shame, and at managing the child's aggressions.[27]

  Ambivalent children alternate proximity-seeking behaviors with angry, rejecting behaviors – perhaps punishing the caregiver for being unavailable. Because these caregivers do not function as a reliable, secure base, the children can become preoccupied with the caregiver's emotional states to the point of not feeling free to play and explore independently. As this child displays heightened emotionality and dependence, she succeeds in drawing the caregiver's attention.[28] The child becomes addicted to

© Copyright 2009 by Shirley Jean Schmidt, MA, LPC. All rights reserved. Duplication in any form without permission is prohibited.

the caregiver, and addicted to strategies to influence the caregiver to change. The ambivalent child learns that fear will bring attention, so she looks for things to be afraid of.[29] Sroufe observed two types of ambivalent preschoolers: (1) those who were fidgety, impulsive, tense, with poor concentration, and easily upset by failures; and (2) those who were fearful, hypersensitive, clingy, lacking in initiative, and prone to give up easily.[30] These children were too preoccupied with their own needs to have any feelings for the children around them. They were highly dependent, exhibiting a weak sense of self. Their disruptive behavior often angered other children. Aggressive encounters evoked a panic response, which made them easy targets for future bullying. The preschool teachers described the ambivalent children as ineffective, emotionally immature, and incapable of following rules. Ambivalent children worry about themselves and their intrusive caregiver, often becoming the *parentified child*. The child may be afraid of going to school, not because something at the school is frightening, but because she fears losing her caregiver, or worries that her caregiver will become unbearably lonely while she is away.[31] Adults who had an ambivalent attachment style in childhood are said to have a *preoccupied state of mind with respect to attachment* in adulthood.[32] Main observed that these adults, when asked to discuss childhood experiences (including painful interactions with parents), would discuss disturbing attachment experiences to excess. They would go on and on about parents' failings, taking far more than the usual conversational turn, demonstrating their preoccupation with anger. They exhibited a lack of coherence by not answering the questions asked; by wandering off topic; or by oscillating between positive and negative evaluations of a caregiver, in rapid succession. They appeared incapable of objectivity, insight, or genuine understanding about their attachment wounds, and were consequently unable to discuss them fruitfully or skillfully. They resorted to blame of self or others. Their sense of self appeared closely linked to unresolvable disturbing experiences with their parents.

Children who grow up with an ambivalent attachment to caregivers become adults who are preoccupied with problematic emotional connections and attachments – both past and present, who are overly dependent on others, and who lack the ability to manage their own emotions and impulses.

- ### *Disorganized/Unresolved Attachment*

In addition to the three childhood attachment styles listed above (secure, ambivalent, or avoidant) a child may have a *disorganized attachment* to caregivers.[33] The disorganized attachment status is a secondary classification, applied in addition to the child's primary attachment status. For example, a child may be secure-disorganized, ambivalent-disorganized, or avoidant-disorganized. Caregivers who have unresolved traumas and losses can slip into an unresolved, anxious, dissociated state of mind. In this *unresolved state of mind*, the *dissociated caregiver* cannot provide a child with a secure base or safe haven. Infants identified as disorganized demonstrated unusual behaviors upon reunion with their mother following a brief separation. Examples of these unusual behaviors include sequential or simultaneous contradictory behaviors (e.g. avoidance and contact-seeking gestures); incomplete approaches to the caregiver; unusual body movements or posturing; fearful or dazed facial expressions; and rapid changes in affect.[34] Main and Hesse attributed this disorganization to unresolved caregiver behaviors that frighten the child. They reasoned that, if a caregiver arouses a child's fear, it places the child in an unresolvable paradox, because the caregiver to go to for safety is the also the source of the fear.[35] Karlen Lyons-Ruth *et al.* advanced two alternative hypotheses. First, that unresolved caregivers might display competing or contradictory strategies for caring for the child, much as disorganized children display competing or contradictory attachment strategies. Second, that any caregiver behaviors (e.g. rejection, neglect, intrusion) that were unable to calm a child's fear, would also be potentially disorganizing, whether or not those caregivers behaviors actually elicited the fear. Unresolved adults become disoriented, illogical, and incoherent during discussions of abuse or loss.[36]

Children who are not offered a safe haven from fearful arousal often become dissociated adults. As they experience traumas and losses in adulthood they are unable to resolve them, because their disorganized mental models and internal representations lack the means to do so.[37]

- ### *Earned/Autonomous Secure Attachment*

Bowlby writes, "Fortunately the human psyche, like human bones, is strongly inclined towards self-healing. The psychotherapist's job, like that of the orthopedic surgeon's, is to provide the conditions in which self-

© Copyright 2009 by Shirley Jean Schmidt, MA, LPC. All rights reserved. Duplication in any form without permission is prohibited.

healing can best take place."[38] Individuals with any of the insecure attachment categories listed above can achieve "earned" secure/autonomous attachment status. Individuals who have earned secure/autonomous attachment status have finally made sense of their childhood wounds with the help of one or more supportive relationships and/or psychotherapy.[39] They are able to understand, organize, and discuss painful childhood attachment relationships in a coherent way. (The term "earned" does not refer to "deserving.")

Caveat about Attachment Styles

Each attachment style described above reflects a relationship with a single caregiver. For example, an infant could be securely attached to her nanny, avoidantly attached to her father, and ambivalently attached to her mother. The attachment styles outlined above describe these classifications in their purest form. While they are helpful categories for attachment researchers, in reality, many people do not fit these classifications exactly as described. A given individual may exhibit behavior patterns from more than one attachment classification.[40] This is understandable considering that different ego states can have different mental models, formed by the internalized representations of different significant caregivers.

Rupture and Repair

Relationships between children and caregivers will naturally involve times of disconnection. These small traumas may or may not be followed by reconnection and repair. Loving, attuned caregivers recognize and respond to these disconnections with soothing and comfort, which leads to the necessary repair. Avoidantly attached children have rejecting caregivers who lack the willingness or ability to provide the needed reassurance to effect a repair. Ambivalently attached children have intrusive caregivers who persist in making reparative contact, but who do so without sufficient sensitivity or attunement. Because the caregiver is misattuned, the child becomes overwhelmed, and attempts to initiate a repair fail. Disorganized children may have frightening caregivers who are unable to affect a repair because they are the source of the fear. This leaves the child over-aroused, in a state of despair.[41]

Neurobiology of Attachment and Attunement

Two branches of the autonomic nervous system (ANS) help control the body's state of arousal. The *sympathetic branch* is associated with excitatory, arousing affect. It induces physiological responses that increase heart rate, respiration, sweating, and states of alertness. The *parasympathetic branch* is associated with inhibitory, de-arousing, energy-conserving affect. It induces physiological responses that decrease heart rate, respiration, sweating, and states of alertness.

Excited states of mind (sympathetic branch) predominate in the first year of life, during moments of intense non-verbal attunement between a child and her loving, attuned caregiver. Inhibited states of mind (parasympathetic branch) predominate in the second year, when a child becomes more mobile, and caregivers prohibit risky exploration. For example, when the child reaches for a hot stove, mother will yell "No!" For a child to learn self-regulation, caregivers must balance the child's need for excitatory mental-state alignment with the need for inhibitory prohibitions.

The *orbitofrontal cortex* (OFC) is the part of the brain just behind the eyes. It is the only cortical structure with direct connections to the cingulate gyrus, hypothalamus, the amygdala and brainstem nuclei; thereby constituting the rostral (extended) limbic system. The lower limbic structures (hypothalamus, amygdala and brainstem) provide automatic, primitive, survival reflexes (e.g. fight or flight) while the higher rostral limbic structures (OFC and cingulate gyrus) allow for fine-tuned adjustments in emotional perception and affect management.[42] Because of its strategic anatomic location, the OFC is able to integrate these higher and lower limbic processes into a functional whole. The OFC is especially sensitive to face-to-face communication and eye contact. Because it serves as an important center of appraisal, it has a direct influence on the elaboration of states of arousal into various types of emotional experience. Understanding the OFC is crucial to understanding emotional self-regulation and neural integration.[43]

Caregiver attunement appears to have a direct impact upon a child's OFC.[44] When a happy excited toddler is about to touch a hot stove, and the caregiver yells "No!", the OFC puts on the brakes. The toddler contracts in

© Copyright 2009 by Shirley Jean Schmidt, MA, LPC. All rights reserved. Duplication in any form without permission is prohibited.

shame. Shame can be understood as a sudden shift from sympathetic system activation (the accelerator) by an *internal* "Go!", to parasympathetic system activation (the brakes) by an *external* "Stop!"[45] The attuned caregiver comforts the upset child, and lovingly explains that hot stoves can cause painful burns. This helps restore the child-caregiver alignment, which leads to a release of the brakes (the parasympathetic system is deactivated). Once the emotional repair with the caregiver has been completed, the child feels free to return to exciting play and exploration (the sympathetic system is reactivated). There is a healthy balance between the activation of the accelerator and the application of the brakes – which is the essence of affect regulation. The child successfully integrates this upsetting experience by concluding that, while her caregivers might not always like what she does, they always like her. As this child becomes an adult her OFC will be able to regulate the sympathetic "accelerator" and the parasympathetic "brakes," without an attuned caregiver present to guide the process.

When a caregiver responds with disgust or displeasure to a child's bid for attunement, the child shifts into an escalating state of shame. This is a serious relationship break, and if unrepaired, will lead to mental models that cannot self-regulate shame, and that inhibit the spontaneous expression of "true self." [46]

The OFC plays an important role in many brain functions.[47] When developing in the care of loving, attuned parents, it functions very differently than when developing in the care of misattuned, rejecting, or intrusive parents. This point is illustrated in the table below.

An optimally-developed OFC plays a role in the following benefits:	A non-optimally-developed OFC may play a role in the following problems:
▪ The regulation of emotion;	▪ Impaired regulation of emotion;
▪ The appraisal of stimulus to make meaning of events; [48]	▪ Impaired appraisal of stimulus. Problems making meaning of events;
▪ Engagement in emotionally attuned communications;	▪ Difficulty engaging in emotionally attuned communications;
▪ Sensitivity to others' subjective experience;	▪ Difficulty sensing others' subjective experience;
▪ Moral reasoning; and	▪ Poor moral reasoning; and
▪ *Response flexibility*, the ability to adapt to the internal and external environment with appropriate behavioral and/or cognitive responses. [49]	▪ Inflexible responses resulting in a failure to adapt to internal and external environments.

An optimal-functioning emotion-regulating OFC develops as child-caregiver psychobiological states are attuned.[50] There can be neurobiological consequences when this does not happen. Excessive, unregulated arousal (whether from the sympathetic or parasympathetic branch) will interfere with the maturation of the child's right hemispheric structural systems that mediate socioaffective self-regulation. Reductions in the levels of neurotrophic catecholamines during critical periods (first two years) of corticolimbic maturation produce alterations in the structural development of the OFC. Extreme hormonal alterations induce "developmental overpruning" of the sympathetic ventral tegmental and/or parasympathetic lateral tegmental limbic circuits that it dominates. The release of stress hormones leads to excessive death of neurons in the crucial pathways involving the cortico-limbic structures – the areas responsible for emotional regulation.

The orbitofrontal region plays an important role in response flexibility. This refers to the brain's ability to adapt to the internal and external environment with appropriate behavioral and/or affective responses. This appears to require the integrative capacities of the orbitofrontal region in order to functionally link the associational cortex, limbic circuits, and brainstem areas. In this manner, the orbitofrontal region enables the more complex "higher order" processing of the left dorsolateral prefrontal cortex to be integrated with the "lower order" functions of the deeper structures. The region functions as a neural pathway that links a wide array of perceptual regulatory and abstract representational regions of the brain.[51]

Siegel defines integration as the "functional coupling of distinct and differentiated elements into a coherent process or functional whole."[52] Adaptive and flexible ego states can be both highly differentiated *and* functionally united. He describes ego states that are stuck in unresolved trauma as "...functionally independent, an isolation

© Copyright 2009 by Shirley Jean Schmidt, MA, LPC. All rights reserved. Duplication in any form without permission is prohibited.

that may have preserved the ability of the individual to function in the face of traumatic experiences."[53] If trauma leads to the isolation of ego states, it follows that the neural integration of those ego states should lead to healing. Siegel favors psychotherapies that encourage the bilateral integration of information across the right and left hemispheres of the brain, as well as integration of here-and-now with past-present-future awareness.[54]

The orbitofrontal region plays a key role in facilitating neural integration. It makes sense that a psychotherapy that helps it to function optimally should increase the probability of adaptive neural integration occurring. The OFC thrives in the care of loving, attuned caregivers in childhood. It appears to respond well to nurturing in adulthood too – whether the loving, attuned caregivers are internal or external.

Attachment References

1. Bowlby, J. (1969). *Attachment. Volume I of Attachment and Loss.* New York: Basic Books.
2. Ainsworth, M.D.S., Blehar, M.C., Waters, E., & Wall, S. (1978). *Patterns of attachment: A psychological study of the strange situation.* Hillsdale, NJ: Erlbaum.
3. Bowlby, J. (1969). *Attachment. Volume I of Attachment and Loss.* New York: Basic Books.
4. Schore, A. (1994). *Affect regulation and the origin of self: The neurobiology of emotional development.* Hillsdale, NJ: Erlbaum.
5. Siegel, D.J. (1999). *The developing mind: Toward a neurobiology of interpersonal experience.* New York: Guilford Press.
6. Siegel, D.J. (1999). *The developing mind: Toward a neurobiology of interpersonal experience.* New York: Guilford Press.
7. Bowlby, J. (1969). *Attachment.* Volume I of *Attachment and Loss.* New York: Basic Books.
8. Hofer, M.A. (1994). Hidden regulators in attachment, separation and loss. In N.A. Fox (ed.), The development of emotion regulation: Biological and behavioral considerations. *Monographs of the Society for Research in Child Development,* 59(2-3, Serial No. 240), 192-207.
9. Bowlby, J. (1969). *Attachment.* Volume I of *Attachment and Loss.* New York: Basic Books.
    Siegel, D.J. (1999). The *developing mind: Toward a neurobiology of interpersonal experience.* New York: Guilford Press.
10. Isabella R.A., Belsky J. & von Eye A. (1989). Origins of infant-mother attachment: An examination of interactional synchrony during the infant's first year. *Developmental Psychology,* 25, 12-21.
11. Del Carmen R., Pedersen F., Huffman L. & Bryan Y. (1993). Dyadic distress management predicts security of attachment. *Infant Behavior and Development,* 16, 131-147.
12. Belsky J., Rovine M. & Taylor D. G. (1984). The Pennsylvania Infant and Family Development Project, III: The origins of individual differences in infant-mother attachment: Maternal and infant contributions. *Child Development,* 55, 718-728.
13. Malatesta C. Z., Grigoryev P., Lamb C., Albin M. & Culver C. (1986). Emotional socialisation and expressive development in pre-term and full-term infants. *Child Development,* 57, 316-330.
14. Isabella R.A., Belsky J. & von Eye A. (1989). Origins of infant-mother attachment: An examination of interactional synchrony during the infant's first year. *Developmental Psychology,* 25, 12-21.
15. O'Connor M., Sigman, M. & Kasari, C. (1992). Attachment behavior of infants exposed prenatally to alcohol: Mediating effects of infant affect and mother-infant interaction. *Development and Psychopathology,* 4, 243-256.
16. Sroufe L.A. (1996). *Emotional development: The organization of emotional life in the early years.* New York: Cambridge University Press.
17. Sroufe, L.A. (1983). Infant-caregiver attachment and patterns of adaptation in preschool: The roots of maladaptation and competence. In M. Perlmutter (Ed.) *Minnesota Symposium in Child Psychology.* 16, pp.41-83. Hillsdale, NJ: Erlbaum Associates.
18. Fonagy P., Steele M., Moran G., Steele M. & Higgitt A.C. (1991). The capacity for understanding mental states: The reflective self in parent and child and its significance for security of attachment. *Infant Mental Health Journal,* 13, 200-216.
19. Main, M. & Goldwyn, R. (1998). *Adult attachment scoring and classification system.* (V 6.3). Unpublished manuscript, University of California at Berkeley.
20. Siegel, D.J. (1999). *The developing mind: Toward a neurobiology of interpersonal experience.* New York: Guilford Press.
21. Ainsworth, M.D.S., Blehar, M.C., Waters, E., & Wall, S. (1978). *Patterns of attachment: A psychological study of the strange situation.* Hillsdale, NJ: Erlbaum
22. Main, M. & Goldwyn, R. (1998). *Adult attachment scoring and classification system.* (V 6.3). Unpublished manuscript, University of California at Berkeley.
23. Main, M., & Weston, D. R. (1981). The quality of the toddler's relationship to mother and to father: Related to conflict behavior and the readiness to establish new relationships. *Child Development,* 52, 932-940.
    Schore, A. (2003). *Affect dysregulation and disorders of the self.* New York: W.W. Norton and Company.
24. Main, M., & Stadtman, J. (1981). Infant response to rejection of physical contact by the mother: Aggression, avoidance and conflict. *Journal of the American Academy of Child Psychiatry,* 20, 293.
25. Sroufe, L.A. (1983). Infant-caregiver attachment and patterns of adaptation in preschool: The roots of maladaptation and competence. In M. Perlmutter (Ed.) *Minnesota Symposium in Child Psychology.* 16, pp.41-83. Hillsdale, NJ: Erlbaum Associates.

© Copyright 2009 by Shirley Jean Schmidt, MA, LPC. All rights reserved. Duplication in any form without permission is prohibited.

26. Main, M. & Goldwyn, R. (1998). *Adult attachment scoring and classification system*. (V 6.3). Unpublished manuscript, University of California at Berkeley.

27. Schore, A. (2003). *Affect dysregulation and disorders of the self*. New York: W.W. Norton and Company.

28. Schore, A. (2003). *Affect dysregulation and disorders of the self*. New York: W.W. Norton and Company.

29. Karen, R. (1998). *Becoming attached: First relationships and how they shape our capacity to love*. New York: Oxford.

30. Sroufe, L.A. (1983). Infant-caregiver attachment and patterns of adaptation in preschool: The roots of maladaptation and competence. In M. Perlmutter (Ed.) *Minnesota Symposium in Child Psychology*. 16, pp.41-83. Hillsdale, NJ: Erlbaum Associates.

31. Bowlby, J. (1973). *Separation: Anxiety and Anger*. Volume II of *Attachment and Loss*. New York: Basic Books.

32. Main, M. & Goldwyn, R. (1998). *Adult attachment scoring and classification system*. (V 6.3). Unpublished manuscript, University of California at Berkeley.

33. Main, M., & Hesse, E. (1990). Parents' unresolved traumatic experiences are related to infant disorganized attachment status: Is frightened and/or frightening parental behavior the linking mechanism? In M. Greenberg, D. Cicchetti, & E.M. Cummings (Eds.), *Attachment in the preschool years: Theory, research and intervention* (pp. 161–184). Chicago: University of Chicago Press.

34. Lyons-Ruth, K. & Jacobvitz, D. (1999) Attachment disorganization: Unresolved loss, relational violence, and lapses in behavioural and attentional strategies. In *Handbook of Attachment* (eds J Cassidy & P Shaver), pp. 520-555. New York: Guilford Press.

35. Main, M., & Hesse, E. (1990). Parents' unresolved traumatic experiences are related to infant disorganized attachment status: Is frightened and/or frightening parental behavior the linking mechanism? In M. Greenberg, D. Cicchetti, & E.M. Cummings (Eds.), *Attachment in the preschool years: Theory, research and intervention* (pp. 161–184). Chicago: University of Chicago Press.

36. Lyons-Ruth, K., Bronfman, E., & Parsons, E. (1999). Atypical maternal behavior and disorganized infant attachment strategies: Frightened, frightening, and atypical maternal behavior and disorganized infant attachment strategies. In J. Vondra & D. Barnett (Eds.), Atypical patterns of infant attachment: Theory, research, and current directions. *Monographs of the Society for Research in Child Development*, 64(3, Serial No. 258).

37. Moran, G., Pederson, D., and Krupka, A. (2005). Maternal unresolved attachment status impedes the effectiveness of interventions with adolescent mothers. *Infant Mental Health Journal*, 26(3), 231-249.

38. Bowlby, J. (1988). *A secure base*. New York: Basic Books, p. 152.

39. Main, M. & Goldwyn, R. (1998). *Adult attachment scoring and classification system*. (V 6.3). Unpublished manuscript, University of California at Berkeley.

40. Siegel, D.J. (1999). *The developing mind: Toward a neurobiology of interpersonal experience*. New York: Guilford Press.

41. Siegel, D.J. (1999). *The developing mind: Toward a neurobiology of interpersonal experience*. New York: Guilford Press.

42. Schore, A. (2003). *Affect dysregulation and disorders of the self*. New York: W.W. Norton and Company.

43. Siegel, D.J. (2003). An interpersonal neurobiology of psychotherapy: The developing mind and the resolution of trauma. In M. F. Solomon & D. J. Siegel (Eds.), *Healing trauma: attachment, mind, body and brain* (pp. 1-56). New York: Norton.

44. Schore, A. (1994). *Affect regulation and the origin of self: The neurobiology of emotional development*. Hillsdale, NJ: Erlbaum.

45. Hofer, M.A. (1994). Hidden regulators in attachment, separation and loss. In N.A. Fox (ed.), The development of emotion regulation: Biological and behavioral considerations. *Monographs of the Society for Research in Child Development*, 59(2-3, Serial No. 240), 192-207.

46. Schore, A. (2003). *Affect dysregulation and disorders of the self*. New York: W.W. Norton and Company.

47. Siegel, D.J. (2003). An interpersonal neurobiology of psychotherapy: The developing mind and the resolution of trauma. In M. F. Solomon & D. J. Siegel (Eds.), *Healing trauma: attachment, mind, body and brain* (pp. 1-56). New York: Norton.

48. Damasio, A. (1994). *Descartes' error: Emotion, reason, and the human brain*. New York: Grosset/Putnam.

49. Mesulam, M. M. (1998). Review article: From sensation to cognition. *Brain*, 121, 1013-1052.

50. Schore, A. (1994). *Affect regulation and the origin of self: The neurobiology of emotional development*. Hillsdale, NJ: Erlbaum.

51. Siegel, D.J. (2003). An interpersonal neurobiology of psychotherapy: The developing mind and the resolution of trauma. In M. F. Solomon & D. J. Siegel (Eds.), *Healing trauma: attachment, mind, body and brain* (pp. 1-56). New York: Norton.

52. Siegel, D.J. (2003). An interpersonal neurobiology of psychotherapy: The developing mind and the resolution of trauma. In M. F. Solomon & D. J. Siegel (Eds.), *Healing trauma: attachment, mind, body and brain* (pp. 1-56). New York: Norton, p. 41.

53. Siegel, D.J. (2003). An interpersonal neurobiology of psychotherapy: The developing mind and the resolution of trauma. In M. F. Solomon & D. J. Siegel (Eds.), *Healing trauma: attachment, mind, body and brain* (pp. 1-56). New York: Norton, p. 45.

54. Siegel, D.J. (2003). An interpersonal neurobiology of psychotherapy: The developing mind and the resolution of trauma. In M. F. Solomon & D. J. Siegel (Eds.), *Healing trauma: attachment, mind, body and brain* (pp. 1-56). New York: Norton.

© Copyright 2009 by Shirley Jean Schmidt, MA, LPC. All rights reserved. Duplication in any form without permission is prohibited.

Section 4: Background Material on Prenatal Introjection

Prenatal Introjection

According to Siegel, *explicit memory* can be verbal, episodic and/or semantic. It requires conscious awareness for encoding.[1] It involves a subjective sense of self, of time, and of "recalling." It includes factual memories (e.g. names of each state) and autobiographical memory (e.g. 1980 trip to Paris). In contrast, *implicit memory* is nonverbal and procedural. It includes behavioral, emotional, perceptual, and perhaps somatosensory memory. It lacks a subjective experience of self, of time, or of "recalling." Focused attention is not required for encoding. While children begin to collect and recall explicit memories about age two, implicit memories begin forming in the womb. Both types of memories contribute to the formation of mental models of the world. The explicit memories contribute consciously, while the implicit memories contribute unconsciously.

In his book, *The Secret Life of the Unborn Child,* Thomas Verny writes that an unborn baby is capable of learning, hearing, responding to voices and sounds, and responding to love.[2] The baby is an active, feeling human being, sensitive to parents' feelings about him. He cites several research projects relevant to the DNMS. Monika Lukesch, at Constantine University in Frankfurt, followed 2000 women through pregnancy and birth. The mothers came from the same economic background, had the same intelligence level, and received the same degree and quality of prenatal care. Lukesch observed that the mothers who had wanted a family had children who were physically and emotionally healthier, at birth and afterwards, than the children of rejecting mothers. Gerhard Rottmann, at the University of Salzburg, placed each of 141 pregnant mothers in one of four emotional attitude categories based on psychological testing that measured the mother's conscious and unconscious desire to have the baby. The *Ideal Mothers* who wanted their babies both consciously and unconsciously had the easiest pregnancies, the most trouble-free births, and the healthiest offspring – physically and emotionally. The *Ambivalent Mothers* appeared to others to want their babies, but were privately ambivalent. An unusually large number of their babies had both behavioral and gastrointestinal problems. The *Cool Mothers* reported they were not ready to become mothers (e.g. due to financial problems or career plans), but actually wanted their babies. An unusually large number of their babies were apathetic and lethargic. The *Catastrophic Mothers* did not want to be pregnant. Their babies had the most devastating medical problems during pregnancy, and bore the highest rate of premature, low birth weight, and emotionally disturbed infants.

The *Avon Longitudinal Study of Parents and Children,* is a prospective, community-based study that has followed a cohort of 7144 women since pregnancy. The women delivered their baby between April 1, 1991, and December 31, 1992. The women were asked to self-report levels of anxiety and depression at repeated intervals during and pregnancy. Then parents assessed their children's behavioral/emotional problems at age 4. After statistically accounting for a number of confounding effects, such as smoking, alcohol abuse, birth weight, maternal age, and socioeconomic factors, the researchers, O'Conner, Heron, and Glover, found that the women who reported feeling highly anxious during pregnancy were twice as likely as non-anxious women, to have children with behavioral difficulties, depression, and anxiety.[3]

Prenatal Introjection References

1. Siegel, D.J. (1999). *The developing mind: Toward a neurobiology of interpersonal experience.* New York: Guilford Press.
2. Verny, T. & Kelly, J. (1981). *The secret life of the unborn child.* New York: Dell Trade Paperback.
3. O'Connor, T., Heron, J., Glover, V., & the ALSPAC Study Team. (2002). Antenatal anxiety predicts child behavioral/emotional problems independently of postnatal depression. *Journal of the American Academy of Child and Adolescent Psychology, 41*(12), 1470-1477.

© Copyright 2009 by Shirley Jean Schmidt, MA, LPC. All rights reserved. Duplication in any form without permission is prohibited.

Section 5: Popular Ego State Psychotherapies

Psychosynthesis

Psychosynthesis, developed by Roberto Assagioli, is an approach focused on the integration of previously separate elements into a more unified whole.[1] Those separate elements range from the lower unconscious subpersonalities (pre-programmed, contradictory aspects of self) to the superconscious (inspiration, guidance, comfort, strength, peace, hope, wisdom). Much of Psychosynthesis is aimed at recognizing and harmonizing subpersonalities. Methods commonly used include honoring parts of self, acknowledging and meeting subpersonality's needs, guided imagery, body awareness and movement, symbolic art work, journal-keeping, training of the will, goal-setting, dreamwork, development of the imagination and intuition, gestalt, ideal models, and meditation.

Transactional Analysis

Transactional Analysis, developed by Eric Berne, is based on the idea that human personality is made up of three distinct ego states (Parent, Adult, and Child).[2] Each ego state is a set of related thoughts, feelings, and behaviors from which we can understand interpersonal and intrapsychic dynamics. Berne believed decisions made in childhood in the interest of survival could become self-limiting and result in dysfunctional behavior. The Parent ego state has two parts, the Nurturing and the Controlling Parent, and the Child ego state has two parts, the Adapted and the Free Child. The Nurturing Parent is comparable to the DNMS *adaptive introject*; the Controlling Parent is comparable to the DNMS *maladaptive introject*, the Adapted Child is comparable to the DNMS *reactive part*; and the Free Child is comparable to a reactive part that's become totally unstuck.

Gestalt Therapy

Gestalt Therapy, developed by Fritz Perls, invites clients to integrate and accept parts of their personality they have disowned or denied.[3] Perls believed a *top dog* (controlling, blamer part of self) and an *underdog* (victim, complainer part of self) are in constant internal conflict. His top dog is considered an introject of societal authority figures and parents conveying "should" and "shouldn't" messages. The underdog resists the top dog's messages. The empty chair technique is a role-play used to reduce the internal conflict. The client engages these conflicted parts of self in dialogue by playing the top dog in one chair, talking to the underdog in another chair. The internal conflict resolves as both parts come to understand and accept each other.

The SARI Model

The SARI Model, developed by Maggie Phillips and Claire Frederick, is a four-stage approach for the treatment of clients with ego state conflicts and dissociative disorders.[4] SARI is an acronym for each stage, starting with stage one, *safety* and *stabilization*; stage two, *accessing* the trauma and related resources; stage three, *resolving* traumatic experiences and *restabilization*; and stage four, personality *integration* and the creation of a new *identity*. Phillips & Frederick advocate the use of clinical and Ericksonian hypnotherapy at each stage of treatment.

Internal Family Systems Therapy

Internal Family Systems Therapy, developed by Richard Schwartz, evolved out of the observation that patients had an internal system of parts of self that interacted just like members of a family. [5] This approach is based on the idea that each person has a core Self that contains crucial leadership qualities (e.g. curiosity, competence, clarity, confidence, compassion, acceptance), and other parts of self which fall into three categories. These categories include Exiles (young traumatized parts which embody pain, terror, and fear, which are isolated from the rest of the system), Managers (parts that control situations and relationships in an effort to protect exiles from feeling hurt or rejection), and Firefighters (parts that engage when Exiles are activated in an effort to control and extinguish their feelings). Therapy is designed to unburden parts so a client can be effectively led by the Self.[6]

© Copyright 2009 by Shirley Jean Schmidt, MA, LPC. All rights reserved. Duplication in any form without permission is prohibited.

Voice Dialogue

Voice Dialogue, developed by Hal and Sidra Stone, aims to expand a client's ability to act consciously.[7] The therapy is designed to help a client develop an "Aware Ego" that is able to make choices by taking the views of opposing selves into consideration. Those contrasting views come from Primary Selves (responsible for executive functioning and decision-making) and Disowned Selves (repressed vulnerable parts of self), that are often in direct conflict. The goal of Voice Dialogue is not to change parts of self, but to bring sufficient awareness to internal dynamics that harmony can replace conflict. One aspect of this work involves honoring the parts, acknowledging and meeting their needs.

Ego State Therapy

Ego State Therapy, developed by Jack and Helen Watkins, is based on the belief that ego states constitute a "family of self" within an individual.[8] Hypnosis and family/group therapy techniques are used to resolve conflicts between ego states. Internal negotiations may use directive, behavioral, abreactive, or analytic or humanistic techniques of treatment, usually under hypnosis. Dependent ego states are helped to find internally the nurturing needed to heal. According to Watkins & Watkins, as internal needs are satisfied and conflicts are resolved, the internal family becomes happy and the whole person is well adjusted.

Inner Child Psychotherapy

Inner Child Psychotherapy is based on the idea that adults who suffered neglect, abuse, or unmet needs from childhood can heal past hurts by nurturing their child ego states. In his book *Homecoming*,[9] John Bradshaw outlines methods for using a "wise and gentle old wizard" self to adopt and nurture an infant self, a toddler self, a pre-school self, a school-age self, and an adolescent self. Nancy Napier's books *Recreating Yourself*[10] and *Getting Through the Day*[11] suggest ways to connect to an optimal future self and to identify and embrace disowned child parts of self. Lucia Capacchione wrote several books proposing non-dominant hand drawing and writing to connect to and heal the inner child.[12] Some others who have promoted inner child healing work include Bishop & Grunte,[13] Chopich,[14] Hay,[15] Levin,[16] Missildine,[17] Paul,[18] Taylor,[19] and Whitfield.[20]

Ego State Therapies References

1. Assagioli, R. (1975). *Psychosynthesis: A manual of principles and techniques*. London: Turnstone Press.
2. Berne, E. (1961). *Transactional analysis in psychotherapy, a systematic individual and social psychiatry*. New York: Grove Press.
3. Perls, F.S., Hefferline, R.F., & Goodman, P. (1951). *Gestalt therapy: Excitement and growth in the human personality*. New York: Dell.
4. Phillips, M., & Frederick, C. (1995). *Healing the divided self: Clinical and Ericksonian hypnotherapy for post-traumatic and dissociative conditions*. New York: W.W. Norton & Company.
5. Schwartz, R. C. (1995). *Internal family systems therapy*. New York: Guilford Press.
6. Schwartz, R. C. (1995). *Internal family systems therapy*. New York: Guilford Press.
7. Stone, H. & Stone, S. (1993). *Embracing our selves: The voice dialogue manual*. Nataraj Publishing.
8. Watkins, J. G., & Watkins, H. H. (1997). *Ego states: Theory and therapy*. New York: Norton.
9. Bradshaw, J. (1990). *Homecoming: Reclaiming and championing you inner child*. Bantam Books.
10. Napier, N. (1990). *Recreating your self: Building self-esteem through imaging and self-hypnosis*. New York: Norton.
11. Napier, N. (1993). *Getting through the day: Strategies for adults hurt as children*. New York: Norton.
12. Capacchione, L. (1991). *Recovery of Your Inner Child: The Highly Acclaimed Method for Liberating Your Inner Self*. New York: Simon & Schuster/Fireside.
13. Bishop, J. & Grunte, M. (1991). *How to love yourself when you don't know how: Healing all your inner children*. Pure Gold Publishing.
14. Chopich, E.J. (1990). *Healing your aloneness: Finding love and wholeness through your inner child*. San Francisco: Harper.
15. Hay, L.L. (1990). *Self-Esteem: Motivational Affirmations for Building Confidence and Recognizing Self-Worth*. (The Subliminal Mastery Series/Audio Cassette/706) Hay House, Inc.
16. Levin, P. (1988). *Cycles of Power*. Deerfield Beach, FL: Health Communications Inc.
17. Missildine, W.H. (1991). *Your inner child of the past*. Pocket Books.
18. Paul, M. (1992). *Inner bonding: Becoming a loving adult to your inner child*. San Francisco: Harper.
19. Taylor, C.L. (1991). *The inner child workbook: What to do with your past when it just won't go away*. J P Tarcher.
20. Whitfield, C.L. (1989). *Healing the child within: Discovery and recovery for adult children of dysfunctional families*. Health Communications.

© Copyright 2009 by Shirley Jean Schmidt, MA, LPC. All rights reserved. Duplication in any form without permission is prohibited.

Section 6: Typical Developmental Needs Table

Some Typical Developmental Needs

Conception to Birth

- Parents want the baby
- Parents prepared to bond with baby
- Parents lovingly talk, sing to baby
- Parents happy about baby coming

- Mother eating well
- Mother exercising enough
- Mother refrains from unhealthy acts
- Mother supported by father

- Parents emotionally prepared for baby
- Parents financially prepared for baby
- Parents who can meet their own needs and manage own emotions

Birth to 1 Year

- Good food
- Safety
- Attunement

- Warmth and closeness
- Appropriate response to cries
- Consistent nurturing

- Loving eye contact
- Respectful caregivers
- Positive attention

1 Year to 3 Years

Plus all birth to 1 year needs

- Reassurance
- Supervised play
- Unconditional acceptance
- Loving correction

- Conversation
- Praise
- Stimulating exploration
- Freedom of expression

- Structure
- Consistency
- Freedom to develop self control
- Repair of relationship breaks

3 Years to 6 Years

Plus all birth to 3 year needs

- Encouragement and praise
- Approval for accomplishments
- Validation of perceptions

- Opportunities to make things
- Opportunities to master motor skills
- Freedom to express emotions

- Help processing through emotions
- Age-appropriate limits
- Patient caregivers

6 Years to 12 Years

Plus all birth to 6 years needs

- Support for exploring the world
- Encouragement to develop opinions
- Encouragement to express ideas

- Help solving problems
- Help developing social skills
- Age-appropriate responsibility

- Learning opportunities
- Intellectual challenges
- Physical challenges

12 to 18 Years

Plus all birth to 12 years needs

- Age-appropriate independence
- Age-appropriate limits and rules

- Support for finding sense of identity
- Permission to separate from parents

- Support for making education and occupational decisions

© Copyright 2009 by Shirley Jean Schmidt, MA, LPC. All rights reserved. Duplication in any form without permission is prohibited.

Section 7: Typical Misunderstandings That Block Processing and Suggestions for Correcting Them

Misunderstandings Unique to the Resource Development Protocol

Client has confused the words "protective" and "overprotective."
Show client the difference with her own experiences of being <u>appropriately</u> protective.

Client has confused the notion of "being nurturing to others" with "being exploited by others."
Show client the difference with her own experiences of being <u>appropriately</u> nurturing.

Client has assumed a skill must be applicable all the time, with everyone, to be endorsable.
Explain to client that a skill can be endorsed if it is ever applied with a loved one, from the most adult self, even for short periods of time. It does not matter that the skill is not applied at other times.

"I wasn't very good at protecting my kids. I don't think I have a Protective Self."
Explain to client that if she has ever been appropriately protective of a loved one, while in her <u>most adult self</u>, even for short periods of time, then she has the potential to be protective again in the future. So for the purposes of connecting to a PAS, it does not matter that there were also times she was not protective. What matters is that she can recall times she was protective.

"There's no point in developing Resources because they won't be real."
Explain that the Resources are about real skills contained in real neural networks. If a client's love and affection for her cherished loved one is real, then the Resources are real as well.

"I prefer to experience my Resources as fictional beings because they'd be better caregivers than I am."
Ask the client if her cherished loved one believes she is an adequate caregiver when she is in her <u>most adult self</u>. If so, her Resources should be as good as or better than fictional Resources.

"If I admit to having adult skills, I'm bragging. Bragging is bad and should be punished."
Explain the difference between bragging, self-absorption, and conceit, versus self-confidence, self-esteem, and self-assurance. (There may also be an introject involved, threatening to punish bragging.)

Misunderstandings Unique to the Conference Room Protocol

"Inviting an introject forward puts child parts at risk."
Reactive parts often fear that the introjects who are going to be invited to the conference table, are a threat. Offer to separate the reactive parts and introjects with a protective "glass wall" across the table. In addition, reactive parts can be informed that, while an introject costume may appear threatening, the danger is just an illusion. The child wearing the costume is not a threat at all.

Misunderstandings Unique to the Needs Meeting Protocol

"There's no point in doing the needs meeting work because it won't be real."
Explain that the Resources are real neural networks that can be nurturing and protective of wounded child parts in the same real way the most adult self can be nurturing and protective of her cherished loved one.

"I can't process my anger or grief without being overwhelmed." (Step 8)
Explain the *Processing Emotions by Needs Meeting* routine.

"Anger is a bad emotion." (Step 8)
Some clients believe that bad emotions, like anger, must be avoided. Explain that emotions are not good or bad, they are comfortable and uncomfortable, pleasant and unpleasant. When managed appropriately, every emotion can serve a valuable purpose – even anger. (This may be a message from a maladaptive introject.)

"Only bad people express anger." (Step 8)
Validate that mean people can hurt others in anger. Then explain that healthy people can express anger in healthy ways – with skill and respect for others. (This may be coming from a maladaptive introject.)

"I'd be just like my (*wounding role model*) if I show my anger." (Step 8)
Explain that there is a difference between expressing anger skillfully versus unskillfully. Her wounding role model expressed anger unskillfully and destructively. In contrast, skillful expression of anger is not disrespectful. It can be constructive and healing. Furthermore, the loving compassion of the Resources can help the anger process through.

© Copyright 2009 by Shirley Jean Schmidt, MA, LPC. All rights reserved. Duplication in any form without permission is prohibited.

"If I express my anger I'll be disloyal." (Step 8)

Some children grow up being told that any negative emotions they expressed towards or about parents is a sign of being ungrateful or disloyal. These clients may have trouble acknowledging unexpressed and unresolved anger or grief about unmet childhood needs. Explain that the expression of anger about wounding parental behaviors is natural and appropriate – whether or not the parents agree. (There may also be an introject threatening to punish child parts for being disloyal.)

"Bonding with a caregiver will inevitably lead to betrayal or abandonment." (Step 9)

Remind the child parts that the Resources would not betray or abandon their cherished loved one. (There may also be an introject threatening to betray or abandon child parts if they get too close.)

"If I bond with the Resources I'll be smothered or engulfed." (Step 9)

Explain that bonding to loving, attuned Resources is not smothering or engulfment. Invite the child parts to notice that the Resources totally understand her aversion, and grant her explicit permission to feel it as long as she needs to. Explain they want her to express whatever emotion comes up, without pressure to feel any other way. (There may also be an introject threatening to smother or engulf child parts.)

"It's not okay for the Resources to hurt when I hurt." (Step 9)

Have the child parts ask the Resources if they are okay with hurting when they hurt. When the Resources say "yes," the aversion may soften. Ask the child parts if they would feel distressed seeing their favorite kitten or puppy hurt, and if so, would that be okay? The child parts may then see it is a normal appropriate reaction. Help the child parts understand that the hurt experienced in empathy for a loved one is a good hurt. Tell the child parts that parents who cannot manage emotions well are more likely to shame or punish a child for "making them hurt." In contrast, the Resources can manage emotions quite well.

Misunderstandings Common to all the Protocols

"I'm afraid I'll lose a familiar sense of identity."

Say something like: "You'll never be without a sense of identity. While you maintain your old familiar negative identity, based on (*feeling lonely, depressed, etc.)* the Resources will help create a new one, based on self-esteem and self-confidence. Anything of value from your old sense of identity will be integrated into your new identity. Once your new identity is strong enough, everything about your old identity that no longer helps you will be naturally and automatically discarded. How does that sound?" This usually resolves the fear.

"I had to meet my own needs in childhood. Doing the DNMS means I'll have to meet my own needs again. I don't want to do that. It's time for someone else to meet my needs."

When child parts voice this concern they need to know that they will not be expected to meet their own needs, the Resources will do that for them.

When adult clients voice this concern they need to know that when a young child gets connection, soothing, and nurturing needs met by parents, in the brain **special neural networks** form (which mimic the loving parents) and **special neural pathways** form (which communicate that mimicked love to other parts of the brain). As parents meet these needs over time, these neural networks and pathways become stronger and better developed, and eventually facilitate self-soothing. When this child is an adult, these neural pathways help in the management of painful emotions, especially at times of crisis or loss. A child who does not get these needs met well, may not develop these neural networks and pathways well enough for self-soothing, and may have great difficulty as an adult, managing even mildly painful emotions. The DNMS appears to help establish these pathways in adulthood. That means that, even if they were not formed well in childhood, they can be formed and strengthened now. The result is an adult brain capable of managing emotions well – the same brain the client would have had if those needs had been met in childhood.

"If I get unstuck from childhood, my abusive parents are off the hook."

Tell the child parts that adults' abusive behavior towards children is never excusable. In a perfect world parents would be held accountable for abusive behavior, but that does not always happen. Fortunately the child parts can get unstuck whether parents pay for their crimes or not.

"The Resources would (or will) eventually abandon me like everyone else has."

The client is probably projecting a wounding role model onto the Resources. Ask client if she is going to abandon her cherished loved one eventually. (There may also be an introject threatening abandonment.)

"Authority figures cannot be fully trusted – not even my Resources."

The client is probably projecting a wounding authority figure onto the Resources. Ask client if she is trustworthy with her cherished loved one. (There may also be an introject who cannot be fully trusted.)

"The Resources would (or will) act just like my wounding parents."

The client is probably projecting wounding parents onto the Resources. Ask client if she wounds her cherished loved one while in her most adult self. (There may also be an introject mimicking dysfunctional parents.)

© Copyright 2009 by Shirley Jean Schmidt, MA, LPC. All rights reserved. Duplication in any form without permission is prohibited.

"The Resources would (or will) expect me to meet their needs."
The client is probably projecting a needy caregiver onto the Resources. Ask client if she expects her cherished loved one to meet her needs. (There may also be a needy parental introject involved.)

"The Resources would (or will) be perpetrators, and I'll be their victim."
The client is probably projecting a perpetrator onto the Resources. Some child parts may only know of two roles in a relationship – perpetrator and victim. Ask client if she victimizes her cherished loved one. (There may also be a perpetrator introject involved.)

"The Resources would (or will) impose their agenda on me."
The client is probably projecting a wounding caregiver onto the Resources. Ask client if she imposes an agenda on her cherished loved one. (There may also be an introject threatening to impose an agenda.)

"If I feel closely connected to the Resources, the intimacy will inevitably lead to betrayal."
The client is probably projecting an earlier betrayal onto the Resources. Ask client if she would ever betray her cherished loved one because of an intimate connection. (There may also be an introject associated with a betrayal.)

"If I connect to Resources or get unstuck, I'll have to be perfect all the time."
Ask client if she would ever expect her cherished loved one to be perfect all the time. Explain client has the freedom to be imperfect after connecting to Resources or getting needs met. (There may also be an introject insisting on perfection.)

"If I connect to Resources or get unstuck, I'll have to meet other's needs at the expense of my own."
Explain that healing involves learning to set good boundaries. Ask client if she would allow her special loved one to meet others' needs at the expense of her own? (There may also be an introject threatening to harm parts that assert themselves.)

"If I connect to Resources or get unstuck, I'll have to disconnect from my family."
Explain that the level of connection to family members will always be the client's choice. There is no fixed, predictable outcome. All options are open and each option gets evaluated on a case-by-case, moment-to-moment basis.

"If I connect to Resources or get unstuck, I'll have to be to be responsible for everything."
Ask the client if she would ever expect her cherished loved one to be responsible for everything. Explain that with the Resources' help, she can learn appropriate responsibility. (There may also be an introject involved insisting on over-responsibility.)

"If I connect to Resources or get unstuck, I'll have to assert myself all the time."
Explain that is not wise to be assertive all the time. Sometimes it is smart to keep quiet. Part of being appropriately protective is knowing when to do which. Ask client if she would expect her cherished loved one to be assertive all the time. (There may also be an introject threatening to harm parts that assert themselves.)

"If I connect to Resources or get unstuck, I'll be more vulnerable. People will take unfair advantage of me."
Explain that being appropriately nurturing is also about setting good boundaries. (There may also be a introject involved that takes unfair advantage of vulnerable people.)

"If I connect to Resources or get unstuck, I'll stop meeting my parents' needs and lose my connection to them."
Explain that while the relationship to parents may change, it is not certain that the connection will be lost. It is more likely that the relationship will improve as she is better able to stay in her most adult self around them. (There may also be an introject threatening rejection.)

"If I connect to Resources or get unstuck, I'll start setting boundaries and people will reject me."
Explain that setting good boundaries can improve relationships. Those who cannot tolerate boundaries do not make good company. (There may also be an introject threatening rejection.)

"If I connect to Resources or get unstuck, I'll come out of hiding. Then people will see how inadequate I am and reject me."
Ask client if she considers herself inadequate caring for her cherished loved one, or if her special loved one sees her as inadequate. (There may also be a rejecting introject involved.)

© Copyright 2009 by Shirley Jean Schmidt, MA, LPC. All rights reserved. Duplication in any form without permission is prohibited.

Appendix C:
Stabilizing Techniques for Unstable Clients

While the DNMS protocols are not inherently risky or likely to destabilize clients, some clients who are highly dissociative are often easily triggered. Guiding fragile clients to connect to loving, supportive Resource ego states will have a stabilizing effect in the long run. When that takes a while to accomplish, a few short-term interventions may be necessary to keep them grounded.

Decompensation is often defined as a stress-induced failure of psychological defense mechanisms. For example, in session you may see a client become overwhelmed with fright, experience sudden-onset nausea, or become frozen and non-verbal. The trigger may be an *external* stressor that you can see, such as a client's divorce papers, or an *internal* stressor that you cannot see, such as a threatening father introject. Clients who decompensate in the middle of a session have usually shifted into a wounded child ego state that does not know the current environment is relatively safe. Once back in an adult ego state, a client will feel more grounded. This book is not intended to teach the complexities of working with highly dissociative clients, but this section will provide a few techniques for stabilizing clients who decompensate in the middle of a session, and for preventing future occurrences.

- ### *Invite the Client Back into Her Most Adult Self*

  This is the simplest intervention. Say to the client something like, "Come back into your most adult self," or "It's safe to come back into your most adult self now. Come back into the present moment." It may be necessary to say it several times.

- ### *Invite Verbal Clients to Describe the Room*

  Invite the client to look around the room. Ask simple questions like, "What color is the carpet? What color is the wall? Is it hot or cold in here? What time does the clock say it is?" This can help pull the client out of the past and into the present moment.

- ### *Invite Non-Verbal Clients to Notice the Room*

  If a client is in a nonverbal state, say things like, "Notice the many colors in the room," "Notice the texture of the sweater you're wearing," "Notice the sensation of your feet touching the floor," and "Notice the sound of the birds singing outside the window." This can help pull a client into the present without having to answer questions.[1]

- ### *Ask Questions the Client Can Answer Only from Her Most Adult Self*

  Ask the client questions she can only answer from her most adult self. For example, "How much do you think this chair cost?" or "Who is the Secretary of State?" or "What is a zip drive?" A question like "What is your mother's name?" would not be helpful, because a child part could answer it. It is better to ask questions *you know* only the adult self can answer. For example, ask a computer professional to describe a zip drive, ask a mechanic to explain fuel injection, and ask a lawyer to explain tort reform. It may be necessary to ask many questions before the client begins to return to an adult ego state.

- ### *Engage the Client in a Sensorimotor Activity*

  Invite the client to engage in a sensorimotor activity. For example, if you have a TASPER, you can invite the client to push and pull on the TASPER. Have her look in your eyes while you smile and say, "Bring yourself back into your most adult self, back into your body, back into this room, back into (2009)." If you're working with a client on the phone, for example, who is in crisis at home, you can have her twist a towel or push on a wall. If there is another person around, the client can push on the person's hands while making eye contact. A sensorimotor activity can help ground the client in the body.

© Copyright 2009 by Shirley Jean Schmidt, MA, LPC. All rights reserved. Duplication in any form without permission is prohibited.

- *Apply the Adult Body Intervention*

  Engage the upset child part in a dialogue. Start by asking to speak to the child part that's upset. Ask how old she is. Then apply the Adult Body Intervention as described on page 65. This can help the child part see that now that she's in an adult body she has power and protection she did not have in childhood.

- *Invite the Client to Notice the Supportive Relationship*

  Invite the client to notice the relationship she has with you.[2] Say something like, "Notice that it's just me and you in the room. The same you that came in today talking about your frustration at work; and the same me that empathically listened to you talk about that frustration." If the client seems frightened, it might help to say, "I can see you're afraid. If you look at me, you'll notice that I'm not afraid. The fear you're experiencing is related to something from the past. Notice there is no danger here in this room right now. (The Resources and) I are completely here for you. Just let that feeling of fear run its course, as you notice we're both safe in this room right now."

- *Connect the Child Part to the Resources*

  If a client has already successfully connected to one or more robust Resources, those Resources can be called upon to comfort an upset child part. Say to the child part something like, "Now little one, notice the Resources are coming to your side right now. Notice they're here to protect you and comfort you. As long as the Resources are here – you're safe. They will not let anything harm you. They understand exactly how you feel right now. Their hearts are filled with empathy and compassion. Notice they're here to provide whatever reassurance and support you need right now." This can help the child part feel supported by competent caregivers. It's helpful to follow this with the Adult Body Intervention (see above). Sometimes, when a client is in a very dissociated state, access to Resource ego states is temporarily blocked. This will not work if a client cannot access her Resource ego states.

- *Calming the Client with a Scent Paired with a Calm State of Mind*

  Our olfactory nerve cells connect directly to the brain's olfactory cortex, where memory and emotion can link with the sense of smell. It can be helpful to pair a *favorable scent* with one or more client *Resources*. For example, after completing the Resource Development Protocol you could invite the client to smell something pleasant, while anchoring (with ABS) *that smell to the good feeling* of being connected to the Resources. Later, when the client is upset about something, smelling the scent will immediately link her to the positive memory and emotion of connecting to the Resources. That can have an instant calming effect. It can be like putting the Resources on speed dial!

  Before a client has connected to her DNMS Resources, you can pair a scent with a Provisional Resource, or with the safety of being in the therapy office. The particular scent is not important, so long as the client likes it. It could be a perfume, spice, or tea. Ideally it should be something the client can keep in a pocket (like a small container of ground cloves), and smell anytime she is distressed.

- *Exchange a Few Jokes*

  This intervention is not a good *starting point*, but once a client has recovered from the extreme upset, exchanging a few quick jokes or stories that have nothing to do with the therapy processing can be a helpful distraction. This can serve to further ground the client in her ordinary, adult state of mind.

- *Switch the Dominance of the Introject Threatening the Child Part*

  Sometimes a client decompensates when a wounded child part perceives a significant internal threat – for example from a hostile introject. Once the child part feels safely contained by the Resources (above intervention) it may help to ask her to look to the right to see who she is reacting to. When an introject appears, you can switch the dominance. This can (at least temporarily) stop the internal threat. You can do this type of crisis intervention in the office and in crisis phone calls.

© Copyright 2009 by Shirley Jean Schmidt, MA, LPC. All rights reserved. Duplication in any form without permission is prohibited.

- **Guide the Client to Establish a Safe Place for all Child Parts to Hang Out**

This intervention can be applied with your more fragile clients in advance of a crisis – ideally within the first few treatment sessions. It can help to *prevent* emotional breakdowns and better *manage* those that do occur. Invite the client to establish a safe place for all the wounded child parts to hang out. This should be a special place, such as a resort, an island, a beach house, a day care, a scout camp, or some other place with positive associations – a place a child would very much want to visit. For example, a place with an art room, a reading room, a play room, a kitchen, bedrooms, a swimming pool, a movie theater, a roller rink, a Ferris wheel, a go-cart course, or anything else the child parts might want. Invite the client to populate the place with many competent caregivers (e.g. the DNMS Resources or Provisional Resources). It should be a fun place where child parts can feel confident they'll get their physical, emotional, and intellectual needs met by the safe setting, and by the Resources stationed there. Once a client has gotten a good mental picture and a positive felt sense about this place, ask if it would feel good to strengthen the good feeling with ABS. Once a client has established this safe place, you can teach her to manage upset child parts during the week by tucking them in to this safe place. When a client decompensates, it may help to send the upset child parts into the arms of Resources who are waiting for them in this safe place. It's important that child parts experience this as a place of wonder that they deserve for being intrinsically good – as opposed to a place of exile for being bad. They must also understand that this is not their final home; rather this is a safe place for them to wait until the DNMS protocols help them heal.

DNMS therapist, Joan Bacon, also uses this safe place intervention. She finds it helpful to place a conference room in this place.[3] (Later it will become the room used in the Conference Room Protocol). Provisional Resource(s) are always there to help child parts feel safe until DNMS Resources have been established. Bacon will invite the child parts to place a blackboard or whiteboard in the room. They are invited to leave messages for her on the board – directly or anonymously. She'll invite the client to check the board for messages just before beginning DNMS work. She finds that this can serve as another effective way to identify processing blocks before beginning a protocol.

This intervention can serve as a significant tool for lovingly containing upset child parts. Some clients may argue that, because this is an imaginary place, it can't really help. Explain that, while this place does not literally exist, it provides real containment for neural networks holding disturbing emotions. All clients who have done this have told me their child parts felt lovingly contained in their safe place. Some have even told me their constant internal chatter stopped when they tucked child parts in to their safe place.

- **Consider a Biological Cause**

Clients who seem to be perpetually unstable, who frequently decompensate, and/or who do not improve with psychotherapy may have an underlying biological cause. What triggers a symptom can give you a clue. For example, a client may feel especially symptomatic a few days before starting her period; after becoming perimenopausal; during the winter months; or right after eating a particular food.

Psychological symptoms can come from medical problems such as hypoglycemia, sleep apnea, malnutrition, seasonal affective disorder, drug/alcohol toxicity, hemochromatosis, mercury toxicity, certain tumors and head injuries, hypothyroidism, and other hormone imbalances. Become informed about the signs of underlying biological problems and be prepared to refer clients for appropriate testing and treatment. Notice these are conditions that anti-depressants will not treat.

Many clients have symptoms caused by *both* childhood wounds and current biological imbalances. For example, an overweight client who manages her childhood incest trauma by eating a lot of processed foods and sugar may experience significant psychological symptoms from malnutrition, unstable blood sugar, and untreated sleep apnea. As long as her body is out of balance, the volume on any unresolved emotional wounds will be much louder. Resolving such biological imbalances can be as important, or even more important, than healing childhood wounds.

1. Suggestion contributed by Donna Stanley and Joan Bacon in 2008.
2. Suggestion contributed by Donna Stanley in 2008.
3. Suggestion contributed by Joan Bacon in 2008.

© Copyright 2009 by Shirley Jean Schmidt, MA, LPC. All rights reserved. Duplication in any form without permission is prohibited.

Appendix D:
Preparing Clients for the DNMS

Screening Clients for the DNMS

While many clients are drawn to the DNMS, some are not. Some clients reject the idea of parts of self, some are dead-set on a particular therapy (e.g. EMDR, hypnosis, CBT) and refuse to discuss DNMS, and some need basic help (e.g. personal safety coaching, trust building) more than DNMS. Some presenting problems are clearly targets for the DNMS, and some are not. For example, unwanted symptoms can come from organic brain dysfunction (e.g. head injury), chronic physical stress (e.g. chemotherapy), and inherent temperament (e.g. hypersensitivity). These conditions can be exacerbated when a maladaptive introject is also a source of problems. The DNMS can help relieve symptoms generated by maladaptive introjects – whether they were formed in childhood or adulthood. But the most significant introjects are formed in childhood around unmet developmental needs. The DNMS can help motivated clients with issues clearly linked to unmet developmental needs and wounding introjects, regardless of the initial diagnosis or ego strength.

Explaining the DNMS to Clients

You have many options for explaining the DNMS to clients. You first option is to tell them about it, without the benefit of visual aids. Since clients seem to understand it better when they see the concepts illustrated, you have a number of visual-aid options. (1) You can give clients the two introductory handouts below (pages 218 and 226). You can go over the material in session, and/or let them take it home to read. (2) You can explain the DNMS background and protocols with the help of the 75-page Flip Chart, which serves as a paper "slide show." (3) You can invite your client to watch the 25-minute, narrated, DNMS slide show at www.dnmsinstitute.com. This slide show describes most of the DNMS. (4) You can invite your client to watch the 1-hour, narrated, slide show that is Module 1 (Background & Overview) of the 7-module DNMS Home Study Course. It's on a CD that you can show clients on your office computer or lend clients to watch at home. It covers all the protocols. (See Appendix F for more information about the Course and the Flip Chart.)

A client's reaction to this information should be considered when determining if the DNMS is the correct intervention. Ego state therapy will not work without a client's belief in, and commitment to, the process. If a client insists she has no ego states, no parts of self, or no parts of self stuck in the past, the DNMS will not be appropriate – even if she does have child parts stuck in the past.

Taking a History for the DNMS

Start treatment by getting a history. Ask about the most significant relationships – especially those from the developing years. Include questions about how family members related to the client (e.g. loving, abusive, neglectful, rejecting, enmeshing); how family members related to themselves (e.g. self-critical, self-sabotaging, self-soothing); how family members related to each other (e.g. mutually supportive, mutually destructive); how family members related to people outside the family (e.g. supportive or destructive); and how people outside the family related to the client (e.g. supportive or destructive). Answers to these questions should give you a pretty good idea of where a client's current strengths and weaknesses have come from.

For the purposes of the DNMS, a primary caregiver is generally defined as anyone who is 100% responsible for a child's well being. This would, of course, include legal guardians (usually parents), but may also include others who assumed a significant role in the care of the client in childhood (e.g. nannies, grandparents). Be especially mindful to collect a lot of information about relationships with clients' primary caregivers. Clients' introjected caregivers are often the most significant factors in their mental health – for better or worse.

© Copyright 2009 by Shirley Jean Schmidt, MA, LPC. All rights reserved. Duplication in any form without permission is prohibited.

The Developmental Needs Meeting Strategy: What It Is and How It Works

Background

The DNMS was developed by Shirley Jean Schmidt, MA, LPC, a psychotherapist in private practice in San Antonio, Texas. It is a therapeutic approach based on what is known about how a child's brain develops within a healthy family. It was designed to treat present-day problems that originated with unmet childhood needs. The DNMS has been found helpful for treating depression, anxiety, panic disorder, social phobias, substance abuse, complex post-traumatic stress disorder, relationship problems, obsessions/compulsions, sexual abuse, eating disorders, dissociative disorders, borderline personality disorder, sexual addiction, self-injurious behavior, and complicated grief. It has also been used to resolve memories of painful physical, emotional, or sexual traumas that were inflicted by a person. A brief explanation of this therapy, its specialized terminology, and the concepts it is built on are presented here.

Getting Stuck in Childhood

This model is based on the assumption that children have physical, emotional, social, and intellectual needs at each stage of development. When caregivers meet those needs well, children thrive. When caregivers fail to meet needs well enough, they suffer. The degree to which developmental needs were not adequately met is the degree to which a child can become stuck in childhood. *Being stuck* means that behaviors, beliefs, or emotions connected to the unresolved childhood wounds of unmet developmental needs can get triggered today. For example, you may feel like an adult one minute – then something upsetting happens and suddenly you see the world through the eyes of a sad, angry, or fearful child. The more stuck we are in childhood, the more we have unwanted behaviors, beliefs, and emotions.

The DNMS is an ego state therapy designed to treat a wide range of motivated clients, regardless of initial diagnosis or ego strength. This includes clients with complex *trauma wounds*, such as those inflicted by verbal, physical, and sexual abuse, and *attachment wounds*, such as those inflicted by parental rejection, neglect, and enmeshment. A child may become stuck even if loving, well-meaning caregivers fail to parent well enough, because: a child's needs are particularly complex or obscure, a caregiver has unresolved emotional issues, a caregiver is under extreme stress, and/or there are hardships (e.g. financial problems, health problems, natural disasters, war) which make it impossible for a caregiver to meet needs he/she would otherwise be able to meet.

Children get confused when their needs are ignored, misunderstood, or trivialized by their caregivers – whether intentionally or unintentionally. When this happens often enough, a child will get stuck in those experiences. When there is a good match between a child's needs and a caregiver's parenting skill, the child will grow up feeling secure. When such a match is not so good, a child may grow up feeling wounded.

Parts of Self

Everyone has parts of self. Perhaps you have experienced ambivalence, where one part of you wants to eat cake while another part wants to diet. You may have noticed that you have different states of mind for different roles – perhaps you have a professional work self, which is different from a playful parent self, which is different from a romantic spouse self.

Healthy parts of self form in response to positive, affirming relationships with caregivers who are loving and attuned. They live in the present; feel and manage the full range of emotions; hold positive beliefs about self and world; engage in appropriate/desirable behaviors; and have an adaptive point of view. *Wounded parts of self* form in response to traumas, and to negative, wounding relationships with caregivers who are abusive, neglectful,

© Copyright 2009 by Shirley Jean Schmidt, MA, LPC. All rights reserved.   Duplication and distribution of this page is allowed.

rejecting, and enmeshing. They live in the past; are stuck in painful emotions; hold negative, irrational beliefs about self and world; engage in unwanted or inappropriate behaviors; and have a maladaptive point of view.

Parts of self that are stuck in the past can have competing agendas, which lead to internal conflicts. These conflicts can generate unwanted behaviors, beliefs, and emotions. The DNMS aims to calm such internal conflicts by getting wounded parts of self unstuck.

DNMS Resource Parts of Self

In the DNMS, special guided meditations are used to help a client connect to three positive, healthy Resource parts of self: a Spiritual Core Self (or Core Self), a Nurturing Adult Self, and a Protective Adult Self.

The Spiritual Core Self: This Resource is considered the core of one's being. It is the part of self experienced during meditation, prayer, yoga, peak spiritual experiences, enlightening near-death experiences, and profound connections with nature. Some people believe this is a part of self that existed before the body arrived and will exist after the body dies. The following qualities, commonly experienced during deep prayer or meditation, are characteristic of the Spiritual Core Self:

- Sense of interconnectedness to all beings
- Sense of completeness and wholeness
- Sense of safety and invulnerability
- No ego, no struggles
- Non-judgmental, non-critical
- All things and events are equally special

- No desires or aversions
- Unconditional, effortless happiness
- Unconditional, effortless acceptance
- Unconditional, effortless loving kindness, compassion
- Timeless, cosmic wisdom and understanding
- Timelessness; present moment is precious and full

Connecting to this Resource does not require a belief in God or spirituality. Clients averse to notions of faith or spirituality can be guided to connect to a *Core Self*. But for those of faith, this Resource would be the part of self that resonates with divine love from a higher power.

The Nurturing & Protective Adult Self: Most people have all the skills needed to be a good enough caregiver, whether they are aware of it or not. A caregiver skill that was applied just once in the past can be applied again in the future. The DNMS uses two guided meditations to heighten awareness of these skills. One meditation strengthens a Nurturing Adult Self (a part of self that can competently nurture a loved one), the other strengthens a Protective Adult Self (a part of self that can competently protect a loved one). The process is anchored in a personal memory of a meaningful relationship – current or past – a favorite time when all or most of the skills on a list of 24 caregiver skills and traits (e.g. empathy, understanding, patience, compassion, courage) were naturally, effortlessly, and appropriately applied.

Healing Circle: Once a client has established each Resource, all three are invited to come together as a team, to form a Healing Circle. Later, wounded child parts will be invited inside the Circle where the Resources will provide the emotional repair necessary to help them get totally unstuck.

The Healing Circle

Spiritual Core Self

Protective Adult Self

Nurturing Adult Self

© Copyright 2009 by Shirley Jean Schmidt, MA, LPC. All rights reserved. Duplication and distribution of this page is allowed.

Reactive Parts of Self

Parts of self that form in reaction to wounding caregivers are called **reactive parts**. Some reactive parts hold raw emotions, like anxiety, terror, anger, sadness, hopelessness, grief, despair, and shame. Some hold details of traumatic experiences. Some reactive parts engage in "coping" behaviors such as overeating, starving, complying, intimidating, overachieving, drinking, withdrawing, etc. All reactive parts have good intentions, no matter how problematic their behavior may be. Clients notice the problems created by reactive parts. These are the problems they want therapy to fix, such as: depression, withdrawing, perfectionism, eating disorders, substance abuse, anxiety, anger, and trauma memories.

Introjects

It is normal for a child to be curious, engaged, and eager to observe and learn from caregivers. Children automatically and unconsciously form mental representations that mirror the caregivers they observe. These mental representations are called **introjects**. Newly discovered *mirror neurons* appear to explain how this happens. It is not a choice; it is a biological reflex. When children mirror caregivers who are supportive, loving, and kind, they thrive. But when children mimic caregivers who are unkind, neglectful, abusive, rejecting, or unable to meet developmental needs, they suffer.

Parts of self that mirror wounding caregivers are called *maladaptive introjects*. These introjects can act out the same abuse, neglect, or dysfunction of the caregiver on other people and/or reactive parts. This is like a child wearing a costume she doesn't like but cannot take off; or playing a role she doesn't like but cannot stop playing. The introject costume's message does not match the child's true nature – to be in respectful harmony with self and others. Maladaptive introjects are very wounded and stuck in the past.

Maladaptive Introject

Reactive Parts and Maladaptive Introjects Interact

In childhood, many unwanted behaviors, beliefs, and emotions get generated by reactive parts in reaction to wounding caregivers, and the maladaptive introjects that mirror them.

When stressful experiences happen in adulthood, the maladaptive introjects that formed in childhood can get activated, and deliver a caregiver's wounding message to reactive parts. This keeps the reactive parts overreacting.

© Copyright 2009 by Shirley Jean Schmidt, MA, LPC. All rights reserved.   Duplication and distribution of this page is allowed.

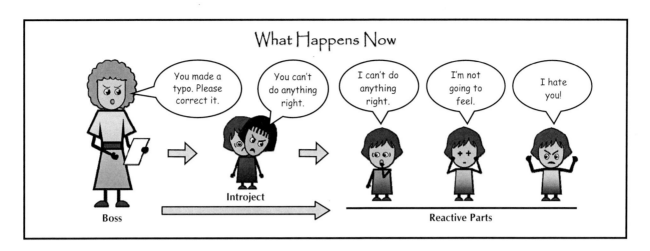

Getting Unstuck

The DNMS focuses a lot of attention on getting maladaptive introjects totally unstuck by guiding the Resources to provide them the emotional repair they need to heal. This repair work involves meeting needs, processing through painful emotions, and establishing an emotional bond. As the Resources provide for these needs, the introjects begin to feel safe, wanted, and loved. As they heal, they stop mirroring the wounding caregiver and begin to express their own good true nature instead. Because their good true nature does not evoke internal conflicts, it does not aggravate reactive parts. As maladaptive introjects heal, they transform into parts of self that are loving and supportive. As they get totally unstuck, the associated reactive parts experience great relief, and their unwanted behaviors, beliefs, and emotions abate.

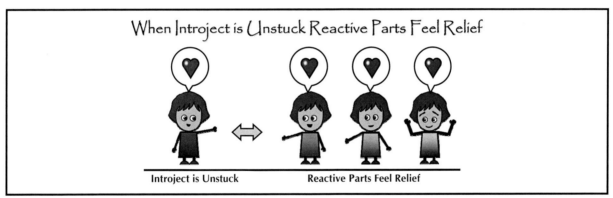

Clients are then better prepared to respond to adulthood stressors without wounded child parts overreacting. Clients can simply respond to their world from their most adult self. No wounded child parts react.

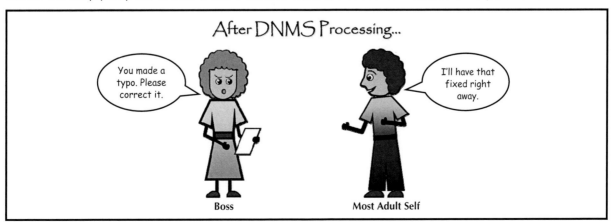

© Copyright 2009 by Shirley Jean Schmidt, MA, LPC. All rights reserved. Duplication and distribution of this page is allowed.

The Switching the Dominance Protocol

This is a multipurpose protocol used often during the DNMS. A maladaptive introject is made up of two components: (1) a costume that mimics an unfriendly caregiver, and (2) an innocent child self underneath, reluctantly wearing it. Initially the costume is dominant. By speaking to the child part under the costume and applying a series of mini-interventions, the therapist can help the child part understand that the costume is just an illusion of that caregiver, and not a real threat at all. As the child part begins to understand this, the costume appears smaller and less important. Eventually it appears so small and so unimportant that the child part can put the remains of it in her pocket and feel control over it for the first time. When this occurs the dominance has been switched from the costume to the child part that was under it.

Selecting Child Parts for Needs Meeting Work

A secure attachment to a primary caregiver is a child's most important developmental need. Unmet attachment needs can be the source of many problems, such as insecurity, anxiety, depression, dissociation, self-sabotage, emotional shutdown, emotional overwhelm, and relationship problems. The DNMS focuses particular attention on identifying and remediating unmet attachment needs. The core of the DNMS is a *Needs Meeting Protocol* that consists of 20 steps. This protocol helps get maladaptive introjects unstuck from the past by meeting their developmental needs. But first the client and therapist will select the most important wounded child parts to process. This selection process often begins with the *Attachment Needs Ladder* questionnaire.

Attachment Needs Ladder

This questionnaire was born from the assumption that the most efficient healing will occur when the most wounding caregiver/introject attachment messages are identified and processed first. It lists negative beliefs a client might acquire in childhood if attachment needs were not met well. They are listed on the Ladder by themes, in order of importance. The themes are:

- Rung 1 – Existence
- Rung 3 – Sense of Self
- Rung 2 – Basic Safety
- Rung 4 – Relationship to Others

Clients are asked to rate how true each negative belief feels, from 0-10, one, at moments when they have felt especially vulnerable. The beliefs are rated and processed one Rung at a time. If/when beliefs on a single Rung are found to feel true, the Conference Room Protocol is used to locate the introjects that keep those beliefs alive.

The Conference Room Protocol

Clients are asked to get a mental picture of a conference room, with a conference table and chairs. The Resources are invited into the conference room. Next, the reactive parts that hold the negative beliefs that

© Copyright 2009 by Shirley Jean Schmidt, MA, LPC.   All rights reserved.   Duplication and distribution of this page is allowed.

were rated above zero on the Attachment Needs Ladder questionnaire (e.g. "I cannot tolerate being alone," "I cannot tolerate criticism," and "I cannot tolerate rejection") are invited into the conference room, to sit on one side of the table. The most upset reactive part is asked to look at the empty spot across the table to see the part of self she is reacting to. The maladaptive introject that is upsetting the reactive part will appear in that spot. Information about the introject, such as the message it is delivering and who it is mimicking, is collected. Then the dominance of the introject is switched. Afterwards the therapist speaks to the next most upset reactive part at the table. This reactive part is asked to look at the empty spot across the table to see the part of self she is reacting to. These steps are repeated until the dominance of each maladaptive introject, associated with each reactive part at the table, has been

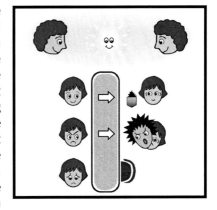

switched. Once this protocol is complete, all parts at the table will feel a sense of relief and the internal disturbance around the targeted issue will be substantially calmed. The client is then invited to select one or more parts of self from the conference room, to begin the Needs Meeting Protocol.

The Needs Meeting Protocol

The Needs Meeting Protocol begins when the selected introjects are invited into the Healing Circle. Once in the circle the therapist will guide the Resources to meet their developmental needs (e.g. safety, love, attunement, nurturing, validation, respect), help them process through painful emotions (e.g. anger and grief), and establish an emotional bond. As the child parts make a loving connection to the Resources, they become totally unstuck from the past.

Resources Meet Developmental Needs

Resources Process Painful Emotions

Resources Form an Emotional Bond

Child Parts Become Totally Unstuck

© Copyright 2009 by Shirley Jean Schmidt, MA, LPC. All rights reserved. Duplication and distribution of this page is allowed.

Follow-up and Repeat the Process

Once the Needs Meeting Protocol is complete the unwanted behaviors, beliefs, and emotions associated with a targeted issue typically abate. Clients are asked follow-up questions to verify a healing shift has occurred. Typically the wounding messages that were delivered by the introject masks are no longer disturbing. The negative beliefs that felt true in the beginning no longer feel true. The targeted issue seems like a much smaller problem. When one issue is resolved, the client is invited repeat these steps with another, then another until all therapy goals have been met.

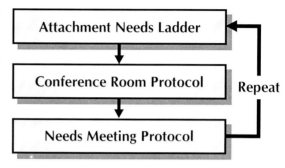

Alternating Bilateral Stimulation

Alternating bilateral stimulation (ABS) is applied throughout the DNMS to strengthen all positive experiences (including enhancing internal resources and positive beliefs about self). In 1989, Francine Shapiro discovered that *rapid side-to-side eye movements* could be used to help desensitize trauma memories. Eye movements became a cornerstone of the Eye Movement Desensitization and Reprocessing (EMDR) therapy. Shapiro also observed that rapid eye movements could help strengthen positive beliefs about self. Both *alternating bilateral tactile and auditory stimulation* were discovered to be effective alternatives to eye movements during EMDR therapy. Now, all three modalities are considered forms of ABS.

Harvard sleep researcher Robert Stickgold proposed that ABS accomplishes the same type of memory consolidation that occurs during rapid eye movement (REM) sleep. During REM sleep associations between neural networks can become activated and strengthened. He postulated that isolated neural networks can more easily connect to positive adaptive neural networks when ABS is applied. The use of ABS during the DNMS appears to help facilitate communication between child parts and Resources, and to strengthen positive feelings and beliefs.

Most clients prefer to do the DNMS with their eyes closed, so ABS is usually applied as alternating bilateral tactile or auditory stimulation. It is usually applied with an electronic device called a *TheraTapper™*. The TheraTapper™ consists of a small control box attached by six-foot wires to two handheld pulsers with small, enclosed motors which vibrate in an alternating fashion. From a six-foot distance, the therapist can change the intensity, length, and speed of the pulses, or start and stop the tactile ABS. The TheraTapper™ pulsers can be applied anywhere on the body bilaterally (e.g. in each hand, under each leg, in each sock). Auditory ABS is usually applied with alternating bilateral sounds or tones coming through headphones.

DNMS versus EMDR: Even though the DNMS uses alternating bilateral stimulation it is neither EMDR nor a form of EMDR. The DNMS protocols have little in common with EMDR protocols. The DNMS is intended for symptoms that grew out of unmet childhood needs - such as neglect, abuse, rejection, enmeshment, and unskillful parenting. EMDR was designed to desensitize trauma, and works best for symptoms related to single-incident traumas that are not related to unmet childhood needs.

How Does the DNMS Work?

The strengths or weaknesses in a relationship between a parent and a child will affect the development of the child's brain. Loving, attuned caregivers will positively influence the way a young brain develops the neural pathways that facilitate the self regulation of emotions. When present, these neural pathways ensure that a child will be able to explore the world, separate from parents, and mature in healthy ways. If these neural pathways are not formed, or not formed well enough, a child will grow up feeling insecure, and the development of normal behaviors (play, exploration, and social interactions) may be impaired. DNMS therapy appears to

© Copyright 2009 by Shirley Jean Schmidt, MA, LPC. All rights reserved.   Duplication and distribution of this page is allowed.

construct – in wounded adults – the neural pathways for the regulation of emotions that should have been formed in childhood. After DNMS therapy, clients report feeling more integrated and whole, and better able to manage their emotions.

Before the DNMS begins, wounded child parts, who are isolated and stuck in the past, suffer with painful issues from unresolved childhood wounds. During the DNMS, they make a healing connection with loving, attuned Resources who are grounded in the present. When the healing is complete, the child parts report feeling totally unstuck. As they interact with the Resources they too come into the present moment. The resulting emotional repair may be accomplished by neural integration.

Unusual Communication Style

Throughout many of the DNMS protocols the therapist communicates directly with individual wounded child parts, and facilitates communication between those child parts and Resources. Because this is not the way people usually talk to each other, it can seem odd at first, but clients get used to it when they see how effective it is.

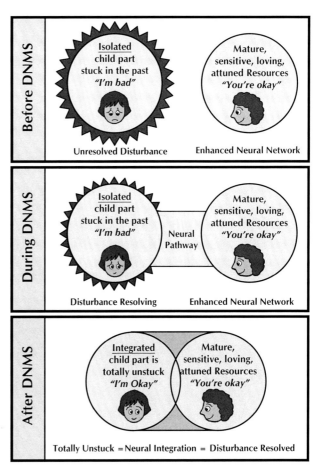

How Long Does DNMS Take?

DNMS is not usually short-term therapy, but it does appear to be efficient, taking much less time than traditional talk therapy. The length of treatment depends on a person's therapy goals, the number of unmet developmental needs, and the availability of internal Resources. Many clients progress quickly, but sometimes fears about the therapy process or outcome can slow the process. Processing blocks can usually be cleared quickly and easily, but sometimes it takes awhile.

Published Research

To date there are currently two published, peer-reviewed journal research articles about the DNMS. The first is the *Developmental Needs Meeting Strategy: A New Treatment Approach Applied to Dissociative Identity Disorder*, published in the Journal of Trauma and Dissociation in December 2004. The second is the *Developmental Needs Meeting Strategy: Eight Case Studies*. Published in *Traumatology* in March 2007. Both articles are posted at the DNMS web site, www.dnmsinstitute.com.

In Conclusion

This description of the DNMS offers hope to adults who may be experiencing unwanted behaviors, beliefs, and emotions that originated in unmet childhood needs. DNMS therapists world-wide have found this model to be an effective means of healing old wounds.

© Copyright 2009 by Shirley Jean Schmidt, MA, LPC. All rights reserved. Duplication and distribution of this page is allowed.

The Needs Meeting Protocol in Pictures

Selecting Ego States for Processing
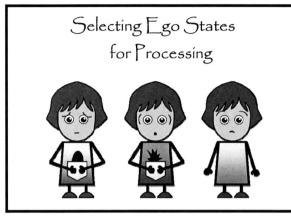

Connecting to the Healing Circle

Into the Healing Circle

Strengthening Sense of Safety

Meeting Needs

Meeting More Needs

Processing Strong Emotions

Resolution of Strong Emotions

© Copyright 2009 by Shirley Jean Schmidt, MA, LPC. All rights reserved. Duplication and distribution of this page is allowed.

The Needs Meeting Protocol in Pictures (continued)

Strengthening Bonds

Strengthening Bonds

Strengthening Bonds

Return to Wounding Experience

Return to Care of Resources

Back and Forth

Strengthening a Positive Belief

Tucking In

© Copyright 2009 by Shirley Jean Schmidt, MA, LPC. All rights reserved. Duplication and distribution of this page is allowed.

Appendix E:

Therapist Worksheets & Forms

Worksheets in Appendix D may be copied and used in
clinical practice by the owner of this book.

Duplication and distribution to others is prohibited.

The handouts, worksheets, and forms from
Appendices D & E are also available to download at
www.dnmsinstitute.com/doc/dnmstherapistworksheets.pdf.

© Copyright 2009 by Shirley Jean Schmidt. All rights reserved. Personal use copy allowed. Distribution without permission is prohibited.

Resource Development Protocol Worksheet

All notes to therapist are in italics. All statements to be spoken to client are in **black bold type**.

Step 1:   ***Explain the Resource Development Protocol***

Define each of the three Resources and briefly describe the meditations to connect to them.

Step 2:   ***Invite Client to Identify Moments of Competently Nurturing and Protecting***

Show the list of 24 skills. Invite client to identify ordinary experiences of applying all skills naturally, effortlessly, and appropriately – at the same time – while in his/her most adult self. Discuss any of the skills on the list that the client is not aware of owning.

Step 3:   ***Discuss Potential Processing Blocks***

Sometimes while connecting to Resources, concerns or fears about the processing will arise. Unconscious fears can be expressed by the sudden arrival of a body disturbance such as unpleasant sensations, dissociation, distracting thoughts, numbness, or sleepiness. That may or may not happen to you, but if it does, please tell me about it, even if it doesn't seem important. You're welcome to have concerns or fears – just let me know if they come up. I'll want to address them right away. Okay?

Step 4:   ***Invite Client to Connect to each Resource – In Client's Preferred Order***

Which Resource would you like to connect to first?
- ❏ *Begin connecting to the Spiritual Core Self*
- ❏ *Begin connecting to the Nurturing Adult Self*
- ❏ *Begin connecting to the Protective Adult Self*

Step 5:   ***Bring All Three Resources Together To Make a Healing Circle***

Picture these three Resources together in a circle, and tell me what you notice. *Then:* **Does it feel like they can work together as a team?**
- *If images or body sensations are disturbing, go to Overcoming Blocks Flowchart.*
- *If images and body sensations are positive, apply ABS and say:* **Notice this. Let it get as strong as it wants to. Tell me when it's strengthened all the way.** *Once fully strengthened say:* **You now have a team of Resources to provide comfort, reassurance, and soothing. In the future these Resources will be able to help wounded child parts get all their needs met.**

Connecting to the Spiritual Core Self

Before beginning <u>any one</u> of the SCS meditations:

When you think about beginning the meditation now, to connect you to your Spiritual Core Self, what do you notice in your body? *If there is no disturbance or a benign disturbance, begin a meditation. If there is a body disturbance suggestive of a block, go to the Overcoming Processing Blocks Flowchart.*

Alternative #1: The Regular Spiritual Core Self Meditation

In a very gentle, slow, soothing voice, say: **(Think about your special, spiritual experience.) Close your eyes (if that's comfortable) and take a deep breath. Now get in touch with the center of your being... that place within you that is quiet... peaceful... and still. And in this place... it's possible you'll connect to your spiritual core. Your spiritual core has been with you from the beginning... it's the essence of who you are... your core of goodness. Pure... resilient... and whole. And your body knows exactly how to connect you. Notice as you connect to this part of you, and when you're ready, tell me what you notice.**
- *If body sensations are disturbing, go to the Overcoming Processing Blocks Flowchart.*
- *If body sensations are positive, apply ABS and say:* **Notice that good feeling. Let it get as strong as it wants to. Tell me when it's strengthened all the way.** *Once fully strengthened ask:* **Do you get a mental picture of this part of you?** *If the mental picture does not appear as light or energy, this may not be the Spiritual Core Self being sought, and another intervention* may be required.*

© Copyright 2009 by Shirley Jean Schmidt. All rights reserved. Personal use copy allowed. Distribution without permission is prohibited.

Alternative #2: The Core Self Meditation

In a very gentle, slow, soothing voice, say: **(Think about your special, transcendent experience.) Close your eyes (if that's comfortable) and take a deep breath. Now get in touch with the center of your being... that place within you that is quiet... peaceful... and still. And in this place... it's possible you'll connect to your core self. Your core self has been with you from the beginning... it's the essence of who you are... your core of goodness. Pure... resilient... and whole. And your body knows exactly how to connect you. Notice as you connect to this part of you, and when you're ready, tell me what you notice.**

- *If body sensations are disturbing, go to Overcoming Processing Blocks Flowchart.*
- *If body sensations are positive, apply ABS and say:* **Notice that good feeling. Let it get as strong as it wants to. Tell me when it's strengthened all the way.** *Once fully strengthened ask:* **Do you have a mental picture of this part of you?** *If the mental picture does not appear as light or energy, this may not be the (spiritual) core self being sought, and another intervention* may be required.*

Alternative #3: Breath Meditation

In a very gentle, slow, soothing voice, say: **There is a place in your mind that is quiet, peaceful, and calm. It's always been there, even though you may never have noticed it. You'll get there by simply watching your breath. First, deliberately inhale, noticing how it takes muscle tension to do this. You have to do a little work to get the air into your lungs. Now release the air, and notice that all you have to do is let go. Just let yourself float down, while the air leaves your body. Notice how good it feels just to let go. Now take another breath, and again notice that muscle tension is needed. Then let go, and just float down. Notice that right at the bottom of your breath, right at the point where you stop exhaling, there is a still moment, a moment where nothing is happening, where all is quiet, calm, peaceful. Okay, now just breathe again, and watch for that point, at the bottom of your breath. Now, breathe again, and this time when you get to the bottom of your breath, just sit there a moment or two, still and quiet, not breathing. Notice what that feels like, what your mind is like: empty, quiet and calm. So, now as you keep breathing, just stay connected to this calm and quiet part of you, now that you've found it... and when you're ready, tell me what you notice.**

- *If body sensations are disturbing, go to Overcoming Processing Blocks Flowchart.*
- *If body sensations are positive, apply ABS and say:* **Notice that good feeling. Let it get as strong as it wants to. Tell me when it's strengthened all the way.** *Once fully strengthened ask:* **Do you have a mental picture of this part of you?** *If the mental picture does not appear as light or energy, this may not be the (spiritual) core self being sought, and another intervention* may be required.*

Alternative #4: Spiritual Core Self List Meditation

In a very gentle, slow, soothing voice, say: **(Think about your special, spiritual experience.) Close your eyes (if that's comfortable) and take a deep breath. Now get in touch with the center of your being... that place within you that is quiet... peaceful... and still. And in this place... it's possible you'll connect to a sense of interconnectedness to all beings... a sense of completeness and wholeness... of safety and invulnerability. A place where all things and events are equally special... a place of no desires or aversions... no ego or struggles. A place of unconditional, effortless, happiness, acceptance. A place of loving kindness and compassion. Notice as you connect to this part of you, and when you're ready, tell me what you notice.**

- *If body sensations are disturbing, go to Overcoming Processing Blocks Flowchart.*
- *If body sensations are positive, apply ABS and say:* **Notice that good feeling. Let it get as strong as it wants to. Tell me when it's strengthened all the way.** *Once fully strengthened ask:* **Do you have a mental picture of this part of you?** *If the mental picture does not appear as light or energy, this may not be the (spiritual) core self being sought, and another intervention* may be required.*

*Possible interventions to apply if the SCS does not appear as light or energy:

- *Invite client to contrast this picture with a picture of the Spiritual Core as a ball of light or energy.*
- *Invite client to "remove" body from the picture to see the Spiritual Core as the light or energy that remains.*
- *Invite client to notice the Spiritual Core is not a loving, divine, higher power (e.g. Jesus); it is the part of self that resonates with love from this higher power.*
- *If client has an aversion to changing the picture, ask:* **If you could comfortably picture your Spiritual Core Self as light or energy, what would you lose or what bad thing would happen?** *Handle any blocks revealed with the Overcoming Processing Blocks Flowchart.*

© Copyright 2009 by Shirley Jean Schmidt. All rights reserved. Personal use copy allowed. Distribution without permission is prohibited.

Connecting to the Nurturing Adult Self

Before beginning the Nurturing Adult Self meditation, ask:

When you think about beginning the meditation now, to connect you to your Nurturing Adult Self, what do you notice in your body? *If there is no disturbance or a benign disturbance, begin the meditation. If there is a body disturbance suggestive of a block, go to the Overcoming Processing Blocks Flowchart.*

The Nurturing Adult Self Meditation:

Think about (*that familiar experience of being naturally, effortlessly, and appropriately nurturing*) **as I name each skill on the list. Nod or say "yes" with each skill you know you possess. Stop me if I name a skill you believe you don't have, or if you feel any discomfort that suggests a block is arising. Close your eyes (if that's comfortable) and take a deep breath. Now get in touch with the following skills and traits, which you already have, including your ability to be empathic... compassionate... understanding... accepting... patient... nurturing... warm... open... able to attune... good at listening... good with boundaries... reliable... trustworthy... confident... respectful... appropriately responsible... problem-solver... action-taker... decision-maker... logical... strong... courageous... protective... and grounded (or centered). Now, bring all these skills together into a single sense of self, your Nurturing Adult Self, and when you're ready, tell me what you notice.**

- *If body sensations are disturbing, go to Overcoming Processing Blocks Flowchart.*

- *If body sensations are positive, apply ABS and say:* **Now I'm going to read the list again, with the** (*TheraTapper*) **on. Again I want you to think about** (*that familiar experience of being naturally, effortlessly, and appropriately nurturing*) **as I name each skill on the list. You don't have to nod or say "yes" this time, just listen to each item and let each strengthen. Stop me if you feel a discomfort that suggests a block is arising. Now get in touch with the following skills and traits, which you already have, including your ability to be empathic... compassionate... understanding... accepting... patient... nurturing... warm... open... able to attune... good at listening... good with boundaries... reliable... trustworthy... confident... respectful... appropriately responsible... problem-solver... action-taker... decision-maker... logical... strong... courageous... protective... and grounded. Now, bring all these skills together into a single sense of self, your Nurturing Adult Self, and tell me when it's strengthened all the way.** *When client says "okay," ask:* **What do you notice?** *OR* **How does that feel in the body?**

  - *If body sensations are disturbing, go to Overcoming Processing Blocks Flowchart.*

  - *If body sensations are positive, apply ABS and say:* **Notice that good feeling. Let it get as strong as it wants to. Tell me when it's strengthened all the way.** *Once fully strengthened ask:* **Do you have a mental picture of this part of you?**

    - *If the mental picture looks like an ordinary picture of the client, in his/her most adult self, nurturing a cherished loved one or holding the potential to nurture a loved one, the Nurturing Adult Self connection is complete.*

    - *If the mental picture portrays the Nurturing Adult Self as something other than self, say:* **For just a moment, hold your mental picture of this (Not-Self) Resource next to an ordinary picture of you nurturing** (*your cherished loved one*)**. Which image feels the most comfortable and powerful in the body?**

      - *If the client prefers to envision this Resource as self, the Nurturing Adult Self connection is complete.*

      - *If the client has an aversion to envisioning this Resource as self, ask:* **If you could comfortably picture your Nurturing Adult Self as who you are caring for** (*your cherished loved one*)**, what would you lose or what bad thing would happen?** *Handle any blocks revealed with the Overcoming Processing Blocks Flowchart.*

© Copyright 2009 by Shirley Jean Schmidt. All rights reserved. Personal use copy allowed. Distribution without permission is prohibited.

Connecting to the Protective Adult Self

Before beginning the Protective Adult Self meditation, ask:

When you think about beginning the meditation now, to connect you to your Protective Adult Self, what do you notice in your body? *If there is no disturbance or a benign disturbance, begin the meditation. If there is a body disturbance suggestive of a block, go to the Overcoming Processing Blocks Flowchart.*

The Protective Adult Self Meditation:

Think about (*that familiar experience of being naturally, effortlessly, and appropriately protective*) **as I name each skill on the list. Nod or say "yes" with each skill you know you possess. Stop me if I name a skill you believe you don't have, or if you feel any discomfort that suggests a block is arising. Close your eyes (if that's comfortable) and take a deep breath. Now get in touch with the following skills and traits, which you already have, starting with your ability to be protective... courageous... strong... logical... decision-maker... action-taker... problem-solver... appropriately responsible... respectful... confident... trustworthy... reliable... good with boundaries... good at listening... able to attune... warm... open... nurturing... patient... accepting... understanding... compassionate... empathic... and grounded (or centered). Now, bring all these skills together into a single sense of self, your Protective Adult Self, and when you're ready, tell me what you notice.**

- *If body sensations are disturbing, go to Overcoming Processing Blocks Flowchart.*

- *If body sensations are positive, apply ABS and say:* **Now I'm going to read the list again, with the** (*TheraTapper*) **on. Again I want you to think about** (*that familiar experience of being naturally, effortlessly, and appropriately protective*) **as I name each skill on the list. You don't have to nod or say "yes" this time, just listen to each item and let each strengthen. Stop me if you feel a discomfort that suggests a block is arising. Now get in touch with the following skills and traits, which you already have, starting with your ability to be protective... courageous... strong... logical... decision-maker... action-taker... problem-solver... appropriately responsible... respectful... confident... trustworthy... reliable... good with boundaries... good at listening... able to attune... warm... open... nurturing... patient... accepting... understanding... compassionate... empathic... and grounded (or centered). Now bring all these skills together into a single sense of self, your Protective Adult Self, and let it get as strong as it wants to. Tell me when it's strengthened all the way.** *When client says "okay," ask:* **What do you notice?** *OR* **How does that feel in the body?**

  - *If body sensations are disturbing, go to Overcoming Processing Blocks Flowchart.*

  - *If body sensations are positive, apply ABS and say:* **Notice that good feeling. Let it get as strong as it wants to. Tell me when it's strengthened all the way.** *Once fully strengthened ask:* **Do you have a mental picture of this part of you?**

    - *If the mental picture looks like an ordinary picture of the client, in his/her most adult self protecting a cherished loved one or holding the potential to protect a loved one, the Protective Adult Self connection is complete.*

    - *If the mental picture portrays the Protective Adult Self as something other than self, say:* **For just a moment, hold your mental picture of this (Not-Self) Resource next to an ordinary picture of you protecting** (*your cherished loved one*). **Which image feels the most comfortable and powerful in the body?**

      - *If the client prefers to envision this Resource as self, the Protective Adult Self connection is complete.*

      - *If the client has an aversion to envisioning this Resource as self, ask:* **If you could comfortably picture your Protective Adult Self as who you are protecting** (*your cherished loved one*), **what would you lose or what bad thing would happen?** *Handle any blocks revealed with the Overcoming Processing Blocks Flowchart.*

© Copyright 2009 by Shirley Jean Schmidt. All rights reserved. Personal use copy allowed. Distribution without permission is prohibited.

The Nurturing Adult Self & Protective Adult Self Skills Defined

Empathic	Able to understand, be aware of, be sensitive to, and vicariously experience the feelings, thoughts, and experiences of others. *
Compassionate	Able to be sympathetically conscious of another's distress, together with a desire to alleviate it. *
Understanding	Able to achieve a grasp of the nature, significance, or explanation of something; able to show a sympathetic or tolerant attitude toward something. *
Accepting	Able to receive willingly, to give admittance or approval to, or to endure without protest or reaction. *
Patient	Able to bear pains or trials calmly or without complaint. Able to manifest forbearance under provocation or strain. Not hasty or impetuous. Steadfast despite opposition, difficulty, or adversity. *
Nurturing	Able to supply nourishment*, both physical and emotional.
Warm	Able to readily show affection, gratitude, cordiality, or sympathy. *
Open	Able to be readily accessible, usually with a generous attitude. Willing to hear and consider. Responsive. Free from reserve or pretense. *
Able To Attune	Able to read nonverbal behavior (body language, tone of voice, and so on) and respond appropriately, with empathy.
Good At Listening	Able to hear something with thoughtful attention and give it consideration. *
Good with Boundaries	Able to set appropriate limits on other's behavior to create safety and comfort for self and others.
Reliable	Able to be relied on, dependable. *
Trustworthy	Able to be trusted. Worthy of confidence, dependable. *
Confident	Self-assured or self-reliant, having confidence in and exercising one's own powers of judgment. *
Respectful	Able to treat someone with respect, giving particular attention or consideration, or showing high regard or esteem. * Able to be courteous.
Appropriately Responsible	Able to answer for one's conduct and obligations. Able to choose between right and wrong.* Not assuming more responsibility than is appropriate.
Problem-Solver	Able to acknowledge a problem and map a plan to get it solved.
Action-Taker	Able to use available resources to take action to solve a problem.
Decision-Maker	Able to select one option, after thoughtful consideration of many.
Logical	Able to reason.* Able to be rational.
Strong	Not easily injured or disturbed, solid; not easily subdued or taken.* Resilient.
Courageous	Able to use mental or moral strength to venture, persevere, and withstand danger, fear, or difficulty. *
Protective	Able to cover or shield from exposure, injury, or destruction. Able to guard. *
Grounded/Centered	Able to be "in the body", in present time, with a sense of peace and stability.

*From Merriam-Webster Online Dictionary, 2002

© Copyright 2009 by Shirley Jean Schmidt. All rights reserved. Personal use copy allowed. Distribution without permission is prohibited.

Switching the Dominance Protocol Worksheet

All notes to therapist are in italics. All statements to be spoken to client are in **black bold type**. *For a thorough explanation of each step and instructions for handling complications, refer to Chapters 4 and 7.*

Step 1: Permission to Speak to the Child Behind the Mask

I'm guessing there's a little one behind that mom costume. Is that right? *Then:* **May I speak to the child behind the** (*role model*) **mask (or costume)?**

Step 2: Welcoming the Child Behind the Mask

Hey little one, I want you to know that I see you, and I know that you're good. And I know the difference between you and this costume. What's it like to hear that? *Then:* **Do you like or need this costume? Does it serve a useful purpose?**

- *If "yes," this is a reactive mimic. Find the introject this part is reacting to and start over at Step 1.*
- *If "no," proceed to Step 3.*

Step 3: Contrasting the True Nature of the Child with the Dysfunction of the Mask

Let's talk about the ways that you're different from this costume. <u>*Tailor about three questions specifically to the costume's message, so the costume will not agree with the child.*</u> *Here are some sample openings:*

Do you believe caregivers should _____ **?**	**Does the costume agree?**
Do you believe it's okay for caregivers to _____ **?**	**Does the costume agree?**
Do you believe children should _____ **?**	**Does the costume agree?**

See how different you are from the costume?

Step 4: Getting the Child Part's Age

So little one, how old are you?

Step 5: Explaining the Illusion of Significance

When you were age ___, your (*role model*) **was real, his/her invalidating, wounding messages were real, and the wounds his/her messages inflicted were real. While your** (*role model*) **was behaving this way, your brain was making a recording of him/her; like filming a home movie. That recording became encapsulated in the mask. So the mask looks and sounds like your** (*role model*)**, but it's not your** (*role model*)**. It's just a recording of him/her behaving this way. But every time this recording plays, it evokes some very painful emotions. Right? That emotional reaction creates the illusion that the costume is real, important, and wounding, just like your** (*role model*) **was. Now watching a scary movie may make you feel afraid, but that doesn't mean you're really in danger, does it – because a movie is not real life. And this mask isn't real life either. If you don't like a movie, you can turn it off. When you understand the truth – that this mask it is no more real than a movie, you can turn it off. How does that sound?**

Step 6: Checking on the Appearance of the Mask

Does the costume look any different now? *The first time it looks different say:* **See? It already appears less important. That's proof what I'm saying is true.**

Step 7: Mini-Interventions Help Shift Dominance

Use any one or all of these interventions, to eliminate the animation, and to reduce it to pocket size.

- *Ask the Resources:* **So little one, ask the Resources if they believe the costume can hurt you now?** *When they say the costume is not dangerous, ask:* **What's it like to hear them say that?** *Recheck costume's appearance.*
- *Adult Body Intervention:* **Do you know you're in an adult body now? Look at your hands (or look in this mirror). Is this what you expected to see?** *If "no" say something like:* **As a child your parents were in total control of your life, weren't they? They told you what to eat, when to eat it, what to wear, when to sleep. They were in control of who came to the house and who you spent time with. The younger you were, the more control they had. Right? But now that you're in an adult body, you make those decisions. You decide**

© Copyright 2009 by Shirley Jean Schmidt. All rights reserved. Personal use copy allowed. Distribution without permission is prohibited.

what to eat, when to eat it, what to wear, when to sleep. You decide who to spend time with and who to stay away from. What's it like to think about that?   *Recheck costume's appearance.*

- *Photo not dangerous:* **If I gave you to hold, either a** (*scorpion*) **or a photo of a** (*scorpion*), **which would you choose?** *When child part says "photo," ask:* **Why?**   *Recheck costume's appearance.*

- *More metaphors:* **Notice the costume is just a hologram. You can pass your hand right through it.**   *OR* **The costume is about a real as a character in a novel.** *OR* **The costume is like a tape recording or a photo of your** (*role model*). *Recheck costume's appearance.*

- *Additional validation:* **When you were age ___, your** (*role model*) **was real, his/her invalidating, wounding messages were real, and the wounds his/her messages inflicted were real. But notice that, unlike your real** (*role model*), **this costume is no more real than a movie.** *Recheck costume's appearance.*

- *Once all the animation is gone, suggest the child play with the costume.* **Grab a corner of that fabric and wave it around your head and dance, as the Resources play some peppy music.** *OR* **Lay out what's left of the costume on the floor and dance on it.**   *Recheck costume's appearance.*

Step 8: Assessing the Mask's Animation

If I were to poke at the costume, what would happen? Would it try to kick me, would it yell at me?
If animation is gone <u>and</u> costume is smaller than a lunchbox, go to Step 9. Otherwise return to Step 7.

Step 9: Highlighting the Child Part's Importance

So little one, who's in charge now, you or what's left of the costume? Who's alive and real, you or what's left of the costume? Who matters now, you or what's left of the costume? Who has power now, you or what's left of the costume? *Recheck costume's appearance.*

- *If costume is small enough to pocket, and is devoid of a role model image, go to Step 10.*
- *If costume is too large to pocket, or has a bit of role model image remaining, return to Step 7.*

Step 10: Pocketing the Remains

Would you have any aversion to putting what's left of the costume it in your pocket now?

- *If there is <u>any aversion</u>, hesitation, or reluctance at all – even subtle, return to Step 7.*
- *If there is <u>no aversion</u>, say:* **Now put it in your pocket. Does that feel okay? Now pat on your pocket and say "I'm in charge now."** *Apply ABS.* **Tell me when that's strengthened all the way.**

Step 11: Orienting the Child Part and Tucking In

- *If doing the Conference Room Protocol:* **I'd like to help you get totally unstuck from the remains of this costume, at the perfect time. I'm not sure when that will be – hopefully soon. In the meantime, let's check across the table and see how the** (*x-year-old*) **reactive part is doing.** *Say to the reactive part something like:* **A few minutes ago, you reported feeling pretty stuck. Between 0-10, how stuck are you feeling right now?** *Record this new rating on the Conference Room Map.*

- *If clearing a Resource Development block:* **The Resources we're working on establishing will be able to help you get totally unstuck from this costume at the perfect time. Would you be willing to tuck in for a while now, so I can finish getting the Resources ready? Find a nice warm safe place to tuck in to – a good, safe, place to wait until the next time you're needed.**

- *All other processing:* **I'd like to help you get totally unstuck from this costume at the perfect time. I'm not sure when that will be, hopefully soon. Would you be willing to tuck in for now? Find a nice warm safe place to tuck in to. You can tuck in with the Resources if you like. Just find a good, safe, place to wait until the next time you're needed.**

Step 12: Temporary Nature of the Shift

While this intervention has helped this little one get partly unstuck from the mask, we'll have to do the Needs Meeting Protocol later, to help her get totally unstuck. Until then, the mask could reanimate and start delivering the ugly message again. But even if that happens it's STILL harmless, and we can easily switch the dominance back again, in just a few minutes.

© Copyright 2009 by Shirley Jean Schmidt. All rights reserved. Personal use copy allowed. Distribution without permission is prohibited.

The DNMS Attachment Needs Ladder

Client Name: _____   Start Date: _____

To administer this questionnaire: This is a list of negative beliefs wounded children might acquire in childhood when attachment needs are not met well. Show these pages to your client. Point out that the four Rungs (Existence, Basic Safety, Sense of Self, and Relationship to Others) are listed in order of importance. Explain you will address one Rung or Section at a time, eliciting 0-10 ratings on each statement. A rating of 10 means a statement feels totally true. Discuss various prompts you might employ to ensure ratings come only from *wounded* parts of self. A prompt might focus attention on ***disturbing childhood events***, ***disturbing recent events***, or ***disturbing future events***. Write below each prompt you use. Once a Rung or Section has been rated, invite the client to disclose and rate any additional beliefs relevant to that theme.

Rung 1 – Existence

When you think about_____
_____
_____does the statement_____feel true?

O R

Are there any wounded child parts that believe the statement _____ is true?

A N D

If yes, How true does it feel when it feels the most true?

	Date:	Date:	Date:	Date:	Date:
1. I don't exist.	___	___	___	___	___
2. I shouldn't exist.	___	___	___	___	___
3. It's not safe to exist.	___	___	___	___	___
4. I don't deserve to exist.	___	___	___	___	___
5. Shame on me for existing.	___	___	___	___	___
6. I'm so alone, there's no point in existing.	___	___	___	___	___
7. My existence is completely irrelevant.	___	___	___	___	___
8. My existence is completely unimportant.	___	___	___	___	___
9. My existence is completely unacceptable.	___	___	___	___	___
10. _____.	___	___	___	___	___
11. _____.	___	___	___	___	___
12. _____.	___	___	___	___	___

Rung 2 – Basic Safety

Section A: Physical (and/or Sexual) Safety

When you think about_____
_____
_____does the statement_____feel true?

O R

Are there any wounded child parts that believe the statement _____ is true?

A N D

If yes, How true does it feel when it feels the most true?

	Date:	Date:	Date:	Date:
1. There is no safe place for me - *physically (and/or sexually).*	___	___	___	___
2. I am completely vulnerable - *physically (and/or sexually).*	___	___	___	___
3. Everyone is frightening - *physically (and/or sexually).*	___	___	___	___
4. Everyone is dangerous - *physically (and/or sexually).*	___	___	___	___
5. I don't deserve to be safe - *physically (and/or sexually).*	___	___	___	___
6. Everyone is out to *physically (and/or sexually)* hurt me.	___	___	___	___

© Copyright 2009 by Shirley Jean Schmidt. All rights reserved. Personal use copy allowed. Distribution without permission is prohibited.

7. I must mistrust everyone to stay *physically (and/or sexually)* safe.   ____ ____ ____ ____

8. I must hide to stay *physically (and/or sexually)* safe.   ____ ____ ____ ____

9. I must be invisible to stay *physically (and/or sexually)* safe.   ____ ____ ____ ____

10. I must be a pleaser or peacemaker to stay *physically (and/or sexually)* safe.   ____ ____ ____ ____

11. I must be intimidating to stay *physically (and/or sexually)* safe.   ____ ____ ____ ____

12. I must keep my guard up all the time to stay *physically (and/or sexually)* safe.   ____ ____ ____ ____

13. I must be ready to threaten or attack all the time, to stay *physically (and/or sexually)* safe.   ____ ____ ____ ____

14. _____ .   ____ ____ ____ ____

15. _____ .   ____ ____ ____ ____

Section B: Emotional Safety

When you think about_____

_____   **O R**   Are there any wounded child parts that believe the statement ____ is true?   **A N D**   *If yes,* How true does it feel when it feels the most true?

_____does the statement_____feel true?

	Date:	Date:	Date:	Date:
1. There is no safe place for me - *emotionally*.	____	____	____	____
2. I am completely vulnerable - *emotionally*.	____	____	____	____
3. Everyone is frightening - *emotionally*.	____	____	____	____
4. Everyone is dangerous - *emotionally*.	____	____	____	____
5. I don't deserve to be safe - *emotionally*.	____	____	____	____
6. Everyone is out to *emotionally* hurt me.	____	____	____	____
7. I must mistrust everyone to stay *emotionally* safe.	____	____	____	____
8. I must hide to stay *emotionally* safe.	____	____	____	____
9. I must be invisible to stay *emotionally* safe.	____	____	____	____
10. I must be a pleaser or peacemaker to stay *emotionally* safe.	____	____	____	____
11. I must be intimidating to stay *emotionally* safe.	____	____	____	____
12. I must keep my guard up all the time to stay *emotionally* safe.	____	____	____	____
13. I must be ready to threaten or attack all the time, to stay *emotionally* safe.	____	____	____	____
14. _____ .	____	____	____	____
15. _____ .	____	____	____	____

Rung 3 – Sense of Self

Section A: Personal Identity

When you think about_____

_____   **O R**   Are there any wounded child parts that believe the statement ____ is true?   **A N D**   *If yes,* How true does it feel when it feels the most true?

_____does the statement_____feel true?

	Date:	Date:	Date:	Date:
1. I don't have a self.	____	____	____	____
2. I shouldn't have a self.	____	____	____	____

© Copyright 2009 by Shirley Jean Schmidt. All rights reserved. Personal use copy allowed. Distribution without permission is prohibited.

3. I don't deserve to have a self.
4. Shame on me if I want a self.
5. I must not be seen or heard.
6. I must not grow.
7. I must not individuate.
8. I must not have needs.
9. I don't matter.
10. I must rely on others to tell me who I am.
11. I must rely on others to tell me what I feel. (e.g. angry, sad)
12. I must rely on others to tell me what I like. (e.g. red vs. blue)
13. I must rely on others to tell me what to believe.
14. It's acceptable for me to be an object, but not a person.
15. _____ .
16. _____ .

Section B: Enmeshment

When you think about_____
_____
_____does the statement_____feel true?

O R

Are there any wounded child parts that believe the statement _____ is true?

A N D

If yes, How true does it feel when it feels the most true?

Date: Date: Date: Date:

1. I must let others smother or engulf me.
2. I must not set or maintain interpersonal boundaries.
3. I must do for others, even when it's not good for me.
4. _____ .
5. _____ .

Rung 4 – Relationship to Others

Section A: Preoccupied Attachment – *Needs too much closeness*

When you think about_____
_____
_____does the statement_____feel true?

O R

Are there any wounded child parts that believe the statement _____ is true?

A N D

If yes, How true does it feel when it feels the most true?

Date: Date: Date: Date:

1. I must depend on others to feel secure.
2. I must get lots of attention from others to feel secure.
3. I must be emotionally close to others to feel secure.
4. I cannot tolerate being alone.
5. I cannot tolerate rejection.
6. I cannot tolerate people leaving me.

© Copyright 2009 by Shirley Jean Schmidt. All rights reserved. Personal use copy allowed. Distribution without permission is prohibited.

7. I cannot tolerate criticism.
8. Others must comfort me when I'm feeling upset or insecure, because I cannot comfort myself.
9. Others must meet my emotional needs, because I cannot.
10. _____ .
11. _____ .
12. _____ .

Section B: Preoccupied and/or Dismissive Attachment

When you think about_____ _____ _____does the statement_____feel true?

O R

Are there any wounded child parts that believe the statement _____ is true?

A N D

If yes, How true does it feel when it feels the most true?

	Date:	Date:	Date:	Date:

1. I am, and always will be, completely alone.
2. People will accept me if I don't have needs.
3. People will reject me if I have needs.
4. People will inevitably ignore me.
5. People will inevitably disappoint me.
6. People will inevitably reject me.
7. People will inevitably abandon me.

Section C: Dismissive Attachment – *Needs too much distance*

When you think about_____ _____ _____does the statement_____feel true?

O R

Are there any wounded child parts that believe the statement _____ is true?

A N D

If yes, How true does it feel when it feels the most true?

	Date:	Date:	Date:	Date:

1. I must rely solely on myself.
2. I must not depend on others.
3. I must not get emotionally close to others.
4. I must not let others get emotionally close to me.
5. I must not ask for comfort, advice, or help.
6. I must not share my private thoughts/feelings.
7. I must not show others how I feel deep down.
8. I must comfort myself when I'm upset, because others cannot.
9. I must meet my own emotional needs, because others cannot.
10. _____ .
11. _____ .
12. _____ .

© Copyright 2009 by Shirley Jean Schmidt. All rights reserved. Personal use copy allowed. Distribution without permission is prohibited.

The Conference Room Map

Client _____ Date Began _____

Rung or Current Problem _____

Age _____

Mood _____

Stuck now? _____

After SDP? _____

After NMP? _____

Introject of _____ Part's age _____

Message _____

_____

_____

_____

0-10, how disturbing is message now? _____ After NMP? _____

Dominance switched? ❑ Partial _____ ❑ Complete _____
                                    date   date

Age _____

Mood _____

Stuck now? _____

After SDP? _____

After NMP? _____

Introject of _____ Part's age _____

Message _____

_____

_____

_____

0-10, how disturbing is message now? _____ After NMP? _____

Dominance switched? ❑ Partial _____ ❑ Complete _____
                                    date   date

Age _____

Mood _____

Stuck now? _____

After SDP? _____

After NMP? _____

Introject of _____ Part's age _____

Message _____

_____

_____

_____

0-10, how disturbing is message now? _____ After NMP? _____

Dominance switched? ❑ Partial _____ ❑ Complete _____
                                    date   date

Age _____

Mood _____

Stuck now? _____

After SDP? _____

After NMP? _____

Introject of _____ Part's age _____

Message _____

_____

_____

_____

0-10, how disturbing is message now? _____ After NMP? _____

Dominance switched? ❑ Partial _____ ❑ Complete _____
                                    date   date

Age _____

Mood _____

Stuck now? _____

After SDP? _____

After NMP? _____

Introject of _____ Part's age _____

Message _____

_____

_____

_____

0-10, how disturbing is message now? _____ After NMP? _____

Dominance switched? ❑ Partial _____ ❑ Complete _____
                                    date   date

There may not be a 1-to-1 correlation between **negative belief** and **reactive part** and **introject**. For example, 3 beliefs may be held by 1 reactive part; 1 reactive part may be reacting to 2 introjects; 2 reactive parts may be reacting to 1 introject. Use as much or as little of this template as needed. Use additional pages if needed.

Conference Room Protocol Worksheet

*All notes to therapist are in italics. All statements to be spoken to client are in **black bold type**. For a thorough explanation of each step and instructions for handling complications, refer to Chapters 5 and 7.*

Select a Target Issue

Invite your client to select a target issue, either a specific current problem or old attachment wounds. If choosing a current problem, the client may opt to make and rate a list of associated negative beliefs. If choosing to work on old attachment wounds, have the client rate a Rung of the Attachment Needs Ladder.

Step 1: Explain the Process for the First Time

Provide a general overview of all the options and steps for selecting ego states for processing. Then invite your client to choose a target issue, either a specific current problem or old attachment wounds. Just before starting the Conference Room Protocol with a client the first time, go over each of the following points: (a) there may or may not be one reactive part per belief, (b) client must accurately disclose how the reactive parts look coming into the conference room, whether or not the mental picture makes sense, (c) there may or may not be one introject per reactive part, (d) a reactive part that appears across the table (instead of an introject) will be asked to report who he/she is reacting to, and (e) the reactive parts are separate and distinct from the child parts wearing costumes. (This point should be made with a color-coded drawing.)

Step 2: Record Information in the Conference Room Map

Start filling in the Conference Room Map Template with the client's name, date, and issue or Rung.

Step 3: Connect to Resources

Connect to your Resources. (Let me know if you need my help connecting.) Tell me when you're connected. *Once connected, apply ABS.* **Tell me when that's strengthened all the way.** *Once strengthened, stop ABS.*

Step 4: Picture the Conference Room

Picture a conference room with a table and chairs. Now picture the Resources in the conference room. Tell me when you've got the picture.

Step 5: Check for Processing Blocks

When you think about beginning this conference room work with the child parts connected with (the target issue), for the purpose of identifying and working with the associated introjects, what do you notice in your body now?

- *If the body is clear, go to Step 6.*
- *If disturbing body sensations indicating a processing block is present, ask:* **Would it help if we were to erect a protective glass wall or one-way mirror across the middle of the conference room, so you would be protected from any introjects that shows up at the table?** *If "yes" say:* **Good, we'll do that. We can also place Resources on both sides of the table.**

  - *If this calms the concern go to Step 6.*
  - *If this does not calm the concern, go to the Overcoming Processing Blocks Flowchart.*

Step 6: Invite Parts Into the Conference Room

- *If processing with a list of negative beliefs say:* **I'd like to invite into the conference room, to sit on one side of the table, all the parts of self who believe the following statements....** *then read the list.* **When you're ready, tell me what you notice.**

- *If processing without a list of negative beliefs say:* **I'd like to invite into the conference room, to sit on one side of the table, all the reactive parts who are connected to (the problem). When you're ready, tell me what you notice.**

*Record any available details (e.g. mood, age) on the **Conference Room Map**.*

© Copyright 2009 by Shirley Jean Schmidt. All rights reserved. Personal use copy allowed. Distribution without permission is prohibited.

Step 7: Engage the Most Upset Reactive Part

Which reactive part seems to be the most upset now? (*or* Which reactive part needs my attention first?) *Then:* May I speak to this part? *When permission is granted, say to this part:* Welcome, I'm glad you're here. How old are you? What kind of mood are you in? *Then:* I'm guessing you've been stuck in the past a long time. Is that right? *When part answers "yes" ask:* 0-10, how stuck are you?

Record these answers on the Conference Room Map and draw in a face to represent the part's mood.

I'd like to help you get unstuck, and you can help me. When you're ready, take a look at that empty spot across the table from you. In a moment you'll see appear in that spot the part (or parts) of self that you're reacting to. When you're ready, tell me what you notice.

Step 8: Classify the Part of Self that Appears Across the Table

When a part appears ask something like: What does this part look like? What is it saying? What kind of mood is it in?

- *If it appears as a metaphor (e.g. a monster, witch, blankness, darkness) ask:* Does (this metaphor) have a message for you? *Then:* Does this message remind you of someone?
- *If it is silent, ask:* If this part's body language or facial expression could be translated into words, what would that message be?

Determine whether this is another reactive part *or* an introject. *See Clues to Classifying Parts of Self table below. If in doubt, ask:* Are you reacting to someone or mimicking someone?

If another reactive part appears say: I'd like for you to move to the other side of the table, to sit with the other reactive parts. Would that be okay? *Once the reactive part has moved, say:* Welcome, I'm glad you're here. How old are you? What kind of mood are you in? *Then:* I'm guessing you've been stuck in the past a long time. 0-10, how stuck are you? *Record these answers on the Conference Room Map and draw in a face to represent the part's mood.* I want to help you get unstuck, and you can help me do that. When you're ready, take a look at that empty spot across the table from you. In a moment you'll see appear in that spot the part (or parts) of self that you're reacting to. When you're ready, tell me what you notice. *Again determine whether the part that appears across the table is definitely a reactive part or probably an introject.*

When a presumptive introject appears, proceed to Step 9.

Step 9: Collect Information about the Presumptive Introject

Ask the reactive part (or client) something like: Who is this part mimicking? What message is this part conveying? 0-10, how disturbing is this message now? What mood is this part conveying?

Record this information on the Conference Room Map. Draw the mask's expression.

> **NOTE:** The **wounding message** should reveal one or more of the following:
> – Contempt for the child.
> – A threat to emotional safety.
> – A threat of physical harm.
> – An inappropriate assignment of responsibility.
> – A caregiver's negative belief about self.
> – A faulty notion about the world.

Step 10: Switch the Dominance

Go to the Switching the Dominance Protocol Worksheet. When the dominance has been switched, go to Step 11 below.

Step 11: Repeat Steps 7-10

Repeat Steps 7-10 until all the reactive parts at the table have identified all the associated introjects. Then double check that all the reactive parts are actually in the conference room.

- *If processing* with *a list of negative beliefs say:* I'm going to re-read the list of negative beliefs you endorsed. Let me know if you feel we've identified all the reactive parts connected to these statements. If we've left anyone out, let me know, so we can bring them into the conference room now. *Then re-read the list.*

- *If processing* without *a list of negative beliefs ask:* Are you aware of any additional reactive parts connected to (this problem)?

If one or more additional reactive parts *are identified, repeat Steps 7-10 with each new part. If* no additional reactive parts *are identified, proceed to Step 12.*

© Copyright 2009 by Shirley Jean Schmidt. All rights reserved. Personal use copy allowed. Distribution without permission is prohibited.

Step 12: Prepare for the Needs Meeting Protocol

Now we're ready to start the needs meeting work. There are (x) introjects and (y) reactive parts at the conference table. Ultimately we'll want to process all (x) introjects. We can work with one at a time, or we could work with several together. In addition, we can process one or more of the reactive parts along with the introjects, but they will likely get totally unstuck automatically as the introjects heal – so including them in the needs meeting work is optional. What do you think would be best?

- *If starting the Needs Meeting Protocol later, tuck in all parts with:* **Thanks to each of you for your hard work today. I'd like each of you to find a nice warm safe cozy place to tuck in to. You can tuck in separately, each with your very own set of Resources, or tuck in as a group. Just find a good safe place to wait until the next time you're needed.**

- *If starting the Needs Meeting Protocol immediately, tuck in just the parts that the client has chosen to exclude from the processing.* **I'd like to invite** (name each one) **to find a nice warm safe cozy place to tuck in to. You can tuck in separately, each with your very own set of Resources, or tuck in as a group. Just find a good safe place to wait until the next time you're needed.**

Then say to the chosen child parts remaining in the room: **Let's take the table out of the room. Little ones, gather together in the center of the room, and let the Resources surround you.**

Then: **When you think about beginning the Needs Meeting Protocol now, to help these little ones get totally unstuck, what do you notice in your body?**

- *If the body has a* <u>disturbing sensation</u> *indicating a processing block is present, go to the* **Overcoming Processing Blocks Flowchart.**
- *If the body is* <u>clear</u>*, start the Needs Meeting Protocol with Step 4:* **Does it feel safe here with the Resources? Notice that sense of safety. Tell me when it's strengthened all the way.**

Clues to Classifying Parts of Self

Clues That Differentiate Introjects & Reactive Parts	Powerless Reactive Part	Controlling Reactive Part	Controlling Reactive Mimic	Maladaptive Introject
Part (mask) looks like wounding role model.	No.	No.	Yes.	Yes.
Conveys wounding message (typically a "you" message).	No.	Yes – In reaction to a role model's message.	Yes –Mimicking a role model's message.	Yes –Mimicking a role model's message.
Reacting or mimicking?	Reacting.	Reacting.	Both.	Mimicking.
Mask (or costume) present.	Maybe.	Maybe.	Yes.	Yes.
Issues warnings, threats, commands, or admonitions.	No.	Yes.	Only if the wounding role model issued them.	Only if the wounding role model issued them.
Reveals behaviors, beliefs, or emotions suggestive of being wounded. ("I" statements).	Yes.	No.	No.	Not usually.
Mask is part of a valued coping strategy created by child part wearing it. *	If a mask is present – yes.	If a mask is present – yes.	Yes.*	No.*

*Assessed in Step 2 of the **Switching the Dominance Protocol**

© Copyright 2009 by Shirley Jean Schmidt. All rights reserved. Personal use copy allowed. Distribution without permission is prohibited.

Needs Meeting Protocol Worksheet

All notes to therapist are in italics. All statements to be spoken to client are in **black bold type**. *For a thorough explanation of each step and instructions for handling complications, refer to Chapters 6 and 7.*

Say to clients new to the protocol:

- **Sometimes during this protocol, concerns or fears about the processing will arise. Unconscious fears can be expressed by the sudden arrival of a body disturbance such as unpleasant sensations, dissociation, distracting thoughts, numbness, or sleepiness. That may or may not happen to you, but if it does, please tell me about it, even if it doesn't seem important. You're welcome to have concerns or fears – just let me know if they come up. I'll want to address them right away.**

- **During this protocol, the Resources will be meeting needs in present time – in (20XX). Please let me know, if at any point, your mental pictures suggest the Resources are meeting needs in the past, rather than in present time. For example, if you picture the Resources meeting needs in your childhood home. We want to make sure that child parts are getting their needs met in the Healing Circle now, because the Resources can't change the past.**

- **At some point during this protocol, painful emotions will likely come up. One option for processing emotions gets the body involved. I suggest doing this by** (*pulling on this TASPER*). **This intervention is based on the idea that a child being physically or emotionally wounded has an urge to fight or flee. When fighting back is forbidden, or physically impossible, the urge gets submerged in the body – often for years.** (*Pulling on the TASPER*) **involves the body in the processing. It helps to express and resolve the physical and emotional tension. If we get to a point that it might help to use this, I'll ask you if you want to try it. I'm just letting you know about it now, so I don't have to interrupt the processing to tell you about it later.**

- **I'll be asking a lot of questions as we go through the protocol. Most of them will be addressed to the child parts we'll be working with. It's very important that each question is answered honestly and authentically. If I ask a question you cannot answer, just tell me you don't know the answer. For example, if I ask what a child part looks like, and you can't see the part, don't tell me what you think it should look like, tell me you can't see it. It's important for the child parts to personally feel the Resources meeting their needs. Let me know if they don't. If we engage in a protocol step that you don't like, or if you start to feel uncomfortable, please tell me. As soon as I know about a processing problem I can take steps to fix it.**

Step 1: Connecting to Resources   ABS On

Set up for ABS as needed (e.g. adjust TheraTapper ™ settings to suit client).
Connect to your Resources. (Let me know if you need my help connecting.) Tell me when you're connected. *Once connected, apply ABS and say:* **Let that get as strong as it wants to. Tell me when it's strengthened all the way.** *When the client says "okay," stop ABS.*

Step 2: Checking for Processing Blocks   ABS Off

When you think about beginning the needs meeting work now, with (*the selected parts of self connected to the target issue*), **what do you notice in your body?**

- *If the body is* clear *go to Step 3.*
- *If the body is a* little apprehensive but not blocked *go to Step 3.*
- *If the body is* contracted or uncomfortable *go to the* **Overcoming Processing Blocks Flowchart**.

Step 3: Inviting the Child Parts into the Healing Circle   ABS Off

Inviting Introjects Forward

First orient the client with: **By the time we had finished switching the dominance of these introjects, all the masks were pocketed. When I invite them forward today, the masks might still be pocketed, they might be a little bigger than before, or they might be big again – completely reanimated. As each introject comes forward, tell me what you notice.**

Invite each introject, one at a time: **I'd like to invite to approach the Resources, the** (*x-year-old*) **we worked with** (*last week*), **the one that was mirroring your** (*wounding role model*), **delivering the message,** (*You're not good enough*). **When you're ready, tell me what you notice.** *When the part appears ask the client:* **What do**

© Copyright 2009 by Shirley Jean Schmidt. All rights reserved. Personal use copy allowed. Distribution without permission is prohibited.

you notice? Is the mask still in the pocket? *Then speak with the child part wearing the costume:* **Hey little one. Thanks for coming. Take a look at the Resources. Do they look safe to you?** *Then:* **Would you like to get up close... right in between them?** *Then:* **Good. Move in close.** *Once inside the circle ask:* **Does it feel safe here?** *Then:* **Good. (Just hang out here. I'll be back with you in a moment.)**

Once all the introjects are in the Healing Circle, begin inviting any reactive parts forward. If none have been selected, go to Step 4.

Inviting Reactive Parts Forward

Invite all the selected reactive parts at once, by age and mood (e.g. sad, angry, fearful).

I'd like to invite to approach the Resources, the (<u>sad x-year-old</u>)**, the** (<u>fearful x-year-old</u>) **and the** (<u>angry x-year-old</u>)**.** *Once they have come forward ask:* **Do the Resources look safe? Would you like to get up close?**

Then: **Good. Move in close.** *Once inside the circle ask:* **Does it feel safe here?** *If it feels safe, go to Step 4.*

Step 4: Strengthening the Sense of Safety   (ABS On)

Apply ABS and say to the child parts: **Notice the sense of safety and comfort here. Let it get as strong as it wants to. Tell me when it's strengthened all the way.** *When they say "okay," stop ABS.*

Step 5: Asking for a Generalization Effect   (ABS Off)

I'm guessing these wounding messages were delivered over many developmental stages, not just (<u>ages x-y</u>)**. Is that right?** *When the client agrees say:* **Brain, please allow all the work we do today with the** (<u>x-y-year-olds</u>)**, to apply to all developmental stages affected by these messages from** (<u>the wounding role models</u>)**.**

Step 6: Explaining the Process   (ABS Off)

So little ones, I'm guessing you've been stuck in the past for a long time. Does that sound right to you? *When they agree say:* **If it were possible to get unstuck, would that interest you?** *Then:* **Notice the Resources. Notice they're real, notice they're here for you, and notice they can help you get unstuck because they can meet needs for you now that were not met well in the past. Think back to being** (<u>ages x-y</u>)**. Think about needs you had at that time that were met well... and needs that were not met well... and when you're ready, tell me what you need most, right now.**

Step 7: Meeting Needs   (ABS On)

Will likely answer Step 6 with a single need (e.g. love, empathy, safety). Say something like: **Can the Resources** (<u>meet that need</u>) **now?** *When they say "yes," turn on ABS and say:* **Good. Notice that. Let it get as strong as it wants to. Tell me when it's strengthened all the way.**

When they say "okay," say: **Good. And what else do you need?** *When they answer with another need, something like:* **Can the Resources** (<u>meet that need</u>) **now?** *When they say "yes," say:* **Good. Notice that. Tell me when it's strengthened all the way.**

After meeting a few needs, check for processing problems. Ask the client:

How's this processing going? Do the Resources and child parts seem mostly vivid or mostly vague?
- *If mostly* <u>vivid</u>, *continue meeting needs.*
- *If mostly* <u>vague</u>, *ask:* **If the Resources could meet the needs of these child parts now, is there something you'd lose or something bad that would happen?** *If there is a block, go to the* **Overcoming Processing Blocks Flowchart** *and clear it, then continue meeting needs.*

Are the Resources meeting needs in the past or in the present?
- *If meeting needs in the present, continue with the processing.*
- *If meeting needs in the past, invite child parts to notice that the Resources are actually meeting needs in the present, then continue meeting needs.*

Again say: **Good. And what else do you need?** *When they answer with another need, say something like:* **Can the Resources** (<u>meet that need</u>) **now?** *When they say "yes," say:* **Good. Notice that.**
Repeat this questioning until about 10-15 needs have been met.

© Copyright 2009 by Shirley Jean Schmidt. All rights reserved. Personal use copy allowed. Distribution without permission is prohibited.

To prepare for Step 8 ask: **Do you need caregivers who want you to feel and express the full range of emotions?** *Then:* **Do the Resources want you to feel and express the full range of emotions?** *Then:* **Good. Notice that.** *Then:* **Do you need caregivers who can help you process through painful emotions, like anger or grief?** *Then:* **Can the Resources help you process through painful emotions?** *Then:* **Good. Notice that.**

Ask about changes in appearance: **As you picture these little ones now, is there anything different about their appearance? Have the masks/costumes changed? Are there any remains left in the pockets?** *Then ask the client:* **What do you notice in your body now?**

- *If the* <u>child parts appear happier</u>, *if the* <u>masks/costumes appear either smaller or gone</u>, *and if the* <u>body feels more relaxed and calm</u>, *then a* **substantial shift** *has occurred. Proceed to Step 8.*

- *If the child parts appear serious or gloomy, or if the masks/costumes appear exactly the same size, meet more needs in Step 7 until a substantial shift has occurred.*

- *If a* <u>new</u> *body disturbance is reported, ask:* **If the** (*body disturbance*) **could talk, what would it say?**
  - *If not, find and clear the associated block, then meet more needs until a substantial shift has occurred.*
  - *If so, proceed to Step 8.*

Step 8: *Processing Painful Emotions*   ABS On

Say to the child parts: **Your experiences with your** (<u>wounding role models</u>) **were pretty upsetting, weren't they? I wonder if you might have some unresolved painful emotions connected to those experiences – maybe anger or grief?** *If necessary, read the introject messages aloud.*
  - *If they report a* <u>readiness to process the emotions</u>, *say:* **Which emotion would you like to process first – anger or grief?**
  - *If they report* <u>blocked access to emotions</u>, *say:* **I understand that you have some unresolved grief or anger to process, but access to these emotions is blocked. We can actually process them in a way that does not require you to fully access them. Which emotion would you like to explore first – anger or grief?**
  - *If they report a* <u>fear of contacting the emotions</u>, *say:* **I understand you're afraid of contacting these emotions. I know a way we can process them without you having to fully feel them. You won't even have to cry. It's very gentle. It involves the Resources meeting more needs. Let's give it a try. If you don't like it, we can stop. Which emotion would you like to explore first – anger or grief?**
  - *If they* <u>deny having unresolved emotions</u>, *say:* **I understand your grief and anger may be completely resolved and you have nothing left to process through, but I'd like to pursue this a little bit, just in case there might be something left to work through. If you did have some unresolved emotions buried, which would you like to explore first – anger or grief?**
- *If they are* <u>unwilling</u> *to explore emotion processing, look for and clear the associated blocks.*
- *If they* <u>answer</u> *"anger" or "grief," proceed with the processing.*

So little ones, if you could feel the (*anger or grief*) **completely and fully in your body now, how intense would it be, from 0-10, where 10 is the most intense you could imagine and 0 is none at all?** *When they answer with a rating, ask:* **Which of your** (*wounding role models'*) **behaviors are most connected to that** (*rating*)? *Figure out the unmet, need then ask:* **Can the Resources** (*keep you safe*) **now?** *When they say "yes," say:* **Good. Notice that. Tell me when it's strengthened all the way.** *Once it has strengthened say:*

So little ones, if you could feel the (*anger or grief*) **completely and fully in your body now, how intense would it be, 0-10?** *When they answer with a rating, ask:* **Which of your** (*wounding role models'*) **behaviors are most connected to that** (*rating*)? *Figure out the unmet need, then ask:* **Can the Resources** (*keep you safe*) **now?** *When they say "yes," say:* **Good. Notice that. Tell me when it's strengthened all the way.**
- *Repeat this questioning until both grief and anger are zero.*

> *If child parts express intense despair about the past, say:* **Notice that the Resources completely understand what you're saying and feeling. They totally support you and honor your emotions. Express them any way you need to.** *As the processing unfolds, softly add:* **...feel their compassion, empathy, and support... they completely understand... just let it heal.** *After awhile ask:* **Does this seem to be processing through?**
>
> - *If it is still underway, say:* **Good. Just feel that empathy and support.**
> - *If the disturbance is escalating, ask if adding a sensorimotor activity would help.*
> - *If/when it feels complete, return to Processing Emotions by Meeting Needs.*

© Copyright 2009 by Shirley Jean Schmidt. All rights reserved. Personal use copy allowed. Distribution without permission is prohibited.

When both anger and grief are zero say to the child parts: **Would you be willing to check for completeness by** (*pulling on the TASPER*)**? If the emotion has completely resolved, you should know right away because it will feel good to pull. If there are any unresolved emotions left, pulling should bring them to the surface so we can finish them off. How does that sound?**

Once the sensorimotor activity is set to go, say: **Notice your connection to the Resources. Think about those things your** (*wounding role models*) **did or said to make you sad and angry, and when you're ready, pull.** *As the child parts pull, say:* **And if there is anything you wished you could have said to your** (*wounding role models*) **then, but knew you couldn't, you can say it out loud now.**

Once the anger and grief have processed through, ask the client: **As you picture these little ones now, is there anything different about their appearance? Have the masks/costumes changed? Are they still in the pockets?** *Then ask:* **What do you notice in your body now?** *If all is well, go to Step 9.*

Step 9: Bonding with the Resources

`ABS On`

Now little ones, look into the eyes of the <u>Nurturing Adult Self</u>**. What do you see in his/her eyes?** *When answer is positive, say:* **Good. And notice that, as you're looking into his/her eyes, he/she's looking into your eyes, seeing straight into your hearts. Do you feel a bond forming?** *When they say "yes," say:* **Good. Notice that bond. Tell me when it's strengthened all the way.** *Then:*

Good. Now little ones, look into the eyes of the <u>Protective Adult Self</u>**. What do you see in his/her eyes?** *When answer is positive, say:* **Do you feel a bond forming?** *When they say "yes," say:* **Good. Notice that. Tell me when it's strengthened all the way.** *Then:*

Good. Now little ones, look into the eyes of the <u>(Spiritual) Core Self</u>**. What do you see in his/her eyes?** *When answer is positive, say:* **Do you feel a bond forming?** *When they say "yes," say:* **Good. Notice that. Tell me when it's strengthened all the way.** *Then:*

Good. Now notice the (*number*) **of you together. Do you feel a** <u>group bond</u>**?** *When they say "yes," say:* **Good. Notice that group bond. Tell me when it's strengthened all the way.** *Then:*

I'd like to explain what a bond is. This means when you hurt the Resources hurt. They don't want to hurt and they don't want you to hurt, so they will do whatever they have to do, as quickly as they can, to help you feel better. How does that sound to you? *When they say "great!" say:* **Think about that. Tell me when it's strengthened all the way.**

Step 10: Heightening Awareness of the Adult Body

`ABS On`

So little ones, do you know you're in an adult body now? *Whether they say "yes" or "no," say:*
Take a moment to notice your hands. Now wiggle your fingers. Notice – those are <u>your</u> **fingers. (OR Look in this mirror. Now touch your nose. Notice that's** <u>your</u> **nose.) Is this what you expected to see?**

- *If they are* <u>aware</u> *of being in an adult body, ask:* **What does it mean to be in an adult body now, compared to being in a child body then?** *If they understand adult choices, freedoms, protection, etc. say:* **Good. Think about all this. Tell me when it's strengthened all the way.** *Go to Step 12.*

- *If they are* <u>partially aware</u> *or* <u>unaware</u> *of the adult body, ask:* **As a child your parents were in total control of your life, weren't they? They told you what to eat, when to eat, what to wear, when to sleep. They were in control of who came to the house and who you spent time with. They made up the rules and punished you if you broke the rules. The younger you were, the more control they had. Right? But now that you're in an adult body, you make those decisions. You decide what to eat, when to eat it, what to wear, when to sleep. You decide who to spend time with, and who to stay away from. You make up the rules now, right? What's it like to think about that?** *If their reaction is favorable, say:* **Good. Think about all this. Tell me when it's strengthened all the way.** *Go to Step 11.*

Step 11: Checking In

`ABS On`

So little ones, I'm guessing when we started you felt pretty stuck. How stuck do you feel now? Somewhat stuck, somewhat unstuck, mostly unstuck, or totally unstuck?

- *If* <u>somewhat stuck</u> *or* <u>somewhat unstuck</u>, *look for unexpressed blocks.*
- *If* <u>mostly unstuck</u>, *proceed to Step 12.*
- *If* <u>totally unstuck</u>, *say:* **I hear you believe you're totally unstuck. In fact you may be. But I have a few more steps to take you through. If you're totally unstuck they'll go very quickly, but if you're still a little stuck, we'll catch it and clear it. How does that sound?** *Then proceed to Step 12.*

© Copyright 2009 by Shirley Jean Schmidt. All rights reserved. Personal use copy allowed. Distribution without permission is prohibited.

Step 12: Returning to the Wounding Experiences

Explain the process: Now little ones, so far everything we've done has been in the presence of the Resources. To find out if there's any remaining disturbance I'll be asking you to disconnect from the Resources for just a moment, so you can revisit (*those wounding experiences*) from the past – just as they were back then, without your Resources present for support. You'll do this for just a moment, long enough to tell me how much disturbance comes up, then you'll come right back to the Resources. Are you okay with that?

- *If the child parts* are okay *with this, say:* **Good. Now little ones, disconnect from the Resources for just a moment and, when you're ready, bring your attention back to** (*those wounding experiences*) **from** (*ages x-y*), **remembering them just the way they were back then, when you didn't have Resources present for support. How much disturbance comes up now, from 0-10, where 0 is none and 10 is the worst disturbance you can imagine?**
    - *If the rating is 0 proceed to Step 15.*
    - *If the rating is above 0, ask:* **Which of the** (*wounding role models'*) **behaviors is most connected to that** (*1-10 rating*)**?**

- *If the child parts* are not okay *with this, say:* **Okay. So we can do this in a way that's comfortable for you, without leaving the company of the Resources. Now little ones, if you were to bring your attention back to** (*those wounding experiences*) **from** (*ages x-y*), **remembering them just the way they were back then, when you didn't have Resources present for support, and if you could feel the disturbance completely and fully in your body now, how intense would it be, from 0-10, where 0 is none and 10 is the worst disturbance you can imagine?**
    - *If the rating is 0 there is a processing block to find and clear.*
    - *If the rating is above 0, ask:* **Which of the** (*wounding role models'*) **behaviors is most connected to that** (*1-10 rating*)**?**

Step 13: Returning to the Care of the Resources

Figure out the unmet need from the answer given in Step 12. Then say something like: **So little ones, now bring your attention back to the Resources. Can the Resources** (*meet that need*) **now?** *When they say "yes,"* say: **Good. Notice that. Tell me when it's strengthened all the way.** *Then go to Step 14.*

Step 14: Repeating Steps 12 & 13

- *If the child parts are* okay with disconnecting *from the Resources, say:* **Good. Now little ones, once again disconnect from the Resources, and when you're ready, revisit** (*those wounding experiences*) **from** (*ages x-y*). **Remembering them just the way they were back then, when you didn't have Resources present for support, 0-10, how much disturbance comes up now?**
    - *If the rating is 0 proceed to Step 15.*
    - *If the rating is above 0, ask:* **Which of the** (*wounding role models'*) **behaviors is most connected to that** (*1-10 rating*)**?** *Figure out the unmet need and say:* **So little ones, bring your attention back to the Resources. Can the Resources** (*meet that need*) **now?** *When they say "yes," say:* **Good. Notice that. Tell me when it's strengthened all the way.** *Repeat.*

- *If the child parts are* not okay with disconnecting *from the Resources, say:* **Good. Now little ones, if you were to revisit** (*those wounding experiences*) **from** (*ages x-y*), **remembering them just the way they were back then, when you didn't have Resources present for support, and if you could feel the disturbance completely and fully in your body, 0-10, how intense would it be now?**
    - *If the rating is 0 there's a block to clear unless they are now willing to disconnect from Resources.*
    - *If the rating is above 0, ask:* **Which of the** (*wounding role models'*) **behaviors is most connected to that** (*1-10 rating*)**?** *Figure out the unmet need and say:* **So little ones, bring your attention back to the Resources. Can the Resources** (*meet that need*) **now?** *When they say "yes," say:* **Good. Notice that. Tell me when it's strengthened all the way.** *Repeat.*

Step 15: Shifting Attention Back and Forth

Okay little ones, now shift your attention back and forth between (*those wounding experiences*) **from the past when you had no Resources for support, and the Resources' care now... back and forth, and back and forth... and when you're ready, tell me what you notice.**

© Copyright 2009 by Shirley Jean Schmidt. All rights reserved. Personal use copy allowed. Distribution without permission is prohibited.

- *If no disturbance remains, ask:* **Are you saying there is <u>absolutely no disturbance</u> in your body when you revisit** (*those wounding experiences*)**?**

- *If some disturbance remains, say:* **Keep shifting your attention back and forth. The remaining disturbance will either go away, or it won't go away. When you're ready, tell me which is happening.**

- *If dismissive of remaining disturbance, say:* **It sounds like you still have some aversion to revisiting** (*the wounding experiences*)**. Keep shifting your attention back and forth. That remaining aversion will either go away, or it won't go away. When you're ready, tell me which is happening.**

- *If using the Resources to insulate from remaining disturbance, say:* **The fact that you believe you need the protection tells me that you haven't processed this disturbance all the way through yet. How much disturbance would you feel if you didn't have their protection and support right now?**

- *If/when the child parts report that <u>absolutely no disturbance</u> comes up proceed to Step 16.*

- *If the child parts report <u>any disturbance or aversion at all</u>, ask:* **Of your** (*wounding role models'*) **behaviors, which is most connected to the disturbance that remains?** *Figure out the unmet need and say:* **Now bring your attention back to the Resources. Can the Resources** (<u>meet that need</u>) **now?** *When they say "yes," say:* **Good. Notice that. Tell me when it's strengthened all the way.** *Once the need is met, return to the start of this step and invite them to shift attention back and forth again.*

Step 16: Checking In   `ABS On`

Ask the child parts: **So little ones, are you feeling mostly unstuck or totally unstuck now?**

- *If <u>mostly unstuck</u>, the process is not complete. Find out why.*

- *If <u>totally unstuck</u> ask the client:* **As you picture these little ones now, is there anything different about their appearance? (If we were to take the child parts out to a playground, which would they prefer to do, play on the swings and jungle-gym, or sit at the picnic table with the Resources?)**

  - *If they are <u>not engaged in age-appropriate play</u>, the process is not complete. Find out why.*

  - *If <u>engaged in age-appropriate play</u> ask the client:* **Is there anything left of the masks or costumes?**

    - *If <u>any shred of the masks or costumes remain</u>, the process is not complete. Find out why.*

    - *If <u>the masks or costumes are gone</u>, ask the client:* **What do you notice in your body now?**

      - *If there is any <u>emotional disturbance</u>, the process is not complete. Find out why.*

      - *If the body feels <u>clear and relaxed</u>, go to Step 17.*

Step 17: Strengthening a Positive Belief   `ABS On`

So little ones, when you think about what we've done today – what you've learned and how you've grown – what positive belief do you know to be true about you now? *Then:* **How true does it feel, 0-10?** *Then:* **Good. Think about these words. Tell me when they've strengthened all the way.**

Step 18: Tucking In the Child Parts   `ABS Off`

- *If protocol is <u>complete</u>, say:* **So little ones, I want to thank you for all your hard work today. You've been very courageous and have done a marvelous job of working through this old stuff. It sounds like you're totally unstuck. If it turns out you're not, or if you need additional help, I'll be happy to help you in a future session. In a few moments I'm going to invite you to tuck in. Is there anything you'd like to say or ask before you tuck in?** *Then:* **Now find a nice, warm, cozy, safe place to tuck into. You can tuck in with your Resources if you like. Just find a good safe place to wait until the next time you're needed.**

- *If protocol is <u>unfinished</u>, say:* **So little ones, I want to thank you for all your hard work today. You've been very courageous and have done a marvelous job of working through this old stuff. I understand we have more work to do to get you totally unstuck. I promise to help you with that in a future session. In a few moments I'm going to invite you to tuck in. Is there anything you'd like to say or ask before you tuck in?** *Then:* **Now find a nice, warm, cozy, safe place to tuck into. You can tuck in with your Resources if you like. Just find a good safe place to wait until the next time you're needed.**

© Copyright 2009 by Shirley Jean Schmidt. All rights reserved. Personal use copy allowed. Distribution without permission is prohibited.

Step 19: Counting Up

If client does not seem fully present ask: **Would you like for me to count up from 1-5?**

- *If "yes," say:* **One, coming up slowly. Two, a little more alert, and little more awake. Three, notice your body in the chair, notice your hands... your feet... your breath. Prepare to open your eyes. Four, letting your eyes open. Notice colors... notice sounds... notice your body in the chair... feeling a little more awake, a little more alert...** *once eye contact is made...* **and five, completely and totally awake and alert.** *Go to Step 20.*

Step 20: Checking on the Outcome

Refer to the Conference Room Map...

- *For each introject processed ask:*
  How disturbing is (*your wounding role model's*) **message _____ now, 0-10?**
- *For each relevant reactive part that did not participate in the needs meeting ask:*
  With respect to (*your wounding role model's*) **message _____ how stuck is the** (*x-year-old*) **reactive part now?**

If processing from the <u>Attachment Needs Ladder</u>...

- *Re-rate each belief from Rung you just processed, starting with the original prompt:*
  When you think about (*disturbing event x*) **how true does the statement _____ feel now, 0-10?**
- *If the client can identify an unwanted behavior, belief, or emotion connected to this Rung, ask:*
  When you think about (*the unwanted behavior/belief/emotion*)**, is your reaction any different now?**

If processing from a <u>specific current problem</u>...

- *If the client gave you a list of beliefs associated with the current problem, re-rate each item:*
  How true does the statement _____ feel now, 0-10?
- *Ask about changes in perception of the problem:*
  When you think about (*the current problem*)**, is your reaction any different now?**

Sample Responses...

When child parts express a need...	Follow up with...
To be wanted.	Do the Resources want you now?
To be validated.	Can the Resources validate you now?
For some independence.	Can the Resources grant you age-appropriate independence?
For parents who are sane.	Are the Resources sane caregivers now?
For my opinions to be valued.	Do the Resources value your opinions now?
To be comforted when I'm upset.	Can the Resources comfort you when you're upset?
For permission to express myself.	Will the Resources allow and encourage self-expression now?
For parents to pay attention to me.	Can the Resources give you the attention you need now?

If the child parts answer "yes" to...	Follow up with...
Do you need to be protected?	Can the Resources protect you now?
Do you need positive attention?	Can you get positive attention from the Resources now?
Do you need caregivers who want you?	Do the Resources want you now?
Do you need caregivers who validate you?	Can the Resources validate you now?

If the child parts disclose...	Follow up with...
My parents ignored me.	Can the Resources pay attention to you now?
They wouldn't listen to me.	Can the Resources listen to you now?
My parents fought all the time.	Do the Resources know how to resolve conflicts?
My mom was verbally abusive.	Will the Resources always treat you with respect?
My dad's punishments were brutal.	Can the Resources provide loving corrections?
They let grandpa sexually abuse me.	Can the Resources protect you now?
My needs weren't important to them.	Are your needs important to the Resources now?
Mom expected me to meet her needs.	Can the Resources meet their own needs?

© Copyright 2009 by Shirley Jean Schmidt. All rights reserved. Personal use copy allowed. Distribution without permission is prohibited.

Needs Meeting Protocol: Session Notes

Client: _____ CR Map Date(s): _____ NMP Date(s): _____

Introjects: _____

Reactive Parts (optional): _____

NEEDS MEETING: *Blacken the ☐ below next to each need met in Step 7*

☐ ○ △ Safety/Protection	☐ ○ △ Peaceful environment	***Caregivers who...***
☐ ○ △ To be wanted/valued	☐ ○ △ Safe environment	☐ ○ △ can manage their own emotions
☐ ○ △ Respect	☐ ○ △ Age-appro. boundaries	☐ ○ △ can meet their own needs
☐ ○ △ Attunement	☐ ○ △ Age-appro. responsibility	☐ ○ △ put your needs above their wants
☐ ○ △ Unconditional love	☐ ○ △ Age-appro. freedoms	☐ ○ △ are nurturing, caring, loving
☐ ○ △ Unconditional accept.	☐ ○ △ Age-appro. expectations	☐ ○ △ are consistently respectful
☐ ○ △ Loving connection	☐ ○ △ Age-appro. guidance	☐ ○ △ are good at listening
☐ ○ △ Understanding	☐ ○ △ Age-appro. privacy	☐ ○ △ are mature, respons, grown-ups
☐ ○ △ Empathy/compassion	☐ ○ △ Age-appro. supervision	☐ ○ △ take respons. for their behavior
☐ ○ △ Warmth/affection	***Permission/encouragement to...***	☐ ○ △ see reality clearly
☐ ○ △ Positive attention	☐ ○ △ develop autonomy	☐ ○ △ respond to reality appropriately
☐ ○ △ Support	☐ ○ △ develop/express a self	☐ ○ △ will help you meet your potential
☐ ○ △ Praise	☐ ○ △ express opinions	☐ ○ △ know which behaviors need
☐ ○ △ Reassurance	☐ ○ △ take age-appro. risks	correction and which don't
☐ ○ △ Encouragement	☐ ○ △ learn from mistakes	☐ ○ △ provide loving correction when
☐ ○ △ Validation	☐ ○ △ enjoy life	correction is needed
☐ ○ △ _____	☐ ○ △ _____	☐ ○ △ _____
☐ ○ △ _____	☐ ○ △ _____	☐ ○ △ _____
☐ ○ △ _____	☐ ○ △ _____	☐ ○ △ _____
☐ ○ △ _____	☐ ○ △ _____	☐ ○ △ _____
☐ ○ △	☐ ○ △ _____	☐ ○ △ _____

Before processing emotions...

☐ ○ △   Do you need caregivers who want you to feel and express the full range of emotions?

☐ ○ △   Do you need caregivers who can help you process through painful emotions, like anger or grief?

APPEARANCE: _____   **BODY:** _____

PROCESSING EMOTIONS: *Blacken ○ above for each anger need met; Blacken △ above for each grief need met*

ANGER level: _____	***GRIEF/SADNESS*** level: _____
Processed anger with Resources' support:	Processed grief with Resources' support:
○ **with** or ○ **without** a sensorimotor activity	△ **with** or △ **without** a sensorimotor activity

☐ Anger and grief processing tested for completeness with a sensorimotor activity.

APPEARANCE: _____   **BODY:** _____

BONDING: ☐ NAS   ☐ PAS   ☐ SCS   ☐ Group   ☐ Explanation

ADULT BODY: ☐ Knew about adult body   ☐ Resources explained adult body   ☐ Therapist explained adult body

BLOCKS

Block #:	Details: _____	Block #:	Details: _____
	_____		_____
Step #:	_____	Step #:	_____
	_____		_____
☐ Misunderstanding	_____	☐ Misunderstanding	_____
☐ Reactive Part	_____	☐ Reactive Part	_____
☐ Maladaptive Introject	_____	☐ Maladaptive Introject	_____

© Copyright 2009 by Shirley Jean Schmidt. All rights reserved. Personal use copy allowed. Distribution without permission is prohibited.

CHECKING IN: ☐ Somewhat stuck   ☐ Somewhat unstuck   ☐ Mostly unstuck   ☐ Totally unstuck

PENDULATING: *Blacken the ☐ below next to each need met in Steps 12-15.*

Steps 12-14 disturbance level changes _____

Step 15:   ☐ All body sensations gone   ☐ Met more needs before body sensations gone

☐ Safety/Protection	☐ Peaceful environment	***Caregivers who...***
☐ To be wanted/valued	☐ Safe environment	☐ can manage their own emotions
☐ Respect	☐ Age-appropriate boundaries	☐ can meet their own needs
☐ Attunement	☐ Age-appropriate responsibility	☐ put your needs above their wants
☐ Unconditional love	☐ Age-appropriate freedoms	☐ are nurturing, caring, loving
☐ Unconditional acceptance	☐ Age-appropriate expectations	☐ are consistently respectful
☐ Loving connection	☐ Age-appropriate guidance	☐ are good at listening
☐ Understanding	☐ Age-appropriate privacy	☐ are mature, responsible grown-ups
☐ Empathy/compassion	☐ Age-appropriate supervision	☐ take responsibility for their behavior
☐ Warmth/affection	***Permission/encouragement to...***	☐ see reality clearly
☐ Positive attention	☐ develop autonomy	☐ respond to reality appropriately
☐ Support	☐ develop/express a self	☐ will help you meet your potential
☐ Praise	☐ express opinions	☐ know which behaviors need a correction and which don't
☐ Reassurance	☐ take age-appropriate risks	
☐ Encouragement	☐ learn from mistakes	☐ provide loving correction when correction is needed
☐ Validation	☐ enjoy life	
☐ _____	☐ _____	☐ _____
☐ _____	☐ _____	☐ _____
☐ _____	☐ _____	☐ _____
☐ _____	☐ _____	☐ _____

CHECKING IN: ☐ Mostly unstuck   ☐ Totally unstuck   ☐ Child parts playing   ☐ Mask/costumes gone   ☐ Body clear

POSITIVE BELIEF: _____   How True, 0-10? _____

TUCKING IN: ☐ Completed NMP on: _____   **COUNTED UP:**   ☐ Yes   ☐ No

CHECKING ON OUTCOME:

☐ How disturbing are the introject messages now? _____

☐ Unless just processed, how stuck are the reactive parts now? _____

☐ Re-rate negative beliefs: _____

☐ Status of unwanted behavior, beliefs, or emotions: _____

BLOCKS

Block #: ____ Details: _____ Step #: _____ _____ ☐ Misunderstanding _____ ☐ Reactive Part _____ ☐ Maladaptive Introject _____	Block #: ____ Details: _____ Step #: _____ _____ ☐ Misunderstanding _____ ☐ Reactive Part _____ ☐ Maladaptive Introject _____

UNFINISHED PROTOCOL

Date: _____ How True, 0-10? _____ ☐ Tucked in Positive Belief: _____ _____ _____	Date: _____ How True, 0-10? _____ ☐ Tucked in Positive Belief: _____ _____ _____
Date: _____ How True, 0-10? _____ ☐ Tucked in Positive Belief: _____ _____ _____	Date: _____ How True, 0-10? _____ ☐ Tucked in Positive Belief: _____ _____ _____

© Copyright 2009 by Shirley Jean Schmidt. All rights reserved. Personal use copy allowed. Distribution without permission is prohibited.

Some Typical Misunderstandings That Block Processing

Misunderstandings that Can Block Resource Development

- Confusing the words "protective" and "overprotective."
- Confusing the notions of "being nurturing to others" with "being exploited by others."
- Assuming a skill must be applicable all the time, with every one, to be endorsed.
- I wasn't very good at protecting my kids. I don't think I have a Protective Self.
- There's no point in developing Resources because they won't be real.
- I prefer to experience my Resources as fictional beings because they'd be better caregivers than I am.
- If I admit to having adult skills, I am bragging. Bragging is bad and should be punished.
- If I connect to Resources I'll have to be perfect all the time.
- If I connect to Resources I'll have to meet other's needs at the expense of my own.
- If I connect to Resources I'll have to disconnect from my family.
- If I connect to Resources I'll have to be to be responsible for everything.
- If I connect to Resources I'll have to assert myself all the time.
- If I connect to Resources I'll be more vulnerable. People will take unfair advantage of me.
- If I connect to Resources I'll stop meeting my parents' needs and lose my connection to them.
- If I connect to Resources I'll start setting boundaries and people will reject me.
- If I connect to Resources people will expect me to protect them, then they'll reject me when they see I can't.
- If I connect to Resources I'll come out of hiding. Then people will see how inadequate I am and reject me.

Misunderstandings that Can Block Conference Room and Needs Meeting Protocols

- There's no point in doing the needs meeting work because it won't be real.
- I can't process my anger or grief without being overwhelmed.
- I'd be just like (*wounding role model x*) if I show my anger.
- Bonding with a caregiver will inevitably lead to betrayal or intolerable loss.
- It not okay for the Resources to hurt when I hurt.
- If I get unstuck, I'll have to be perfect all the time.
- If I connect to Resources or get unstuck, I'll have to meet other's needs at the expense of my own.
- If I get unstuck I'll have to disconnect from my family.
- If I get unstuck I'll have to be to be responsible for everything.
- If I get unstuck I'll have to assert myself all the time.
- If I get unstuck I'll be more vulnerable. People will take unfair advantage of me.
- If I get unstuck I'll stop meeting my parents' needs and lose my connection to them.
- If I get unstuck I'll start setting boundaries and people will reject me.
- If I get unstuck I'll people will expect me to protect them, then they'll reject me when they see I can't.
- If I get unstuck I'll come out of hiding. Then people will see how inadequate I am and reject me.

Misunderstandings that Can Block Any Protocol

- I'm afraid I'll lose a familiar sense of identity.
- I had to meet my own needs in childhood. Doing the DNMS means I'll have to meet my own needs again.
- I don't want to do that. It's time for someone else to meet my needs.
- If I get unstuck from childhood, my abusive parents are off the hook.
- The Resources would (or will) expect me to meet their needs.
- The Resources would (or will) eventually abandon me like everyone else has.
- Authority figures cannot be fully trusted – not even my Resources.
- The Resources would (or will) act just like my dysfunctional parents.
- The Resources would (or will) be perpetrators, and I'll be their victim.
- The Resources would (or will) impose their agenda on me.
- If I feel closely connected to the Resources, the intimacy will inevitably lead to betrayal.

© Copyright 2009 by Shirley Jean Schmidt. All rights reserved. Personal use copy allowed. Distribution without permission is prohibited.

Overcoming Processing Blocks Flowchart

Begin this flowchart if a client reports an unpleasant body sensation, dissociation, distracting thoughts, numbness, sleepiness, or some other complaint suggestive of a processing block, just before beginning or during a DNMS protocol. If ABS is on, turn it off.

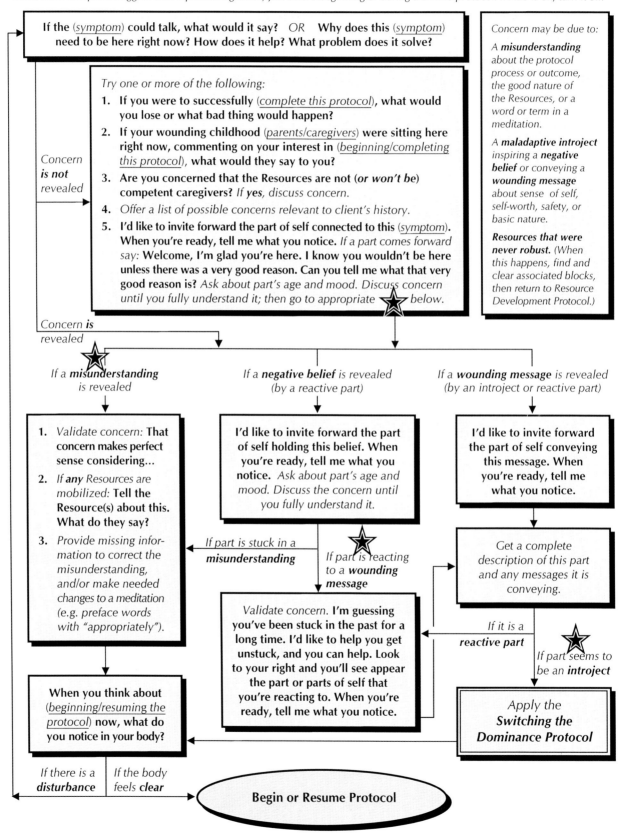

If the (symptom) **could talk, what would it say?** *OR* **Why does this** (symptom) **need to be here right now? How does it help? What problem does it solve?**

Concern may be due to:

*A **misunderstanding** about the protocol process or outcome, the good nature of the Resources, or a word or term in a meditation.*

*A **maladaptive introject** inspiring a **negative belief** or conveying a **wounding message** about sense of self, self-worth, safety, or basic nature.*

Resources that were never robust. *(When this happens, find and clear associated blocks, then return to Resource Development Protocol.)*

Try one or more of the following:

1. **If you were to successfully** (complete this protocol)**, what would you lose or what bad thing would happen?**
2. **If your wounding childhood** (parents/caregivers) **were sitting here right now, commenting on your interest in** (beginning/completing this protocol)**, what would they say to you?**
3. **Are you concerned that the Resources are not (*or won't be*) competent caregivers?** *If yes, discuss concern.*
4. *Offer a list of possible concerns relevant to client's history.*
5. **I'd like to invite forward the part of self connected to this** (symptom)**. When you're ready, tell me what you notice.** *If a part comes forward say:* **Welcome, I'm glad you're here. I know you wouldn't be here unless there was a very good reason. Can you tell me what that very good reason is?** *Ask about part's age and mood. Discuss concern until you fully understand it; then go to appropriate ★ below.*

Concern **is not** *revealed*

Concern **is** *revealed*

★ *If a **misunderstanding** is revealed*

★ *If a **negative belief** is revealed (by a reactive part)*

*If a **wounding message** is revealed (by an introject or reactive part)*

1. *Validate concern:* **That concern makes perfect sense considering...**
2. *If **any** Resources are mobilized:* **Tell the Resource(s) about this. What do they say?**
3. *Provide missing information to correct the misunderstanding, and/or make needed changes to a meditation (e.g. preface words with "appropriately").*

I'd like to invite forward the part of self holding this belief. When you're ready, tell me what you notice. *Ask about part's age and mood. Discuss the concern until you fully understand it.*

I'd like to invite forward the part of self conveying this message. When you're ready, tell me what you notice.

If part is stuck in a **misunderstanding**

★ *If part is reacting to a **wounding message***

Get a complete description of this part and any messages it is conveying.

Validate concern. I'm guessing you've been stuck in the past for a long time. I'd like to help you get unstuck, and you can help. Look to your right and you'll see appear the part or parts of self that you're reacting to. When you're ready, tell me what you notice.

If it is a **reactive part**

★ *If part seems to be an **introject***

Apply the **Switching the Dominance Protocol**

When you think about (beginning/resuming the protocol) **now, what do you notice in your body?**

If there is a **disturbance**

If the body feels **clear**

Begin or Resume Protocol

© Copyright 2009 by Shirley Jean Schmidt. All rights reserved. Personal use copy allowed. Distribution without permission is prohibited.

DNMS Tools & Home Study Course

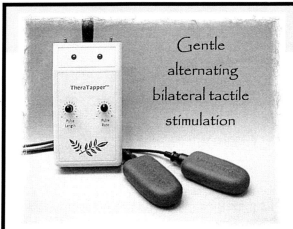

Gentle alternating bilateral tactile stimulation

The TheraTapper™

Features of the Design:

Six-Foot Long Disposable Wires
When a wire wears out merely unplug it from the control box and the pulsers and throw it away! You can buy replacement wires from us or from any store that sells audio accessories!

High/Low Pulse Intensity Switch
High intensity pulse is great for standard EMDR. Low intensity pulse is wonderful for calming, meditating, or sleeping.

Easy-Grip Pulsers
2.4"x1.25"x0.6" oval pulsers - great size for holding in hands!

Adjustable Pulse Rate
For a slower pulse rate lengthen the pause between pulses. For a faster pulse rate shorten it.

Adjustable Pulse Length
Choose from a wide range of pulse lengths.

Blinking LEDs
Real-time visual feedback about pulse length and rate.

Uses Long-Lasting AA Batteries
Get 100+ hours of tapping on 1 pair of AA alkaline batteries.

The **TheraTapper**™ provides alternating bilateral stimulation (ABS) for DNMS and EMDR therapy. It consists of a control box connected to two small (hand-holdable) pulsers by disposable six-foot wires. The pulsers vibrate in an alternating fashion to provide a gentle tactile stimulation which many find soothing and relaxing. The stimulation is comparable to the vibration of a pager or cell phone. Each TheraTapper™ purchased comes with an extra set of wires and a zippered canvas carrying case. Batteries are included. One month warranty on the wire, and a one year warranty covers manufacturing defects on the control box and pulsers.

The TASPER

Therapist's Aid for Sensorimotor Processing for Emotional Release

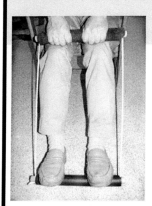

The TASPER is a tool for therapists who wish to help clients achieve emotional resolution with a sensorimotor activity. The TASPER consists of two 14-inch long padded bars connected by two ropes. During emotion processing, clients pull on one bar while pushing against the other bar with their feet. They can pull and push against their own strength. Clients may have a more complete experience of processing strong emotions with the TASPER because all the major muscles are involved. The TASPER is a quiet alternative to beating a pillow with a bat. The lengths of the ropes are easily adjusted.

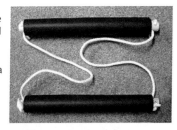

DNMS Flip Chart

This 75-page, illustrated paper "slide show" provides clients a systematic introduction to the DNMS. It provides background information, defines parts of self, the Resources, reactive parts, and introjects. It explains the Switching the Dominance Protocol, the Attachment Needs Ladder, the Conference Room Protocol, the Needs Meeting protocol, and more.

To Place an Order

For more information about any of these items, or to place an order, call the DNMS Institute at 210-561-7881 or go to www.DNMSInstitute.com

The DNMS Home Study Course

The 7-module Home Study Course teaches therapists how to competently execute each DNMS protocol. Each module consists of a narrated slide show and an illustrated study guide.

- Each **slide show** explains key concepts with animated illustrations. Review questions are provided throughout the slide shows, so you can check your comprehension of the material. Modules 3-7 demonstrate the protocols with recordings of real sessions.

- Each **study guide** provides an illustrated outline of all the material covered in the slide shows. The Module 2-7 study guides include long lists of study questions and answers.

Module 1: DNMS Background and Overview
This module consists of a 63-minute slide show and a 19-page study guide. It provides a brief description of the basic principles, goals, and limitations of the model, and a brief overview of the theoretical underpinnings. It includes an overview of the DNMS protocols and procedures, including interventions for overcoming processing blocks. It provides an overview of the model for therapists who are considering studying the DNMS, beginning the Course, and/or wanting another tool for explaining the DNMS to their clients.

Module 2: Ego State Therapy Basics
This module consists of a 80-minute slide show and a 28-page study guide with 40 study questions and answers. It provides all the background material on ego state therapy needed for understanding and executing the DNMS protocols taught in Modules 3-7.

Module 3: Resource Development Protocol
This module consists of a 91-minute slide show and 24-page study guide with 40 study questions and answers. It provides an in depth description of the Resource Development Protocol and instructions for handling potential complications. An audio track of a 30-minute Resource development session is embedded in the slide show.

Module 4: Switching the Dominance Protocol
This module consists of a 137-minute slide show, a 35-page study guide with 50 study questions and answers, and a Switching the Dominance Protocol work-sheet. It includes a detailed discussion of each protocol step and instructions for handling potential complications. Two audio tracks (57 minutes) of sample sessions are embedded in the slide show.

Module 5: Selecting Ego States for Processing
This module consists of a 143-minute slide show and 39-page study guide with 40 study questions and answers, an Attachment Needs Ladder form, a Conference Room Map template, and a Conference Room Protocol worksheet. It explains how to use the Attachment Needs Ladder questionnaire and how to execute the Conference Room Protocol. It includes guidance for handling a number of potential complications that can arise while administering the questionnaire or during the Conference Room Protocol. A 49-minute audio track of a real session is embedded in the slide show.

Module 6: Needs Meeting Protocol
This module consists of a 149-minute slide show and 43-page study guide with 40 study questions and answers, a Needs Meeting Protocol worksheet, and a guide for taking notes during a needs meeting session. It provides a detailed description of each step in the Needs Meeting Protocol, including instructions for handling potential complications. A 39-minute audio track of a real needs meeting session is embedded in the slide show.

Module 7: Overcoming Processing Blocks
This module consists of a 116-minute slide show and 19-page study guide with 20 study questions and answers. It provides the core information needed to identify and handle processing blocks that are due to misunderstandings, mal-adaptive introjects, and issues with the Resources. It provides information for handling blocks that was not already covered in Modules 3-6. An Over-coming Processing Blocks Flowchart simplifies the learning process. Nine audio tracks (63 min) of real examples of handling blocks are embedded in the slide show.

Complete Course (Modules 1- 7)
The complete course comes with all seven modules, as described above. The study guide comes in a three-ring binder. The 7 slide shows will come on your choice of 7 individual CDs or a single DVD.

Home Study Course Endorsements

Richard Holcomb, Registered psychologist from Christchurch, NZ wrote: *Excellent self-paced learning program carrying the potential to teach ten times as much as a 3-day course. I would highly recommend this course as the best way to start learning DNMS.*

Joan Bacon, MA, Psychologist from Emmaus, PA wrote: *As someone who has been practicing the DNMS since 2000, I found the Home Study Course to be a great way to learn about changes in the DNMS model, and to sharpen my DNMS skills. The Course format, of slide shows and study guides, was the perfect way for me to explore the depths of the DNMS. The material was presented in a clear and precise way - much easier to digest than studying a book. I found the detailed guidance about handling protocol complications especially helpful. I really appreciate all the time and energy Shirley Jean has put into creating this Course.*

Donna Stanley, LCSW from Chapel Hill, NC wrote: *The DNMS Home Study Course will revolutionize DNMS training. It is complete, thorough, and user-friendly. Through graphics, recordings of real sessions, study questions, slides, and printed material this Home Study Course is able to convey the complexity of the DNMS in a clear and learnable manner. It is well worth the investment.*

Sandra Helpsmeet, MS, LMFT from Eau Claire, WI wrote: *This course is a masterpiece! When Shirley Jean first said she was going to write a self-study course for learning the DNMS, I was doubtful as to whether such a multi-faceted therapy could be condensed in that way. I don't learn well by just reading, and I had found the workshops of demonstrations and practice sessions invaluable. However, the course is so well structured, so complete, and so full of examples, including recordings of actual sessions, that I have continued to learn from it. And there is no chaff—each sentence carries important information. The best part is that it is always available, so I can easily look up something I have forgotten or catalyze my creativity when I am stuck with a client.*

Bill Solz, LCSW, CASAC, from Bellmore, NY wrote: *The DNMS Home Study Course is a very comprehensive overview of an exciting modality. Although I have actively been utilizing DNMS with my clients for the past three years, I have found the Course to be additionally enlightening. It has been inspired by both valuable additions to the protocol, combined with more in depth understanding. The slide show presentation is extremely user-friendly, and I have derived great value from the written material. I believe this Course can serve as a great introductory means for clinicians who are interested in first learning this exciting and life altering modality. I would also recommend the complete Home Study Course to those therapists who have already attended previous trainings. Thanks again to Shirley Jean for all her efforts promoting meaningful and comprehensive healing to those who can benefit.*

Home Study Course Continuing Education Credits

The full 7-Module DNMS Home Study Course is sponsored by **R. Cassidy Seminars** (RCS) for 20 CE credit hours. In order to receive a Certificate of Completion, participants who purchase the Home Study Course must pay a $45 RCS fee, complete and pass the post-test, complete an evaluation form, and provide an Attestation Statement (verification of completion). The $45 fee can be paid when the Course is purchased, or when the Certificate of Completion is needed. The post-test, evaluation form, and Attestation Statement can be completed on-line. This course has been approved for CE credits for most Psychologists (APA), Social Workers (ASWB), Professional Counselors (NBCC), Marriage and Family Therapists (NBCC), and Chemical Dependency Counselors (NAADAC). RCS, the CE provider, maintains responsibility for this program. For a complete description of who can obtain CEs for this Course, and other relevant information, go to **www.dnmsinstitute.com/ces**.

Other Home Study Course Information

- When you order a single module you'll get a single CD with the slide show, and the printed study guide, punched with holes for your 3-ring binder. When you order the whole course, the study guides come in our three-ring binder. You can get your 7 slide shows on a single DVD, or on 7 individual CDs. The DVD or CDs will play on most Windows-based and Macintosh computers. They will not play in a CD or DVD player.

- To get an idea of how the narrated slide shows work, go to **www.dnmsinstitute.com/dnmsintro.html** and watch the free 25-min *Introduction to the DNMS* slide show.

To Order the Home Study Course

To order one or more modules, or the whole Course, contact the DNMS Institute at 210-561-7881, or use our on-line order form at **www.dnmsinstitute.com**. Therapists who took a DNMS Institute workshop between 2002 and 2006 may be eligible for a discount. Call for details.

Index